Elementary Social Studies

A PRACTICAL APPROACH TO TEACHING AND LEARNING

SIXTH EDITION

Ian Wright

University of British Columbia

PEARSON

Prentice
Hall

Toronto

National Library of Canada Cataloguing in Publication

Wright, Ian, 1941–
    Elementary social studies : a practical approach to teaching and learning / Ian Wright. — 6th ed.

Includes bibliographical references and index.
ISBN 0-13-124089-7

    1. Social sciences—Study and teaching (Elementary) I. Title.

LB1584.5.C3W75 2005   372.83'044   C2004-903516-9

0-13-124089-7

Vice President, Editorial Director: Michael J. Young
Acquisitions Editor: Christine Cozens
Marketing Manager: Ryan St. Peters
Associate Editor: Paula Drużga
Production Editor: Richard di Santo
Copy Editor: Martin Townsend
Proofreader: Kathleen Richards
Production Coordinator: Peggy Brown
Page Layout: Heidi Palfrey
Art Director: Julia Hall
Cover and Interior Design: Miguel Acevedo
Cover Image: Magma Photo

    4 5   RRD   09 08 07 06 05

Printed and bound in the USA.

Contents

Preface

This book is not a text in the usual sense of the word. Textbooks usually require you to absorb information first and then carry out certain activities, such as answering questions based on the text's content. Maybe this is how you learned social studies in school. The assumption in most methods texts is that if you read about the theory and practice of social studies teaching, you will become an effective teacher. However, this book is based on the assumption that if you are actually *involved* in social studies activities, you are more likely to understand and implement these activities in your classroom. In other words, this book encourages you to "learn by doing" and to *reflect critically* on what you are doing.

The emphasis, then, is on the procedures and standards of critical thinking as they pertain to the areas of intellectual standards and personal and social values in the social studies. The philosophy behind this text is that students of all ages should be actively engaged in finding, applying, interpreting, analyzing, synthesizing, and evaluating information in order to make rational decisions.

I hope this book challenges you to think critically about what you teach and how you teach it, in addition to providing you with many practical ideas.

ORGANIZATION

This book is divided into five parts. In Part 1 you are introduced to the nature of social studies and some rationales for teaching it. You will learn that there is no one agreed-upon definition of the term "social studies" and that differing definitions are based on differing views of what constitutes the educated person. These views are, in turn, based on disparate assumptions about the nature of knowledge, how people learn, what defines a good person, what the ideal society would consist of, and what is important to know in order to be an educated person. Throughout, you are asked to reflect on what you believe, what factors in your background may have contributed to your beliefs, and the contexts in which you will be teaching. In this way, you should begin to develop your own philosophy for teaching the social studies.

In the second part of the book, you are introduced to the teaching of empirical and conceptual claims and the intellectual standards associated with them. Empirical claims are statements about what *was*, *is*, or *will be* the case. If they are believed to be true, then we call them facts. For example, stating "This book has 500 pages" is an empirical claim because it asserts that something is the case, even though it is not true. "Ottawa is the capital of Canada" is an empirical claim that also happens to be true. What we want students to do is evaluate empirical claims so that they can determine which ones to believe. Therefore, we should introduce them to some of the intellectual standards usually found in the skills or applications sections of social studies curricula. These standards include validity, reliability, logic, accuracy, precision, lack of bias, and having enough evidence to support a conclusion. Similarly, because we need to teach students to use language effectively and to be clear about the concepts they use, you are introduced to ways of helping students develop conceptual clarity. Throughout, you are asked to think critically about empirical and conceptual matters so that you can help your students do the same.

Part 2 begins with a broad overview of how to *plan* for instruction. Once this plan is in place, then you have to decide on the teaching methods you will use to realize your objectives. As the "lecture" is a very familiar and efficient method, Chapter 5 is devoted to helping you present didactic instruction in meaningful and interesting ways. I also introduce you to Kieran Egan's "Teaching as Story Telling" approach and try to help you and your students use textbooks in interesting and critical ways. Because one major component of any lesson will be the teaching of the concepts students need to know, Chapter 6 is devoted to teaching and learning concepts. Although in a talk we may tell students what a particular word means, when we want students to fully grasp a concept, more than a dictionary definition is needed. In this chapter, I point out that no learning can occur unless students understand the meanings of the words in any sentence. For example, you could not make any sense of the statement "Ottawa is the capital of Canada" if you did not know what the term "capital" means.

As a teacher, you will ask yourself many questions: What are the best examples to teach this concept? What information will my students require to study this topic? What are the most thought-provoking questions I can pose to my students? Similarly, you should encourage students to ask their own questions. Chapter 7 focuses on these matters.

Both student- and teacher-originated questions are meant to be answered. One major approach is to have students find out the answers themselves. I label this "inquiry learning and teaching," and it is the focus of Chapter 8. As any empirical claim needs to be tested for its truth value, I introduce you to some of the intellectual standards that students need to learn and to critical thinking approaches and activities that will help you teach these standards. Often in inquiry activities, students work together in groups, so Chapter 9 helps you plan cooperative learning activities and introduces you to some of the dispositions needed to create a community of inquiry in your classroom. Of course, knowledge of methodology makes no sense unless there is "content" to teach. General teaching methods are given disciplinary substance in the following chapters. Chapters 10 and 11 present rationales, organizing principles, and teaching strategies for two key disciplines: history and geography. Both disciplines can be taught via field studies, which are the subject of Chapter 12. To help you teach students how to make connections between the information learned—whether it be in history, geography, or any other subject—Chapter 13 is devoted to ways students can create generalizations, cause-and-effect relationships, and syntheses.

Once you understand these chapters, then you are in an excellent position to begin to develop a unit plan where the emphasis is on facts, concepts, generalizations, and intellectual standards. Chapter 14 provides several examples.

The last chapter in Part 2 explores the philosophy and methodology of assessment. You need to know if students have realized your lesson or unit objectives, not only for report card purposes, but also because you can use assessment information to improve your teaching. In addition, students also need to note their own progress.

Whether your topic is families, Canada, pollution, or ancient Greece, you and your students will require information. In Part 3, Chapter 16 provides a wealth of ideas for obtaining and evaluating many information sources, including websites. There are also ideas for student interpretation of images. This chapter can be referred to at any time because it is relevant to every other chapter.

Part 4 deals with matters of value through the medium of decision making. In a number of chapters, I outline approaches to values education and explore the value questions that arise in citizenship, multicultural, global, human rights, peace, gender, conflict resolution, and law-related education. I believe that the examination of value issues should be the major goal of social studies. If we want to develop responsible and rational citizens, then we have to help students deal with the myriad value problems that confront them in everyday life as well as those that will confront them in the future. Knowing about Canadian history or world geography is of little use unless that knowledge is put to work. Such knowledge is most worthwhile when it helps students create a better world for themselves and others and for future generations.

Part 5 provides a detailed framework for unit planning that goes beyond the conveying of information. It includes discussions, with examples, of unit rationales and the scope and sequence of a unit. Sample unit episodes, some involving value questions, are also presented. In a modest way, the book's various ideas are pulled together so that you can see how you can interweave them yourself. Receiving further emphasis in this section are the writing of objectives and ways to motivate student interest in a topic.

At the end of each part is a list of relevant websites. No doubt there are hundreds of others that would be useful for teaching social studies and I would welcome hearing from you about them so that I can keep as up to date as possible.

Answers to questions in the text as well as a selected bibliography, organized by topic, appear at the end of the book.

Critical thinking and integration with other subject areas are emphasized throughout. To arrive at conclusions about social phenomena, students will have to bring information to bear from many other subject areas, both in the sciences and in the arts. In addition, it is suggested throughout that students be encouraged to search for data in a variety of sources and to present their conclusions in a variety of forms—written, pictorial, and oral. *Elementary Social Studies* demonstrates that many "authentic learning" objectives can be realized through social studies.

I hope you find this text both exciting and challenging. I wish you well in your chosen career.

SUPPLEMENTS

Elementary Social Studies is supplemented by an Instructor's Manual that can be downloaded from Pearson Education Canada's protected Instructor Central website, at **www.pearsoned.ca/instructor**.

ACKNOWLEDGMENTS

I am indebted to my social studies instructors at the Universities of Calgary and Alberta; to my colleagues at the University of British Columbia, especially Joanne Nysland in the Education Library, who knows so much about social studies resources; to my students who have endured my classes and the use of previous editions of this book, and who tell me how it ought to be written; and to the people who provided illustrative materials, especially Pierre Caritey and Nick Murphy for their graphics. I am also indebted to the reviewers, who helped in the development of this revision: Sharon Abbey, Brock University; Larry Glassford, University of Windsor; and Vicki Green, Okanagan University College. I also acknowledge the fine work of my copy editor, Martin Townsend, who considerably improved the book and ensured that egregious errors were obliterated. Many thanks to the staff at Pearson Education Canada, without whom this book would never have happened: Christine Cozens, Richard di Santo, Paula Drużga, Kathleen Richards, Ryan St. Peters, and Cas Shields. And last but not least, special thanks to Carol for her support and her love.

IAN WRIGHT

Vancouver, British Columbia
November 2003

chapter one

What Is
Social Studies?

Imagine you have a class of elementary school students (you can choose which age level) and are free to plan and implement your own one-year social studies program. What will you do? How you answer this question depends upon what you think about several factors: what "social studies" means, what the goals of social studies should be, and what students are capable of learning. In answering these questions, you will draw upon your background experiences, and you should reflect on how these influence your decisions and whether the influence is positive or negative. For example, if you learned social studies in your secondary school through reading a textbook and having teachers lecture you, then these methods will be very familiar to you, whether you liked them or not. If you disliked these methods, you might find yourself rejecting them without considering the positive results they can have if used wisely. Or if you liked these methods you might reject others that can produce meaningful learning. All these factors are related. Suppose we decided that it is a worthwhile goal to teach our Grade 4 students about the Quebec conscription crisis during World War I; then someone might legitimately ask if Grade 4 students could make much sense of the topic. (This does not mean, of course, that the topic is not worth teaching at another grade level.) Similarly, a decision to teach Grade 6 social studies students to play the recorder simply because they are capable of learning to play it might also be questioned. Although teaching the recorder is a worthwhile endeavour, it does not fall under the "social studies" label. Let us first look at how you define social studies.

Activity 1-A

1. What words, phrases, or images come to mind when you think of "social studies"? Write down one word or phrase, or draw an image, in each of the segments of the reaction wheel.

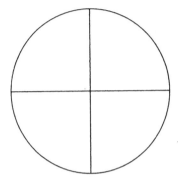

2. Exchange your reaction wheel with a peer. Try to clarify what your peer means by his or her reactions. What experiences led to these reactions?

3. What do you remember studying and doing in social studies lessons in your schooling?

   Did you enjoy social studies? Why or why not?

   Do you think you learned anything of importance? Why or why not?

   Do you want to teach social studies in the ways that it was taught to you? Why or why not?

4. If necessary, rewrite or redraw your reactions so that they are clear and understandable.

5. In a large group (five or more people), collect all reactions. Try to classify these into *the knowledge you learned*, *the skills you learned*, and *expressions of attitude*. Looking just at the knowledge classification, can you agree on what social studies is?

Knowledge: What one "knows"	Skill: What one "does"	Attitude: How one "feels" (what evaluations one makes)

You may find that your group is able to agree on what the knowledge base of social studies is, at least in general terms. You have all studied some history and geography in social studies and may remember making models of Egyptian pyramids or colouring maps of Canada. There is not likely to be much disagreement that such activities as colouring maps of Canada or building models of the pyramids could be construed as social studies activities. However, not all activities fall so clearly under the social studies label.

Activity 1-B

Read the following. Which of these situations would you consider to be social studies? Indicate your answers on the chart that follows, and then refer to the Answers to Activities section in the back of the book.

1. To teach a simple statistical procedure, the teacher has organized students to conduct a survey on people's attitudes toward litter in order to discover whether males and females differ significantly in their attitudes.
2. Students are creating a mural to display what they learned on a field trip to a farm.
3. Students are acting out the arrival of some of the first settlers in New France.
4. Students are listening to a nurse tell them how to apply a tourniquet.
5. Having read a story about the life of two children in Japan, students are answering comprehension questions in their notebooks.
6. To develop citizenship skills and attitudes, students are discussing how to welcome a new immigrant from India to their class.
7. Students are reading a fairy tale from China.
8. Students are learning songs sung by children in Israel.
9. Students are making scale drawings of their classroom.
10. Students are collecting food for the local food bank.

Situation	Social Studies	Not Social Studies	Not sure	Reason
1.				
2.				
3.				
4.				
5.				
6.				
7.				
8.				
9.				
10.				

You will notice that in all the above situations students are engaged in some sort of activity. But it is not the activity itself that constitutes social studies; students could read, act, discuss, draw, and listen in any subject. Rather, it is the content of the activity and the reason(s) for doing it that lead us to conclude that it is social studies. If the goal of reading a story about the life of two children in Japan is to develop students' abilities in phonics, then it is a language arts activity. If the goal is to teach about how children live in Japan, then it probably fits under the social studies label.

DEFINITIONS OF SOCIAL STUDIES

It is unlikely that everyone in your class has arrived at exactly the same definition of social studies. Experts in the field, who spend an inordinate amount of time trying to define social studies, also disagree.[1] The definitions that follow attest to this.

1. The social studies are the social sciences simplified for pedagogical purposes.[2]

2. Social Studies should furnish the forum for the analysis and evaluation of normative propositions or value judgments about man [*sic*] and society.[3]

3. Social studies is the integrated study of the **social sciences** and humanities to promote civic competence. Within the school program, social studies provides coordinated, systematic study drawing upon such disciplines as anthropology, archeology, economics, geography, history, law, philosophy, political science, psychology, religion, and sociology, as well as appropriate content from the humanities, mathematics, and natural sciences. The primary purpose of social studies is to help young people develop the ability to make informed and reasoned decisions for the public good as citizens of a culturally diverse, democratic society in an interdependent world.[4]

4. Social Studies is a composite subject based on history and geography and the social science disciplines…. [T]he overarching aim of social studies is citizenship education.[5]

5. Social studies is the interdisciplinary integration of social sciences and humanities concepts for the purpose of practicing citizenship skills on critical social issues.[6]

6. The social studies is that part of the elementary and high school curriculum which has the primary responsibility for helping students to develop knowledge, skills, attitudes, and values needed to participate in the civic life of their local communities, the nation, and the world.[7]

7. A study of people and their relationships with their social and physical environments. The knowledge, skills, and values developed in social studies help students to know and appreciate the past, to understand the present, and to influence the future.[8]

8. Social Studies is the integration of history, the social sciences, and the humanities to promote civic competence.[9]

9. The social studies are concerned exclusively with the education of citizens. In a democracy, citizenship consists of two related but sometimes disparate parts: the first socialization, the second countersocialization.[10]

10. Social studies is a school subject that assists students to acquire the basic knowledge, skills, and attitudes needed to be responsible citizens. The content of social studies draws upon history, geography, economics, other social sciences, the behavioural sciences, and the humanities.[11]

11. Social studies seeks to examine and understand communities, from the local to the global, their various heritages and the nature of citizenship within them.[12]

12. Social studies provides coordinated, systematic study drawing upon such disciplines as anthropology, economics, geography, history, political science, psychology, and sociology, as well as appropriate content from the humanities, mathematics, and the natural sciences. Social studies recognizes and validates the importance of the individual disciplines in providing awareness and perspectives to help students understand issues and problems. The social studies curriculum provides the multidisciplinary lens through which students examine issues affecting their lives from personal, academic, pluralistic, and global perspectives.[13]

13. Social studies is the study of people in relation to each other and the world in which they live. In Manitoba, social studies comprises the disciplines of history and geography, draws upon the social sciences, and integrates relevant content from the humanities. As a study of human beings in their physical, social and cultural environments, social studies examines the past and present, and looks toward the future. Social studies helps students acquire the skills, knowledge, and values necessary to become active democratic citizens and contributing members of communities, locally, nationally, and globally.[14]

14. Social studies should bring to the foreground the problems of knowledge, power, culture, and difference that have animated the humanities and social sciences over the past 20 years, and, along with them, the complex and theoretically rich tasks of teaching students how to read the texts that structure their lives, and write the ones that might restructure the world.[15]

Activity 1-C

What have the above definitions got in common? On what points do they disagree? Create a chart that outlines these agreements and disagreements, using the categories of "Disciplines included," "Other content included," "Rationales," and "Objectives." Then look at your own province's curriculum guide and ascertain where, if at all, it fits.

There are variations in these definitions. This is because there are disagreements about what disciplines make up social studies, what the major goals should be, and how citizenship is to be defined.[16] Yet, in spite of their differences, all these definitions either state explicitly that social studies includes the study of human beings in social settings, using knowledge drawn from (at least) the social sciences, or they imply that social studies requires this knowledge (e.g., to solve social problems). This is the *knowledge base* of social studies. But a definition does not tell us *why* we should teach social studies or what the goals of teaching the subject should be. Nor does it tell us what we could or should teach from the vast array of possible social studies knowledge.

A BRIEF HISTORY OF SOCIAL STUDIES

The goals we aim for are those thought to be worth pursuing by makers of public policy; teachers make curriculum decisions on the basis of these goals. Some of the definitions above state what these goals should be. For example, several of them claim that the purpose of social studies is education for citizenship. The US National Education Association—the association credited with the "invention" of social studies—identified this as the primary goal for social studies education in 1916. This same goal is espoused presently by the US National Council for the Social Studies and by most of the ministries of education in Canada. Education for citizenship is thus viewed by most educators as the raison d'être for the social studies.

This goal has been the traditional one for the subject throughout its history in Canada.[17] Beginning in the western provinces in the 1920s and in Ontario in 1937, social studies was the name given to an interdisciplinary approach to the teaching of history, geography, the social sciences, and civics. Canadian social studies educators have been strongly influenced by their American counterparts. In the early days of the subject, in the 1930s and 1940s, there was an emphasis at the policy level on "child-centred" or "progressive" educational ideas, with activity-oriented curricula in which children worked together on projects. These ideas relied heavily on the theories of the American philosopher John Dewey. In the 1960s, Canadian educators were influenced by the "structure of the disciplines" movement in the United States. Here, curricula were based on the various social studies disciplines, and students were taught to think and act like historians, geographers, political scientists, and so on. Another important influence was Hilda Taba (see Chapter 6), whose ideas on organizing curricula around key concepts were, and still are, accepted by many curriculum developers.

The reliance on ideas from the United States was challenged in the late 1960s, especially by Hodgetts.[18] On the basis of his somewhat flawed research, Hodgetts concluded that civic education and the teaching of history needed a great deal of improvement. The Canadian Studies Foundation, created in 1970 as a result of his efforts, produced a profusion of curriculum materials. Provincial curricula began to focus more sharply on Canadian content, and Canadian publishers started to produce more materials on Canadian history and geography. Aspects of this movement can still be found in Canadian education, but the "structure of the disciplines" approach has given way to new concerns. In the last 20 years, Canadian society has awakened to such problems as racism, sexism, environmental degradation, and the demand for First Nations self-government, and has had to face the spectre of the separation of Quebec from the rest of Canada. Thus, new curricula have been developed, ranging from a focus on value issues to a renewed emphasis on history and geography. New themes such as multicultural, anti-racist, global, law-related, human rights, environmental, economic, and Maritime and Pacific Rim studies have been included as the political climate has changed at the national and provincial levels. These changes have not always been put into widespread practice. There are many constraints on implementation and these have to be considered in any analysis of the history of social studies.[19] Yet, despite changes over the years, the key concern of the social studies—**citizenship education**—has remained constant.[20] And this is despite the criticism that citizenship education is too broad an idea, as it is an overarching goal of schooling, and there is no agreed-upon body of content that makes up citizenship education.[21]

Activity 1-D

Create a time line outlining the changes in Canadian social studies since the 1920s. Underneath this time line, draw another one indicating the political and social factors that you think influenced the changes in the social studies curriculum.

THE PROBLEM OF DEFINING SOCIAL STUDIES

Even though we may all agree on the broad knowledge base of the social studies, we may not agree on what the citizenship goals of social studies should be. Should social studies education develop passive citizens who do not criticize the existing social order? Or, as Engle and Ochoa ask, should its purpose consist of socialization and then countersocialization (by which the authors mean "a learning process designed to foster independent thought and social criticism"[22])? Other social studies experts may agree with Engle and Ochoa that education for citizenship should be the goal of social studies, but they have very different ideas on what constitutes a "good citizen." In Canadian social studies curricula, the notion of active citizenship has generally been de-emphasized, and where it has been included, there may well be a gap between what is prescribed and what actually goes on in classrooms. Sears[23] tells of a situation in New Brunswick in 1995 where students were threatened with disciplinary action if they signed a petition calling for a change in the school rules. As Sears states, "Hardly a ringing endorsement for getting involved."

A similar problem arises when we consider other aspects of these definitions. Consider those that include a prescription for teaching history. What are the aims of this teaching to be? Are students to know only what great men, and a few women, did in the past? Are they to be taught to understand how historians work? Or is history aimed at raising important social and political issues to help students understand that "history is an ongoing attempt to make sense of why we are here and what our actions should be"?[24] Similar questions arise in defining the other disciplines included in the social studies and in conceptualizing multicultural and global education (see Chapters 20 and 21).

As we have seen, we may all agree, broadly speaking, on the knowledge base of the social studies, but what is actually taught will depend on our goals. Although it is a useful exercise to find out how other citizens, students, and curriculum developers define social studies, the definition question is not an empirical one; it is a question of value. Thus, the question that is the title of this chapter—"What is social studies?"—might be better rephrased as "What *should* social studies be?"

OTHER ACTIVITIES

1. Look at the social studies curriculum guide for your province. How is "social studies" defined? Does the definition change according to grade level? What disciplines are included in the curriculum?

2. Look at any other social studies curriculum guide and/or social studies texts or kits. How is "social studies" defined? Does the definition differ from the one in your province? If so, what difference, if any, does this make to the objectives, content, and teaching methods outlined in the guide, text, or kit?

3. Ask students in an elementary school, teachers, consultants, parents, professors, or school trustees for their definitions of "social studies." Differentiate between what people say social studies *is* and what they say social studies *ought* to be. Compare your responses with those of another person who interviewed a different group of people. How do you account for the similarities or differences? How can you explain the differences between what people say social studies is and what they say it should be?

4. In discussing social studies with peers, try to determine how their experiences have led them to their views about the subject.

NOTES

1. P. Seixas, "Review of research in social studies," in V. Richardson, ed., *Handbook of Research on Teaching* (Washington, DC: American Education Research Association, 2001).

2. E. Wesley and S. Wronski, *Teaching Social Studies in High Schools* (Boston: Heath, 1958), p. 3.

3. B. Massialas, *Inquiry in Social Studies* (New York: McGraw-Hill, 1966), p. 24.

4. The definition approved by the House of Delegates of the National Council for the Social Studies, 1992. Quoted in *The Social Studies Professional* January/February (1993), p. 3.

5. D. Welton and J. Mallan, *Children and Their World: Strategies for Teaching Social Studies*, 4th ed. (Boston: Houghton Mifflin, 1992), p. 2.

6. J. Barth, "Beliefs that discipline the social studies," *International Journal of Social Education* 6:2 (1991), p. 19.

7. J. Banks, *Teaching Strategies for the Social Studies*, 4th ed. (New York: Longman, 1990), p. 3.

8. Saskatchewan Education, *Report of the Social Sciences Reference Committee* (Regina: Saskatchewan Education, 1984), p. 1.

9. M. Mcguire, "Board seeks members' comments," *The Social Studies Professional* March/April (1992), p. 1.

10. S. Engle and A. Ochoa, *Education for Democratic Citizenship: Decision-Making in the Social Studies* (New York: Teachers College Press, 1990).

11. Alberta Education, *Alberta Social Studies Curriculum* (Edmonton: Alberta Education, 1990). ednet.edc.gov.ab.ca/studentprograms

12. Ontario Ministry of Education and Training, *Social Studies Grades 1–6* (Toronto: Ministry of Education and Training, 1998). www.edu.gov.on.ca/eng/document/curricul/social/social.html

13. Atlantic Provinces Education Foundation, *Foundation for the Atlantic Canada Social Studies Curriculum* (Atlantic Provinces Education Foundation, no date), p. 2.

14. Manitoba Education and Youth, *The Framework for Learning Outcomes in Social Studies (K–8)* (Winnipeg: Manitoba Education and Youth, 1988), p. 3.

15. P. Seixas, p. 561.

16. I. Wright, "What sort of question is 'What is social studies?' and how do we go about answering it?" *International Journal of Social Education* 13:1 (1999), pp. 66–76.

17. P. Clark, "Social studies in English Canada: Challenges and prospects in historical context," in A. Sears and I. Wright, eds., *Challenges and Prospects for Canadian Social Studies* (Vancouver: Pacific Educational Press, 2004).

18. A. Hodgetts, *What Culture? What Heritage? A Study in Civic Education in Canada* (Toronto: Ontario Institute for Studies in Education, 1978).

19. See C. Cornbleth, "What constrains meaningful social studies teaching?" *Social Education* 66:3 (2002), pp. 186–190.

20. G. Tomkins, "The social studies in Canada," in J. Parsons, G. Milburn, and M. van Manen, eds., *A Canadian Social Studies* (Edmonton: Faculty of Education Publication Services, University of Alberta, 1983).

21. A. Marker and H. Mehlinger, "Social studies," in P. Jackson, ed., *Handbook of Research on Curriculum* (New York: Macmillan, 1992).

22. S. Engle and A. Ochoa, p. 31.

23. A. Sears, "Social studies in Canada," in I. Wright and A. Sears, eds., *Trends and Issues in Canadian Social Studies* (Vancouver: Pacific Educational Press, 1997), p. 23.

24. G. de Leeuw and B. Griffith, "An historical approach to human understanding," *History and Social Science Teacher* 25:4 (1990), pp. 187–192.

GLOSSARY OF KEY TERMS

A glossary of key terms will be provided at the end of each chapter. Please note that for each glossary in the chapters that follow, these short definitions cannot always do justice to the complexity of some of the terms.

Citizenship education — a "contested" concept with meanings ranging from inculcation of loyalty to the state to social activism.

Social sciences — usually anthropology, history, sociology, geography (the non-physical part), political science, and economics are deemed social sciences.

chapter two

Social Studies:
Why Bother?

Robert Howard, who teaches social studies methods courses at the University of Washington in Tacoma, begins his first class with the following activity.[1]

Activity 2-A

Write down the most important things in your life.
How many of them are included or could be included in the social studies curriculum?

Howard concludes that most of the things that his students mention fall under the social studies umbrella and thus social studies is the most important subject in the curriculum. Yet, what is most important in a person's life may not be educationally significant. Look at your list and then decide which of them are significant enough to be included in the social studies curriculum. Given that social studies can be defined to include everything that is known about people and their interactions, the following question arises: What should we teach? The answer to this will depend upon how we construe the purposes of social studies. What do you think the goals of social studies should be?

Activity 2-B

Indicate your degree of agreement or disagreement with each.

	Strongly agree	Agree	No opinion	Disagree	Strongly disagree
The main task of social studies is to preserve and transmit the cultural heritage.					
Social studies should provide learners with an understanding of decision-making processes so that they may become effective decision makers.					
Social studies should teach about social phenomena; it should not manipulate students' attitudes and values.					
Social studies should help students understand the structure of the social sciences.					
Social studies should teach children to be good Canadian citizens by being patriotic and obeying the laws of the land.					
Social studies should provide learners with an awareness of possible futures and the roles they might play in developing these futures.					
Social studies should teach history and geography so that students understand their place in the world.					
Social studies should teach a body of tested principles and generalizations about human relations and societies.					
Social studies should teach students to make rational decisions about personal and social issues and to act upon their decisions.					
Social studies should provide students with the skills necessary to solve problems and to become independent learners.					
Social studies should develop students' abilities to deal with questions of "What ought to be?" and "What can I do about it?"					

You may find that you agree with all the above statements to some extent. If you analyze the beliefs and value judgments that underlie each of the statements, however, you may find that some of them are incongruent. Can you strongly agree that students should both "obey the laws of the land" and "make rational decisions about personal and social issues and act upon their decisions" if a student's decision is to break a law? If you look at other statements with which you agree, you may find similar incongruities.

Whether differing aims are a result of differing definitions of social studies or vice versa is, perhaps, of little importance. What is important, however, is that each definition and its concomitant aim(s) are embedded in a larger conception of social studies. These conceptions will include beliefs about how students learn, what constitutes truth, what values are appropriate to hold, and so on.

CONCEPTIONS OF SOCIAL STUDIES

Look at the following three lesson plans. Even though the topic is the same in each, the objectives, instructional activities, and assessment methods are very different.

Activity 2-C

The following lesson plans are all for a Grade 4 class in a rural community. The class has 26 students with a variety of ethnic backgrounds: 21 students with various European backgrounds, three students of Indo-Canadian origin, and two First Nations students. There are 13 males and 13 females. One ESL student has special lessons during language classes but is with the class for all other lessons. Another student is dyslexic. All students are engaged in a unit on the history of Canada.

Lesson Plan A

Objectives:

- Students will recall important facts about the explorations of Jacques Cartier.
- Students will work quietly and independently at their desks.
- Students will read the text for important facts.

INTRODUCTION: Ask students to tell you what they learned about Cabot as the first European explorer of Canada. Explain to students that they will now be learning about the second great explorer—Cartier.

BODY OF THE LESSON: Using a map, pictures of Cartier and his ship, and blackboard notes, tell students about Cartier's first voyage. Have students copy the notes into their books. Then ask students to read about Cartier's second voyage in their textbooks and answer the following questions:

- When did Cartier carry out his second voyage?
- Where did Cartier go on his second voyage?
- What happened to him and his crew?

CULMINATION: When students have finished answering the questions, collect their books and tell them that tomorrow they will be given a True/False test on what they have learned about Cartier and Cabot.

ASSESSMENT: Mark the notes and answers to the questions for neatness and accuracy.

Lesson Plan B

Objectives:

- Students will understand why Cartier explored North America.
- Students will write a diary of one of Cartier's voyages as if they were members of Cartier's crew.

- Students will empathize with the life of a sailor on one of Cartier's voyages.
- Students will comprehend, interpret, and analyze information to answer questions.
- Students will work effectively in groups.

INTRODUCTION: Remind students of what they discovered about Cabot and why he came to North America. Ask students to guess why other explorers would want to come to North America. List their responses on the board.

BODY OF THE LESSON: Students will get into their groups (equal number of males and females; one student helps the student with dyslexia, and the ESL student has special reading materials for the activity). Each group reads different materials, including some facsimiles of original documents, to determine if their guesses about Cartier's motives were correct.

Invite students to share their findings on Cartier's motives and then draw their attention to the map of Cartier's two voyages on the blackboard. Briefly describe what Cartier did on the voyages. Have students pose questions about the voyages and then have them divide into teacher-chosen groups. Using materials provided, two groups study the first voyage and two groups study the second voyage. Each group works with materials developmentally appropriate for the group. Students who are at a concrete stage will have straightforward descriptive materials; those at a more abstract level will have materials that use metaphors and analogies. When students have answered the questions, have them put their findings into a diary format (group writing project) as if they were actually on the voyage.

CULMINATION: Have each group of students read one paragraph from their diary and then ask them how they would assess their work. Have students generate a list of criteria for diary assessment and then use these criteria to assess their work.

ASSESSMENT: Students will be observed in their groups, and a checklist will be used to assess participation and research skills based on the developmental level of each student. Diaries will be assessed on the basis of the criteria generated in class and the developmental level of the students.

Lesson Plan C

Objectives:

- Students will describe and evaluate the story of Cartier from the point of view of the French and the Native people.
- Students will analyze the relationships between the French and Native people, noting the colonizing mentality of the French leaders.
- Students will empathize with the Native people.
- Students will work in self-chosen groups or individually to create a chart noting the similarities and differences between the Native and French accounts.
- Students will use research skills to realize the first two objectives.

INTRODUCTION: Remind students about the last lesson, where they found out that Europeans carried out the exploration of North America for the purposes of obtaining power and wealth. Inform students that they will now be carrying out a case study of one explorer, Cartier.

BODY OF THE LESSON: Students choose to work in groups or individually. They read an account of Cartier's voyages written from the French point of view plus an account from the Native point of view. The readings have a lot of graphics and for those who learn best through listening, there are audiotapes. The student with dyslexia works with a partner, and the ESL student is given "simplified" reading material as well as an audiotape so that he can record his answers. Students determine what the similarities and differences are between the two accounts, note them on their charts, and hypothesize why they exist.

CULMINATION: Students share their findings with each other. Ask students whether it is possible to state whether one account is more reliable than the other. Discuss why there can be many accounts of the same event and that it is impossible to tell which is true. Note that the stories of the people with the least power are often ignored. Have students give examples from their own experiences. Discuss how the power of the colonizing Europeans determined the treatment accorded the Native people. Ask students for other examples of colonization that they know about. Students then work on their charts to bring them up to a standard they think would warrant their being placed in their portfolios. Tell students that they will be studying other explorers and their relationships with Native people and how this, and other factors, contributed to the present marginalized state of many First Nations people.

ASSESSMENT: Students who wish to do so place their charts in their portfolios. Anecdotal records are kept of students who make significant comments in the discussion. For example, a student's comment that the French would view the Native people as "savages" because they were not Christians would be recorded.

Which of the teachers of lessons A, B, and C would be most likely to

a) vote for a middle-of-the-road party?

b) vote for a right-wing party?

c) vote for a left-wing party?

d) believe that knowledge is the product of an inquiring mind and its interactions with the environment and that knowledge will change as students develop and we learn more?

e) believe that knowledge is "out there" and that there are absolute truths?

f) believe that students construct their own knowledge, that there are multiple truths, and that there is no way of really determining which belief is truer than another?

g) negotiate classroom rules based on the belief that there are no absolute values and that rules have to be negotiated?

h) lay down rules based on a belief that there are absolute values that all people should follow?

i) believe that students develop through stages and that their views change as they develop?

j) believe in a behaviourist theory in which what is taught is presented in a highly structured way and what is learned is learned through reinforcement and practice?

k) believe that learning is highly personal and that people construct their own truth?

l) believe that people are born *tabula rasa* (with a blank-slate mind on which society writes its knowledge)?

Now look at the Answers section at the back of the book to see what I think the most reasonable responses are.

According to Barr, Barth, and Shermis,[2] three traditions or **conceptions of social studies** can be identified:

1. social studies as **Citizenship Transmission**
2. social studies as **Reflective Inquiry**
3. social studies as **Social Science**

Social Studies as Citizenship Transmission

In this conception, the aim is to instill in students the knowledge and values thought necessary for good citizenship. Through the study of history, government, and the students' own community and country, students are to learn the virtues of being responsible, patriotic, loyal, and respectful citizens. The basic instructional approach is didactic: teachers pass on knowledge selected by an external authority (e.g., the province's ministry of education) through lectures and activities based on student reading of a textbook.

This Citizenship Transmission conception is based on several assumptions: that there are irrefutable societal values (such as respect for authority) that students have to accept; that reality is objective (not based on the subjective views of individuals) and essentially unchanging; and that wisdom from the past must be transmitted to future generations. Presumably, children are born as *tabulae rasae*—their minds are "blank slates" on which the knowledge and values necessary for citizenship will be written. Alternatively, children are born with a propensity for being "bad" (the idea of "original sin" fits in with this view) and must be taught to be "good." This conception has received attention recently especially in the United States, where E.D. Hirsch[3] is promoting the view that there is a body of content (which he refers to as the "civil religion") that all students must learn if they are to be considered "good" Americans. Similarly, in Canada, various interest groups are calling for more "content" (especially Canadian history and geography) to be taught so that students become "good" Canadian citizens.

Social Studies as Reflective Inquiry

In this conception the aim is to develop rational decision makers in the social-political context. The focus is on structured and disciplined inquiry into the problems and issues that children face in their day-to-day lives—problems that have their counterparts in the wider world. In this conception it is not assumed that values are finite and absolute. Values can change. Similarly, knowledge is also changeable: it is constructed by the learner through the interaction of the content presented and the learner's developing mental powers. Children are not born "bad" or as "blank slates" but with potential that can be channelled in appropriate directions according to their developmental levels. Further, it is assumed that if students are presented with relevant problems, they can be taught to use their developing rational powers. They have the right to apply these powers in making their own decisions. This conception is child-centred.

Social Studies as Social Science

The aim in this conception is for students to become effective citizens by acquiring knowledge from the social sciences and the skills of social scientists. Thus, the content chosen for study consists of concepts and research methodologies that students are to apply to problems derived from these disciplines. The focus is on the academic aspect of the social studies. It is assumed that the social sciences best explain human behaviour and that students can use these explanations in becoming good citizens. Behind this conception lies the belief that knowledge can be organized into discrete disciplines and that truth can be determined through the use of social science research methodologies.

Social Studies as Critical Reflection

Barr, Barth, and Shermis do not consider one recent conception of social studies. Clarke[4] labels this the **Critical Reflective** approach, the goal of which is to empower people so that they can take action to solve societal ills. Clarke argues that students are presently socialized into holding the beliefs and ideologies of the dominant groups in society, and that opposing beliefs are ignored. Thus, students are taught to be non-critical and to accept the existing distribution of power in society. What students need to learn is to be critical, to participate in civic affairs, and to take the actions needed to bring about social justice. They must take into account the stories of those who are oppressed and marginalized. This conception assumes that knowledge is constructed by groups who share common interests. What qualifies as truth is relative to a group; there is no absolute knowledge. However, although some values are relative, underlying moral principles are not. Concerns for social justice, human dignity, and freedom are universal, even though the ways they are conceptualized and applied as a basis for action can be a matter of disagreement and debate. This postmodern conception and variations of it are receiving considerable attention in educational theory, although it is rarely found in curriculum documents or learning materials.

Activity 2-D

Now that you are familiar with the four differing conceptions of social studies, identify the conception that would be congruent with each of the following statements. Then turn to the Answers section.

1. The content to be learned in the social studies should be determined by an authority and passed down to students by the teacher.

2. It is better to evaluate students on how they think rather than on the products of their thought.

3. By reading stories of great men and women of the past, students will learn the requirements for being good citizens.

4. By reading the stories of people who are oppressed or ignored in society, students will realize that there are differing realities.

5. Learning how historians arrive at their answers to historical questions will help students solve contemporary social problems.

6. Students should be tested on their knowledge of facts, and their performance should be compared against national norms.

7. The two most powerful psychological theories are behaviourism (human behaviour is a direct function of the environment, and learning is defined according to the quantity of information acquired) and social learning theory (learning is a gradual accumulation of patterns of behaviour through imitation and modelling).

8. If students are presented with problems that are relevant to them, they are more likely to be motivated to learn and to create solutions that are meaningful to them.

9. All knowledge is shaped by human interests. Dominant groups in society use their self-interested knowledge to subjugate other groups and individuals.

These four conceptions are "ideal types." Rarely will you find pure examples of each. Rather, social studies curricula tend to incorporate aspects of more than one of them, although there is little evidence that the Critical Reflective view receives much attention. The other three conceptions receive varying degrees of emphasis. All elementary school social studies curricula in Canada (of which I am aware) include the study of history and geography and some study of the research methodologies used in these disciplines, such as oral history and field studies. All include the teaching of critical thinking. All incorporate the values thought necessary for being an effective citizen of Canada. Curricula vary in the degree of emphasis accorded history, critical thinking, citizenship, and so on. There are other ways of categorizing conceptions of social studies (for example, see Case,[5] who identifies categories of social initiation, social reformation, personal development, and academic understanding; or the research of Goodman and Adler,[6] who found that elementary teachers held six different conceptions). However, these four—Citizenship Transmission, Reflective Inquiry, Social Science, and Critical Reflection—do provide a useful way of looking at social studies.

DEVELOPING A RATIONALE

To answer the question as to which is the most appropriate conception, we have to develop a rationale. We have to argue that the aims of one particular conception of social studies are more appropriate than the aims of another. We must provide evidence that the assumptions of how children learn in one conception are more believable than those in another. We must decide between competing conceptions with respect to the nature of truth and how knowledge is constructed. These questions are not specific to social studies; they are relevant to the entire educational enterprise. To answer them, we need to develop our own philosophy of education. This is a complex endeavour. The example below demonstrates how one teacher (T) justifies teaching about the local community by answering questions posed by a pre-service teacher (PT).

T: I've decided to teach my Grade 2 students about the local community.

PT: What specifically will you be emphasizing?

T: Well, the role of people in the community and how they all work together to make the community work.

PT: Which people will you be focusing upon?

T: The mayor, police officers, firefighters.

PT: Aren't most of these people male?

T: Well, yes they are. But I will point out that women can be elected as mayor and can be firefighters and police officers.

PT: Why do you think students need to know this?

T: Students need to understand that women can contribute just as much to the community as men. And they need to learn that we are all interdependent.

PT: Why is this important?

T: Because we live in an interdependent world, and we all have to rely on each other if we are to have a better society. So students will have to think through how their community works and see if it can be improved.

PT: How do you think your study of the community will do this?

T: In a number of ways. Students will learn about different roles in the community and how they all relate; they will have to think through how the community might be improved; and they will see what their roles might be in bringing about these changes.

PT: Do you think your students can understand this?

T: Oh yes, by this age they can realize that they depend on people in the community for their food, shelter, safety, and so on. And they are able to understand the consequences if someone in the community does not perform their role. And they do have ideas about how their community could be made better.

PT: Do you have other reasons for teaching about the community?

T: I think students can begin to think about roles, and as you pointed out, how males tend to dominate many roles. However, I will make sure that students can understand some of the reasons for this, and what changes women can make and have made. Anyway, girls ought to have the same opportunities as boys. In fact, I may persuade some girls to begin thinking about jobs as firefighters. *[T. laughs.]*

PT: And boys as secretaries in the mayor's office?

T: Hadn't thought about that!

PT: How would you define "community"?

T: Well, I think as I have already said it is about people living and working together in interdependent relationships.

The above dialogue reveals that T has a number of reasons for including the study of the local community in the social studies curriculum. Notice that some of the initial reasons are supported with "higher order" reasons—for example, that understanding community roles can lead to an understanding of interdependence. T is also asked to clarify terms— to say what is meant by "community." T is also asked whether students are capable of understanding what is to be taught. Throughout, T has presented a series of arguments to justify the teaching of a particular topic. For example:

Conclusion: I ought to teach about the local community.

Reason: Through the study of the local community, students will understand the importance of interdependence.

Because T believes the reason to be a good one, T must also believe that learning about interdependence is significant. When asked to justify this belief, T presents yet another argument. You will find out more about arguments in later chapters.

Activity 2-E

Write a dialogue similar to the one above. Start with "I have decided to teach (state the topic) to my Grade (state the grade level) students." Then interrogate yourself or have a partner pose questions as to why you made this decision.

Now that you have some familiarity with the four conceptions of social studies and how to construct a rationale, try the next activity.

Activity 2-F

A committee has been formed in your school to look at the goals of social studies for your school. There are four people on the committee. Choose to be person A, B, C, or D *before* you read the role cards below. Read your role card and play the role. Your task is to persuade the committee to accept your goal and the conception of social studies in which the goal lies. Then create a *very brief* outline for a social studies curriculum for a particular grade level, listing four major goals and suggesting four topics to be taught, four major skills to be incorporated, and four important values to be stressed.

Person A

You believe that social studies should teach children to be good citizens. Your goal is to develop children who are patriotic, law-abiding, democratic, and knowledgeable about current events. You believe in the Citizenship Transmission conception of social studies.

Person B

You believe that social studies should teach children how to find information for themselves and how to interpret and evaluate that information so that they can solve problems and make their own decisions. You believe in the Reflective Inquiry conception of social studies.

Person C

You wish students to study history and geography in a disciplined way. You believe that if students can think like historians and geographers, they will be better equipped to understand their environment and their own place in it. You believe in the Social Science conception of social studies.

Person D

You think that the ultimate goal of social studies is for students to critique the existing social order and take actions that will lead to equality and justice for all people. You believe in the Critical Reflective conception of social studies.

The next activity asks you to develop a rationale for a specific aspect of social studies. Even though you will be starting with this straightforward task, you will have to apply "higher order" reasons to justify your decision. Eventually you will be appealing to your own complex philosophy of education.

Activity 2-G

Choose something—a topic, an ability, an attitude—that you think would be worthwhile to teach to a group of students. List your reasons for teaching it and, where appropriate, try to answer the following questions. (The questions are not in hierarchical order.)

1. What do I mean by "X"? ("X" is a key term in your reasoning, e.g., What do I mean by "respect," or "cooperation," or "history"?)
2. Do I believe that students don't already know what I intend to teach them? Have I any evidence for this?
3. Are students capable of learning what I intend to teach? Have I any evidence for this?
4. What value position am I assuming in giving a particular reason? Is this value defensible?
5. If students didn't learn what I intend to teach, would they be disadvantaged? Why or why not?
6. How is what I intend to teach relevant to students' lives? What does "relevance" mean in this case?
7. Do students really need to know what I intend to teach them? Why?

In synthesizing Chapters 1 and 2, we can see a number of significant goals.

- *Knowledge of the content of social studies*

  It is clear that in all the definitions of social studies and the rationales for teaching it, subject matter knowledge is important. Even though the exact nature of what should be taught is disputed, no social studies educator would say that subject matter knowledge should not be taught.

- *The abilities and skills needed to obtain, process, and present this knowledge*

  If students are to collect and use social studies information, then they need to be able to locate it, classify it, analyze it, and present it in reports, maps, graphs, or other formats.

- *The intellectual standards needed to evaluate this knowledge*

  All social studies curricula in Canada call for students to be critical thinkers. **Intellectual standards** will require that students examine information for its logic, plausibility, reliability, and accuracy. They will also require students to be clear, coherent, open-minded, and fair-minded.

- *The personal and social values required to resolve issues and evaluate value claims and actions*

  All social studies curricula also emphasize the resolution of social issues or call on students to be good citizens who will make responsible decisions. This will require students to critically examine their own values and the values of society.

- *The citizenship action competencies to put decisions into practice*

The raison d'être for social studies is citizenship. This entails that people take actions in democratic and responsible ways. To do this requires competencies such as making persuasive presentations, knowing where to obtain information, understanding how political institutions work, and evaluating how actions impinge on self and others.

In Chapter 3, you will see how these five broad goals can provide a framework for organizing a social studies curriculum.

We must remember that social studies is but one subject among many, that education is lifelong, and that the school can't "do it all." Further, although we may formulate what we consider to be a justifiable rationale for a particular goal of social studies, we need to keep open minds because our reasons and reasoning may change as we reflect upon our teaching practices. Rationale building is complex, but it can't be ignored. We should be able to give good reasons for what we do in the name of social studies.

OTHER ACTIVITIES

1. What rationales are presented in your province's social studies curriculum? Are they based on the Citizenship Transmission, the Reflective Inquiry, the Social Science, or the Critical Reflective conception of social studies?

2. Very often surveys are taken of public opinions on education. Commissions are convened to advise provincial governments on educational matters. Or assessments of students' knowledge about social studies are carried out by ministries/departments of education. If such information is available, which conceptions of social studies underlie the results of the surveys or commissions, or the interpretations placed on the results? Are these conceptions consistent with those of your provincial curriculum?

3. Ask students in an elementary school why they think they have to study social studies. Compare their comments to rationale statements in your provincial curriculum.

4. According to the latest recommendations of the National Commission on Social Studies in the United States,[7] history and geography should provide the framework for social studies. Selective studies of the history, geography, government, and economic systems of the major civilizations should receive coverage at least equal to the study of the United States (substitute "Canada" here for purposes of answering the questions below). Integration of other subject areas with the social studies should be encouraged. Are these recommendations desirable? Are they feasible to implement?

5. Find out from other professional bodies (e.g., your provincial social studies organization) what they think the goals of social studies are and/or should be. Compare these goals with those in your provincial curriculum guide. How would you account for the similarities and differences?

NOTES

1. R. Howard, "The shrinking of social studies," *Social Education* 67:4 (2003), p. 285.

2. R. Barr, J. Barth, and S. Shermis, *Defining the Social Studies* (Washington, DC: National Council for the Social Studies, 1977).

3. E. Hirsch, *Cultural Literacy: What Every American Needs to Know* (New York: Vintage Books, 1988).

4. M. Clarke, "A critically reflective social studies," *The History and Social Science Teacher* 25:4 (1990), pp. 214–220.

5. R. Case, "Elements of a coherent social studies program," in R. Case and P. Clark, eds., *The Canadian Anthology of Social Studies* (Vancouver: Pacific Educational Press, 1999).

6. J. Goodman and S. Adler, "Becoming an elementary social studies teacher: A study of perspectives," *Theory and Research in Social Education* 13:2 (1985), pp. 1–20.

7. National Commission on Social Studies in the Schools, *Charting a Course: Social Studies for the 21st Century* (Report of the Curriculum Task Force of the National Commission on Social Studies in the Schools, Washington, DC, 1989).

GLOSSARY OF KEY TERMS

Conceptions of Social Studies — a set of assumptions about the major objectives of social studies and how they should be realized:

Citizenship Transmission — teaching a decided-upon body of information via didactic means with the intent to socialize the student into the conventions of the society.

Critical Reflection — teaching students that there are many points of view and that all must be heeded, especially those of the disadvantaged and marginalized. The focus is on social justice.

Reflective Inquiry — teaching students how to inquire into problems that face them so that they can decide what actions to take.

Social Science — using the traditional disciplines to teach students how to be good citizens.

Intellectual standards — standards for judging the truth, reliability, validity, plausibility, clarity, and coherence of the knowledge we use and create.

chapter three

What Should a Social Studies Curriculum Look Like?

It is clear that the content of social studies includes knowledge from many disciplines. As we can't teach all of this knowledge, we have to make curriculum choices. But how? In the previous chapter, we looked at some broad goals for social studies and some different conceptions of social studies. These goals and conceptions provide the framework for the development of a curriculum. So, if you view social studies as the teaching of the social sciences, then the curriculum you design will reflect knowledge and skills drawn from these disciplines. If you accept the Reflective Inquiry conception, your curriculum will be built around problems for students to resolve. But goals such as learning "knowledge and skills of the social sciences," "solving problems," and helping students "become good citizens" are too broad to serve as guides to classroom teaching. How does one translate these goals into operational terms for a particular group of students?

How we translate goals into practice will depend upon a number of considerations. First and foremost, there are the curriculum guides that every province produces. These either state, in quite specific terms, what to teach or provide guidelines to follow. In both cases, teachers are contractually bound to follow what the curriculum guide stipulates. There may also be prescribed textbooks or other learning materials. Thus, teachers should become familiar with all the prescriptions of the provincial or territorial ministry/department of education curriculum.

Activity 3-A

What does your social studies curriculum guide prescribe? How much choice do you have?

STUDENT CAPABILITIES

One key consideration in the design of curriculum guides and our own lessons will be the capabilities of our students. If what we intend to teach is beyond students' abilities, then there is no point in teaching it. Thus, we have to take into account the intellectual maturity of elementary students.

Activity 3-B

What do the following vignettes tell us about the capabilities of students in the early grades of elementary school?

TEACHER: Where's Ontario?
STUDENT: In Toronto.

TEACHER: Dinosaurs once roamed the earth.
STUDENT: Were there dinosaurs when you were young, teacher?

TEACHER: We're going to visit the zoo.
STUDENT: How far is the zoo?
TEACHER: About 50 kilometres.
STUDENT: Is that a long way?

   As Piaget[1] reports, a six-year-old believed that "Mountains made themselves all alone. So that we can skate."[2] Other young children interviewed by Piaget had their own explanations for physical phenomena. Consider the following exchange about the creation of clouds:

PIAGET: And where does the steam for the clouds come from?
STUDENT: When you cook soup.
PIAGET: Does cooking soup make the clouds?
STUDENT: The steam goes out and it takes water with it.

   Consider these conversations:

TEACHER: Let's see, it's noon here, so it's 2:30 p.m. in Newfoundland.
STUDENT: How can that be? Did they miss lunch?

TEACHER: Define "climate."
STUDENT: It means how much rain and sun there is.

TEACHER: What about barometric pressure?

STUDENT: Uh?

TEACHER: How do you think this person feels? *[Shows a picture of a boy crying at a birthday party.]*

STUDENT: He feels happy.

TEACHER: Why do you think so?

STUDENT: Well, I'd feel happy if it was my birthday.

TEACHER: Draw a map of your desk and chair.

STUDENT:

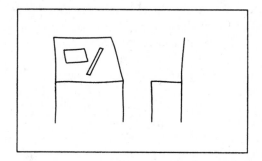

These vignettes demonstrate that young elementary students (and some older ones too) have concepts of time and space that differ from those of most adults, and they have problems taking the perspective of another person (role-taking). They also define words from a limited knowledge and conceptual base.

There is also evidence that students—at least in the US, where the two authors of a recent study conducted their research—have limited understanding of the basic concepts of food, shelter, and clothing.[3] Primary students, generally speaking, did not know why people lived in different kinds of housing or ate different kinds of food, although they could explain why people needed shelter and food. They did not know where electricity, cloth, and many food products came from or how they were produced. They were not aware of the geographical and cultural influences on food and shelter. The authors suggest that we should do a much better job of explaining why there are differences and similarities in food, shelter, and clothing around the world and they have developed materials to teach these.[4]

We have to take into account the capacities of our students and what research says about these. In this regard, one recent phenomenon has been brain-based teaching and learning,[5] and teachers have been encouraged to buy into expensive packages. However, as Bergen states, "… the best judge of effective classroom practice is not the neuroscientist, but the knowledgeable and experienced teacher."[6]

Activity 3-C

Obtain examples of students' work in social studies or interview students about their knowledge of social studies content. What conceptions do they have of the content they have studied? How do they conceive of time and space? What explanations do they have for historical events, for climatic phenomena, for social phenomena, and so on? Look at the maps drawn by students in Chapter 11 and the web on Peru in Chapter 4 and infer those students' knowledge and abilities.

STUDENT AND SOCIAL CHARACTERISTICS

In addition to beliefs about what capacities students have, beliefs about student characteristics such as class, ethnicity, and gender affect how the curriculum is developed and then implemented by teachers. There is evidence that children from working-class backgrounds[7] and from minority cultures[8] are viewed by some teachers as having low self-esteem and poor attention spans. Teachers may also perceive working-class children as having less facility with language than their middle-class counterparts. Evidence also suggests that teacher expectations about the abilities of boys and girls differ,[9] and that teachers can reinforce sexual stereotypes.[10] Recent studies are indicating that boys, because they are more boisterous, perceive themselves to be less liked than girls in elementary classrooms.[11]

In addition, we should consider the social makeup of Canada. According to Statistics Canada,[12] the population of urban areas is increasing, especially in suburbs; cities such as Toronto and Vancouver have a population of foreign-born people of 44 and 38 percent, respectively; women hold 65.2 percent of new jobs, although men still hold 53.4 percent of all jobs; more couples are living common-law and there are more same-sex couples living together; and we think that a sense of nationhood is important. We must also remember that we are finding more special needs students in our classrooms.[13] These and other characteristics of our society will influence the types of students we have in our classes, the ways in which we teach these students, and the social studies curriculum.

CURRICULUM ORGANIZATION

Another consideration is how to *organize* the content of the curriculum. The terms **scope** (what is to be taught, and the depth and breadth of what is to be taught) and **sequence** (the order in which knowledge, skills, and attitudes are taught) are frequently used to describe the organizational pattern of a curriculum. It should be noted here that there is ambiguity in the use of the term "scope." Sometimes it is used to refer to the topics (family, community, geography of Canada, etc.) and the skills and attitudes to be taught. Sometimes it refers to the depth and breadth of what is to be taught, e.g., the inclusion in Canadian geography of a detailed study of each of the regions and a section on interpreting topographical maps.

Case[14] points out that there are a number of strands that could be used in organizing a social studies curriculum.

1. A **disciplinary strand** would consist of history, geography, and other social sciences.

2. A **dimension-based strand** would involve topics that cross disciplinary boundaries. Examples would be social phenomena such as conflict or peace; social roles such as citizen or worker; social institutions such as families or governments; and regional studies such as the Rockies or Southeast Asia.

3. Finally, there are **concern strands**—also known as **issue-based strands**—where the emphasis is on controversial topics. Examples would be in global, human rights, peace, multicultural, or environmental education where the objective is to suggest solutions to issues.

Using these strands will entail having students obtain and present information. If we wish students to evaluate information, then we have to teach them the intellectual standards to do this. We would have to teach them the standards of validity, logic, plausibility, relevance, and so on and how to apply these to the information they use. And if we want students to consider issues and take action on them, then such personal and social values as equality, fairness, and respect will have to be explored. Thus, using the major goals identified at the end of Chapter 2, a curriculum could be organized in the following way with the goals relating to whichever strand is emphasized:

Goals	Disciplinary knowledge	Interdisciplinary dimensions	Interdisciplinary issues
Content knowledge			
Information gathering and reporting			
Intellectual standards			
Personal and social values			
Active citizenship			

Whatever strands are used, there has to be a grade-by-grade sequence. Most elementary school curricula in Canada and the United States organize their social studies programs on the basis of **expanding horizons**. This view of scope and sequence is based on the assumption that children should start with what they know—themselves and then their families—and then move outward in space to the community and eventually the world. Kieran Egan criticizes the expanding horizons view, arguing that what children know best are such concepts as "good" and "bad," and "love" and "hate," and that these, and the child's power of imagination, should be the basis for organizing the curriculum.[15] In his book *Teaching as Story Telling* he outlines how his ideas could be put into practice.[16] Egan's concerns about the rigid and lockstep manner in which the expanding horizons approach has been implemented are valid. For example, Grade 1 children *can* examine events that would be construed as beyond the boundaries of a study of families, and they *can* grapple with abstract ideas, either within a story format or through other activities.

Expanding Horizons

Another way of organizing a curriculum is a scope and sequence based on **spiralling concepts**.

In this framework, chosen concepts are dealt with at increasing levels of sophistication as students move through the grades. Thus, at Grade 1, students would deal with concepts such as family, tradition, rules, continuity, etc., at their level of sophistication, whereas Grade 5 students would deal with them at their level. In this spiralling concepts framework the concepts are often chosen from the scope of the expanding horizons approach; that is, in Grade 1 the concepts are related to studies of families, in Grade 2 to community studies, and so on. When this rigid pattern is chosen, Egan's criticisms of the "expanding horizons" view apply.

Another way of sequencing, applicable to historical content, is chronology. Students study their family history in Grade 1 and their community history in Grade 2. Then, starting at Grade 3 or 4, students learn about the history of Canada in chronological fashion. Study of the first inhabitants is followed by learning about the first European explorers and settlers, and so on. Then, at about Grade 6 or 7, students begin another chronological sequence with the study of the first humans and first civilizations, and continue in Grades 8 through 12 to follow a chronological history, usually of Europe and North America. In Ontario,[17] the sequence moves from a study of pioneers in Canada to Medieval Europe, to ancient civilizations at Grade 5, followed by a study of Native peoples and the European exploration of Canada.

A curriculum may be organized by amalgamating a number of different organizational patterns. In Canada, when history is the topic, the "expanding horizons" model is often melded with spiralling concepts and with chronology. Further, the scope may consist of topics that pertain to a single discipline or to topics that require a multidisciplinary or integrated disciplinary approach. The examples that follow reflect various provincial approaches to curriculum design.

The Atlantic provinces base their curricula on the Foundation for Atlantic Canada Social Studies Curriculum.[18] This is organized around several key concepts:[19]

- Citizenship, Power, and Governance
- Culture and Diversity
- Individuals, Societies, and Economic Decisions
- Interdependence
- People, Place, and Environment
- Time, Continuity, and Change

Quebec organizes the curriculum around key competencies sequenced in three cycles, with each cycle consisting of two elementary years:[20]

- Cycle One competency: to construct his/her representation of space, time, and society
- Cycles Two and Three competencies: to understand the organization of a society in its territory; to interpret change in a society and its territory; to be open to the diversity of societies and their territories.[21]

Each of these competencies is fleshed out with specific content, techniques, and evaluative criteria.

Ontario[22] divides its curriculum into two major themes, each with its own sequence:

Heritage and Citizenship

Grade 1: Relationships, Rules, and Responsibilities

Grade 2: Traditions and Celebrations

Grade 3: Pioneer Life

Grade 4: Medieval Times

Grade 5: Early Civilizations

Grade 6: Aboriginal Peoples and European Explorers

Canada and World Connections

Grade 1: The Local Community

Grade 2: Features of Communities around the World

Grade 3: Urban and Rural Communities

Grade 4: The Provinces and Territories of Canada

Grade 5: Aspects of Government in Canada

Grade 6: Canada and Its Trading Partners

Manitoba sequences the curriculum as follows:[23]

Kindergarten: Being Together

Grade 1: Connecting and Belonging

Grade 2: Communities in Canada

Grade 3: Communities of the World

Grade 4: Manitoba, Canada, and the North: Places and Stories

Grade 5: People and Stories of Canada to 1867

Grade 6: Canada: A Country of Change (1867 to Present)

Grade 7: People and Places in the World

Manitoba plans to implement a new curriculum guide[24] for Kindergarten to Grade 8 by spring 2005. Here, the organizing framework consists of the following concepts: Identity; Culture; Community; The Land; Places and People; Historical Connections; Global Interdependence; Power and Authority; and Economics and Resources.

Saskatchewan[25] organizes its curriculum like this:

Grade 1: Families

Grade 2: Local Community

Grade 3: Community Comparisons

Grade 4: Saskatchewan

Grade 5: Canada

Grade 6: Canada's Global Neighbours

Grade 7: Canada and the World Community

Twenty major concepts are intertwined throughout the sequence with some having more emphasis in one grade level, some in another.[26]

Concept	Grades						
	1	2	3	4	5	6	7
Beliefs							
Causality							
Change	X		X			X	X
Conflict							
Culture	X			X			
Decision making			X	X	X		
Distribution					X		X
Diversity		X	X	X	X	X	
Environment		X	X				
Identity	X			X	X	X	
Institution				X	X	X	
Interaction						X	X
Interdependence			X		X		
Location				X		X	X
Needs					X	X	X
Power							X
Resources					X		X
Technology				X			
Time		X			X	X	
Values				X	X	X	X

Alberta[27] specifies topics in each grade:

Grade 1: Me and Others: my school, my family, other Canadian families

Grade 2: People Today: people nearby, people in Canada, people in the world

Grade 3: Communities: my community in the past, communities needing each other, special communities

Grade 4: Alberta: its geography and people, its history, a comparative study with Quebec

Grade 5: Canada: its geography and people, exploration and settlement, links with other countries

Grade 6: Meeting Human Needs: local government, Greece (an ancient civilization), China (Pacific Rim nation)

As in some other provinces, the social studies curriculum in Alberta is under review.[28] The new curriculum is to be implemented in stages with K–3 being in force in 2005, Grades 4 and 7 in 2006, Grade 5 in 2007, and Grade 6 in 2008. The topics will be the following:

Kindergarten: Being Together

Grade 1: Citizenship: Belonging and Connecting

Grade 2: Communities in Canada

Grade 3: Connecting to the World

Grade 4: Alberta: The Land, People, and Stories

Grade 5: Canada: The Land, People, and Stories

Grade 6: Democracy: Action and Participation

Grade 7: Canada: Origins, Histories, and Movement of People

In British Columbia[29] each grade is organized around five themes:

• Applications of Social Studies
• Society and Culture
• Politics and Law
• Economy and Technology
• Environment

In each grade there are a number of objectives for each theme, and teachers choose objectives from one or more of these to develop their units of study.

PRINCIPLES OF CURRICULUM ORGANIZATION

Whatever organizational pattern is used, it should be remembered that students learn best if the information is

• limited in amount
• structured around and related to a key idea or concept
• thought about in a critical way
• related to what they already know
• applied to new contexts

In choosing the scope and sequence of a curriculum, logical criteria must be considered. A student may have the capacity to memorize "15° of longitude is equivalent to one hour of time," but to *understand* this the student must comprehend, at least, that the earth rotates on its axis every 24 hours (approximately) and that there are 360° in a circle. It is logically necessary to know some things before one can begin to know other things. Therefore, in sequencing anything we have to ask, "In order to know X, what do students have to know prior to studying X?" Having ascertained this, then we have to find out whether students actually have this prior knowledge. If they haven't got it, then we will have to teach it.

Activity 3-D

How is the scope and sequence of the social studies curriculum in your province organized? Are any reasons given for the organizational scheme? Do you think the reasons are good ones? What skills are emphasized in the curriculum in your province? How are they sequenced? Do you think that the sequence is a realistic one? Is there any evidence that children learn these skills in the sequence outlined in the curriculum guide?

A further consideration is the number of objectives that can be realized through the study of a particular topic. It is usually better to strive for multiple objectives because such a method is efficient (it allows, for example, teaching language arts skills through writing a report in social studies) and comprehensive (allowing students to develop knowledge at the same time as they develop skills and attitudes).

Your own knowledge, abilities, and interests are important in curriculum development. If you have recently visited another country, and the curriculum calls for the study of another culture, you are probably going to be more enthusiastic about studying the country you visited than one you haven't. Moreover, you are likely to have up-to-date information about the culture. Having current information about the topic being studied is another key criterion for choosing to study X rather than Y.

School and community pressures may also be an issue. Does the school administration require the teaching of certain topics? Does the community want particular controversial issues avoided? The mere mention of "values education" may raise ire in some communities. Factors such as the social makeup of the community and the students have to be considered. If there is prejudice in the community, it has to be dealt with. If a political event occurs—a strike, a government action that divides the community, a war—it has to be dealt with in a way that is sensitive to both educational goals and the needs of students. This is especially true in light of recent events such as SARS, terrorism, mad cow disease, West Nile virus, and so on, all of which have affected or can affect student lives.

Broader public pressures also influence curriculum decision making. Recently, public concerns have been raised about multiculturalism, the environment, Canada–US relations, trade with Pacific Rim countries, global education, and human rights. Furthermore, the perceived lack of student knowledge about Canadian history and geography has resulted in curriculum changes in some provinces.[30]

Yet, despite the fact that many people may have provided input for curricula decisions, the most important people, the students, are rarely consulted. No one in Canada, as far as I know, has ever carried out a systematic research study to find out what elementary school students would like to learn, or think is important to learn, in social studies.

Activity 3-E

What would you guess elementary school students would like to study or think would be important to study? Now go and ask at least one student. Have a class collection of the findings.

1. Were your original guesses correct?

2. Are there any topics that a majority of students would like to study?

3. Are any of these topics included in the provincial curriculum guide or texts?

4. Do choices change with age; that is, do Grade 1 students make different choices from Grade 6 students?

5. Should topics that students like to study be included?

6. If there is a vast discrepancy between the actual curriculum and student choices, should you do anything about it? Why or why not? If you think something ought to be done, how would you go about doing it?

7. Are resource materials available to teach the topics chosen by students?

CURRICULUM INTEGRATION

Activity 3-F

Decide which of these vignettes would count as an example of integration. Then look at the Answers section.

a) The teacher looked at the objectives of the Grade 4 curriculum and related them to the planning of her Grade 5 curriculum.

b) The teacher planned a unit on games. Students researched games played in their own society as well as games in other cultures. They played the games in their social studies classes as well as in physical education; by so doing, they realized some physical education objectives.

c) The teacher planned a unit on games. Students drew pictures of games; they learned to spell words related to games; they sang songs about games; they did math problems involving game situations; they wrote stories about games; and in science class, they carried out experiments to determine how much force was required to throw and kick different sorts of balls (baseball, soccer ball, etc.) a certain distance.

d) Students were allowed to choose a topic by relating it to their personal interests.

e) The school was dedicated to multiculturalism but had no firm policies. Teachers in all the grade levels formulated a policy and objectives. They then planned activities to realize those objectives and to include multiculturalism in whichever subject area was the most appropriate.

f) The students studied the history of Canada for 10 weeks, and then they studied the geography of Canada for 10 weeks. They finished the year with a study of a First Nations group.

g) The students studied Peru. They learned about the food, shelter, clothing, religion, government, education, celebrations, and so on and related these aspects to each other to formulate generalizations about Peru.

One of the major ideas in contemporary social studies is **integration**. Of course, social studies has always been an integrated subject as it draws on knowledge from many disciplines, which are also integrated fields of study (e.g., historians study economic, social, cultural, and political events and ideas). In learning social studies, students use skills drawn from other subjects; they put their social studies skills to use in still other areas. The debate today concerns the desirable degree of integration and the question of what is to be integrated.

Curricular integration can include

- the joining together of social studies and language arts into a humanities course
- the teaching of something common to all subject areas (e.g., critical thinking)
- the integration of **student interests** with what students must learn
- the integration of all that is done in the school around a particular "philosophy," such as multiculturalism
- the **vertical integration** of what is being studied now with what was learned in previous grades and what will be learned in the next grade

Thus, when integration is mentioned, it is necessary to determine what sort of integration is being discussed and, especially, why it is desirable.

The following goals can be identified for integration:

* helping students deal with a complex and interconnected world
* helping them see that subject boundaries are artificial
* helping them learn more efficiently

For example, to understand the situation in Kosovo today, one would have to understand (at least) history, geography, economics, religion, and anthropology. While teaching this topic, the goal of efficiency could certainly be met if students also learned and applied map-reading skills.

According to Case,[31] there are four modes of integration:

1. **Fusion** refers to the joining of two elements, as in the example concerning social studies and language arts.

2. **Insertion** is the addition of part of another subject into an existing one. An example would be the teaching of statistics (for purposes of designing survey research and interpreting the results of the research) in social studies.

3. **Correlation** refers to drawing connections between elements that are taught separately, for example, learning about Japan in social studies and doing origami in art class.

4. **Harmonization** refers to a stress on common elements in all or several subject areas, for example, when all teachers focus on the same critical thinking competencies.

Whatever form integration takes, the results must make sense. *More* does not necessarily equal *better*. For instance, many of the so-called integrated units I have seen involve taking a topic and linking everything to it. So, in a unit on bears, students count bears, draw them, write about them, sing songs about them, and so on. This performs no true integrative function.[32] A more sensible integrated unit on bears would draw on knowledge needed to understand bear behaviour and habitats, and how humans have reacted, do react, and should react to them. The degree to which the topic is integrated will depend upon the capacities of the students and on the objectives of the study. Forcing integration onto a topic can be counterproductive. Integration, like many other educational ideas, is complex and requires careful thought before it is undertaken. I have sketched out an integrated unit on pioneers in Chapter 14.

Activity 3-G

To what extent does the curriculum guide in your province integrate social studies into other subject areas? What subjects are integrated into social studies? What form does the integration take (fusion, insertion, etc.)?

Having looked at the range of factors that need to be considered in deciding what to teach, we will move on to the question, "How do I go about teaching?" The rest of this book is devoted to trying to answer this question.

OTHER ACTIVITIES

1. Choose a particular topic (law, environmental problems, multiculturalism, or the treatment of women) that you believe social studies should focus on. Show how you would modify the existing social studies curriculum to include this topic.

2. Suppose your major goal was to develop respect for others at a given grade level. How would you go about doing this, given the curriculum in your province/territory?

3. Choose a topic at the grade level of your choice from your social studies curriculum guide and, using the chart on page 27, show what you would focus on.

4. Using a curriculum guide in another subject, choose a topic at a grade level of your choice and show how you could integrate social studies objectives and activities into this curriculum.

NOTES

1. J. Piaget, *The Child's Conception of the World* (London: Routledge, 1971).

2. The student probably meant "ski" as people do not skate down mountains.

3. J. Brophy and J. Alleman, "Early social understanding: What do children know about food, shelter and other cultural universals?" *Social Education* 66:7 (2003), pp. 453–457.

4. J. Allerman and J. Brophy, *Social Studies Excursions, K–3: Book One; Powerful Units on Food, Clothing and Shelter* (Portsmouth, NH: Heinemann, 2001).

5. S. Gibson and R. McKay, "What constructivist theory and brain research may offer social studies," *Canadian Social Studies* 35:4 (2002). www.quasar.ualberta.ca/css/css_35_4/ARconstructionist_theory.htm

6. D. Bergen, "Brain-based curriculum: Evaluating claims," *Social Education* 66:6 (2002), p. 378.

7. B. Curtis, D. Livingstone, and H. Smaller, *Stacking the Deck: The Streaming of Working-Class Kids in Toronto Schools* (Toronto: Our Schools Our Selves, 1992).

8. G. Gay, "Culturally diverse students and social studies," in J. Shaver, ed., *Handbook of Research on Social Studies Teaching and Learning* (New York: Macmillan, 1991).

9. R. Best, *We've All Got Scars: What Boys and Girls Learn in Elementary School* (Bloomington, Ind.: Indiana University Press, 1983).

10. J. Shapiro, S. Kramer, and C. Hunerberg, *Equal Their Chances: Children's Activities for Non-Sexist Learning* (Englewood Cliffs, NJ: Prentice-Hall, 1981).

11. D. Kindlone and M. Thompson, *Raising Cain: Protecting the Emotional Life of Boys* (New York: Ballantine, 1999).

12. Quoted in the *Globe and Mail*, Saturday, June 7, 2003, F6–9, Focus.

13. H. Taylor and S. Larson, "Teaching students with mild disabilities in elementary social studies," *Social Education* 64:4 (2000), pp. 232–235.

14. R. Case, "Elements of a coherent social studies program," in R. Case and P. Clark, eds., *The Canadian Anthology of Social Studies* (Vancouver: Pacific Educational Press, 1999).

15. K. Egan, "What children know best," *Social Education* 43:2 (1979), pp. 130–139.

16. K. Egan, *Teaching as Story Telling* (London, Ont.: Althouse Press, 1986).

17. Ministry of Education and Training Ontario, *The Ontario Curriculum for Social Studies, History and Geography, Grades 1 to 8* (Toronto: Ministry of Education and Training, 1998). www.edu.gov.on.ca

18. Atlantic Provinces Education Foundation, *Foundation for the Atlantic Canada Social Studies Curriculum* (Atlantic Provinces Educational Foundation, no date).

19. Atlantic Provinces Education Foundation, pp.16–27.

20. Gouvernement du Québec, Ministère de l'Éducation, Québec Education Program, 2001.

21. Gouvernement du Québec.

22. Ministry of Education and Training Ontario, *The Ontario Curriculum for Social Studies, History and Geography, Grades 1 to 8* (Toronto: Ministry of Education and Training, 1998). www.edu.gov.on.ca

23. Manitoba Education and Youth, *The Framework for Learning Outcomes in Social Studies (K–8)* (Winnipeg: Manitoba Education and Youth, 1988).

24. www.edu.gov.mb.ca/ks4/cur/socstud/framework/index.html/html

25. Saskatchewan Education, *Elementary Social Studies: A Curriculum Guide and Activity Guide for the Elementary Level* (Regina: Saskatchewan Education, 1995). www.sasked.gov.sk.ca/curr_inst/social/heritage_network.html

26. Reproduced from *Social Studies: A Curriculum Guide for the Elementary Level* (1995). Reprinted with permission of Saskatchewan Education.

27. Alberta Education, *Social Studies 1–6* (Edmonton: Alberta Education, 1990). ednet.edc.gov.ab.ca

28. Alberta Learning, *Social Studies Kindergarten to Grade 12*. Validation draft, May 2003. www.learning.gov.ab.ca/k_12/curriculum/bySubject/social/default.asp#info

29. Ministry of Education British Columbia, *Social Studies K–7* (Victoria: Ministry of Education, 1998). www.bced.gov.bc.ca/irp

30. Ministry of Education and Training, Ontario, news release, "New curriculum restores history in the classroom, August 26, 1998." www.edu.gov.on.ca/eng/document/nr/98.08/history.html

31. R. Case, "The anatomy of curricular integration," *Canadian Journal of Education* 16:2 (1991), pp. 215–224.

32. Ibid., pp. 215–224.

GLOSSARY OF KEY TERMS

Concern (or issue-based) strand — using issues (e.g., human rights, global warming) to organize the curriculum.

Dimension-based strand — using themes that cross subject boundaries (community or regional studies) to organize the curriculum.

Disciplinary strand — using the traditional disciplines (especially history and geography) to organize the curriculum.

Expanding horizons — basing the curriculum on the view that students first learn about themselves, then their families, their communities, their territory or province, their country, and eventually the world.

Integration — organizing the curriculum in various ways to focus on relationships:

Correlation — drawing connections between elements that are taught separately, e.g., doing origami in art, and studying Japan in social studies.

Fusion — joining of two elements, such as social studies and language arts.

Harmonization — common elements are stressed in several subject areas, e.g., multicultural education in social studies, language arts, art, and music.

Insertion — adding part of a subject to another, e.g., using a mathematical formula to draw a map.

Student interests — relating what is taught to the students' interests.

Vertical — relating what has occurred in a previous grade or topic to the one at hand.

Scope — in a curriculum or lesson, how much is taught and to what depth.

Sequence — the order in which the curriculum or lesson is taught.

Spiralling concepts — basing the curriculum on the progressive development of concepts.

WEBSITES FOR PART ONE

Ministries/Departments of Education

Alberta:
www.learning.gov.ab.ca

British Columbia:
www.gov.bc.ca

Manitoba:
www.edu.gov.mb.ca

New Brunswick:
www.gov.nb.ca/education

Newfoundland:
www.gov.nf.ca/edu

Nova Scotia:
www.ednet.ns.ca

Ontario:
www.edu.gov.on.ca

Prince Edward Island:
www.edu.pe.ca

Quebec:
www.meq.gouv.qc.ca

Saskatchewan:
www.sasked.gov.sk.ca

Teachers' Associations with Social Studies Websites

Alberta Social Studies Council:
www.socialstudies.ab.ca

British Columbia Teachers Association
Social Studies Provincial Specialist Council:
www.bctf.ca/psas/BCSSTA

Nova Scotia Social Studies Teachers'
Association:
http://ssta.ednet.ns.ca

Ontario Association for Geographic and
Environmental Education:
http://oagee.org

Ontario History and Social Sciences
Teachers' Association:
www.ohassta.org

Social Studies and Social Science Organizations

Canadian Council for Geographic Education:
www.ccge.org/ccge/english/home.htm

Historica:
www.histori.ca

The National Association for Social Studies:
www.ncss.org

chapter four

How Do I Get Started?

The broad goals of social studies, the curriculum guide, students, and other factors must all be taken into account when we decide what to teach. The goals can include content knowledge; information gathering, processing, and presenting; intellectual standards; personal and social values; active citizenship; and the disciplinary, interdisciplinary, or issue strands that can be addressed in social studies (see Chapter 3). Taking these goals and strands into account, we can organize our lessons or units on a variety of bases, such as the following:[1]

THEME OR SURVEY

Organizing units on the basis of a **theme or survey** places the emphasis on a) a historical or contemporary event or phenomenon, e.g., the expulsion of the Acadians, the building of the pyramids in Egypt, the fishing industry in Canada; b) a place, for example, my community, Newfoundland, China; or c) a particular time period—early exploration of Canada, Toronto in the early 1900s. Many curriculum guides and textbooks are organized around such themes.

GENERALIZATION

The emphasis is on a broad **generalization** that is developed through the study of one or more samples. "People in a community interact to provide goods and services" is one example of such a generalization. Another is "People adapt their environments to meet their needs, and they, in turn, adapt to their environments." See Chapter 13 for a discussion on how to teach generalizations.

CONCEPT

The focus here is on central **concepts** and how they are related to one particular example or to several. For example, a unit with "tradition" as its focus might look at what this concept means in the contexts of students' families, the community, and other places in the world. A unit with "equality" as its focus might examine this concept as it relates to the treatment of physically disadvantaged people in Canada, or male and female roles in a particular society. Chapter 6 can help you teach for conceptual understanding.

ISSUE

Another way to focus a lesson or unit is on an **issue** or concern where intellectual standards or personal and social values are applied. For example, deciding which account of a particular event is most plausible would entail the use of intellectual standards (see Chapter 8). Deciding whether a shopping mall should be built in the community or what rights students should have in the classroom would involve the use of personal and social values. See Part 4 for ideas on how to develop lessons or units on issues where social and personal values are developed.

INQUIRY

The organizer here can be questions where the answers are known (or at least partially known). Examples could include these: What motivated Europeans to explore North America? What rules govern our community? How are the governments of Canada and Japan similar and different? Chapters 7 and 8 help you implement **inquiry** as an organizer.

PROBLEM

The aim of focusing on a **problem** is to suggest a course of action. How can we make a new immigrant feel welcome in our school? What can we do to clean up garbage in our community? What can we do to help students become more globally aware? Part 4 contains ideas for this focus.

PROJECT

If based on a **project**, a lesson or unit is built around the creation of a model (a Hudson's Bay fort), a newspaper (about the Klondike gold rush), a drama (acting out the arrival of Irish immigrants in Halifax), a mural (showing how the goods we purchase are dependent on foreign sources), or a presentation (using written information and copies of old photographs to show what life was like for children in Winnipeg in the early 1900s).

NARRATIVE

The emphasis here is on a story or other **narrative**. Examples could be stories of another person (a biography or autobiography) or the story of the development of a city or of a particular invention.[2] Kieran Egan[3] has an approach to developing units based on the story form which you can discover in Chapter 5.

Activity 4-A

Look at the objectives for one grade level in your school's social studies curriculum and state how you could plan a lesson or unit based on each of the organizers listed above.

WEBBING

Whichever organizer is chosen, we need to map out what would be required to study the theme, answer the inquiry question, and so on. Here a **web** is a most useful tool.

The first step is to break down the topic into its constituent parts. Suppose we have a Grade 3 class and have been asked to teach about the Inuit in Nunavut using a thematic approach and focusing on the knowledge goals of social studies. What specifically do we teach? We could examine food, shelter, and clothing, but what else would we need to examine in order to build up as complete a picture as possible of the Inuit?

Activity 4-B

What aspects of Inuit life could be studied? Write down what you think ought to be studied to obtain as complete a picture as possible of Inuit life.

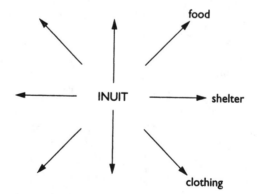

Depending on the objectives of the unit and student abilities, what might appear to be a simple concept like "food" can be broadened to include very powerful concepts that are food-related, such as ritual, community, conceptions of nature, power, cultural transmission, cultural change, exploitation, and needs. Thus, teaching the concept does not merely entail listing examples of Inuit food but rather puts the concept in the wider social, political, spiritual, environmental, economic, and historical contexts. Similarly, depending on student abilities, the other concepts can be related to more abstract and theoretically powerful concepts.

Activity 4-C

If the topic is ancient Greece, and our focus is on knowledge, intellectual values, and the information-gathering goals of social studies, what aspects might be studied?

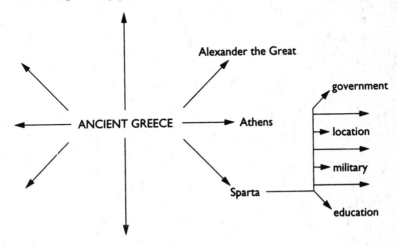

Similarly, powerful abstract concepts such as conflict, power, authority, imperialism, and democracy can be explored through the listed concepts.

Activity 4-D

If our organizer is the issue of how violence in society should be dealt with, and our focus is on personal and social values and citizenship action, what aspects would have to be studied?

What we have done in these activities is break down or analyze our topic into its components so that we can see what could be taught. Of course, decisions will have to be made concerning what will actually be taught, especially as any analysis could be quite complex. If we mapped out a complete picture of the forest industry in Canada, it could include everything from chainsaws to types of trees, to conservation or international trade and tariff regulations. Specifically, what we focus on will depend upon such factors as the age and maturity of students, the time available to teach the topic, suitable resource materials, the curriculum guide, and our philosophy of social studies. But, in each case, a "map" of the territory we wish to cover will be necessary. Without a map we can become hopelessly lost!

This map is also useful to students if they are to derive meaning from what they are studying. Constructing meaning is an interactive process in which learners use their existing conceptual schemas (their knowledge and understandings) to make connections between what they already know and new information. Thus, students with rich background knowledge derive more and deeper meanings from new information than do students with poor background knowledge.[4] One way to help students use their prior knowledge to comprehend new information is to use a technique called **semantic mapping**.[5] Students draw a visual representation of the relationships between concepts and information that they already know. When completed, the map will look much like the ones shown in this chapter. Carried out at the beginning of a new topic, this activity allows us to find out how much students already know. If we wish to make our teaching meaningful to our students, then we have to link it to how students make sense of their world. As the topic is developed in class, students can add to their semantic maps and show how new information is linked to their prior knowledge.

Activity 4-E

Here is a web drawn by a student in Grade 6 during a unit on Peru.[6] What does she know about the topic? How does she understand Peru? What else do you think she needs to know?

PLANNING A UNIT

From these maps and from the focus we choose, we then need to plan our unit. On the basis of our overall objectives, we would decide what aspects to teach and in what depth (scope), and what the sequence would be. Then we would choose our teaching methods and resources. We would also have to decide how to assess student learning. Although there is logic to developing a unit plan (there should be coherence between the objectives, what is taught, how it is taught, and how students would be assessed), we may find ourselves jumping around from one aspect to another as we plan.

Here are two samples based on two ways of organizing a unit. They are not fleshed out in any detail, as specific unit plans will be presented in Chapters 14 and 22 after we have seen what is required to develop and teach them.

Example 1

Grade 3

Goals: Knowledge of social studies information, personal and social values, and information gathering

Strand: Interdisciplinary

Organizer: Theme—place, my community

Aspects: Geography, history, economics, government, people, recreation, religion, education, community services

Overall objectives: Students will describe how members of the community are interdependent with each other and with their physical environment, and how they can help maintain that interdependence. Students will apply research skills.

Through a series of activities in which students pose questions and carry out research to find answers (through field trips and interviewing people in the community), students will learn about the physical geography of their community and how people in the community, including themselves, are influenced by it, and how they influence the environment. Other activities (visits to local industries, the town hall, cultural centres, and so on) will show how people in the community are interdependent. This information will be synthesized so that students build up a more complete understanding of their community and the interactions it is built upon.

Example 2

Grade 5

Goals: Personal and social values, citizenship action

Strand: Interdisciplinary concern

Organizer: Problem—how can we cut down the amount of garbage in our school?

Aspects: Garbage, recycling, motivation to change behaviours; attitudes towards garbage; materials that are trashed; alternative ways of packaging and reducing waste

Overall objectives: Students will devise and monitor ways to reduce the amount of garbage in the school. Students will work together in cooperative problem-solving groups.

Students will ascertain the extent of the garbage problem and student attitudes toward it. They will research ways in which garbage could be reduced and will devise ways to implement their methods in the school. They will evaluate the results.

Note that in both examples, to realize the objectives we would have to develop student understanding of the key concepts; know what the relevant questions are; use a variety of teaching methods and resources; and know how to pull together the various aspects of the unit so that students synthesize and generalize information. Student skills and attitudes must also be developed.

OTHER ACTIVITIES

1. Create a map showing what *could* be studied on a topic at a grade level of your choice. Then decide which of these aspects your class *would* study. Give reasons for your decisions.

2. Develop a plan for a social studies topic of your choice. Will your goals focus on content knowledge, information gathering and presenting, intellectual standards, personal and social values, or citizenship action? Will you organize your plan on the basis of a discipline, an interdisciplinary dimension, or an interdisciplinary concern or issue? Will you organize it around a theme, a concept, a generalization, an inquiry, a problem, an issue, a project, or a narrative?

3. Have elementary students draw a semantic map on a social studies topic they are studying in school. What concepts and information do they provide? How are the maps different or similar? Compare them to determine whether students give the same meaning to the topic.

4. Some provincial social studies curriculum guides provide model unit plans. Review these to ascertain how they are organized. What goals are emphasized? What strands are focused upon? What organizing patterns are used? You could also look at textbooks to see which organizational patterns are prevalent.

NOTES

1. Some of these headings are used in the *British Columbia Social Studies K–7 Integrated Resource Package* (Victoria, BC: Ministry of Education, 1998), p. 6.

2. For lists of suitable literature for history teaching see Chapter 10, and for values education see Chapter 19. *Social Education* 67:4 (2003) includes a list of notable books for children, some of which are appropriate for teaching Canadian social studies curricula.

3. K. Egan, *Teaching as Story Telling* (London, Ont.: Althouse Press, 1983).

4. See K. Camperell and R. Knight, "Reading research and social studies," in J. Shaver, ed., *Handbook of Research on Social Studies Teaching and Learning* (New York: Macmillan, 1991).

5. P. Antonacci, "Students search for meaning in the text through semantic mapping," *Social Education* 55:3 (1991), pp. 174–175, 194.

6. Drawn by Vanessa Disler. Used with permission.

GLOSSARY OF KEY TERMS

Lesson/unit organization — units or lessons can be based upon the following:

    Concept — how a particular concept (e.g., equality) relates to a particular example (treatment of disabled people in Canada).

    Generalization — broad relationship statement (people in a community interact to provide goods and services).

    Inquiry — a question that is answered by students (What motivated early explorers in Canada?).

    Issue — focus on an issue of concern (How should we clean up the community? What should be done to deal with global warming?).

    Narrative — organizing around a story or other narrative such as a biography.

    Problem — focus on courses of action concerning what others or I ought to do (How can I/we produce less garbage in our school?).

    Project — organizing around the creation of something tangible (a mural, a video, a newspaper, a website, a drama).

    Theme — historical or contemporary event (Riel Rebellion, provincial election), time period (early exploration of Canada), place (my community, Newfoundland, China).

Semantic mapping — diagramming the information and concepts students already know; basically the same as webbing.

Webbing — diagramming the elements of a topic and their relationships.

chapter five

Telling It Like It Is:
Exposition and Narrative

Once we have identified our objectives and the content, we have to decide on the best teaching methods. For reasons of familiarity, brevity, and efficiency, or because resource materials are not available, we might "lecture" to students. This does not mean that we stand up in front of the class and read from a prepared paper for 30 minutes. In the elementary classroom, we might talk to students, but we intersperse this with questions, discussion, blackboard notes, and media presentations. Here are some guidelines:

1. Make sure that students know the objectives for the lecture. Tell students at the beginning of the class what the talk is about and what, in particular, they should listen for.
2. Organize the talk so that it contains the main points in a logical order.
3. At the end of the talk, summarize the main points.
4. Make the talk interesting by asking questions, encouraging discussion, and using visual materials.
5. Prepare an activity in which students have to use the information contained in the talk.
6. Speak in a clear, interesting manner.
7. Maintain eye contact with the students.
8. If interest is slipping, ask questions or give students an activity to do.

Activity 5-A

Prepare a 10-minute talk on a topic of your choice. Decide what the main points are and in what order they will be presented. Choose suitable audio-visual aids. Prepare an activity for students to do after your talk. Give your talk to a peer and have him/her evaluate it on the basis of the guidelines above.

The following is an example of an expository lesson plan. It is but one example of this kind of approach.

Grade 3: Rationale for Using an Expository Approach

Expository teaching offers a highly economical way of presenting information. It can synthesize quantities of information, eliminate the irrelevant, concentrate on the significant, and present information in a structured way. The presentation can be highly entertaining and interesting. It can include a variety of visual materials as well as other aids that reinforce important details. Changes in the level of abstraction can be included so that all students, whatever their cognitive capacities, can learn something.

Overall goals

Students will learn that people meet their needs in varying ways and are interdependent.

Students will respect the varying ways that people interact to meet their needs.

Strand

Interdisciplinary with a focus on social roles

Major organizer

The concept of community

Lesson objectives

Students will be able to list three basic needs of people (food, shelter, and clothing) and state how the Hutterites fulfill these needs.

Students will describe how the Hutterites' sense of community helps them meet basic needs.

Introduction

(In the previous lesson, students were introduced to the Hutterites and their history. In this lesson, students are looking at a picture of Hutterites eating a meal in the communal dining room.)

Looking at this picture, we can see that, like you and me, these people need food. What else do they need? At the end of this lesson, you will be able to tell me who these people are, what needs they have, and how they go about fulfilling their needs.

Main body of the lesson

These people are Hutterites *[reviews the term by writing the word on the board]*. This group lives in Alberta *[reviews where Alberta is on the map; relates location to where students live]*. Like you and me, they have certain needs.

(The needs are listed and explanations are given as to how the Hutterites fulfill these needs and their sense of community. Students are questioned about how their own needs are fulfilled and how these methods compare to the Hutterites' ways. Pictures of Hutterites farming, building, sewing, and so on are shown.)

Synthesis

So we have seen that, like you and me, Hutterites need food, clothing, and shelter. They obtain them in their community in ways that may be similar to, or different from, the ways in which we obtain them.

Assessment

Each student is given the following:

1. Name of people talked about: _____
2. They live in the province of _____.
3. It is their idea of com_____ that helps them meet their needs.
4. Fill in this chart:

Need	How I obtain	How Hutterites obtain

Each student should correctly answer questions 1, 2, and 3 and correctly identify how the Hutterites obtain food, shelter, and clothing.

The objective of exposition is for students to learn a body of information. Another way to achieve this objective is to use a cooperative learning activity employing the "jigsaw" technique. For more information on cooperative learning, see Chapter 9. In the jigsaw technique, each student is assigned to a study group and a learning group. In the study groups, each member becomes an expert in a particular body of information. Students then go to their learning groups and teach the rest of the group the content they learned in their study groups. Finally, all students are tested on all the information. The steps in this procedure are as follows:

1. The teacher prepares materials so that the content to be learned is divided into separate parts.
2. Students are placed into learning groups and each student is assigned a number. All the number ones receive one body of information, all the number twos receive a different body of information, and so on.
3. All the number ones meet in a study group, all the number twos meet in another study group, and so on.
4. Members of each study group teach and test one another on the information until they are all experts on it.
5. Students return to their learning groups, and each member teaches the others the information learned in the study groups.

6. All students are tested on all the information.

7. Grades can be assigned on the basis of the average of each student's individual score and the team's average score. For example, if Rita's individual score was 90 and the learning group's average score was 86, then Rita would receive a score of 88. If students are informed at the beginning of this activity that their scores will be partially dependent on the score obtained by the rest of their group, they are more likely to stay on task and ensure that the content is really understood.

EGAN'S STORY-TELLING APPROACH

Another way information can be imparted is to use Kieran Egan's **story-telling approach**,[1] which is used by a variety of teachers across Canada.[2] There are ongoing projects in Ontario, Nova Scotia, Quebec, British Columbia, and Manitoba, where teachers are using the approach to design learning materials. Egan has also written a number of books in which his theory is explored in depth.[3]

Story-telling, or narrative, can be fiction or non-fiction; the term refers to writing that is shaped in story form. If the content is fiction, then students should be apprised of this. A brief example follows, but you should study Egan's book for a full grasp of the theoretical basis of his approach and how best to apply it in your teaching. Egan recommends that any social studies topic can be approached as a good story to be told, as well as a set of objectives to be attained. He suggests certain questions be answered so that a story unfolds.

Identifying Importance

What is most important about this topic? Why should it matter to children? What is affectively engaging about it?

Suppose the unit is "Multiculturalism" and the focus is on Japanese Canadians. In answering the questions above, we could argue that multiculturalism is vital to Canada (see Chapter 20), that it matters to children because they interact with people from a variety of cultural backgrounds, and that the stories of immigrants—their sorrows, their triumphs—can engage children.

Finding Binary Opposites

What powerful binary opposites best catch the importance of this topic?

A number of significant binary opposites could be used: prejudice/tolerance, freedom/oppression, survival/destruction, cooperation/conflict, or unity/diversity. Given that many groups come to Canada to escape oppression and that young children find "oppression" to be a powerful idea (my children were always complaining that they were being oppressed!), the binary opposites "freedom/oppression" will be used here.

Organizing Content into Story Form

What content most dramatically embodies the binary opposites to provide access to the topic? What content best articulates the topic into a developing story form?

Many incidents could be used to show how "freedom/oppression" applies to the history of Japanese Canadians. They were denied the right to vote, excluded from certain jobs, and discriminated against in the fishing industry. But the most telling content concerns their evacuation from the British Columbia coast during World War II. One of the best ways of telling this story is by relating the tale of Joy Kogawa's *Obasan*[4] through the eyes of Naomi, who, with her family, experiences evacuation and subsequent internment. Students could carry out a number of activities based on the story: role-playing particular incidents; discussing the rightness or wrongness of the internment; or writing a diary from the point of view of one of the internees.

Conclusion

What is the best way of resolving the dramatic conflict inherent in the binary opposites? What degree of mediation of these opposites is it appropriate to seek?

In the story, there is a resolution. When the Canadian government ordered the deportation of Japanese Canadians, a decision that was upheld in the courts,[5] the resulting public outcry led to the repeal of the deportation orders on January 26, 1947. Recently, the survivors of the evacuation were granted both financial compensation and a formal apology from the Canadian government.

To extend this activity, we could clarify the two concepts to show, for example, that freedom does not mean licence, and that having to do what you're told does not necessarily mean oppression. We could show how oppressed people have taken political action and have sometimes gained particular freedoms (e.g., in Eastern Europe in 1989). We could look at the lives of immigrant groups and find out how they attempt to get control over their own lives. We could discuss relevant incidents in children's lives in which they see a conflict between freedom and oppression.

Evaluation

How can one know whether the topic has been understood, its importance grasped, and the content learned?

One of the best ways to evaluate student learning would be to have students write a story from the perspective of a member of the Japanese-Canadian community in 1941, telling of the evacuation, life in an internment camp or on a farm, and the deportation orders. Finally, students could state what their feelings are about freedom and oppression in this context. Other evaluation techniques can be found in Chapter 15.

Activity 5-B

Create a lesson plan using Egan's story-telling approach on a topic for a grade level of your choice. The lesson should contain your objectives, an "opener," a brief description of what you will say, activities students will carry out, and a method of evaluation.

1. Identifying importance

   What is most important about this topic?

   Why should it matter to children?

   What is affectively engaging about it?

2. Finding binary opposites

   What powerful binary opposites best catch the importance of this topic?

3. Organizing content into story form

   What content most dramatically embodies the binary opposites to provide access to the topic?

   What content best articulates the topic into a developing story form?

4. Conclusion

   What is the best way of resolving the dramatic conflict inherent in the binary opposites?

   What degree of mediation of these opposites is it appropriate to seek?

5. Evaluation

   How can one know whether the topic has been understood, its importance grasped, and the content learned?

Egan's story-telling approach is a powerful one for teaching history, as it builds on students' experiences with stories, fairy tales, and myths. The major themes in these narratives are typically conflicts between bravery and cowardice, good and evil, and so on. Students are already familiar with these themes from watching television and movies. This eases the task of capturing their imagination and imparting some historical information. As stories consist of causes and effects within a temporal sequence, children can also begin to develop their concepts of historical time and causation. Chapter 10 provides you with other ideas for the teaching of history.

USING THE TEXTBOOK

Many jurisdictions recommend the use of particular textbooks.[6] Textbooks are a mixed blessing. They can certainly make our lives easier and, if used throughout a particular educational jurisdiction, they provide continuity for students and educators and a common basis on which to evaluate student learning. Most texts provide carefully constructed information with plenty of aids for student readers, along with exercises to help them apply new information. Most also come with teacher guides. However, if textbooks are the only source of social studies information, then they limit access to other points of view and can stultify learning. They also might not provide a close match with curriculum objectives as publishers cannot always afford to publish textbooks to suit each province's curriculum. They need to be used carefully.

Your Analysis of the Textbook

The following questions are raised to help you familiarize yourself with the textbook.

1. What are the backgrounds of the authors? What criteria would you apply to judge the authority of the authors? Do these authors measure up to your criteria?

2. What is the content of the book? Given the topic of the book, what content *could* be included? What in your view would be worth knowing about this topic? What content is excluded? What places, people, issues, ideas, events are given prominence? How

much space is devoted to each? How are women, children, the aged, the challenged, the rich, the poor, minorities, people with particular occupations, people of colour, etc., dealt with? What sorts of biases are present? What are the key words in the index and glossary? What biases do they reflect?

3. What visuals are included? Who is depicted (age, sex, ethnicity)? What are they doing? What does this say about the status of the people and the activities depicted?[7] What evidence is there of stereotyping? Of bias? What sorts of graphs, charts, and tables are included? What do they show? What importance is attached to them? Do the visuals distort the data in any way? If so, how?

4. Is there evidence presented for the claims made in the textbook, e.g., through phrases such as "research states …," "according to (a source) …," or "there is evidence that…"? If there is no evidence presented, how would you go about determining the believability of the claims made? Locate at least one major event, person, idea, or place covered in the textbook. Look at the statements made and identify whether there is any evidence presented to support their believability. If no evidence is presented, how would you go about determining the credibility of the claims made? Would the credibility differ according to who was telling the story or presenting the evidence? If so, how? If the story or evidence was likely to differ, is there any way we could determine "truth"? If there is more than one story and the textbook presents only one of them, how would you go about presenting the other stories? In what situations would it be really important to do this? Why?

5. What are the key concepts that a student would have to grasp to understand the information presented? Are these concepts defined? Are the definitions adequate? If the concept is a contested one (people can legitimately differ in the way they define the term), then is this pointed out to readers? How would you go about determining the most appropriate definition?

6. Are there value claims in the textbook, e.g., this is good/bad, this is better/worse, or this should be done? Are arguments presented to support the value claims? If not, what sort of arguments would be required?

7. Is there any content that you would regard as controversial? If so, how is it dealt with? In your view, how should it be dealt with? Where you know a controversy exists, is it mentioned? If not, why do you think it is not raised? Are opposing points of view identified? Are all the differing viewpoints mentioned? If not, which viewpoints receive attention? Why? How is the controversy dealt with? Is it merely stated that there are opposing points of view or do the authors of the text take a position? If so, what is that position? On what is it based? Are there questions posed to the student? If so, what are these? Are they appropriate? Would it help the student resolve the controversy if the questions were answered?

8. Is cause and effect dealt with? If so, how? Are the cause-and-effect relationships believable? Viewed as complex? Seen as problematic? Choose one event about which you are familiar. Review the text and analyze the cause-and-effect reasoning. Is the reasoning sound?

9. Are there any generalization statements? Are these supported with evidence? What sorts of generalization statements are there (see Chapter 13)? What is the evidence to support the generalization? Are there enough instances to justify the generalization?

Does the generalization fit into a larger body of knowledge that is believable? Have any fallacies been committed—for example, hasty generalization (just because one A is a B doesn't necessarily mean that all As are Bs) or fallacy of division (just because a group generally has a certain characteristic doesn't mean necessarily that each individual member of the group has that characteristic)?

10. How was this textbook written, produced, and chosen for student use? Whose vision of education and truth does the textbook represent?

Helping Students Use the Textbook

Students should know how textbooks are written,[8] as this can help them use textbooks well. When the textbook is first introduced to students, you might want students to address some of the following questions and activities:

1. Who are the authors? What are their credentials?

2. When was the text published? If the text had been published some years ago, would there be any difference in the information presented?

3. Have students look at the title and hypothesize what they think they are going to learn. Then look at the chapter headings and check the hypotheses. If it is a history text, have students look at the index for people's names and categorize them (male/female; rulers, politicians, military, religious leaders, scientists, artists, etc.). Review the list and discuss the results. For instance, there are likely to be far more males than females mentioned in history texts. If the text is geographical in focus, ask students what areas receive attention and why the areas studied might be considered important. What areas receive no attention? Why? Here it is important to tell students that textbook authors have to make decisions about what to include. They have to consider the curriculum, the students, and the various guidelines that provinces use to determine which textbooks will be recommended.

4. Have students look at the illustrations. What is emphasized? Why?

5. Who receives the most attention? Ideas on interpreting visuals can be found in Chapter 16.

Depending on the text, we might want to take several approaches. We could ask students to make a web of what they already know or expect to learn when they first read a chapter title. On reading the chapter, they then fill out the web or check their hypotheses. If the text is in the form of a story, then we should ensure that the story flow is maintained. But we should point out that a story is not fact, although it might be based upon facts. We have to ask students how they might check out the "truth" about the events, places, or persons in the story and check other sources. If the text consists of factual accounts, the first thing to do is ensure that the context is clear and that students understand the key concepts in the titles or headings. For example, texts may well provide "openers" or chapter previews that introduce students to the topic and link it to what they have previously learned. You may have to flesh this out so that the new topic is comprehensible to your students. For example, if the account is about a particular place, you might want to go beyond finding it on a map by asking the kinds of questions outlined in Chapter 11. As writers often begin paragraphs with summary statements, have students write these and then use a diagram linking the other information in the paragraphs to the main ideas. An idea here is to use a "herringbone" activity. Here is an example:

Herringbone Activity

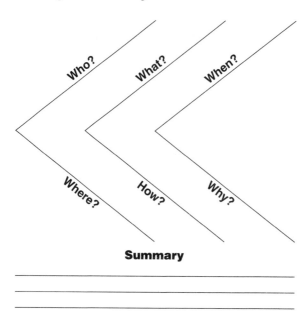

Summary

Another idea would be to have students write the summary statement for the chapter after having read that chapter.

If any of the text is in a sequential order, such as an account of a historical event, have students transfer the information onto a time line (see Chapter 10). Then have them look at the sequence and note what the causes and effects might be. Sometimes the text writer will identify these, sometimes the writer does not. In other cases where there are cause-and-effect claims, have students create a web showing these (see Chapter 13). Where there are comparisons, have students make a chart noting similarities and differences. Point out to students the importance of glossaries and other aids, such as sidebars, to understanding the material. Point out the relationships between the visuals, printed text, captions, and so on.

Any chapter or part of a chapter can be studied as follows: divide the class into learning groups and assign each group a portion of the text. Each group then teaches the content to the other learning groups. What is to be learned can be phrased in question form so that student attention is focused on the relevant content. Another technique, which can be used by pairs of students, is labeled **SQ3R**. This stands for the following:

Survey—read heading(s).

Question—create questions from the heading(s).

Read—orally to find answers.

Recite—discuss answers to questions.

Reread—to check answers and write them down.

In pairs, one student acts as reader, the other as recorder. The recorder asks the questions and listens as the reader reads the relevant materials. They discuss the answers, and the recorder writes down the ones they agree on. Roles are then switched for the next section of the materials.

Whenever we ask students to read materials, we should have a purpose in mind and a framework that can help them understand the information. For example, we could ask students to identify the major concepts, issues, or perspectives in the passage. We can also interrogate the text by asking why the passage was written, what information could have been presented but was not, the perspective of the author, and the biases present (e.g., in a history text how much content is devoted to women?).

OTHER ACTIVITIES

1. One way to teach students information is to play games such as Twenty Questions or Word Bingo. Design a game for a group of students to teach them particular information.

2. Modify a board game such as Snakes and Ladders or Monopoly to teach social studies information.

3. Evaluate a textbook that is used in the jurisdiction in which you will be teaching. Use the questions above as a guideline.

4. Evaluate a textbook passage. Does it constitute a good "lecture"?

5. Take a textbook passage and design an activity that will help students understand it.

NOTES

1. K. Egan, *Teaching as Story Telling* (London, Ont.: Althouse Press, 1986).

2. For information about teachers who use this approach, see http://ierg.net.

3. K. Egan, *Primary Understanding: Education in Early Childhood* (New York: Routledge, 1988). K. Egan, *Romantic Understanding: The Development of Rationality and Imagination, Ages 8–15* (New York: Routledge, 1990). K. Egan, *Children's Minds, Talking Rabbits and Clockwork Oranges: Essays on Education* (New York: Teachers College Press, 1999).

4. J. Kogawa, *Obasan* (Harmondsworth, UK: Penguin, 1981).

5. I. Wright, "Social studies and law-related education: A case study of the Japanese in British Columbia," *The History and Social Science Teacher* 22:4 (1987), pp. 209–214.

6. The Oxford Discovery Series published by Oxford University Press (Toronto) in 2002–2003 (Grade 3, *Discovering Canadian Pioneers* and *Discovering Communities*; Grade 4, *Discovering Castle Days* and *Discovering Canada*; Grade 5, *Discovering Early Civilizations* and *Discovering Canada's Government*; Grade 6, *Discovering First People and First Contacts* and *Discovering Canada's Trading Partners*). The Oxford Outlooks series published by Oxford University Press (Toronto) in 2000–2002 (*Outlooks 3: Our Communities*; *Outlooks 4: Our Beginnings*; *Outlooks 5: Connections Canada*; *Outlooks 6: Global Citizens*; and *Outlooks 7: Ancient Worlds*). The Tapestry Series published by Harcourt Brace (Toronto) in 2000 (Grade 3, *Islands*, *Celebrations*, and *Generations*; Grade 4, *Medieval Times*, *Freshwater Trails*, and *Travel Canada*; Grade 5, *Windows on the Past*, *Making Choices*, and *Town Planner*; Grade 6, *Exploration*, *Marketplace*, and *Leaving Your Mark*). There are also other individual texts such as *Canada Revisited 6: Aboriginal Peoples and European Explorers*, published in 1999 by Arnold Publishing (Edmonton), that are used in some jurisdictions.

7.   P. Clark, "Between the covers: Exposing images in social studies textbooks," in R. Case and P. Clark, eds., *The Canadian Anthology of Social Studies* (Vancouver: Pacific Educational Press, 1999).

8.   J. Parsons. "Helping students learn how textbooks are written," *Canadian Social Studies*. www.quasar.ualberta.ca/css/CSS_35_1/classrom_tips.htm#

GLOSSARY OF KEY TERMS

Expository teaching — imparting information to students in didactic ways, e.g., by lecturing.

SQ3R — an activity in which pairs of students *survey (S)* what is read, create *questions (Q)*, *read (R)* to find answers, *recite (R)* (discuss) answers to questions, and *reread (R)* to check answers before writing them down.

Story-telling approach — a procedure designed by Kieran Egan in which the important element in a topic is identified, binary opposites are found that capture the import of the topic, content is organized into story form, and a conclusion is arrived at that attempts to resolve the conflict between the binary opposites.

chapter six

What Does This Word Mean?
Concept Teaching
and Learning

When we use expository methods, either we tend to assume that students understand key terms or we provide definitions. We do this because we realize that concepts provide the lenses through which we view and understand our world. They are classification devices we use to bring order to the myriad objects, ideas, and events that surround us. They are crucial to the understanding of any statement or question. We cannot answer the questions "Can this garbage be recycled?" or "Was that a fair decision?" unless we know the concepts "recycle" and "fairness." Of course, we would also need to be familiar with the concepts "garbage" and "decision." Understanding any question or statement is one important reason for teaching concepts. There are also other reasons for taking concept teaching seriously.

RATIONALES FOR TEACHING CONCEPTS

We always need to be clear about the concepts we are using. In our own writing, we want to use words clearly so that our readers know what we're trying to say. Suppose I want to write about the benefits of teaching decision making to students. To communicate with my readers, I have to be as clear as possible about "decision making," since it is a term that can be applied to the making of any choice—from what to eat for breakfast, to how Native land claims should be settled. So, if I want to discuss the making of *any* choice, then I should say so; but if I want to focus only on socially significant decisions, then I should stipulate this meaning.

Clarity is also needed when we have to interpret what someone else means in a statement or question. Suppose the headline in the newspaper reads, "Toronto to grow over the next 10 years." I have to read the article to know whether the headline is referring to growth in population, in land area, or in something else before I can understand it.

To demonstrate understanding of a concept, it is not always enough for a student to be able to speak the word or even to use it in a sentence, neither of which means that the student has grasped the concept. I used to teach about the "customs" and "traditions" of various peoples and had a vague idea that these two terms were somehow different. However, it was not until one of my student teachers was asked to differentiate between these terms in teaching about the customs and traditions of people in Mexico that I seriously contemplated these concepts. You will see the result of the student teacher's deliberations, and my own, later in this chapter (in Activity 6-G).

Although the difference between custom and tradition may not strike you as significant, in many contexts meaning is of crucial importance. Disagreements about what is "fair," whether someone was "cheating," or whether certain people are "poor" often revolve around the meaning attached to the terms. A recent example of this concerns "marriage." To many people in Canada, this term should be applied only to the union of a male and female; others argue that it should also pertain to same-sex couples. Eventually there will be a decision concerning how the term shall be used for legal purposes. Judges' rulings on what a particular concept will mean in a given context determine many legal cases. Juries have to decide if, in a particular case, a person was guilty of "murder" or "manslaughter." They have to decide if the facts of the case add up to the definition of one or the other. Are the attributes of "murder" present in the facts of the case, or are the facts more like the attributes of "manslaughter"? As teachers, we have to decide what "excellent" means when assessing a given assignment, or whether the actions of a student constitute "bullying."

In the classroom, teaching any discipline requires us to introduce students to the key concepts of that discipline. For example, to understand history, students need to grasp concepts such as "causation," "time," "change," "continuity," and "chronology." To understand anthropology we need to comprehend and apply such concepts as "culture" and "ethnic." We must remember, too, that different disciplines often use concepts in a technical way. People who are immersed in a particular discipline will have a common understanding of terms that are used somewhat differently in everyday language. For instance, we may use the word "valid" to mean true, but logicians use it to denote an argument in which the conclusion necessarily follows from the premises. In teaching physics, the concept "work" is used very differently from its normal usage. So, in teaching concepts that are relevant to a particular discipline, we have to be aware of how a specific concept is used in that discipline and whether that usage differs from the concept's usage in everyday language.

We must also be on the lookout for words that can fool us. For example, advertisements that promise something for "free" may not give you anything that is really free. Ads for such items as computers and cars often try to persuade you to make a purchase by bombarding you with lots of technical jargon. (Don't you just *have* to buy a computer with an SCSI interface card?) You may remember that during the war in Iraq, we were informed that the dropping of bombs on Baghdad had caused "collateral damage." This piece of jargon was meant to take our minds off the fact that civilians had been killed or injured.

Words have different connotations for different people. Even though a school is, by definition, a place where learning is intended to occur, to some people "school" may have a positive or negative emotive force, evoking pleasurable memories or feelings of loathing. So, in clarifying meaning, we have to be on the lookout for words where the meaning is surrounded by emotional reactions. Even if I loathed my elementary school, it was still a "school"; I do not wish to get rid of "schools" just because mine was an awful place to be.

Most importantly, how words are used affects actions. For example, if certain human beings are regarded as "non-persons," then they will be treated differently from "persons." (Witness the Holocaust.) If taking candy from the local convenience store is not defined as "stealing," then the action may not be deemed wrong by the taker. If someone is deemed not to be a "refugee," then we may not allow that person to stay in Canada. If we label students as "behaviour problems," then we act toward them in particular ways.

Finally, it is crucial to understand that unless we had some understanding of the concepts used in our language, we would be unable to communicate with one another.

The most powerful tool of humankind is language. We use words to communicate information, to control others, to praise, and to condemn. We shape words, and words shape us. Thus, an understanding of the language—i.e., the concepts—of social studies is vital.

Activity 6-A

Note the concepts that are emphasized in the curriculum guide in your province. To which disciplines are these concepts related? Are the concepts listed vital to the understanding of a particular discipline? Can you tell whether these concepts are supposed to be used in specialized ways? If so, what are these specialized ways?

WHAT ARE CONCEPTS?

Before we can teach concepts, we have to know what they are. A **concept** is a mental construct that provides the rules for giving meaning to a word. It is, in one sense, a definition. Thus, if I say, "By 'school' I mean a place where it is intended that learning occurs," I am stating that one of the rules for saying that X is a school is that learning is intended to occur there.

Suppose, however, that I'm not sure what a school is. Then two tasks face me. First, I have to find out what the attributes or characteristics of "school" are and how this term relates to other concepts, such as teaching and learning. Second, I have to know that the building on the corner of the street is a school and not a factory, or a store, or a house. Not only do I have to know what the word means, but I also have to be able to point out examples of the word. Now, imagine that a young child is told by a parent that the building on the corner is a school and that one day she will go to it. What does the child know? All she knows is that this building of a certain shape and size is called a school. She may notice that it has other characteristics, such as a playground, or that children go there, but how does she know it's a *school*, rather than a community centre, or a day-care facility, or any other building that has a playground and children? She has to learn that certain activities go on in a school that differentiate it from other buildings. Eventually, as her knowledge of the concept "school" becomes broader, she will realize that a school's key characteristic is not its particular structure (one can have a school under a tree, in an open field, or in the basement of a home), but rather the activities that take place there. So, in teaching a concept, we have to teach students the attributes that give a term its meaning. Sometimes this is fairly easy. For example, all the shapes below are examples of the concept "triangle."

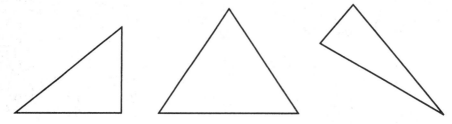

Even though each shape differs from the other two in some respect, they all share the same "triangle rules": closed plane figure, three straight sides. These characteristics or attributes are necessary for the pictured geometric shapes to be called triangles. Whether the triangle is blue and whether it has a dot in it are irrelevant attributes. A triangle must be a closed plane figure with three straight sides. Three sides *alone* do not make a triangle, nor does a closed plane figure *alone*. A triangle must have *both* attributes. These are the **necessary** and **sufficient conditions** of a triangle.

Unfortunately, most concepts in social studies are not this easy. It is not always possible to determine specific necessary and sufficient conditions. There may well be fuzzy boundaries between one concept and a closely related one, even for seemingly simple concepts such as "family." Even though all students will be familiar with this concept, their meanings may be narrow and socio- or ethnocentric.

Activity 6-B

Which of the photos on page 61 would qualify as examples of the concept "family"? How do you know? What would you need to know if you are not sure whether the picture depicts a family? What does "family" mean?

When you have answered these questions, refer to the Answers section.

TEACHING AND LEARNING CONCEPTS

From these activities, you have probably gained some idea of the difficulty that exists in teaching concepts. The idea that pointing at something and saying "That's an X" is *all* that is needed to teach a concept is inadequate. In the "family" example, merely pointing to a picture of a group of people or animals and saying "That's a family" would not be enough. Students have to learn that the concept is complex and can refer to different groups within which certain kinds of relationships exist. Different relationships pertain in different contexts. In some cultures, a family is always an extended one. In our society, a family can refer to a variety of personal relationships. In other contexts, "family" can refer to all members of a group, such as the cat family or the human family.

The context in which a concept is used is significant. One of my colleagues provides an example here. His son had learned the word "no" as a command, so "No, don't touch"

Photo 1

Photo 2

Photo 3

Photo 4

Photo 5

Photo 6

made sense to him. When he began to read, he could point out the "no" at the start of certain signs, and when the rest of the sign was read to him, a message such as NO PARKING made perfect sense. NO THROUGH ROAD, however, was incomprehensible. While the words were no problem, the change in function from "no" as a command to "no" as information giving was something he didn't understand.

Another important matter is raised by the distinction between concrete and abstract. Some educators point out that there are concrete concepts (like "chair") and abstract ones (like "learning"). However, there is no such thing as a concrete concept. There are concepts that refer to concrete things, and there are concepts that refer to abstract ideas. The view that concepts referring to concrete objects are easier to teach and learn than those referring to abstract ideas is also mistaken. Teaching children the concept of "computer," a concrete object, is probably more difficult than teaching them "obey," a rather complex and certainly abstract idea. True, children can become more sophisticated at using particular concepts as they acquire more experience with them, but this does not mean that concepts come in levels, with some more "simple" than others. The fact that some concepts must be taught in advance of others does not necessarily make these prerequisites simpler. And it must always be remembered that a new concept is easier to learn when students are familiar with concepts closely related to the new one and with the context in which the concept is being used.

As noted earlier, unlike "triangle," many concepts cannot be defined in terms of specific, necessary, and sufficient conditions unless we stipulate what these shall be. To return to the "marriage" example, in Canada, this term used to be applied only to the union of a male and a female who were deemed legally old enough to marry. The age limits have changed over time, but the one male and one female requirement had not. Now, in some provinces, gays and lesbians can marry, thus changing the male and female characteristics of the term. This has raised much controversy, and eventually the government will either have to stipulate a new definition of marriage or decide to maintain the old one. Additional difficulties arise with value-laden concepts. As with other concepts, it may not be possible to define these in absolutely specific terms. The context in which they are used is crucial. The concept "good," for example, means different things when you are referring to a good person or a good painting. Although "good" is clearly a value term, not all value concepts are as easy to pick out. Concepts like "cheat," "discriminate," or "manipulate" are also evaluative. In using them, we evaluate events, actions, and policies. We will examine value concepts in more depth in Part 4.

How, then, do we teach concepts? There are two procedures that we can use. The first, **concept development**, helps students classify information pertinent to a particular topic or question into relevant concepts. Using this procedure provides a conceptual structure for the study of a social studies unit or lesson. In some ways it is like a more formalized kind of webbing (see Chapter 4). The second, **concept attainment**, involves the direct teaching of one particular concept.

Concept Development

This procedure, developed by the late Hilda Taba,[1] consists of six steps that eventually lead to the testing of generalizations. We will concentrate on the first three steps and leave the last three until we discuss generalizations in Chapter 13.

Activity 6-C

1. List about 20 items from the following photographs of the Yukon.

2. Select one item and see if any other items will go with it. If so, what will you call this grouping?

3. Continue this process until all the items have been grouped into categories. It is permissible to have a category with only one item in it (e.g., there is only one example of the effects of permafrost, so this item

could be in its own category). Create a chart showing your categories (see below). Explain why you have assigned each category a particular concept label. Review your categories and determine if any are too broad and encompass far too much information. For example, a category labelled "geography" needs to be subdivided into other categories such as landscape and climate.

Category label	Category label	Category label	Category label	Category label
(Items)	(Items)	(Items)	(Items)	(Items)

4. Look at your chart. Can any of the items in one group be placed into another group?
5. Can these items be classified in any other ways? Which concepts would be most appropriate for a study of the Yukon?
6. Get together with one or more of your peers and ascertain whether you agree on the labels. Does it matter if you disagree? Would different labels be equally useful for your purposes?

This may appear to be a simple-minded activity but, as we'll see later in this chapter, the way items are classified differs according to the purposes of the classifier. Whether items are classified appropriately also depends upon the conceptual sophistication of the classifier.

Implementing Concept Development

Students will need items to classify. Young children can classify actual objects or can be given pictures to manipulate physically. Older students can use pictorial or printed material. Students can form their own categories, or we can begin by asking them to state what they see and then list these items on the blackboard. Initially, we need to limit the number of items to between 15 and 30 so as not to overwhelm them. After the items are listed, ask the class to group and label them. We may have ideas as to how the items should be classified. Our students, however, may have different ideas.

Activity 6-D

Below is a list of foods. In how many ways can you classify them?

Peach	Cheese	Pea
Egg	Meat	Milk
Melon	Eggplant	Carrot

1. If you were teaching beginning consonants, what classification scheme would be most appropriate?

2. If you were teaching about Canadian imports and exports, what classification scheme would be most appropriate?

3. If you were teaching about supermarkets/colours/vowel sounds/processed foods/ vitamin content/foods I like, what would be the most appropriate classification schemes?

The classification scheme chosen will depend upon the purpose of the lesson and the perceptions of our students. If, using this list of foods, our purpose was to teach the concepts of "vegetable," "meat," "fruit," and "dairy," but our students wanted to classify according to colour, our job would be to encourage students to see that there are many ways of classifying. We would then help them understand the one that is useful in the context of our lesson.

When using the Taba Concept Development procedure, it is important to remember that even though the labels are concepts used to organize and classify information, the listed items are not necessarily attributes of the concept label. Clearly, in the above activity, a peach is not an attribute of the concept "fruit." A peach is an example of "fruit." The distinction should be kept clear. Students often give an example of the concept when asked for a definition. In using the Taba procedure, students may list items under a concept label when the items are not really examples of that concept label, but are related in some way. For example, if "climate" is the concept, items like "rain" and "snow" fit. "Umbrella" doesn't, even though umbrellas are linked to climatic conditions, since we can make inferences about the climate of a place if we see people using umbrellas.

When teaching concepts, therefore, it is important to teach the attributes of the concept so that the student can recognize examples of it. To do this requires concept attainment procedures.

Concept Attainment

Concept attainment differs from concept development. Concept attainment is used to identify the attributes of a term, i.e., what the term means. Concept development is a technique for helping students classify the myriad phenomena that are part of a place, an event, an institution, a culture, and so on. Thus, in studying the Iroquois, students would list, group, and label what they saw in pictures and arrive at such concept labels as food, government, religion, and celebrations. If students were not clear about what their concept labels meant, then concept attainment would be used to give them a clearer sense of their meaning. For example, in studying the Aboriginal people in Australia, students who have looked at pictures of what Aboriginals traditionally eat have failed to include wichiti bugs within their concept of food because they do not think bugs are food. In fact, they think it is gross to eat bugs. Here, a teacher would have to use a concept attainment method to show students that nutrition is one of the attributes of food, and whether students think something is gross is irrelevant. Grossness is not an attribute we use to determine the meaning of food. However, it is one used for identifying "foods I do not like."

The Direct Teaching of Concepts

One obvious way to teach students the meaning of a concept is to give them a dictionary definition and have them apply this to the information they are learning. Or, students could look up the meaning of a word for themselves. Another direct and more interesting method to teach concepts is to use game formats. Here are some examples:

1. Two or more players identify examples of a concept drawn from the study of a particular culture or area of the world. Pictures provide the information.

   a) Players receive a matrix card with concepts identified at the top and letters of the alphabet down the side.

   b) Players view a picture or series of pictures and attempt to place examples of the concept that begin with the letters of the alphabet listed on the matrix card.

   c) The winner is the player who can correctly complete the most matrix boxes. Here is an example:

South Africa				
	Animals	Vegetation	Economic activity	Landform
Letter A	Antelope			
Letter M			Mining	
Letter T				Table land
Letter D			Diamonds	

2. Another game involves the teacher stating a topic and a concept name. Students have to give an example of the concept; the example must be related to the topic. For example:

Topic: Canada	
Concepts	Examples
Vegetation	Douglas fir, maple
River	St. Lawrence, Saskatchewan, Thompson
Mineral	Gold, coal, nickel

3. In the Market Game, students learn the concepts of "supply," "demand," "profit," and "bargaining" and can learn other important economic concepts such as "surplus," "deficit," "profit," "loss," and "monopoly." This is a simulation game, in that it simulates reality. Players make decisions within an economic system where their actions model what could occur in the real world.[2]

$5	$5	$5

$1	$1	$1	$1	$1

You will need to cut out the money and the "buyer" and "seller" cards. A collection of paper clips, erasers, pencils, and crayons will also be required.

	BUYER	BUYER	BUYER	BUYER
With $20 buy	Paper clips..............1	Paper clips.............2	Paper clips.............2	Paper clips..............1
	Erasers...................2	Erasers....................1	Erasers...................1	Erasers...................2
	Pencils....................3	Pencils....................3	Pencils 1	Pencils 1
	Crayons 0	Crayons..................2	Crayons.................2	Crayons.................2
SELLER	**Paper clips**	**Erasers**	**Pencils**	**Crayons**
	Sell 6	Sell 10	Sell 5	Sell 4
	Cost price $2 each	Cost price $1 each	Cost price $2 each	Cost price $2 each

a) Divide the class into four equal groups of buyers and four equal groups of sellers. Each group of buyers takes one buyer's card and collects $20 in money. Their objective is to purchase all the items listed on their card. Each group of sellers takes one seller's card and the requisite number of paper clips, erasers, pencils, and crayons. Their objective is to sell their products at a profit. Each sellers' group should set up a table and list the prices of the products. Prices can be changed at any time.

b) When the game has started, buyers go to the sellers' tables. Bargaining is permitted.

c) The game ends when a buyers' group collects all the items on their card. This buyers' group, and the sellers' group that makes the most profit, are declared winners.

d) When the game is over, ask the following questions:

Sellers:

- How did you decide what price to set for your products? (concept: profit/loss)
- Did you change the price during the game? Why or why not? (concept: profit/loss)
- Did you sell all your products? Why or why not? (concepts: supply/demand/cost/market)

Buyers:

- How did you decide what price you were willing to pay for each product? (concept: budget/needs/wants)
- Did you bargain with the sellers? Did bargaining result in lower prices? (concept: bargaining)
- Did you obtain all the items on your list? Why or why not? (concepts: supply/demand/need/want)

How could this simulation be adapted so that concepts of inflation, competition, and cooperation are introduced? To what student experiences could this game be related?

Teaching Concept Attainment

Activity 6-E

In order to fully grasp a concept, what must we be able to do? Read the following dialogue and try to ascertain what the teacher is doing to help the student fully grasp the concept of "(hot) desert."

TEACHER: Tell me, what is a desert?

STUDENT: A desert is a place where there is sand and it's hot.

TEACHER: Is this a desert? *[Shows a picture of the Sahara.]*

STUDENT: Yes.

TEACHER: Is this a desert? *[Shows a picture of a beach.]*

STUDENT: Yes.

TEACHER: What about this? *[Shows a picture of the Sahara in a rainstorm.]*

STUDENT: No.

TEACHER: How is that *[beach]* different from this *[Sahara in a rainstorm]*?

STUDENT: This *[beach]* has sand and it's hot and the other one isn't hot.

TEACHER: Is the sandbox in the playground a desert?

STUDENT: No, it isn't big enough. A desert has to be big.

TEACHER: All of these are deserts. *[Shows pictures of deserts.]* Tell me what is the same about all of them.

STUDENT: They are all big and have sand in them. It's hot.

TEACHER: So, could this *[beach]* be a desert?

STUDENT: No, it's not big.

TEACHER: And this one *[Sahara in a rainstorm]*?

STUDENT: There's sand, but it's not hot.

TEACHER: Could it be hot when it is raining? Like a shower in your bathroom?

STUDENT: Guess so.

To understand a concept, students must be able to define the term (state the attributes that give the concept its meaning) as well as give examples of it (state what would qualify as an example of the concept). Consider the concept "island." Students must know that it is a body of land entirely surrounded by water, and that Madagascar and Jamaica are examples of the concept.

As pointed out earlier, a simple way of finding out what a word means is to use a dictionary. Dictionaries, however, define words in their ideal form. Using a dictionary may be inadequate for the purposes of teaching concepts because a) definitions are often circular (value = evaluation, and evaluation = judging on the basis of a value); b) meanings in normal language are ambiguous or vague, and dictionaries cannot point out many of the complexities; and c) dictionary definitions often lack precision. Using concept attainment procedures can help avoid these problems.

Activity 6-F

Below are three examples and one non-example of a particular concept. What might the concept be? After you have looked at them, refer to the Answers section.

1. Jane Smith wanted to live in Canada. She went to the Canadian embassy in London, England, to apply to live in Canada. As she had the appropriate qualifications, she was accepted. Eventually, she became a Canadian citizen. Jane is an example of a/an _____.

2. Liu Chan came to Canada as a graduate student. He liked being here and wanted to stay. However, he had to return to China in order to apply to live here. Eventually, he was accepted. Liu is an example of a/an _____.

3. In the late 1880s, many families came to Canada to escape persecution and economic hardship in Eastern Europe. They intended to stay in Canada and create new lives for themselves. These families are examples of _____.

4. Rajender Singh and his family came to Canada to visit friends and relatives. The family lived in Canada for nine months and then returned to India. Rajender Singh and his family are not examples of _____.

These are the steps for teachers to follow:

1. Having decided on the concept to be taught, we must be able to define the term and know what would qualify as examples of the concept and what would count as non-examples. The non-examples should be items that are closely related to the examples. It would be pointless to contrast "immigrants" with "skyscrapers"; rather, that concept should be contrasted with examples of other people who come to stay in Canada—tourists, visitors, diplomats—but who have no intention of settling here or becoming Canadian citizens. It would also help, where possible, to present a range of examples of the concept, some of which are more concrete than others, or more familiar to students. Examples and non-examples can be in print, picture, or actual object form. We will also have to consider whether our students understand the concepts related to the one we plan to teach. If these concepts are not understood, we will have to teach them.

Then we can teach the concept in an inductive way by proceeding as follows:

2. Show examples of the concept, and ask students if they can use one word (the concept) to describe all the examples (a guessing game). Ask, "Can you think of one word that would describe all of these?" Display non-examples and tell students that these are not examples of the concept. This may help make the game more interesting and may help students make more reasoned guesses.

3. When students have guessed the concept name, ask them to state why the examples can be called by that name. This will lead them to note the attributes of the concept.

Here, it is important to relate the concept to other concepts that are part of the students' prior experience.

4. Show students additional examples and non-examples of the concept, and have them differentiate between them and state why they are examples or non-examples.

5. As an evaluation procedure, students could list the attributes of the concept, find examples and non-examples of the concept, and state why they are examples or non-examples.

Or we could use an expository method where we display the examples of the concept, state that these are examples of concept X, and present a definition. Ask students what is similar about all the examples and help them identify the attributes of the concept. Then, carry out steps 4 and 5 above. For example:

Show students pictures of urban scenes. State, "All of these pictures are examples of the concept 'urban.'" Ask, "What have they all got in common?" When the attributes of "urban" are listed, then introduce some non-examples (a village, a house in the countryside) and tell them that these are not examples. Have students state what attributes of "urban" are missing. Show some more pictures of urban and non-urban scenes and ask them to identify which are urban and which are non-urban. Have them tell you their reasons. Then students should list the attributes of the concept "urban." Finally, they could be given old magazines and asked to cut out examples and non-examples of "urban" and paste them onto paper. Or, using a textbook, they could tell you on which pages pictures of urban scenes occur. Reasons for believing these pictures are examples of the concept could be discussed.

For more sophisticated students, we could introduce examples of "suburbs." Point out that the term "urban" has been modified to describe a phenomenon that is neither urban nor rural, but somewhere in between. We could ask students to think of other words that have been modified to describe situations in which the original word was not quite appropriate. Examples might include "war" and "civil war," or "book" and "booklet."

To help young students learn key concepts, we can pose the following types of questions:

- Can you name a kind of _____?
- Can you give an example of a/an _____?
- How are a/an _____ and a/an _____ alike?
- How are a/an _____ and a/an _____ different?
- How are _____ all the same?

To help you clarify the meaning of the concept you wish to teach, you can ask yourself and your students the following sorts of questions:[3]

- With what terms is X (the concept you wish to teach) synonymous?
- Can X be classified as a kind of _____?
- How does the meaning of X differ from the meaning of _____ (which seems to be similar in meaning)?
- What are the attributes of X? Is _____ a characteristic of things to which X refers?
- What different kinds of X are there? Is _____ a kind of X?
- If I say something is an X, am I ascribing positive or negative value to it?

GUIDELINES FOR CONCEPT ATTAINMENT

There are a few key guidelines that should be followed in concept attainment activities. First, research evidence indicates it is better to present examples of the concept first and to have them remain in view (either in pictorial form or as printed statements) during the activity.[4] Second, the optimal number of examples presented simultaneously should be about four. Third, concepts having few critical attributes are easier to learn than those that have many. Finally, presenting examples and non-examples in verbal form increases the ease of concept attainment. This is because critical properties can be emphasized more easily through verbal means than pictorial ones.

Two major problems occur in concept learning; one is **overgeneralization**, and the other is **overdiscrimination**. Although young children may overgeneralize ("Anything that flies is a bird"), they are more likely to overdiscriminate ("That's not a bird, it's a sparrow"). There is evidence to suggest that a child's ability to determine differences among concepts develops earlier than the ability to determine similarities. While the tendency to overdiscriminate tends to decline with age, the tendency to overgeneralize does not. The Wisconsin Model attempts to explain the development of concept learning.[5]

- **Concrete:** The object is discriminated from other objects.
- **Identity:** The object is generalized to two or more forms of the same thing that look similar.
- **Classificatory:** The objects, although they may look different, are seen to belong to the same class of things.
- **Formal:** The object can be fully defined, and inferred from examples.

Although the ability to understand and use concepts increases with age, this does not mean that young children cannot deal with abstractions. Young children do use words like "fair," "good," "cheat," and so on. They understand "climate" in terms of hot/cold and wet/dry. Older children may be able to discuss wind force and air pressure. They understand these terms at their own level and can be helped to develop conceptual abilities and knowledge through concept attainment activities. What follows are some variations on these activities.

OTHER CONCEPT ATTAINMENT ACTIVITIES

Activity 6-G

What one word could be used in each of the blanks? For a discussion of the concept, see the Answers section.

- It is a _____ in this culture to make reed baskets. For centuries, mothers have taught their daughters to weave. When it appeared that modern technology would lead to the loss of this ancient craft, a revival of interest in this _____ occurred.
- There has been a longstanding _____, based on a strong belief in male supremacy, of excluding women from important roles in Iranian society. When this _____ is flouted, there are serious repercussions.

- Every year on October 3, the Smith family has held a birthday party for Grandma Smith. There is always a cake and presents. This family _____ has been practised for 82 years and is part of a larger cultural _____ of having parties on birthdays.
- Every night John watches the television news. He does not expect his wife or children to do this, and he knows that he can change his behaviour at any time. This practice is not a _____ .

Activity 6-H

Which of the following are examples of the exercise of "power," and which are examples of the exercise of "authority"? When you have decided, turn to the Answers section.

a) The teacher tells the students to line up.

b) The captain of the baseball team says that Catrina can't pitch because she isn't as good as Rachel.

c) Some older children tell Billy to get out of the park.

d) Joel says, "If you don't give me your chocolate bar, I'll get you after school."

e) Mrs. Chan tells her daughter to take out the garbage.

f) A police officer tells Mr. Brown to pull his car off to the side of the road.

g) The school principal says that the teacher must attend the workshop on the new social studies curriculum.

From this activity you can see that agreement about meaning may not always be possible. As pointed out earlier, we may argue about what a particular term should mean. When the meanings are in dispute, we can use critical thinking activities to help students figure out an appropriate meaning. Here is an example:[6]

Question: Was (David Thompson, Laura Secord, Louis Riel, Chief Dan George, etc.) a hero?

In groups, students discuss the characteristics of a hero. They identify people, both real and fictional, whom they think are heroes, and they list their characteristics. The lists are then shared and a class synthesis is created. Where there is disagreement, the characteristic is starred so that when the activity is completed, students can reconsider it.

Students then apply the characteristics to their hero by researching that person's life.

Characteristics of a hero	Hero's actions
Performs an amazing feat	
Possesses special abilities	
Overcomes obstacles	
Etc.	

Another way to have students learn and demonstrate that they have grasped a concept is to have them use a concept map.[7] Here is an example:

Concept Web

WHAT IS IT? Armed conflict between nation states		

OPPOSITE Peace	TERM War	WHAT IS IT LIKE? Armies fight, soldiers and civilians killed or wounded

EXAMPLES World War II The Korean War The Gulf War War against Iraq

From this activity you can see that although you and your students may use such words as "power" and "hero" in speech and may recognize them in print, mere use or recognition does not necessarily mean that the concepts are understood. As teachers, we have to ascertain whether our students have grasped necessary concepts and teach them if they have not.

OTHER ACTIVITIES

1. Design an activity to teach a primary or intermediate-level class a concept that you consider important to learn in the context of the social studies. Give your reasons for choosing this particular concept. State in what context you will be teaching the concept and list the examples you will use and the questions you will ask. Try out your activity on a partner.

2. Formulate a lesson plan to teach the concept "ceremony" to a primary-grade class.

    a) Define "ceremony."

    b) Choose examples that would be meaningful to primary-grade students.

    c) State how you would use these examples and how you might differentiate between "ceremony" and such closely related concepts as "celebration" and "ritual."

3. Write a lesson plan for a grade of your choice on a topic or concept that uses the Taba Concept Development procedure or a concept attainment model. Include the following:

    a) a rationale: Why teach concepts?

    b) objectives: What specifically do you want students to know and do?

    c) the materials you will use

    d) how you will begin the lesson

e) the main body of your lesson: what you and the children will do, in what sequence; how children will be organized (at individual desks, in groups)

f) how you will end the lesson

g) how you might evaluate student learning

h) how you would follow up on your lesson; what you'll do next

4. A teacher is using the Taba Concept Development procedure to introduce a unit on Japan. The students have viewed a videotape on the life of a boy and girl in Tokyo and have listed what they saw. In groups, students are now categorizing and labelling the items. The teacher is working with one group. Critique the teacher's approach. For my assessment, see the Answers section.

TEACHER: I see you have *fish*, *noodles*, and *chopsticks* in one group. What is similar about these?

STUDENT: They all have to do with eating.

STUDENT: They're all food.

TEACHER: Well, what is the best label?

STUDENT: I think fish and noodles should go under *food* and the chopsticks should go somewhere else.

TEACHER: [To another student] What do you think?

STUDENT: Guess so. I wouldn't want to eat chopsticks.

TEACHER: So, what's similar about the food grouping?

STUDENT: They are all things you eat. They're good for you.

TEACHER: Where will the chopsticks go?

STUDENT: We've got a group here of pots, pans, knives, and stuff like that. It could go with them.

TEACHER: Do you remember in the videotape that the chopsticks had beautiful designs on them? Could they go with the group of items labelled *art*?

STUDENT: They could, but I think they fit better with the pots and things. They aren't like paintings.

TEACHER: Do you think your labels are OK?

STUDENT: I think so. If I were in Japan, I'd want to know about their food, how they cooked and ate it, and their art.

STUDENT: I think so too. If a Japanese person came here, she'd want to know what we ate.

NOTES

1. H. Taba, M. Durkin, J. Fraenkel, and A. McNaughton, *A Teacher's Handbook to Elementary Social Studies* (Reading, Mass.: Addison-Wesley, 1971).

2. A variation on this game can be found in D. Brozik and D. Zapalski, "Interactive classroom economics: The Market game." *Social Education* 90:6 (1999), pp. 278–282, in which students have a variety of livestock to barter for other livestock that they require.

3. Adapted from J. Coombs, "Critical thinking and problems of meaning," in I. Wright and C. LaBar, eds., *Critical Thinking and Social Studies* (Toronto: Grolier, 1987).

4. P. Martorella, "Knowledge and concept development in social studies," in J. Shaver, ed., *Handbook of Research on Social Studies Teaching and Learning* (New York: Macmillan, 1991).

5. H. Klausmeier and F. Hooper, "Conceptual development and instruction," in F. Kerlinger and J. Carroll, eds., *Review of Research in Education 2* (Itasca, Ill.: Peacock, 1974).

6. For an example of how this could be used at the upper elementary level, see J. Brien and S. White, "Students explore their conceptions of the heroic," *Social Education* 63:4 (1999), pp. M7–9.

7. R. Schwartz and T. Raphael, "Concept of definition: A key to improving students' vocabulary," *The Reading Teacher* 39:2 (1985), pp. 198–203.

GLOSSARY OF KEY TERMS

Concept — a mental construct that provides the rules for giving meaning to a term.

Concept attainment — a procedure in which students use examples and non-examples of a concept to identify the concept's attributes.

Concept development — a procedure in which students list, group, and label information to develop concepts useful for organizing the study of a particular topic. Eventually leads to the development of generalizations.

Necessary conditions — those attributes, characteristics, or rules of a concept that are required to give the term its meaning: e.g., two necessary attributes of a triangle are that it has three sides and that these sides are straight. These two attributes are not sufficient to give "triangle" its meaning. (See **Sufficient conditions**.)

Overdiscrimination — treating a member of a class of things as if it did not belong to that class: e.g., "That's not a dog; it's a poodle."

Overgeneralization — concluding that because this A is a B, that all As are Bs, when the data do not warrant it.

Sufficient conditions — the required attributes of the concept that give it its meaning. Thus, to say that a triangle, in the geometric sense, has three straight sides and is a closed plane figure is sufficient to establish the shape as a triangle. These are the sufficient conditions for a shape to be called a triangle.

chapter seven

What's the Right Question?
Questions and Questioning

In the previous chapter we looked at teaching the concepts students require in order to make sense of a topic. Both teachers and students will also need information about examples of the concepts as they pertain to a particular topic. If we are studying "climate" as it relates to our community, we could just teach about the climate and then ask questions of students to find out how much they have remembered. Or we could ask questions about the climate to initiate student research or, better yet, have students find answers for questions they generate themselves.

This chapter attempts to help you identify and use questions in the classroom.

Activity 7-A

List 10 questions that could be asked about the photo of a grave marker in Atlin, BC, on the following page.

Presumably, you are familiar with *what?*, *why?*, *where?*, *when?*, and *how?* questions. These are the questions with which we are most familiar and they are very useful questions. But in your list above, did you include any of the following types of questions? (Note that not all the following questions pertain to the photo of the grave marker that follows; they are simply examples illustrating each *type* of question.)

TYPES OF QUESTIONS

Empirical

Answers are in the form of statements about what *is, was,* or *will be* the case. This does not mean that the statements will *necessarily* be true or correct. We may never know the truth about some matters.

Descriptive:
- What is happening? What are those people doing?
- How many of them are there? Is it raining?
- How does S use the term X?
- What does S value?

Comparative:
- How are they similar or different?
- Has X changed?

Historical: These questions are similar to descriptive questions, but they concern the past. Chapter 10 provides examples of significant historical questions.
- When did the first people inhabit North America?

Causal/Correlational:
- What caused that? Why did X happen?
- What has the climate got to do with the vegetation?

Predictive:
- What will happen next? What will it be like in the future? What would happen if...?

Methodological:
- Where can we locate the answer? How can we tackle this problem?

Relevance:
- What has this got to do with me? How does this relate to my life?

Conceptual

Answers are statements about what X means.

- Does A mean the same as B? (Does "taiga" mean the same as "northern forest"?)
- Is A an example of B? (Is this landscape an example of a prairie?)
- Is A an attribute of the term B? (Is a peak an attribute of a mountain?)

Value

Answers are in the form of a judgment where intellectual standards are applied.

- Are our observations reliable?
- Are the data believable?
- Is concept X used appropriately?
- Have we got enough evidence to justify this conclusion?

Or answers are in the form of a judgment where other values (ethical, environmental, religious, aesthetic, prudential) are applied. These will be addressed in Part 4.

- Is X good?
- Is A better than B?
- Should S do X?
- What should be done about X?

Activity 7-B

Pose one question for each of the categories above using the following picture.

The point of asking questions is not only to get students to state what they already know, but also to stimulate further learning and thinking, as illustrated by this next set of questions.

Questions to introduce discussion:

What do you see here? If this picture had been taken 10 years later, what do you think might have changed? What solutions are there to this problem?

Questions to help analyze human behaviour:

What are these people doing? Why are they doing this? Have you done anything like this? How is it done?

Questions to help identify human feelings:

How do these people feel? Why do they feel this way? Have you ever felt this way? When? Do all people have the same feelings in this situation?

Questions to provoke further research:

What questions could be asked? How could answers be found? Is there a problem here? What could be done to solve it? What will we need to know? If you had this problem, what would you do? Why? Are some problems easier to solve than others? Why?

Questions to encourage geographic inferences:

What can we say about the location? Is it hot or cold? Wet or dry? Is it like our own neighbourhood, province, or country? How have people adapted to the environment? How have people adapted the environment to suit themselves?

Questions to encourage historical inferences:

What do you think it was like in the past? Would people have done things differently 100 years ago? What events in the past caused this situation/scene to appear as it does today?

Questions to introduce sequential relationships:

What happened before? What do you think will happen next? Why?

Questions to encourage the making of connections:

How is the new well in the village related to changes in the villagers' way of life? What change in your community has affected how you live?

Questions to broaden understanding and encourage summarization:

What conclusions can we draw from this? Can you make up a sentence to summarize this? If _____ occurred, what might happen? What does this tell us?

Questions to encourage clarity:

Can you say more about that? What do you mean by X?

You will notice that just as there are different types of *questions*, there are also different types of *reasoning* required to answer those questions.

Activity 7-C

Go back to your list of questions in Activity 7-B.

1. Which questions would be easiest to answer? Why?

2. Which questions would be most difficult to answer? Why?

3. What types of reasoning would be required to answer the easiest and most difficult questions? (Reasoning consists of inferring, analyzing, evaluating, interpreting, conceptualizing, and the like.)

4. What intellectual standards (accuracy, plausibility, clarity, logic, fair-mindedness) would you need to apply in order to answer both the most difficult and the easiest questions?

LEVELS OF QUESTIONS

Clearly, those questions to which we already know the answers are easy. If we want to find out what students know, then questions of recall are important. Frequent questioning can lead to gains in student learning.[1] But recall questions don't require any of the reasoning skills identified above. And questions should generate student thinking, not just the recall of specific information. If we want students to evaluate information, to infer, to analyze, and so on, then we have to ask questions that involve more than the recall of information.

Many educators use **Bloom's taxonomy**[2] to identify different levels of questions and the thinking abilities necessary to answer questions at each level. Sanders,[3] who adapted Bloom's taxonomy, lists the following categories. (I use **Sanders's classification** because it divides Bloom's Level 2 into two separate categories, and I find it useful to differentiate Translation and Interpretation. Bloom places both of these under Comprehension.) A typical question is included for each of the categories.

1. **Memory**

   The student recalls previously learned information.

   "Who is the prime minister of Canada?"

2. **Translation**

   The student changes information into a different symbolic form or language.

   "What is the point the artist makes in the cartoon?"

3. **Interpretation**

   The student discovers relationships among facts, generalizations, and concepts. Interpretation involves a reordering or rearrangement of material. It makes use of comparative and cause-and-effect relationships.

   "Prior to European contact, what were the differences and similarities between the shelters of the Haida and Huron peoples?" What might account for these?

4. **Application**

   The student performs a task or solves a problem that requires the application of previously learned information.

   "Use your inquiry skills to answer the following question."

5. **Analysis**

   The student solves a problem by analyzing it into its constituent parts.

   "Is the reasoning in the following quotation sound or unsound?"

6. **Synthesis**

   The student solves a problem that requires original, creative thinking. Synthesis is the assembly of elements and parts so as to form a whole. Synthesis questions encourage students to engage in imaginative, original thinking.

   "How would you solve the problem of litter in the school playground?"

7. **Evaluation**

   The student makes a judgment of good or bad, right or wrong, according to particular criteria or standards such as the intellectual values of

   a) empirical accuracy

      "Have we got the correct measurement?"

   b) conceptual appropriateness

      "Are we using 'equal treatment' here to mean 'exactly the same treatment?'"

   c) logical relationships and internal consistency

      "Is the evidence that constitutes this explanation logically consistent?"

   d) other value principles or standards (e.g., ethical or environmental)

      "Should Canada give aid to people who are starving in Africa?"

Activity 7-D

State whether each of the following examples is an empirical, a conceptual, a logical, or a value question. Specify its level according to Sanders's categorization. Answers are in the Answers section.

a) In what year did Cartier build a settlement in what today is Quebec?

b) What are the major recommendations, and the reasons for them, of *Charting a Course*, the recent report of the National Commission on Social Studies in the Schools?

c) What caused World War II?

d) What is the population of Toronto? (Use the graph provided to answer the question.)

e) What is a harbour?

f) Is unity the opposite of diversity?

g) How should you solve the problem of starvation in Somalia?

h) Should First Nations people have the right to operate their own schools?

i) Should you hit someone whenever you feel like it?

j) If you believed killing was wrong and that capital punishment was a form of killing, would you then believe that capital punishment was wrong?

Whereas Sanders's adaptation of Bloom's taxonomy can be useful in focusing attention on different levels of questions, there are some problems with it. First, it should not be assumed that it is more difficult to answer "higher level" questions than "lower level" ones. The question "Should you hit someone whenever you feel like it?" is an evaluation question, yet is easy to answer for anyone with any moral sensitivity. Second, recall questions can vary in level of difficulty. Some require recall of a specific fact; others require recall of complex bodies of information. Third, it would seem more sensible to have level 2 questions precede level 1 ones because to recall anything meaningfully will require understanding the concepts in what is being recalled. And understanding concepts is a level 2 component. Fourth, merely stating that a question is at a particular level says nothing about the significance of the question. Fifth, just because we ask a higher level question does not mean that students will reply with higher level answers.[4] Sixth, the taxonomy does not mean that we should start with lower level questions and then work up the hierarchy to evaluation questions. It might be perfectly sensible to start with an evaluation question, especially if students know the basic facts. In my view, rather than relying solely on Bloom's taxonomy or Sanders's adaptation of it to tell us something about what will be required to answer a question, we should use the following Question Checklist. And we should do this, because we ought to plan the questions we ask just as we plan other aspects of a lesson. Note that not every checklist question is appropriate for every question you pose.

1. Is the question significant enough to be asked?

2. Will it attract student's attention and engage them?

3. Can the students who will be attempting to answer it answer the question in a satisfactory way?

4. What type of question is it (empirical, conceptual, value)?

5. What information will be needed to answer the question?

6. Is this information available? Where?

7. What concepts (included in the question statement and in the information needed to answer it) will have to be understood to answer the question?

8. What sorts of procedures could be used to answer the question? Do the students know how to carry out these procedures? Which is the best procedure?

9. What sorts of thinking tasks will students have to perform? Will they have to infer, generalize, hypothesize, etc.? Are they capable of performing these tasks?

10. What would qualify as a good answer? To what intellectual or other standards do we appeal?

The last question will involve critical reflection. Students should be introduced to some of the intellectual standards that pertain to evaluating the truth, or believing or accepting various types of claims. For example, some of the ways we can judge the appropriateness of the use of a concept appear in Chapter 6. In Chapter 8, you'll find intellectual standards relevant to judging the accuracy and believability of empirical claims. In Part 4, some standards for justifying personal and social value claims are discussed.

Activity 7-E

Apply the Question Checklist to a question of your choice or to one or more of the following questions, all of which are based on recent provincial social studies curriculum guides.

1. Why do families need rules? (Grade 1, British Columbia)

2. What services and facilities show that individual initiative and/or cooperation are/is valued in a particular community? (Grade 2, Alberta)

3. What are the distinctive geographical features of the prairie region? (Grade 3, Manitoba)

4. How have roles and values changed over the years? (Grade 4, Nova Scotia, in the unit on people and how they change)

5. What is meant by "government"? (Grade 5, Nova Scotia)

6. How does technology affect the lives of people in the Near and Far North? How does it affect life in other regions of Canada? (Grade 5, Manitoba)

7. How do people use the natural environment of Atlantic Canada to make a living? (Grade 6, Prince Edward Island)

8. Should a people, in order to satisfy their needs, be allowed to alter the physical environment of people in other parts of the world? (Grade 7, British Columbia)

Now consider the following questions for a Grade 4 class that is studying the early exploration of North America, and decide which one(s) would best fit the criteria outlined above.

a) What was the sextant used for and how was it used?

b) Suppose you set sail from Europe to North America in the early 1500s. How would you know where you were?

c) Here is a picture (of a sailor using a sextant). What is he doing? What is the instrument he is using?

d) If sailors in the 1500s had a global positioning system, how would this have affected the exploration of North America?

e) Let's suppose you are sailing from Europe to North America in the 1500s, and you have a compass. What else would you need to know to decide in which direction to sail, and how would you learn that information?

CONSIDERATIONS IN POSING QUESTIONS

There are several other important points to be made about questions and questioning. It is clear that the sort of questions we ask will depend upon our objectives. If we want students to recall specific information, then a clearly worded recall question is needed. If we want students to generate a lot of different information, or pose many specific questions, then a broad general question is appropriate. For example, asking the question "What was life like in a fur-trading fort in 1750?" may lead not only to information being given by students but also to questions such as "Where did drinking water come from?" or "Where did people go to the bathroom?" (a serious question asked seriously by a Grade 5 student).

ASKING QUESTIONS ORALLY IN THE CLASSROOM

When we are orally asking questions in a classroom, there are basically two ways of operating:

Individual designated: "Saul, what is _____?"

Group designated: a) "Class, what is _____? Saul, please answer."

b) "Class, what is _____?" *[Student who is not designated by the teacher spontaneously answers.]*

c) "Class, what is _____?" *[Whole class responds en masse.]*

Each of these procedures has its advantages and disadvantages.

Individual

The advantages are that the whole class is alert because nobody knows who is going to be called upon to answer the question; inattentive students are engaged, and a student who is likely to know the answer can answer. A major disadvantage is that favouritism can prevail if only some individuals are called upon by the teacher. (This can be insidious if the favouritism is based on ethnicity, gender, class, or the presumed mental or physical capabilities of a student.) When the student's name is called, the rest of the class may not pay attention to the question or the answer, and shy children may be overlooked entirely. Exclusion of students in a question-and-answer session should be avoided at all costs unless there is a compelling reason for it (such as when a student is experiencing some emotional upset and needs to be left alone for a while).

Group

The advantage is that the entire class is involved initially—every student has the opportunity to answer. The disadvantages are that once a student is chosen to answer the question, the rest of the class may not pay attention to the answer given, and, if an answer is to be given spontaneously, those who know the answer immediately will foreclose on those who need time to think.

Keep these points in mind when you are engaged in question-and-answer sessions and, whichever procedure you adopt, always try to involve as many students as possible. You can achieve this by sharing a single question among several students (so long as the redirection does not give the impression that the first student has the wrong answer), or by posing further questions related to the original one to other students:

TEACHER: Raoul, when did Jean Chrétien become prime minister of Canada?

RAOUL: In 1993.

TEACHER: Susan, is Raoul correct?

SUSAN: Yes.

TEACHER: Fred, are you sure it wasn't 1994?

FRED: I don't think so…. I'm not sure.

TEACHER: Who in the class is sure? Marie?

MARIE: It was in 1993.

TEACHER: Good, we've got the answer and Raoul was correct.

TEACHER: Dorothy, what's the capital of Prince Edward Island?

DOROTHY: It's Charlottetown.

TEACHER: Claude, what makes it the capital?

CLAUDE: The premier lives there.

TEACHER: Is that why Charlottetown is the capital, Sanjit?

SANJIT: No, it's because Parliament is there.

FIONA: *[Spontaneously]* It's the legislature. Parliament is in Ottawa.

TEACHER: Well, class, who is right?

Note that in these exchanges, four or more students can be quickly involved. This "quick-fire" strategy is appropriate only when students do not need time to think about their answers. When time is required for students to reflect, then the teacher should provide adequate "wait-time." Morgan and Saxton[5] state that probably when we find it hard to wait it is because we are not used to silences, or because we think that the question is too hard or not well posed. However, when we do pose questions that demand some thought and we do provide adequate time for students to formulate an answer, then students tend to give longer answers, more students volunteer responses, and student answers are more thoughtful.

One way in which students can be involved in a question-and-answer activity is to use the following cooperative learning strategy. The class is divided into groups of three to five, and each group member is given a number. Each group should be representative of the composition of the class (in ability, gender, ethnicity, etc.). Each group discusses the answer to a question. The teacher then calls upon all students with a particular number (e.g., all number 3s), and designates one of them to provide the answer. This procedure has several advantages. Higher achievers are willing to share their knowledge as they want their group to do well, and lower achievers are likely to listen carefully as they might be called upon to give the answer. Cooperation among students is also enhanced.

Children need rewarding when their answers are correct. Avoid saying "good" or "OK" after every answer; it will become meaningless. Also avoid "No, you're wrong." Instead, say, "That's not quite right; can you clarify that a little more?" or ask another student, "Can you help?" When the correct answer is ascertained, ensure that the student who gave the wrong answer knows and understands the correct one. And watch your body language as this can give students clues as to how you are reacting to their responses.[6]

Student Posing of Questions

Young children are full of questions but their inclination to ask them seems to fade away the longer they are in school. How can we encourage them to be inquisitive? Our attitude helps here as does the classroom climate we foster (see Chapter 9). If we ask good questions and encourage students to ask questions, then students are more likely to think about their own questions.[7] One way is to use the familiar questions "What do I already know about X?" "What would I like to find out about X?" and "What questions do I need to ask to find out about X?" Another idea is to have groups brainstorm questions about a topic, then share the questions and decide which ones would be best. In pairs, students could pose questions about a passage they have read, exchange questions, and answer them. They should then judge the questions they asked using criteria they generate (a list similar to the Question Checklist above could act as these criteria). Having students interview people can also hone their questioning skills (see Chapters 10 and 16), as can having them interview other students who role-play a particular character.

OTHER ACTIVITIES

1. Ask a number of questions about your classroom or a local parking lot, street, or other location. Take one particular question and list the ways this question could be extended. Evaluate your questions for their clarity and importance.

2. Take a particular question from any social studies curriculum and complete a thorough analysis of it.

   a) What sort of question is it (empirical, conceptual, value)?

   b) What concepts would students have to grasp in order to answer the question?

   c) What information would students need to answer the question?

   d) What types of reasoning would students have to demonstrate?

e) What would qualify as a reasonable answer? To what intellectual standards would you appeal to justify your claim that you had a reasonable answer?

NOTES

1. W. Wilen, "Exploring myths about teacher questioning in the social studies curriculum," *The Social Studies* 92:1 (2001), p. 27.

2. B. Bloom, ed., *Taxonomy of Educational Objectives: Handbook 1—Cognitive Domain* (New York: David McKay, 1956).

3. N. Sanders, *Classroom Questions: What Kinds?* (New York: Harper and Row, 1966).

4. W. Wilen, p. 28.

5. N. Morgan and J. Saxton, *Asking Better Questions* (Markham, Ont.: Pembroke Publishers, 1994), p. 83.

6. Ibid., pp. 96–103. The authors also note other behaviours we ought to avoid, such as saying, "Yes, but…" or posing rhetorical questions.

7. Ibid., pp. 112–114.

GLOSSARY OF KEY TERMS

Bloom's/Sanders's Taxonomy:

Analysis — breaking into separate elements.

Application — use of previously learned information to solve a new problem.

Evaluation — judging information, plans, decisions, objects, etc.

Interpretation — discovery of relationships between information.

Memory — recall of information.

Synthesis — assembling elements into a new whole.

Translation — change of information from one form or language to another.

Conceptual — statements or questions about what a word means.

Empirical — statements or questions about what *was*, *is*, or *will be* the case.

Group designated question — question posed to a group.

Individually designated question — question posed to one person.

Value — statements or questions about an evaluation of something, or about what *should be*, or what *should be done*. Example: "What sort of world would be best to live in? What should be done to bring about this world?"

chapter eight

What's the Right Answer? Helping Students Answer Empirical Questions and Develop Intellectual Standards

Having students pose questions, or posing questions ourselves for students to answer, entails that answers be found. One way is to present students with the answers using expository techniques (see Chapter 5). Another way is to have students answer questions by hypothesizing what they think the answer is and then checking their **hypothesis** to ascertain if it is supported. This procedure, called inquiry learning and teaching, is the focus of this chapter.

In the social studies literature, **inquiry** sometimes refers to any procedure whereby students find answers to questions. Thus, looking up the answer in a textbook to a simple and specific question to which the answer is known would constitute inquiry. In this case, the defining attributes of inquiry are that the question is beyond the recall level, according to Sanders's taxonomy (see Chapter 7), and that the student has to find the answer by looking it up in resource materials or by asking someone. At times this is a worthwhile activity, which I label as library research. In this chapter, however, inquiry will be used to denote a procedure in which students generate hypotheses about the answer to a question, and then test them by locating, interpreting, analyzing, and evaluating information.

Sometimes answers will be known (Where did the stones used to build the pyramids in Egypt come from?); sometimes there will be a partial answer (What toys did children play with in ancient Egypt?); and sometimes the answer can only be hypothesized, but some hypotheses will be more plausible than others (How were the pyramids built?). Sometimes a test can be performed to ascertain the answer (Could the pyramids have been built by using gigantic kites to lift the blocks of stone into place?). Sometimes there is no known test to prove or disprove a hypothesis (Did creatures from another planet build the pyramids?). Once a question has been posed and demands an empirical answer (that is, the answer will be a statement about *what is*, *was*, or *will be* the case), hypotheses are generated. Hypotheses are guesses about what the answer will be. We hypothesize that X is the answer and then we test this to see if it is supported.

RATIONALES FOR INQUIRY

As with all teaching methodologies, underlying the use of inquiry procedures are beliefs about how children learn, what constitutes knowledge, and what the aims of education should be. In the next activity, you are asked to identify those beliefs that underlie inquiry procedures. In turn, these beliefs will provide rationales for the use of inquiry procedures. For example, one of the assumptions on which inquiry learning is based is that students are more likely to take ownership of what they learn. If you believe that this is a significant educational objective, then it provides a reason for using an inquiry procedure.

Activity 8-A

If you use an inquiry procedure, which of the following assumptions might you be making? When you have made your choice, refer to the Answers section.

a) All knowledge is absolute.

b) Children learn best when they are finding out their own answers.

c) In a democracy, people have to make decisions. Decision making necessitates the analysis and evaluation of conflicting evidence.

d) Children learn best when they are told the answer.

e) Children learn self-confidence when discovering knowledge for themselves.

f) Children "by nature" are problem solvers.

g) Children learn to think by being taught how to think.

h) Knowledge is a product of continuing inquiry and experimental testing, hence open to re-examination, renewal, and change.

i) Children remember what they've discovered for themselves better than what they've been taught directly.

j) Children are "naturally" curious.

AN INQUIRY METHOD

Suppose you are interested in finding out what motivated your peers in your social studies methods class to become teachers. In that case, the following questions need to be asked as the inquiry procedure is implemented.

1. **Question:** What motivated my peers in my social studies methods class to become teachers? Is the question clear? Do you know what the terms used in the question mean?

2. **Hypothesis:** What do you think the answer(s) is/are?

3. **Organization and data collection:** How will you find out whether or not your hypothesis/hypotheses is/are supported? What information will you need? If you decide to ask your peers, how will you do this? What questions will you ask? How many of your peers will you question? Will you orally question them or use some kind of survey? How can you be sure that your data collection is reliable? Will you work alone or would working in a group be more efficient? If you work with others, how might various tasks be shared?

4. **Data analysis:** How might the information be classified, interpreted, and evaluated? What skills and abilities would you need to make use of the data?

5. **Checking the hypothesis:** Is the hypothesis supported by the information? What will you do if a) your hypothesis is not supported? or b) your conclusion is so tentative that you can neither accept nor reject your hypothesis?

6. **Conclusion:** How might you report your conclusion?

In this inquiry procedure there are several important factors to consider.

The Question

Make sure students understand the question, especially the concepts contained in it. For example, to answer the question "What motivated the first Europeans to explore North America?" students would need to clarify "motivation" and understand that various sorts of mental states—fear, greed, and curiosity—can motivate human behaviour. Without this clarification, the next step would be pointless.

Hypothesizing

Once the question has been clarified, students should hypothesize as to what they think the answer will be. A simple way to start is to have students list what they know about the topic being studied and then ask them what they think they know. They then use this list as the basis of their hypotheses. All hypotheses should be accepted, even if we know they're wrong. One of the reasons for using inquiry strategies in the classroom is that students find it more interesting and challenging to test hypotheses than to merely look up answers in a book—or to rely on a teacher.

Hypothesizing depends upon students' previous knowledge and experiences. It would be pointless to have students hypothesize about Mongolia if students had never heard of Mongolia, just as it would be pointless for them to hypothesize about "motivation" if they did not understand the term. The next activity is designed to show that the quantity and quality of background knowledge make a significant difference to the hypotheses that are generated.

Activity 8-B

Refer to the accompanying map. Place a dot on the map to indicate each place where you think a settlement is located. When you are done, turn to the Answers section.

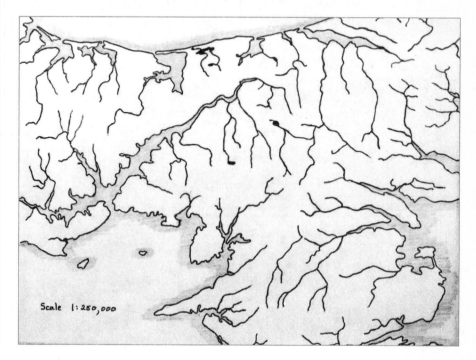

Scale 1:250,000

What previous knowledge did you use to arrive at these hypotheses? To make sensible hypotheses you had to have some ideas why settlements are located in particular places. For example, some reasons are proximity to a water supply, nearness to a sheltered harbour, location at the junction of two important transport routes, or having a good defensive position.

Another way to introduce students to hypothesizing is to use a game format.

Activity 8-C

Imagine you are a member of the British army in Canada in 1818. You are considering settling in Canada, but you'll need the help of the British government to do so. From the following list, decide what you think you will need and put a check mark in the "needs" column. If you think the British government will give you this item, place a check mark in the "individual choice" column. In a group, decide what you think the government would give you and, *if you all agree on the item*, place a check mark in the "group choice" column.

What would the British government provide?					
	I would need	Individual choice	Individual score	Group choice	Group score
free transportation					
radio					
land					
axe					
broadaxe					
money					
mattock					
Bible					
pickaxe					
furniture					
spade					
shovel					
hoe					
scythe					
drawknife					
hammer					
handsaw					
scythe stone					
panes of glass					
putty					
nails					
kettle					
bed tick (mattress)					
blanket					
cooking utensils					
TOTALS					

Check your responses in the Answers section at the end of the book, add up your individual and group scores, and consider these questions:

1. Were the individual and group scores the same or were they different?
2. If the scores were the same, what does this tell you about group decision making?
3. If the scores were different, what does this tell you about group decision making?
4. "Groups are more likely to arrive at better solutions to a problem because there will be more information available." Is this generalization warranted?

This game format can be adapted in several ways. For example, the question could be "What would you expect to find if you visited X *[another country, a museum, a farm, an industrial site, etc.]*?" Students would list their individual hypotheses, decide in a group if their hypotheses were plausible, and use resource materials, or actually visit the site, to find out if their hypotheses were correct. They could check if their individual hypotheses were more or less correct than the group ones and then answer the four questions above.

Data Gathering

Ask students how they are going to find out whether their hypotheses are correct. Ensure that they explore all possible sources. Depending upon the number of resources available and the skills of the students, we can either work with students in the library or we can provide all the materials in the classroom. All students could use the same materials, or groups could be formed. For example, one group could watch a video, another look at pictures, a third read print material, and a fourth use the internet. A variation on this is to use a WebQuest format.[1] In cases where some sort of survey or experiment has to be conducted, ensure first that it is feasible.

Students will need to be taught the skills necessary to use the materials or conduct a survey. They should learn how to locate references in the library and on the internet, and how to use indexes, chapter headings, and subheadings to find specific information. By the intermediate grades, students should be able to use most reference sources and compare sources to see if they agree.

The reading level of resource materials may pose problems. Those students who have difficulties reading can be given simple print material, or another student can help them. Providing pictorial sources is another option for younger readers. Even in the intermediate grades, it may be necessary to paraphrase some reading material. Historical documents, for example, are often difficult for even very able students to read.

The answers to some questions may involve taking surveys (Chapter 16), interviewing people (Chapter 16), doing historical research (Chapter 10), interpreting maps (Chapter 11), or going on a field trip (Chapter 12). In each case, students will have to be taught how to collect information by these means.

Analysis

Once information has been collected, students have to test their hypotheses. They may have to be taught how to classify, interpret, analyze, synthesize, summarize, and evaluate the information. Thinking critically about information and applying intellectual standards are dealt with later on in this chapter.

How the information is organized will depend on the question posed. One way information can be recorded is on an inquiry worksheet.

What did the Haida eat prior to contact with Europeans?		
Hypothesis	Data supporting	Data rejecting and additional data
Fish	Yes, salmon.	Ate shellfish also.
Beef	Didn't have cattle.	
Etc.	Etc.	Etc.

Making charts to display information is one way to prevent the student practice of copying from the source and moving the bones from one graveyard to another. Another way is to use a note-taking format with a piece of paper divided down the middle. In the right-hand column, the students copy the information that supports or refutes a hypothesis. In the left-hand column, they rephrase the information in their own words. The copying problem can also be avoided if at the outset of the inquiry students know that their conclusion must be presented in a way that precludes copying. For example, if students use a **RAFT** writing strategy then they have to write

- in a particular **R**ole (historical figure, journalist, pioneer, world leader)
- to a particular **A**udience (government leaders, newspaper readers)
- using a particular **F**ormat (editorial, letter, poem, newspaper report)
- on a particular **T**opic

Checking the Hypotheses

The conclusions derived from the information must be checked against the hypotheses. Are the hypotheses supported? Can we be sure we are right? Are the hypotheses rejected? Again, can we be sure we are right? Perhaps the evidence to support or reject a particular hypothesis cannot be found. In this case, we may be able to arrive at a tentative conclusion, or we may have to search further to see if we can find an answer. For example, if on the Haida question recorded on the worksheet on page 93, students hypothesize that seagulls were eaten, and no evidence can be found that the Haida either did or did not eat seagulls, then this will have to remain a hypothesis. How will we know whether the conclusion is true or believable? What qualifies as a correct or reasonable answer to an inquiry question?

Here we have to think critically about the information and whether there is enough reliable evidence to support or refute a hypothesis.

APPLYING INTELLECTUAL STANDARDS: THINKING CRITICALLY ABOUT THE INFORMATION

Sometimes it is clear that a particular answer to an inquiry question is correct. There are a lot of facts about which we can agree. All the resources we check contain the same information. Checking other sources and seeing if they agree is one way we can check for accuracy. Our criteria include weight of evidence and consistency of that evidence. However, what do we do if sources are not consistent and they do not agree?

Authority Claims

Activity 8-D

Use at least three different sources to find out the date of Christopher Columbus's birth. Do these sources agree? If not, which source do you think is correct? Carry out the same procedure for the question "Where did Columbus first set foot in the New World?"

Source 1	Source 2	Source 3
Date of birth		

Generally, we rely on authorities to provide us with information. We accept that the information in a textbook is accurate; we believe what experts tell us. Most students will believe what we tell them. I think it is obligatory for us to tell students why we believe that the information we impart to them is accurate; we should have reasons for saying that something is true or believable. We should teach students how to evaluate empirical claims. One way to do this is to focus on the types of information students are exposed to, not only in school but also in their daily lives, and to help them judge its reliability. Disagreements about which information to believe may be a result of authorities (experts on a subject) disagreeing, or people disagreeing about what they observed.

Activity 8-E

Suppose you had to teach the topics listed below. If you had to choose one reference, which would you consider the best? Why? When you have decided on your answer, refer to the Answers section.

1. Topic: Life in China today

   a) A National Geographic movie about life in China, produced in 2002 by two people who spent six months touring the country

   b) A book published in 2000 by the Chinese government extolling the virtues of life in the country

   c) Slides taken by a friend who recently spent two weeks in Beijing and Guangzhou

   d) A 2003 CBC documentary about the building of a dam on the Yangtze River in China

2. Topic: The internment of the Japanese during World War II

   a) A recent prescribed high-school textbook on the history of Canada in the 20th century, in which the history of the internment is discussed up to the granting of compensation by the Mulroney government

   b) The memoirs of a former politician who was instrumental in setting up internment camps

   c) A CBC television documentary made in 1990 about six families who were interned during the war

   d) The autobiography of a Japanese Canadian who, as a child, was interned

For the above activity, you should really choose more than one source because if authorities agree on something, there is a greater likelihood that it is accurate. However, by forcing you to choose one source, my intention was to compel you to think seriously about the criteria you would use to determine what sources of information are likely to be the most reliable.

According to Ennis[2] the following criteria should be applied:
The authority or expert

- has a good reputation
- is making statements that lie in his/her field
- has studied the matter using acceptable procedures
- is aware that his/her statements could affect his/her reputation

Applying these criteria is necessary not only when reading textbooks and other sources of information, but also when people are trying to convince us to believe something or to buy something. Suppose we see a television commercial in which a famous film star is telling us to buy Brand X toothpaste. While the star may be an expert on acting, there is little reason to accept the star's views on dental hygiene. If we did buy Brand X toothpaste because the star told us to, then we would be committing the fallacy of "appeal to authority."

Observation Claims

We do not rely on authorities for all our information. The other major source is observations made by others or by us. These, too, need to be evaluated.

Activity 8-F

Which of the following would you consider a reliable observation? Why? After justifying your choice, turn to the Answers section.

1. a) The umpire in the baseball game said that Rachel was out.
   b) Rachel's mother said she was not out.
   c) The captain of the opposing team said that Rachel was out.
2. a) The driver of the car that hit the bus said the traffic light was green when he went through the intersection.
   b) The driver of a car that arrived at the intersection 10 seconds after the incident said he thought the light was red when the car went through the intersection.
   c) A cyclist who had stopped at the intersection said the car went through a red light.
3. a) Using a measuring tape, the police measured the skid marks of the car that crashed and said, "The car skidded for 20 metres."
   b) A witness to the crash paced out the skid and said, "The car skidded for 15 metres."
   c) Another witness to the crash, who had narrowly avoided being hit by the car, said, "The car skidded for at least 30 metres. It went right by me."

In assessing observation statements, the following criteria should be applied:[3]
The observer

- does not allow emotion to interfere
- has no conflict of interest
- has senses that function properly

- has a good reputation
- uses appropriate observation instruments
- was in a suitable position to observe
- makes statements that are confirmed by others, or are confirmable

Other Intellectual Standards

Students in the elementary school can begin to grasp some intellectual standards by carrying out the following sorts of activities:

1. Compare two or more sources of information for answers to a particular question, or compare two or more newspaper/radio/TV/textbook/etc. accounts of a particular event. For example, ask students to find out the present-day population of Canada. Ask them to present their answers along with complete details about the sources they used.

Population of Canada					
Figure cited	Title of reference	Author	Where published	Date of publication	Date and name of original source

2. Have students witness a given event and write a description of it. For example, have them watch a news clip and then write a newspaper report. Compare the descriptions using the observation criteria listed above. Explore the reasons why people might have different points of view about the event. We all have our own biases, so it is important that students recognize their own and others' biases and judge when a bias leads to unfairness, distortion, prejudice, or closed-mindedness.

Activity 8-G

Which of the following accounts are biased in any of the senses above?

a) "Slugger" Smith hit 32 home runs for the Torpedoes in the 2002 season. "Hits" Wood of the Sharks hit 30, placing him second in the year's standings.

b) "Slugger" Smith was extremely lucky to hit 32 home runs last season. If you remember, most of these came against pretty poor teams and lousy pitching. Without a doubt, the player to praise is "Hits" Wood, who scored all his runs against top league teams and top pitchers.

c) "Slugger" Smith, who hit 32 magnificent homers last season, is probably the greatest ballplayer the Torpedoes have ever had. It was he, and he alone, who took the pennant away from the Sharks. He is so far ahead of "Hits" Wood in home runs that he is in a class all by himself.

3. Richburg, Nelson, and Reid[4] provide an interesting activity with regard to stereotypes in which they ask students to read an account of a person and then provide a physical description of that person. One example presented is about a freshman at Michigan State University who is studying calculus, chemistry, and analytical geometry. The person is expected to finish a Bachelor of Science degree and a medical degree in five years. To find out who this person is, consult the Answers section.

4. Help students distinguish between **primary** and **secondary sources**. Use a concept attainment method to teach students the difference by giving them examples of primary sources and then comparing these with secondary sources. Then hand out the following exercise.

Activity 8-H

Write the letter P beside those items that you think should be classed as primary sources and S for those you think are secondary sources.

a) The Canadian Charter of Rights and Freedoms

b) *Obasan* by Joy Kogawa, a novel about the internment of Japanese Canadians in World War II

c) *Outlooks 3: Our Communities*, a Grade 3 social studies textbook published by Oxford University Press.

d) Minutes of a meeting of the local town council.

It must be remembered that there is not always a clear differentiation between primary and secondary sources. Dhand[5] provides an example in which a witness to an accident tells the story to his parents, who give the account to a newspaper reporter who writes the story. After some editing by the newspaper editor, the story appears. Is the newspaper story a primary source?

5. Encourage students to answer the following types of questions:
    *   *Where* was the evidence found?
    *   *When* was the evidence found?
    *   *Who* reported the evidence?
    *   *How* was the evidence found?
    *   Can the evidence be *checked*? If so, *how*?

6. If inferences are made from information, then ask students whether there is evidence for their inference or whether other **inferences** can be made that are just as plausible. For example, if a picture is shown of people lining up outside a store before it opens, it is plausible to infer that there is a sale. It is also plausible, however, to infer that there is a shortage of goods, and people are lining up to ensure that they obtain their supplies. To discover which inference is true, we'd need more information.

Activity 8-1

Observe the sketch below. Which of the statements that follow are inferences? Of these inferences, which do you think are plausible? Answers are given in the Answers section.

a) The colour of the car is black with white lettering.

b) The lettering on the car says John D. Smith, M.D.

c) Someone is ill in 4122.

d) The car belongs to John D. Smith, M.D.

e) The car is parked outside 4122.

f) John D. Smith lives at 4122.

g) John D. Smith is a doctor.

h) John D. Smith is economically well off.

7. To teach the differences between a descriptive claim, an inference, and a value judgment, we could play this game:

a) One player (the leader) is given a picture and a number of statements identified as descriptions, inferences, or value claims.

b) The other players are each given three cards. One card has "description" written on it, another has "inference," and the third has "value" written on it.

c) The leader displays the picture and reads a statement about it.

d) At a given signal from the leader, each player displays the card that she or he thinks correctly identifies the type of statement read.

e) Players with the correct card receive a point or a token.

f) The player with the most points becomes the winner and the next leader.

Here is an example using this photo:

- The girl is wearing a headband.
- She is happy.
- There are four teepees in the background.
- The girl is going to participate in a ceremony.
- The girl is eight years old.
- Girls should be accorded equal treatment.

Help students avoid making some common fallacies in reasoning. One widely used fallacy is overgeneralization, where it is argued that if one example of something has a particular characteristic, then all similar examples have the same characteristic. For instance, we cannot state that because one doctor is well off, therefore all doctors are well off (see Activity 8–I). Neither can we claim that because something is true of a group, then it is necessarily true for individual members of the group. The fact that Canadian doctors, on average, are near the top of the earning hierarchy doesn't mean that every single doctor is well off.

Another common mistake is called the **black-and-white fallacy**—seeing things only in black and white, ignoring all the shades of grey (e.g., "Either we stop all immigration or there will be no jobs left for people who already live here").

Other common fallacies include **appeals to tradition** ("We did X in the past, so we should do X now"); **appeals to large numbers** ("If the majority of people believe X, then X must be right"); and reasoning that because one event preceded another, then the first must have caused the second. This unsupported assertion of a causal link between events in sequence is labelled *post hoc ergo propter hoc* ("after this, therefore because of this").

An excellent way to draw students' attention to these fallacies is to evaluate advertisements. For example, have students critique advertisements for cars, especially ones that are endorsed by famous people. Students could also compare advertisements for similar products. Comparisons should be made about the intended audiences of each, the images created, the fallacies (if any) committed, the language used, the amount of information conveyed, and possible negative aspects of the product that are not mentioned.

Thinking critically about information takes time and effort, and depends upon having background information. Encouraging students to ask questions and gradually teaching them some of the intellectual standards of critical thought are important throughout our teaching, and they are essential when students are engaged in inquiry procedures.

Unless the information we use is as accurate as possible, we are likely to make serious mistakes that can affect our own lives and those of others. Consider the "simple" matter of being taken in by false advertising—and the far more serious consequences of hateful propaganda for minorities.

TEACHING CRITICAL THINKING

There are several ways we can incorporate critical thinking into the social studies curriculum. One way has been devised by Richard Paul and his colleagues.[6] They take popular lesson ideas and modify them to teach a particular component of critical thinking. Paul and Elder define critical thinking as

> that mode of thinking—about any subject, content or problem—in which the thinker improves the quality of his or her thinking by skillfully taking charge of the structures inherent in thinking and imposing intellectual standards upon them.[7]

They argue that critical thinkers must view issues objectively from the various perspectives of those whose interests are involved. They state that most problems are "multilogical," as they cannot be resolved within a single frame of reference. To identify and define any problem "depends upon some arguable choice among alternative frames of references."[8] Thus, the frames have to be tested using such standards as clarity, accuracy, relevance, significance, completeness, precision, depth, consistency, sound logic, and fairness. Paul and Elder argue that these standards must be applied to the elements of critical thinking (purposes, questions, points of view, information, inferences, concepts, implications, and assumptions), within a framework of intellectual traits (humility, autonomy, integrity, courage, perseverance, empathy, fair-mindedness, and confidence in reason).[9]

Another approach is to use critical challenges. These are problematic situations requiring critical thought. They are based on an approach developed by Sharon Bailin, Roland Case, Jerrold Coombs, and Leroi Daniels,[10] which was adapted for pedagogical purposes for the Critical Thinking Cooperative in British Columbia.[11] The following are examples of such challenges:

- **Concept:** Is Canada really a democracy?[12]
- **Inquiry:** What is the most plausible explanation of how the pyramids were built?

These questions indicate where facts or meanings (concepts) are in dispute and intellectual standards are used to see if we can say that this information is more reliable than other information, or that this meaning of a concept is more appropriate than another. Other critical thinking tasks involve the application of value standards (ethical, aesthetic, etc.). You will find examples of these in Part 4. Any critical challenge must meet certain criteria. These are that the activity 1) requires a judgment be made, 2) is meaningful to students, 3) is embedded in the curriculum, and 4) is focused so that it is not too difficult for students to tackle and students have or can obtain the "tools" necessary to tackle the challenge.[13] The tools required to tackle any critical challenge are as follows:[14]

Background Knowledge   To answer any question requires that students already have or can obtain the knowledge required to answer the question.

Criteria for Judgment   Making a judgment requires the use of criteria. For example, in judging the reliability of observations made by witnesses, we would apply the criteria outlined previously. In judging whether a concept has been used appropriately, we would use criteria outlined in Chapter 6. To judge an account of how the pyramids were built, we would appeal to such criteria as weight of evidence; feasibility (e.g., Could the ancient Egyptians have used this method? Did they have the technology?); archaeological evidence; and the views of scholars.

Critical Thinking Vocabulary　To think critically requires that we use a variety of concepts such as conclusion, inference, and argument. Where answering a critical challenge entails students' using a critical thinking concept, then you have to teach them. For example, if you wished to teach the concept of "inference" you might use an activity akin to the one in Activity 8-I.

Thinking Strategies　Many strategies can be used to answer a critical challenge. One of them, inquiry, is the subject of this chapter. Others include asking an expert, using a problem-solving model, using graphic organizers such as a web, brainstorming, discussing with peers, and role-playing.

Habits of Mind　Unless we are disposed to think critically, there is little point in doing it. Thus, we have to foster **habits of mind**—attitudes such as open-mindedness, fair-mindedness, and respect for evidence. One way to do this is to ensure that we have a classroom climate that is conducive to critical inquiry, a classroom where students' ideas are treated with respect, where students are encouraged to ask questions, and where we model and teach critical thinking strategies and dispositions (see Chapter 9). This conception of critical thinking has been used to develop a series of critical challenge books.[15] There are other ways to teach critical thinking,[16] but the two mentioned above provide the most conceptually and pedagogically sound approaches.

Here is a critical thinking activity that asks you to examine the ways in which you make inferences about classroom interactions and how you would determine which inferences are most reliable.

Activity 8-J

Carry out an inquiry procedure to answer the question "What formal rules and informal conventions govern the interactions in this classroom?"

1. Is the question clear? What would qualify as a "rule"? What would qualify as a "convention"?

2. Generate a hypothesis about what rules and conventions you think govern the interactions in the classroom. Write down your hypothesis.

3. How will you test your hypothesis? If you decide to observe interactions in the classroom, how will you observe whether a rule or convention is or is not being followed? For how long will you observe? How will you ensure that you observe all the likely situations in which your hypothesis could be tested? If you intend to ask people what rules and conventions they think they follow, how will you ascertain this? How will you record your data?

4. Collect your answers according to the decisions made in number 3 above. Decide what you're going to do with the answers—list all of them, classify them, graph them, or tabulate them in some other way.

5. Decide whether the evidence supports your hypothesis. Are you sure your results are reliable? Did you observe for a long enough period? Was your survey thorough enough? If your hypothesis was not supported, can you explain why? What conclusions can you draw? Do they fit in with your (or experts') theoretical under-

standings of the rules and conventions governing group interactions? Do the same rules and conventions operate in different contexts? What factors influence the creation of rules and conventions? What happens when they are not followed?

Questions about the reliability of information and what constitutes a best answer can be raised with young students as well as older ones. Here is an example where primary students inquire into the toys that their grandparents played with and question the validity of their findings. This lesson could well fit into family history projects as outlined in Chapter 10.

Question   What toys did my grandparents play with?[17]

This lesson would be within a history unit on the community. The teacher asks the class what a "toy" is. Answers are discussed and examples of "toys" are given. Students are asked how significant they think toys are in learning history. What do they tell us about children's lives? The students are then asked to guess the answer to the question. As guesses are forthcoming, they are written or drawn on the board or on chart paper. Students then draw one or more of the items they think children played with when their grandparents were children. Where possible, they interview their grandparents to see if their hypotheses are supported. They also use old Sears and Eaton's catalogues. If a hypothesis is supported, the student puts a check mark against the toy. A student who finds a toy that nobody mentioned should draw that toy. Finally, the students share their findings. Other toys that students identified in their research are added to the list. If no evidence can be found for a toy listed by a student, students are asked whether it might have been a toy from another time period, and how they might check this hypothesis. The teacher asks students whether their grandparents might have forgotten some of the toys they played with and tells them that catalogues may not show all the toys that were available. She asks them about toys they play with that are not in toy stores—pieces of wood that are used to represent boats, spears, etc. She asks students whether they think they have the complete answer to the inquiry question.

As further activities, the teacher can have students inquire into whether different ethnic groups played with the same and/or different toys. If actual toys can be obtained, children can play with them and discuss such things as the level of technology involved in producing the toys; whether they are "good" toys; whether toys have changed since their grandparents' time and whether changes have been good or bad; whether there were fewer toys available 50 years ago, and why; how economic status influenced the type and number of toys available to a child; whether there are, and should be, certain toys for boys and certain toys for girls; and how advertising was carried out in the past in comparison with the present and how it influences what children want. Students could also discover what children were playing with in other parts of the world in their grandparents' era. They could carry out a project on the history of toys worldwide with students in groups looking at various parts of the world and then comparing their findings. This topic could culminate in a toy fair in which work done by students is displayed, and other students in the school are invited to come and see the display and play with the toys.

Presenting Conclusions

When the inquiry activity has been completed, students should present their conclusions. Rather than always writing them down, students could use a variety of methods. For example, in Activity 8-J, you could present your answers in the form of a graph (see Chapter 16), showing the number of times various rules and conventions appeared to be at play. The Haida inquiry (pages 93–94) could be answered in the form of pictures or seasonal menus. Other ideas include these:

- writing a diary, letter, poem, newspaper, story, guidebook, journal, travel brochure, or report
- creating a diorama, model, mural, or collage
- creating a play, skit, or radio or television show
- creating a film strip in a shoebox (Cut a window out of a shoebox; insert one dowel through the box above the window and one below, with a long strip of paper attached. The paper has individual pictures that can be displayed through the window one at a time by turning the dowels.)
- preparing a drawing, table, map, chart, diagram, graph, cartoon, painting, or computer graphic
- assembling a booklet
- creating an advertisement
- making a scrapbook
- preparing a menu or an actual meal
- making costumes
- simulating a ceremony
- taking a photograph; making a video or audio recording
- displaying a collection of actual objects
- creating a game or a crossword puzzle
- creating a multimedia presentation on a computer

There is a multitude of ways in which students can present their work. Given that we want students to be excited about social studies, we should allow them to use ways that appeal to them the most.

HELPING STUDENTS CARRY OUT INQUIRY ACTIVITIES

Inquiry procedures have to be taught to students so that they can perform the inquiry activities:

1. Identify a problem that is testable and suitable for their level of maturity.
2. Clarify the question by clarifying the words used in it, i.e., by defining words and/or by giving examples.
3. Hypothesize possible conclusions.
4. Select appropriate research techniques: survey, interview, library research, fieldwork, or actual experiment.
5. Select information pertinent to the question and show a willingness to look at all points of view. Locate information using card catalogues, bibliographies, or online data retrieval systems.
6. "Read" sources of information: skim to find specific information; use headings, topic sentences, and summary statements to distinguish between main and subordinate ideas; draw inferences from information; use and interpret maps, surveys, graphs, historical documents, and pictures.

7. Evaluate information: identify bias and faulty reasoning; use intellectual standards for judging the believability of information.

8. Organize information: use main and supporting evidence; formulate suitable classification schemes; create tables of contents; use appropriate bibliographic formats.

9. Synthesize information: formulate generalizations and cause-and-effect relationships; summarize main ideas; identify information that supports and does not support a hypothesis; recognize the need to change a conclusion when new evidence warrants it; show a willingness to re-inquire if necessary.

10. Present conclusions in a variety of forms: written and verbal reports, graphs, models, charts, diagrams, models, and so on.

THE PROBLEMS AND PITFALLS OF INQUIRY

Although the inquiry procedure has many major advantages, it also has potential pitfalls and problems:

- **lack of time:** Inquiry can be time-consuming; adequate time must be given so that students can explore on their own.
- **lack of resources:** Often resources are lacking, so teachers and students will have to search for pertinent materials.
- **teachers who want to be "in charge":** Teachers should refrain from imposing their "answers" on students. They will have to be supportive and receptive to students' ideas.
- **questions that are too difficult:** Questions must be within the cognitive capacity of students.
- **rigidity:** Despite its many guises, if inquiry is the only method of teaching and learning, it can become boring for students.
- **particular student characteristics:** If students can't find answers or can reach only tentative conclusions, inquiry can have a paralyzing effect on them. Students need to know that there are some questions to which we can find answers, while also realizing that there are some things we don't know. Inquiry has to be introduced gradually to students who are unfamiliar with it. You might start with finding answers to specific questions by using one source, and then advance to posing questions requiring research from many sources. This process could lead to posing more complex questions and, finally, to group inquiry in which questions are answered by groups of students who locate their own resource materials and make decisions about how the inquiry is to proceed.
- **possibility of male bias:** The questions inquired into may be of more import to males than females; insistence on a particular answer may exclude other viewpoints, including feminist ones (see Maher[18]).

All these pitfalls can be avoided through careful teaching and by recognizing and taking into account possible negative biases. They should not dissuade us from using inquiry procedures that actively engage students, and sometimes even excite them, while teaching them many valuable skills. Students are more likely to remember what they learned through inquiry procedures than through more passive methods. Their motivation is enhanced when it is their own questions that are the subject of inquiry.

OTHER ACTIVITIES

1. Write a lesson plan on one of the following questions:
    a) Who works in my school and what jobs do they do? (Grade 1)
    b) What part did the building of the Canadian Pacific Railway play in the history of Canada? (Grade 5)

    Include the following components:

    Opener: How will you motivate interest?

    Hypothesis/Hypotheses: How will you organize for hypothesis making?

    Organization and data collection: How will you organize the class? What data will you use?

    Data analysis: How will students use the data?

    Hypothesis check: How will this be carried out?

    Conclusion: How will students present their findings?

    Finale: How could you continue on this topic?

2. During a class discussion on clothing, the girls claim that they dress better than the boys. They say that boys wear dull-coloured clothing, whereas girls wear bright colours. The question arises, "Do boys in the school wear dull-coloured clothing whereas girls wear bright colours?" How would you use an inquiry approach to help students arrive at a conclusion to this question?

3. Get a picture of yourself as a small child (a two-year-old) and as a ten-year-old. Formulate hypotheses for ages two and ten for each of the characteristics listed on the following chart. Check your hypotheses by asking parents, relations, and friends.

How have I changed?			
	Two-year-old	Ten-year-old	Today
Height			
Weight			
Usual dress			
Hair colour			
Favourite food for...			
breakfast			
lunch			
supper			
Favourite games			
Favourite TV show			
Best friend			
Favourite book			
Hero/heroine			

4. Locate a letter to the editor of a newspaper, or a newspaper editorial, and critique it. What is the writer's conclusion? What reasons are offered for it? Does he or she present enough evidence for the reader to accept the conclusion? Is the evidence accurate? Are concepts clear? Have any fallacies been committed? Do you agree with the conclusion? Why or why not?

NOTES

1. A. Milson and P. Downing, "Webquests: Using internet resources for cooperative inquiry," *Social Education* 65:3 (2001), pp. 144–146. For more on these, see Chapter 16.

2. R. Ennis, *Logic in Teaching* (Englewood Cliffs, NJ: Prentice-Hall, 1963), p. 393.

3. S. Norris, *The Dependability of Observation Statements: Rational Thinking Reports, Number 4* (Urbana, Ill.: Illinois Rational Thinking Project, 1979).

4. R. Richburg, B. Nelson, and J. Reid, "Jump-starting thinking: Challenging student preconceptions," *The Social Studies* 85:2 (1994), pp. 66–69.

5. H. Dhand, "The source method to teach Social Studies," in R. Case and P. Clark, eds., *The Canadian Anthology of Social Studies* (Vancouver: Pacific Educational Press, 1999).

6. R. Paul, A. Binker, and M. Charbonneau, *Critical Thinking Handbook: K–3, A Guide for Remodelling Lesson Plans in the Language Arts, Social Studies and Science* (Rohnert Park, Calif.: Center for Critical Thinking and Moral Critique, 1987).

7. R. Paul and L. Elder, *Critical Thinking: Tools for Taking Charge of Your Learning and Your Life* (Upper Saddle River, NJ: Prentice-Hall, 2001), p. xx.

8. R. Paul, "Dialogical thinking: Critical thought essential to the acquisition of rational knowledge and passions," in J. Baron and R. Sternberg, eds., *Teaching Thinking Skills: Theory and Practice* (New York: Freeman, 1987), p. 138.

9. R. Paul and L. Elder, *Critical Thinking*, p. 50.

10. S. Bailin, R. Case, J. Coombs, and L. Daniels, *A Conception of Critical Thinking for Curriculum, Instruction and Assessment* (Victoria, BC: Ministry of Education, 1993).

11. R. Case and I. Wright, "Taking seriously the teaching of critical thinking," *Canadian Social Studies* 32:1 (1997), pp. 12–19.

12. A Grade 4 class had an interesting time discussing this question. They first defined democracy and then considered whether they could vote and whether they had a say in important decisions in their day-to-day lives. They concluded that life for them was not democratic, so Canada was not democratic either.

13. R. Case and I. Wright, pp. 12–19.

14. Ibid., pp. 14–16.

15. T. McDermid, R. Manzo, and T. Musselle, with R. Case, L. Daniels, and P. Schwartz, eds., *Critical Challenges for Primary Students* (1996), and J. Harrison, N. Smith, and I. Wright, eds., *Critical Challenges in Social Studies for Upper Elementary Students* (1999), (Burnaby, BC: Field Programs Faculty of Education, Simon Fraser University, and Richmond, BC: The Critical Thinking Cooperative).

16. I. Wright, *Is That Right? Critical Thinking and the Social World of the Young Learner* (Toronto: Pippin Publishing, 2002).

17. Where grandparents cannot be questioned, students can use information from the resource materials provided to find out what children played with in the era when their grandparents were children.

18. F. Maher, "Inquiry teaching and feminist pedagogy," *Social Education* 51:3 (1987), pp. 186–193.

GLOSSARY OF KEY TERMS

Appeal to large numbers — arguing that because many people believe something, therefore it is true.

Appeal to tradition — arguing that because something was done in the past, therefore it is right today.

Authority claims — statements made by experts.

Black-and-white fallacy — assuming that there are only two positions on, or solutions to, a problem.

Habits of mind — dispositions such as open-mindedness and fair-mindedness.

Hypothesis — a guess about an answer to a question; a statement about a predicted outcome that is tested by experimental means.

Inference — a statement that goes beyond the given data; to reason from some proposition(s) to another.

Inquiry — sometimes referred to in the social studies literature as any procedure whereby students find answers to questions; often synonymous with problem solving and discovery learning. In this text, inquiry is defined as a procedure in which students test a hypothesis, or hypotheses, about the answer to a question.

Observation claims — statements about what somebody saw.

Post hoc ergo propter hoc — reasoning that as one event preceded another, then the first *must* have caused the second.

Primary sources — those produced at the time an event occurred, e.g., eyewitness accounts.

RAFT — an acronym from the words *Role*, *Audience*, *Format*, and *Topic*; a procedure in which students write in a particular *role* (historical figure, journalist, pioneer, world leader), to a particular *audience* (government leaders, newspaper readers), using a particular *format* (editorial, letter, poem, newspaper report), on a particular *topic*.

Secondary sources — those produced after the event; second-hand sources or those based on interpretations of the primary sources, e.g., a history textbook.

chapter nine

Working Together: Cooperative Learning and Building a Classroom Community

In the last chapter, discussion focused on how students could go about finding answers to questions using inquiry procedures. Sometimes an inquiry is best carried out by individual students; at other times it is better to have groups of students working together in cooperative learning groups. The term **cooperative learning** is used to describe a variety of activities in which students work together on a task. These activities are designed with several objectives in mind: to develop communication skills; to create trust, acceptance, and sharing within the classroom; to lower fear of failure; to develop a commitment to learning; and, especially, to foster individual and group accountability. Proponents of cooperative learning also point out that it can help prepare students to work effectively with the range of people with whom they will interact in their day-to-day lives.[1] These activities are premised on the beliefs that students can learn from each other, that students construct meaning more readily through interaction with others, that students perceive their success as being linked to the success of others, and that cooperation is better than competition.[2]

Research evidence indicates that the objectives of cooperative learning can be realized. As achievement improves, students gain self-esteem and social skills. In addition, they develop positive attitudes toward school in general as well as toward particular subjects and other ethnic groups.[3] Students are helped to make personal sense out of what they are learning through sharing information and teaching it to others.[4] It has also been found that teachers who use cooperative learning activities are more positive about their work than those who do not. They also see less need to discipline students.[5] Because these conclusions are derived from a compilation of results from different studies, it should not be assumed that any one cooperative learning activity would lead to these outcomes. Nevertheless, there are many advantages in using cooperative learning activities. In whole class instruction, a student has an approximately one-in-thirty chance of speaking. However, in a small group, every student has an approximately one-in-four chance. Students are able to help one another and learn from one another. In their lives, both inside and outside school, they will find themselves in group situations; they need to learn how to interact well. Good group relationships are rewarding and enjoyable.

Before launching into cooperative learning activities, we should ask ourselves the following questions:

1. Is the topic appropriate? Cohen[6] suggests that questions posed should have more than one answer, that the task should allow different students to make different contributions, and that a variety of information should be required to carry out the task.

2. How will I ensure that all students can and do contribute? How will I avoid situations in which the high achievers either do all the work and learn more, or decrease their efforts so they are not perceived as "suckers"?

3. What behaviours should students exhibit, and how will I monitor these behaviours?

4. How will the group monitor its own progress?

5. How long should the activity last?

We cannot always expect students to be able to work together without some initial preparation.[7] Students have to be helped to realize the benefits of cooperation. We may have to start off with simple partner activities and progress to more substantial group tasks. Depending on the activity, groups may be formed on the basis of prior friendships, common interests, or common abilities, or on a random basis. Groups should be small in size—three to five members is best. Rules for group learning should be followed: students should help one another; students should not "put down" anyone's contribution; students should encourage each other; students should monitor and evaluate their individual contributions and the overall group effort; and there should be equal participation. You might like to start with small-group activities in which students get to know each other, followed by activities that rely on the participation of all the group members (creating a collage, building a model). Carefully consider group membership. Ideally we want a fairly equal distribution on the basis of gender, ethnicity, and ability. However, we might want to avoid putting certain students together, at least initially, if we know that they do not get on well together. Be prepared to deal with the problems that arise when students work together. Some of these problems, such as "bright" students putting down those who are "less bright," can be avoided by assigning roles to each group member (see the ideas presented later in this chapter).

COOPERATIVE LEARNING STRATEGIES

The following activities are designed to help students begin to work together.

Production Line

Divide students into groups of six. Give each student a sheet of paper and give each group a pair of scissors, a red crayon, a blue crayon, a green crayon, a coin, a pencil (for drawing a circle), and a ruler with a pencil. Each group is to produce six of each of the items shown in the following diagram:

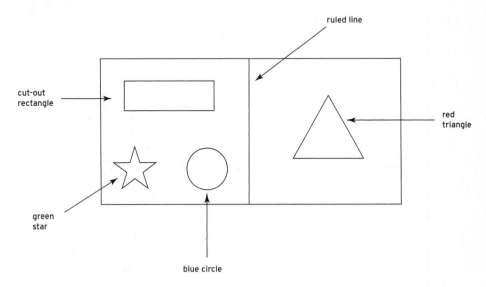

The first group to produce six of each item is the winner.

Usually, each student in each group will attempt to make his or her own item and will "fight" for the materials. The quickest way to produce six items is for each student to have one of the materials (e.g., crayon, ruler, or scissors). As the six pieces of paper are passed from student to student, one student draws a red triangle on each; another draws a ruled line on each, and so on. Specialization is required, with each specialist cooperating with the others to produce a finished product.

Partner Game

Cut out the following shape:

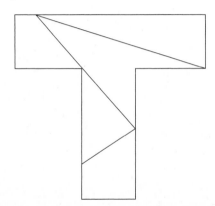

Divide up the class into pairs, and give one member of each pair the cutout shape, and the other the T diagram. The person with the T diagram tells the person holding the shapes how to put the shapes together in the form of the T. Try it—it's not easy.

There are a variety of ways cooperative learning activities can be implemented in the classroom.[8] All the ideas listed below can be used during inquiry procedures as well as in other teaching and learning activities.

- Students in a group are given a topic, and then they identify questions they think are worth investigating. These questions are ranked from most interesting to least interesting, then shared with the whole class, rank-ordered again, and classified. Groups are then created to hypothesize answers to particular questions and to test the hypotheses.

- Within a group, certain students perform particular tasks—one acting as scribe, another as researcher, another as illustrator. Broad questions on which a group is working can be broken down into more discrete questions and hypotheses, with one member of the group becoming a specialist on a specific question. The specialist then teaches the rest of the group, and the information is used to answer the broad question. If several groups are working on the same broad question, then specialists on a particular question from each group can work together. This **jigsaw technique** can also be used when students are required to learn bodies of information (see Chapter 5).

- If a group is working on a particular question, each member can use different resources to test their hypotheses, and findings can be shared. The group then formulates a final answer.

- If a group is working on a particular question, each member of the group can be given information that provides only part of the answer. The information is then synthesized into a final group answer.

- If a group product is required (a report, a chart, a model, a mural), each student can choose to make a particular contribution.

- If students are watching a video, they can be divided into pairs and a **think–pair–share strategy** can be used. The video is stopped and one of the students in each pair summarizes the information, tells the other student what is most interesting, identifies what was confusing, and tries to help the other student understand the information. When the video is stopped the next time, the other student takes on the role of summarizer and clarifier.

- If groups are working on different aspects of the same broad question, each group can teach the rest of the class about their particular topic so that a class answer to the broad question is formulated. For example, if the broad question is "What motivated the first Europeans to explore Canada?" each group tests their hypotheses about a particular explorer. The groups then share their findings with the rest of the class, and the broad question is answered.

- If there are students who need help on a particular aspect of an inquiry procedure, then peer teaching can be used. For instance, if a student needs to be able to read the scale on a map, a classmate who knows how to do this can teach that student.

- If the objective is to help students listen to each other, then a **talking circle strategy** can be used.[9] A topic is discussed by students sitting in a circle. A talking stick is passed around the circle and only the person with the stick can speak. The other students must listen carefully. A person can decline to speak when given the stick and can pass it on to the next student. When speaking, no negative or positive comments can be made about another speaker's comments.

Activity 9-A

Design a cooperative learning activity for either a primary or intermediate class that is studying conservation. Choose one particular aspect of this topic that you consider appropriate for the grade level. Develop a lesson plan that includes your objectives and a detailed description of how the cooperative learning activity would be organized.

It should not be assumed that cooperative learning is designed to stifle conflict. Rather, conditions can be created in which conflict is dealt with in rational ways. The following activity for upper elementary students illustrates one way to do this. It is consistent with Paul's[10] belief that critical thinkers are able to present arguments for all sides of an issue and to enter sympathetically into someone else's point of view.[11]

1. Groups of four are formed and then divided into twos. Each group of two is given a different side of an issue. The pairs then prepare a case to defend their side of the issue. Pairs can meet with other pairs on the same side of the issue to ensure that they've got a strong case.

2. Each pair presents its case to the other members of their group of four; then, each pair can challenge the other pair's arguments.

3. Each pair then presents the strongest argument for the side opposed to the one that it was previously defending.

4. Finally, assigned positions are abandoned and the four students in each group work together to produce a report that summarizes the group's position. Consensus is not required. Each group member should be prepared to justify his or her individual decision to the rest of the class.

Before embarking on cooperative learning, we should carefully consider our objectives and the appropriateness of any particular strategy. Keep in mind that some educators advocate the use of cooperative learning activities for purposes of competition with other groups; others find this unacceptable. Is there any contradiction, for instance, in using cooperative activities in social studies and then emphasizing individual competition in spelling lessons? If cooperative activities are used for purposes of competition, will children believe that cooperation is just another way of getting ahead?

Whatever your answers are to the questions above, it is clear that group activities are worth pursuing in the classroom. Coupled with inquiry procedures, cooperative activities can provide valuable learning experiences for students.

Building a Classroom Community

Cooperative learning strategies have the potential to create a classroom in which groups work well together, but they may not engender the type of classroom where intellectual virtues are fostered. These virtues, such as reasonableness, trustworthiness, and empathic understanding,[12] would lead to students' taking responsibility for the questions they ask and the conclusions at which they arrive. These virtues cannot be taught didactically; they have to be experienced and practised.[13] Sears and Parsons[14] argue that, as teachers, we need to embrace the following principles: that knowledge is subject to change; that any question can be asked; and that awareness and empathy for alternative points of view, tolerance for ambiguity, and skepticism of text are required. Thus, as teachers, we need to admit that we don't know everything and that we should change our minds when necessary. We also need to indicate alternative points of view and, whenever possible, tell students why the information they are learning is worth knowing and the reasons why we believe this information is believable. By modelling such behaviours we can begin to encourage students to adopt the same.

One of the best ways to foster these virtues is through critical thinking (see the previous chapter). This can be carried out through the use of a critical challenge,[15] the redesign of a regular lesson to emphasize a critical thinking problem or question,[16] or the insertion of a critical thinking activity into a lesson. For example, in a study of a particular geographic region, students could be required to ascertain how the area has been affected by humans and what the benefits and disadvantages of this intervention have been. In a current affairs lesson, students could select an issue, research the arguments, and then take a position on the issue. Debating is a good idea here so long as the debate is not viewed as a competition where the winner is assumed to have the right answer.

In any discussion or debate on issues, we need to persuade students that reasons matter. They cannot just say, "Well, that's just my opinion." Richard Paul has a set of questions that focus student attention on reasons.[17] These include "What evidence did I use?" and "How do I know that the conclusion is reliable?"

In open-ended discussions, teachers can ask students whether they agree with another student's response (see Chapter 7 for ideas about how responses to questions can be extended to involve several students). If different reasons are forthcoming, we can ask which reasons are the best. Students also have to learn to ask questions so that the discussion is student-focused rather than teacher-led.[18] Students should also question themselves—"How do I know this is true?" "Is this my best argument?" "Have I considered other points of view?" This encourages reflection and what Lipman calls "self correcting thinking."[19]

Asking questions beyond the level of recall (see Chapter 7) can also lead students to begin to develop the virtues needed for a classroom climate where inquiry and critical thought are honoured. One powerful approach is to ask students how they know that something is true.[20] Students usually look perplexed and often state that it was in their textbook. We should then ask how the textbook author(s) knew it was true and inform students that authors have evidence for their claims. We should then tell students what evidence the author in question was probably using. (For more ideas on interrogating the textbook, see Chapter 5.) As with all teaching, we build on their previous exposure to such questions and give them ample opportunity to learn what might qualify as a reasonable answer to a particular question.

Empathic understanding can be fostered by asking students to consider and reason from different points of view. In discussing any issue, students should be aware of all points of view and should be able to state what these are. For example, if one student disagrees with another, the student should put in her own words the other's opinion. A wonderful example of considering different points of view is to read *The True Story of the 3 Little Pigs! by A. Wolf*, as told to Jon Scieszka.[21] In this story the wolf appears to have very good reasons for blowing down the pigs' houses and eating the inhabitants. Students are asked to consider the story from the wolf's point of view and judge his behaviour. Role-playing can be a powerful strategy here. Literature can also enhance empathy. For example, reading stories of First Nations children can lead to increased understanding of their cultures.

Throughout, we should allow students to have a say in the rules that govern the classroom and, where possible, in the learning activities they pursue. We must build slowly. Students, generally speaking, are not used to thinking critically or to seriously considering the viewpoints of classmates. They like to know the right answer, and often they do not take the ideas of others seriously. It can be disquieting for them to realize that knowledge is often tentative and that debate can be healthy.

Activity 9-B

Design an activity to foster one of the virtues outlined above; for example, one that would help students understand someone else's point of view, or one that would help teach them the rules of discussion so that all students' opinions are heard.

OTHER ACTIVITIES

1. Organize a group issue discussion.
   a) Within a group of four, select a partner and then choose to defend one side of the following issue:
      X: You believe that there should be no competition in social studies classes. You think that the social aspect of social studies should be emphasized, that working together will encourage respect, and that social problems should be solved through cooperative endeavours.
      Y: You believe that competition should be emphasized in social studies because competition creates challenges that motivate students to work hard. Further, you know that to succeed in the world you have to be competitive.
   b) Get together with your partner and write down the three strongest arguments you can think of to support your position.
   c) Within your group of four, argue your case and try to refute the other side's position.
   d) With your partner, write down the three strongest arguments you can think of that support the other side's view, and present these to the other members of your group.
   e) See if your group of four can agree on a position. If you cannot agree, what is the basis of the disagreement? Is there any way it could be resolved if more evidence were available (e.g., the effects of cooperation or competition on students)?
2. Take a topic at a grade level of your choice and design one cooperative learning activity.
3. List some of the behaviours you could exhibit that would encourage students to work together cooperatively and think for themselves.

NOTES

1. J. Myers, "Co-operative learning in history and social sciences: An idea whose time has come," *Canadian Social Studies* 26:2 (1991), pp. 60–64. J. Myers, "Cooperative learning: Putting the 'social' into social studies," in I. Wright and A. Sears, eds., *Trends and Issues in Canadian Social Studies* (Vancouver: Pacific Educational Press, 1997).

2. H. Margolis and P. McCabe, "Using co-operative learning to facilitate mainstreaming in the social studies," *Social Education* 54:2 (1990), pp. 111–114.

3. R. Slavin, "Research on co-operative learning: Consensus and controversy," *Educational Leadership* 47 (1990), pp. 52–55.

4. T. Morton, "Cooperative learning in social studies," in R. Case and P. Clark, eds., *The Canadian Anthology of Social Studies* (Vancouver: Pacific Educational Press, 1999).

5. S. Sharon, ed., *Co-operative Learning: Theory and Research* (New York: Praeger, 1989).

6. E. Cohen, *Designing Groupwork: Strategies for the Heterogeneous Classroom* (New York: Teachers College Press, 1986).

7. T. Morton, *Cooperative Learning and Social Studies: Towards Excellence and Equity* (San Juan Capistrano, Calif.: Kagan, 1996).

8. T. Morton, "Cooperative learning in social studies."

9. J. Orr, "Teaching social studies for understanding First Nations issues, " in A. Sears and I. Wright, eds., *Challenges and Prospects for Canadian Social Studies*, 2nd ed. (Vancouver: Pacific Educational Press, 2004).

10. R. Paul and L. Elder, *Critical Thinking: Tools for Taking Charge of Your Learning and Your Life* (Upper Saddle River, NJ: Prentice-Hall, 2001), pp. 15-17.

11. Ibid., pp. 11–12.

12. Ibid., pp. 4–19.

13. L. Farr Darling and I. Wright, "Critical thinking and the social in social studies," in A. Sears and I. Wright, eds*., Challenges and Prospects for Canadian Social Studies*, 2nd ed. (Vancouver: Pacific Educational Press, 2004).

14. A. Sears and J. Parsons, "Towards critical thinking as an ethic," *Theory and Research in Social Education* 19:1 (1991), 45–68.

15. See, for example, T. McDermid, R. Manzo, and T. Musselle, with R. Case, L. Daniels, and P. Schwartz, eds., *Critical Challenges for Primary Students* (1996), and J. Harrison, N. Smith, and I. Wright, eds., *Critical Challenges in Social Studies for Upper Elementary Students* (1999) (Burnaby, BC: Field Programs Faculty of Education, Simon Fraser University, and Richmond, BC: The Critical Thinking Cooperative).

16. R. Paul, A. Binker, and M. Charbonneau, *Critical Thinking Handbook: K–3, A Guide for Remodelling Lesson Plans in the Language Arts, Social Studies and Science* (Rohnert Park, Calif.: Center for Critical Thinking and Moral Critique, 1987).

17. R. Paul and L. Elder, pp. 124–127.

18. L. Farr Darling and I. Wright.

19. M. Lipman, *Critical Thinking: What Can It Be?* (New Jersey: Institute for Critical Thinking, Montclair State College, 1988).

20. L. Farr Darling and I. Wright.

21. J. Scieszka, *The True Story of the 3 Little Pigs! by A. Wolf* (New York: Viking Kestral, 1989).

GLOSSARY OF KEY TERMS

Cooperative learning — a variety of activities to help students learn together.

Intellectual virtues — these include reasonableness, empathic understanding, the willingness to give reasons for one's conclusions, etc.

Jigsaw technique — an activity wherein groups of students have different pieces of information and have to work together to create a synthesis.

Talking circle strategy — Students sit in a circle to discuss a topic. A stick is passed around and the student who receives the stick can say something or pass it on to the next person. No positive or negative statements can be made about another speaker.

Think–pair–share strategy — students in pairs summarize information and try to help each other understand it.

chapter ten

What Was It Like in the Past?
Teaching and
Learning History

History has often been regarded as the major discipline in the social studies, much to the chagrin of geographers and other social scientists. While teaching history has played an important role, educators and historians[1] have recently complained that there is not enough history in the curriculum, and that what there is, is badly taught. In fact, Ontario has responded to these criticisms by incorporating more history in the social studies.[2] However, in Alberta there is concern that a Ministry of Learning Commission on K–12 Education may neglect consideration of the teaching of history.[3]

Whether these endeavours will result in better teaching is a moot question.

RATIONALES FOR TEACHING HISTORY

Intrinsic Value

People often find the past fascinating. Family histories are traced,[4] and movies and television programs about historical events and people receive a lot of attention. Witness the huge audiences for the made-for-television movie *Roots*, movies based on historical events and characters, and the popularity of the History Channel. People are stimulated by stories of new historical discoveries and especially by findings concerning the origin of the human species. The discovery of "Lucy" in 1974 (the oldest known humanoid skeleton at that time), for example, was reported on the front page of many newspapers. Teachers can build on this almost universal interest in history.

Building Pride in Heritage

Traditionally, history has been taught to instill national pride, an idea that has some power when that pride is justified. This is why, in the past, textbooks have often included stories of heroes and battles won. This is why textbooks today include stories of the contributions to Canada of women, ethnic minorities, and "ordinary" folk. This is why the textbooks in Iraq that extolled the virtues of Saddam Hussein and his Baath party are being replaced so other people and groups are included in the history of Iraq.

Developing a Sense of Identity

History also gives us a sense of identity as individuals and as members of a nation or a cultural or ethnic group—we know where we have come from and can plan for where we want to go. Thus, the teaching of history at the elementary level focuses on family so that students can discover their roots. We now study the history of students' communities, and eventually the whole of Canada, so that students can begin to understand their history and their part in it. As Levstik and Barton[5] state:

> Students who do not see themselves as members of a group who had agency in the past or power in the present, who are invisible in history, lack viable models for the future.

Avoiding Past Mistakes

History can lead us to reflect upon what occurred in the past so that we can try to avoid past mistakes. Consider, for instance, why we teach about some of the atrocities and harm imposed on people in the past (the Holocaust, the internment of the Japanese, the residential schools for Aboriginal children). By teaching about these events, we can help students develop values that are antithetical to the mistreatment of others.

Teaching Inquiry Skills and Critical Thinking

If we teach history using inquiry strategies, then students will have to search for information, judge the reliability of sources, be aware of differing points of view, and decide if there is enough evidence to support a conclusion. For example, in the activity outlined in Chapter 8 where students identify the toys their grandparents played with, it is unlikely that printed sources such as catalogues or newspaper advertisements will indicate all the toys available, especially as some toys were not commercially produced. Thus, students will have to realize that their conclusions may well be incomplete. In the lesson plans outlined in Chapter 2, one teacher has students compare French and Native accounts of Cartier's explorations, thus helping students understand that a historical account is always from someone's point of view.

Making Better Decisions

Students need not only to develop appropriate values about such events as the Holocaust, but also to make decisions about future actions. As the teaching of history helps develop critical thinking abilities (recognizing bias, identifying reliable information, making plausible interpretations), students can apply these to contemporary problems and make more intelligent decisions. Thus, history education is an important part of citizenship education; it not only teaches decision-making skills but also helps students understand the precursors of a problem. Osborne[6] says:

> The main advantage of history is that it enables us to think for ourselves about important issues bearing on the human condition. It makes it possible to see the world as it is (which means understanding how it came to be that way) and to see the world as it might be, while also helping us to think about how to get from one state of affairs to the other. This is what makes the study of history an ideal preparation for democratic citizenship.

Developing Empathy

History can also teach us much about the human condition and thus help develop student empathy. As pointed out above, by teaching about people's inhumanity, we hope to develop values that are positive. By teaching about how people lived in the past, we try to encourage students to see different points of view and gain some understanding of what it would be like to live in a different time period. Here, the use of literature can bring to life people who were famous, infamous, and "ordinary."

However, these rationales are contentious. Michael Bliss,[7] a well-respected Canadian historian, has recently argued that the purpose of history should be the teaching of content about significant events and people in Canadian history. Peter Seixas,[8] in the same journal, puts forward a very different rationale—one based on the raising of historical consciousness.

Activity 10-A

What rationale(s) for the teaching of history is/are presented in your provincial curriculum guide?

Ask a number of elementary school students what importance, if any, they think learning history has, and what they think history is about.

ORGANIZING FOR HISTORY INSTRUCTION

To teach history in a meaningful and interesting way requires that we have a set of **history concepts and questions**. Seixas[9] provides such guiding concepts.

Significance

In choosing what to teach, we decide what is **significant** for students to know. One criterion would be the people and events that have had the most dramatic long-term effects on us. For example, Sir John A. Macdonald and the building of the Canadian Pacific Railroad would qualify. Another criterion would be those people and historical events that connect us as individuals to our present lives. Thus, my Quaker grandfather and the Blitz (when England was bombed by the German air force in World War II) would count as historically significant to me. There may well be a disjuncture between what we consider significant for students to know and what is actually significant to students. Seixas,[10] in his research, has shown that students from diverse backgrounds cite immigration, living in countries other than Canada, and their initial experiences in Canada as being significant. Some students could link these experiences to what is being taught in social studies. One student related his growing up in a village in Portugal to the experiences of early settlers in Canada. Other students could not draw any such relationships. Some expressed dismay that they knew very little about their own family history and the history of the country from which they had emigrated. Clearly, we need to make what we teach in history significant to our students, and so we must draw on their own family histories. For example, if our topic is the building of the CPR, then have students research the impact of railways on their countries of origin. If the topic is communities in Canada and how they develop, then have students research a community in their country of origin by interviewing, where feasible, family and friends. As Seixas states:[11]

> Family history and family experiences had a profound impact on how many of these students understood the past. Unfortunately, their social studies classes have generally neglected these sources of historical understanding.

Seixas is talking about the secondary students he interviewed, but his findings are relevant to elementary school students. We have to find ways to incorporate students' own histories into our curriculum. One way to do this, where feasible, is to have students research their family histories. If parents or guardians are willing, students could create family trees, collect artifacts from their relatives' lives and display these, create a family scrapbook, and link their relatives' lives to what was occurring in the communities in which they lived and the wider world. A time line can be used to do this, as shown in an example given later in this chapter. Then students could research the events that were pivotal in their relatives' lives. For example, if they were involved in the armed services, then which wars or actions did they serve in and what was Canada's role in these? Or if relatives immigrated to Canada, then what was life like in the country of origin and what were the reasons for emigration? Students could also collect images of the environments in which their relatives lived. Here, local archives may be useful. If relatives grew up and lived outside the local community, then online archival photo collections might be of use. Where feasible, relatives could be interviewed, and some might be persuaded to visit the class and talk about their lives. (See Chapter 16 for ideas about interviews.) Another idea is to have students collect family artifacts and put them in a box. Other students then have to identify the objects and place them in chronological order. Preparing a family history can incorporate all the other concepts outlined below.

The following sorts of questions focus on significance:

1. List three significant events in your own life. Why did you choose these? Write an autobiography that links those three events. List three other significant events in your life. Write another autobiography linking them. How are the stories similar and different?
2. Draw a **time line** on which you place significant events in your family history. Why were these events chosen? Ask another family member to draw a time line. Compare the two. Why are there similarities or differences?

3. Create a time line for the history of a particular country. What categories of events (political, military, religious, and recreational) or people (rulers, politicians, military leaders, and sports people) did you include?

4. Create a poster showing four significant events in the history of your community, province/territory, or country. Why did you choose these?

Evidence

What will qualify as a reliable account of a historical event or a plausible description of an artifact? Should students believe the history depicted in movies, the textbook accounts of events, and the stories of the past as told by their families? For example, Seixas[12] has shown how students interpret the movie *Dances with Wolves*, and Justice[13] demonstrates the historical inaccuracies in the movie *Gangs of New York*.

One way to draw attention to **evidence** is through oral history projects. Arruda[14] states that students get richer and more interesting information through talking to someone. They will also get insights into people's lives—lives not always examined in textbooks. Elementary students have carried out some very successful work interviewing people who have lived in the community for a long time.[15] They can also visit historic sites and museums, and study old maps, letters, newspapers, and other documents to gain some understanding of the problems of, and criteria for, deciding what is the most reliable account of a given event or the best description of an artifact. This background can then be used in the later grades to judge "traces" and "accounts." Seixas[16] uses these terms to denote the difference between public or private documents and artifacts that we use as a basis for our historical interpretations and the accounts that historians, moviemakers, textbook writers, and others provide. If students are to interpret and evaluate traces and accounts, they need to be taught some of the criteria for judging evidence (Chapter 8). They can be presented with two or more conflicting accounts of the same event and can begin to consider questions of historical interpretation. Many textbooks now present these sorts of accounts, describing, for example, how the Native people viewed European explorers, as well as the reactions of explorers to Native people.

Closer to home, students can be asked to describe what they saw in the playground at recess and to compare descriptions so that they realize that their vantage point and biases influence what they see. Students could also be asked to describe what they saw on a television program and to compare the descriptions. As a fun activity, have students select an everyday object and pretend that archeologists find it in the year 4000. How will they describe it? Here is what could be said about a home entertainment centre:

> This huge artifact dominated one wall of the building, and all activities were directed toward it. It clearly had religious significance to the ancient Canadians. Although a large number of gods could be contacted from this altar, the favourites appeared to be TSN and MTV. There were impact marks on the top and sides of the altar, indicating that some communication consisted of hitting it. Communication was continued after death as a communicator box could be placed in the hands of the deceased. Below the glass face of the altar were spaces for offerings, and around the perimeter of the room were boxes that allowed the gods to communicate to the worshippers from all directions.

The realization that different points of view exist is an important lesson for elementary students, and students are capable of understanding this in the later grades. According to Lee and Ashby,[17] students progress through stages from viewing history as given—it is just "out there"—to thinking that history cannot be known as we were not there to see it, or history can be known only on the basis of available evidence, to later stages of realizing that the biases and choices of the authors create differences.

Questions

1. Examine an artifact and identify, where possible, when it was made and used, what it was made of, what it was used for, who made it, who used it, and what importance it had in its original context. State reasons for your conclusions.

Activity 10-B

Examine this photograph. What do you think the photographer was trying to say? What did the photographer want viewers to think when they viewed the photo? Give reasons for your answers.

2. How would you find out what your community was like 100 years ago?

3. How would you write an account of the meeting between Cartier and Chief Donnacona that reflects each of their points of view?

Continuity and Change

Change is a constant. Even though there is **continuity** in some ideas, roles, and institutions, these concepts change over time, and often entire ideas, roles, and institutions may be radically altered. Students must come to see how changes can affect many aspects of life. Consider, for example, a modern technological advance such as the computer. By tracing its relationship to work, education, leisure, the roles of men and women, industry, economics, and so on, students can see the profound effects of change. How students view change will depend upon their experiences. A refugee from Kosovo will have a very different view of change from a student who has grown up in a fairly stable middle-class environment. Young children often find it difficult to understand the causes of a particular change, especially when it is divorced from their own experiences and when the causes are complex. Often they see a change as inevitable and not due to any human agency.[18] Teachers can help students deal with causation by presenting the precursors to an event and asking students to identify which ones were possible causes. Further, historical events can be linked to things that students are familiar with so that analogies can be drawn. For example, in discussing why people were motivated to immigrate to Canada, we can ask students what might motivate *them* to move to a new location.

Questions

1. Examine these three photos of the same scene taken at three different time periods. What is similar? What is different? What do you think accounts for these similarities and differences?

2. Examine something that is no longer in use. Why is it not used any more? What, if anything, has replaced it? How has the change affected our lives?

3. Arrange events, pictures, and photos in the order in which you think they occurred. Give reasons for your decision.

4. Have groups of students choose a particular phenomenon (clothing, household utensils, education, etc.) in a particular area (a community, a country), trace its development, and identify the stimuli and impediments to the changes. Groups could compare their findings and ascertain whether there are any stimuli or impediments to change that can be generalized.

Activity 10-C

Draw a diagram tracing the impact of one technological advance, ancient or modern.

Progress and Decline

When changes occur, we are likely to make evaluations. We talk about the "good old days" as if recent changes have been negative. We applaud the technological inventions that mean we do not have to perform tedious jobs. History textbooks often assume that history is about **progress**. Yet, there are those who argue that some changes have been for the worse—for instance, the "erosion" of family values, the **decline** in church attendance, and the possibility of human cloning. Students have to identify the criteria they would use to judge changes. (Part 4 is devoted to helping students make value judgments.)

Questions

1. Examine a historical photo, picture, or account. Have matters improved or worsened since then? In what ways? For whom?

2. Decide whether a historical phenomenon (what was worn at a particular period of time, how people were governed or educated) was better or worse than that same phenomenon is today.

3. Show how one change (human rights legislation, the abolition of slavery) has improved life.

Empathy and Moral Judgment

When students read about people in the past, they realize that much was different. They may also assume that people reacted to their world in much the same ways they do. People in the past had different belief systems and interpreted their world in ways different from our own. Students have to realize this by understanding as clearly as possible the context in which a historical character acted. It is pointless to role-play the meeting between Cartier and Chief Donnacona unless we know that Cartier thought Native people were "*sauvages*." We cannot impose our own beliefs and motivations on historical characters even though this makes them familiar to us. Thus, we have to keep asking whether characters would really have felt this way, given the context in which they acted. This applies when we are judging not only the *feelings* but also the *actions* of characters. However, just because a historical character did what he or she thought right, given the context of the times, does not mean that the action was right. Even though slavery was an accepted practice in the past, that does not mean it was morally defensible, even then. Seixas[19] sums up this principle in the following way:

> As with the problem of historical empathy, our ability to make moral judgements about history requires that we entertain the notion of a historically transcendent human commonality, a recognition of our humanity in the person of historical actors, at the same time that we open every door to the possibility that those actors differ from us in ways so profound that we perpetually risk misunderstanding them.

One way of helping students develop **empathy** (or historical perspective-taking) is through role play. Although young children find this difficult, as they tend to view the world from their own egocentric viewpoints, there is evidence that older students can empathize with historical characters.[20]

Another way historical empathy can be developed is through historical fiction.[21] For example, reading *Ghost Train*[22] to students can engender understanding, anger, and sadness about the plight of Chinese labourers in the building of the CPR. As pointed out above, however, any story should be chosen carefully so that students do not get erroneous information. Levstik and Barton[23] provide a set of criteria for selecting historical fiction.

- Does the book tell a good story?
- Is the book accurate and authentic in its historical detail, including the setting and the known events of history?
- Is the language authentic for its time?
- Is the historical interpretation sound?
- What voices are missing?
- Does the book provide insight and understanding into current issues as well as those in the past?

These authors also provide a structure for students to take on the perspective of another person.[24] Students pretend they are historical characters (real or imagined) and use the stem structure to write about the person:

- I am _____.
- I wonder _____.
- I hear _____.
- I see _____.
- I want _____.
- I am _____.

This is followed by I pretend, I feel, I touch, I worry, I cry, I am, I understand, I say, and I dream.

Activity 10-D

On the following page is a photo of William Miner, who was a train robber in Canada. He was captured when bungling a train robbery in 1906. This photo was taken after his capture. What did the photographer want to say about Bill Miner? How do you think

Miner felt? Could he have felt pride in his accomplishments, exasperation at being caught, and at the same time apprehension about his future? Or do you think he dreamed of escaping? See the Answers section for details on Miner's life.

Questions

1. What did the author of a particular historical account think of (slavery, Native peoples, the building of the CPR)?

2. Write an account of an event from the perspective of a particular person, for example, from the perspective of an Aboriginal person in Dawson City during the Klondike gold rush.

3. How were the beliefs of (Egyptian priests) different from ours?

4. Use the stem structure outlined above and pretend you are a child who has just arrived in Canada from China in 1900.

Agency

Agency refers to the ability to make changes. In traditional history textbooks, it was often only the rich and powerful who were viewed as agents of change. Historians and, to an extent, history textbooks are now emphasizing the lives of "ordinary" people and how they shaped their environments, brought about change, and played a part in history. Thus, history texts now tell the stories of women, the poor, the working class, children, and ethnic groups—those previously marginalized in textbooks. These stories demonstrate to students that it is not just the rich and famous who can bring about significant changes. Davis[25] makes this point well:

> If you spend most of your historical study learning about famous missionaries, explorers, kings and queens, politicians, financiers, writers and inventors, you pick up the message that the life of the average peon is unimportant. If, in addition, you are from a humble background yourself, you pick up the additional message that you and your folks are not that memorable either.

He goes on to conclude that history should include the lives of ordinary people so that they receive the recognition they deserve.

Questions

1. Do you think you have changed somebody else's life in a positive way? If not, do you think you could do this in the future?

2. Which people have made significant changes in history? What conditions enabled them to bring about these changes?

3. If you could bring about one change, what would it be? Why? How would you effect this change?

4. Has the person in a historical picture (for example, a medieval farmer, a monk, or a seamstress) made a difference to the path of history? How?

Activity 10-E

Using the picture below, generate at least one question from each of the categories above (significance, evidence, continuity and change, progress and decline, empathy,

and historical agency) and suggest answers to them. Share your questions and answers with another person or group and discuss any differences. If answers differ, how would you determine which answer is the best or most plausible?

This is a photo of the first radio car on the CNR in 1924. Passengers could put on headphones and listen to the radio as they travelled.

TEACHING TIME AND CHRONOLOGY

In teaching any historical topic, it is necessary to locate it in time. The concept of "time" is a difficult one for children to grasp, but research indicates that young children can and do understand historical time in several ways (see Downey and Levstik[26]). Young children conceive of time not only in terms of their daily lives—going to bed, watching cartoons on television on Saturday—but also in terms of "dinosaur times" or "when people lived in caves." They recognize the passage of time by identifying a number of discrete points that they put in a sequence—for example, events in their own lives such as birthdays; important cultural festivals such as Christmas, Hanukkah, or Diwali; and times when they were in the hospital or when a sister or brother was born. So one way to teach children about historical time is to have them create a personal time line and use this as a reference for the **chronology** of historical events.

Other ideas include the sequential ordering of a series of artifacts. A colleague of mine has a collection of money, postcards, and letters from an aunt. He asks students to place them in sequential order and figure out the life history of his relative. Students really get involved in this activity, especially because they can *touch* the items. Students could also be given pictures of a particular phenomenon over time (costumes, implements of war, kitchen utensils) and be asked to place them in chronological order. For other ideas on the teaching of time, see Muir[27] and Burlbaw.[28]

Activity 10-F

Create a time line for your own life. Compare your time line to that of a peer. Did you mention the same sorts of events? Why or why not?

Underneath your time line, create another one listing important events that occurred in Canada during your lifetime. Again, compare this with a peer's. Did you mention the same events? Why or why not?

Now, extend your time line into the future. What do you want to be able to place on your time line one year from now, 10 years from now, and 20 years into the future? Do the same for your Canada and world time lines.

If possible, create time lines for your parents and grandparents. Relate their lives to events in Canada and the rest of the world.

Not only do time lines help students locate events in sequence; they also help them "see" duration. Children have difficulty in understanding how long a year is, let alone a century or a millennium. Time lines can show duration in spatial terms. In Near Eastern and European prehistory, for instance, the Stone Age (approximately 1 million BC to 3000 BC) takes up more space on the time line than the Bronze Age (approximately 3000

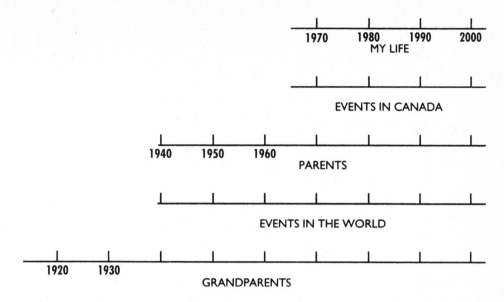

BC to 1000 BC), which means it lasted longer. To help students understand the concepts of "BC" and "AD," it is necessary to tell them that in many Western cultures AD (Anno Domini) dates from the time that it is believed Christ was born. So the years 1 to 100 are in the first century AD (there is no zero century), the years 101 to 200 are in the second century, and so on. The publication date of this book is 2004, in the 21st century. Once this idea has been grasped, then the idea of BC becomes more understandable. Again, there is no zero century BC; we have to count backwards from 1 BC. To find out how long ago something occurred "Before Christ," we have to add the AD and BC figures. So, if it is correct that the first people came to North America around 10 000 BC, then that was approximately 12 000 years ago.[29]

OTHER ACTIVITIES

1. Choose a historical character with whom you are familiar and create a time line for that person's life. Underneath this time line, create another one that shows what other events were happening in the world during that character's lifetime.

2. Have elementary students of different ages construct time lines of their own lives. Compare results and explain why there are differences or similarities (besides the difference of age) among the time lines.

3. In outline form, suggest what sources of information elementary students could use to write a history of a community with which you are familiar. What activities could students carry out to obtain this information?

4. Choose a particular topic in Canadian history from the social studies curriculum and find out what was occurring in another part of the world at that time. Suggest ways you could relate these events to your topic and how you might help your students gain a more global perspective on history.

NOTES

1. J. Granatstein, *Who Killed Canadian History?* (Toronto: HarperCollins, 1998). Also see P. Clark, "Clio in the curriculum: The jury is out," *Canadian Social Studies* 32:2 (1998), pp. 45–51. For an excellent history of the teaching of history in Canadian schools, see D. Morton, "Teaching and learning history in Canada," in P. Stearns, P. Seixas, and S. Wineberg, eds., *Knowing, Teaching and Learning History* (New York: New York University Press, 2000). And Osborne's columns in *Canadian Social Studies* also often deal with the history of teaching history in Canada.

2. Ministry of Education and Training, Ontario. Website: www.edu.gov.on.ca

3. S. Gibson and A. von Heyking, "History teaching in Alberta schools: Perspectives and prospects," *Canadian Social Studies* 37:2 (2003). www.quasar.ualberta.ca/css/css_37_2/ARhistory_alberta_schools.htm

4. When the Church of Latter-day Saints placed their database on the internet, they were flooded with calls from people who wanted to trace their ancestors.

5. L. Levstik and K. Barton, *Doing History* (Mawwah, NJ: Erlbaum, 1997), p. 2.

6. K. Osborne, "The teaching of history and democratic citizenship," in R. Case and P. Clark, eds., *The Canadian Anthology of Social Studies* (Vancouver: Pacific Educational Press, 1999).

7. M. Bliss, "Teaching Canadian national identity," *Canadian Social Studies* 36:2 (2002). www.quasar.ualberta.ca/css/Css_36_2/ARteaching_canadian_national_history.htm

8. P. Seixas, "The purposes of teaching Canadian history," *Canadian Social Studies* 36:2 (2002). www.quasar.ualberta.ca/css/Css_36_2/ARpurposes_teaching_canadian_history.htm

9. P. Seixas, "The place of history within social studies," in I. Wright and A. Sears, eds., *Trends and Issues in Canadian Social Studies* (Vancouver: Pacific Educational Press, 1997).

10. P. Seixas, "Historical understanding among adolescents in a multicultural setting," *Curriculum Inquiry* 23:3 (1993), pp. 301–327.

11. P. Seixas, "Making sense of the past in a multicultural classroom," in R. Case and P. Clark, eds., *The Canadian Anthology of Social Studies* (Vancouver: Pacific Educational Press, 1999).

12. P. Seixas, "Confronting the moral frames of popular film: Young people respond to historical revisionism," *American Journal of Education* 102 (1994), pp. 261–285.

13. B. Justice, "Historical fiction to historical fact: *Gangs of New York* and the whitewashing of history," *Social Education* 67:4 (2003), pp. 253–256.

14. T. Arruda, "In their own voices: Exploring social history through oral narrative," in R. Case and P. Clark, eds., *The Canadian Anthology of Social Studies* (Vancouver: Pacific Educational Press, 1999).

15. See M. Hickey, "And then what happened, Grandpa? Oral history projects in the elementary classroom," *Social Education* 55:4 (1991), pp. 216–217.

16. P. Seixas, "The place of history within social studies," in I. Wright and A. Sears, eds., *Trends and Issues in Canadian Social Studies* (Vancouver: Pacific Educational Press, 1997), p. 118.

17. P. Lee and R. Ashby, "Progression and historical understanding among students ages 7–14," in P. Stearns, P. Seixas, and S. Wineberg, eds., *Knowing, Teaching and Learning History* (New York: New York University Press, 2000).

18. T. Lomas, *Teaching and Assessing Historical Understanding* (London: Historical Association, 1990).

19. P. Seixas, p. 124.

20. M. Booth, "A critique of the Piagetian approach to history teaching," in C. Portal, ed., *The History Curriculum for Teachers* (London: Falmer, 1987).

21. For sources of such stories see I. Aubrey, *Notable Canadian Children's Books*, 1988 and 1989 Supplements (Ottawa: National Library of Canada, 1992). You might also look at reviews of children's books that appear periodically in newspapers such as *The Globe and Mail*. Chapter 4 of S. Egoff and J. Saltman, *The New Republic of Childhood: A Critical Guide to Canadian Children's Literature* (Toronto: Oxford University Press, 1990) is another useful guide. Penney Clark also provides an extensive list of historical fiction suitable for elementary students in her article "Literature and Canadian history: A marriage made in heaven," *Canadian Social Studies* 37:1 (2002). www.quasar.ualberta.ca/css/css_37_1/ARliterature_canhistory_marriage.htm

22. P. Yee, *Ghost Train* (Toronto: Groundwood Books, 1996).

23. L. Levstik and K. Barton, p. 95.

24. Ibid., p. 130.

25. B. Davis. "Teaching the general level student: History and work—rewriting the curriculum," in R. Case and P. Clark, eds., *The Canadian Anthology of Social Studies* (Vancouver: Pacific Educational Press, 1999), p. 320.

26. M. Downey and L. Levstik, "Teaching and learning history," in J. Shaver, ed., *Handbook of Research on Social Studies Teaching and Learning* (New York: Macmillan, 1991).

27. S. Muir, "Time concepts for elementary school children," *Social Education* 54:4 (1990), pp. 215–218, 247.

28. L. Burlbaw, "An unfolding timeline," *Canadian Social Studies* 26:4 (1992), pp. 158–160.

29. However, there is purported evidence from Brazil that human habitation was much earlier—50 000 years ago. See E. Dewar, *Bones: Discovering the First Americans* (Toronto: Vintage Canada, 2001), and A. McIlroy, "Who were the first Americans?" *The Globe and Mail*, September 6, 2003, p. F10.

GLOSSARY OF KEY TERMS

Chronology — the order in which events occurred.

History concepts and questions:

    Agency — seeing oneself as able to make changes and have an impact on history.

    Continuity and change — what has changed and what has remained more or less the same.

    Empathy — putting oneself into the position of historical characters to try to understand their perspectives.

    Evidence — what will qualify as a reliable account or plausible interpretation of a historical event.

    Progress and decline — what is regarded as an improvement and as a retrogression.

    Significance — what is important in a historical event or time period.

Time line — a visual portrayal of events in chronological order of a given time period.

chapter eleven

Getting Involved in Places: Teaching and Learning Geography

Geography is considered one of the major disciplines in social studies, and all provincial curricula contain geography-related objectives. However, there is great variation in the importance devoted to them. For example, according to Jon Bradley,[1] the Quebec elementary curriculum gives overarching status to geography in grades 3–6, whereas others give it far less emphasis.

There are several good reasons for the inclusion of geography in the curriculum.

RATIONALES FOR TEACHING GEOGRAPHY

Intrinsic Value

The places we know are imbued with meanings: the school we attend; the house where we live; the place where we met our spouse. Often we are fascinated by places we don't know, and we search out information. Rather like babies who explore their spaces, often with great enthusiasm, we want to see what is around the corner or over the hill. We are in awe when we see the Rockies, an Atlantic storm, or a prairie sunset. The geography of places appeals to the human spirit.

Value for Personal Decision Making

Being able to read a map helps us plan trips and find our way around. Having mental maps helps us locate places in the world and give meaning to them. For example, without knowing where Kosovo is, I may have no idea of the significance of the recent war there. Knowing about landforms, the direction of the sun, and weather patterns can help us choose where to buy a house or locate a business. Geographic knowledge is also useful in occupations such as urban planning, agriculture, business, disease control, waste disposal, and teaching.

Value for Social Decision Making

As citizenship involves making decisions about matters of public policy, knowledge of geography is essential. We cannot comprehend First Nations' land claims, the effects of global warming, or the destruction of the Amazon rain forest without knowledge of geography. Learning how people live on the earth helps us figure out which arrangements might work best for us. Studying the global consequences of our actions helps us understand the interrelationships between people and their habitats.

These rationales are the basis of objectives for geography education. The Geography Education Standards Project[2] provides a comprehensive and significant list of these objectives. For Grades K to 4, students are expected to know about the characteristics and purposes of geographic representations and how to use and analyze them; the locations of major places in their community and the world; the physical and human characteristics of places and how they interact; the concept of region; how to describe their own community from different perspectives and how people's perceptions of places vary; the major components of the earth's physical systems; the components of ecosystems; the distribution of populations and the causes and effects of human migration; how culture affects the way people live and how cultures change; factors influencing economic activities and settlement patterns; and resource distribution and whether or not resources are renewable.

If you teach a geographical topic, the Standards are a great source of information, not only of what students should know, but also of geographical information and skills. As the Standards were published by *National Geographic*, the illustrations are wonderful.

ORGANIZING FOR GEOGRAPHY INSTRUCTION

There are several foci we can take in organizing for instruction in geography.[3]

Study of a Particular Landscape

Landscape study is an in-depth analysis of a specific place (e.g., a local community, a farm). Students study the landform, the ways in which humans have modified the landscape, and how the landscape has influenced human activities.

Activity 11-A

Using your own location (campus or neighbourhood), study its landscape by answering the following questions:

1. What would you find on the site that is unlikely to be shown on a map of the area? If possible, create a map that depicts these features.

2. How is this area different from where you live? From another area?

3. Is this area suitable for a range of purposes (e.g., to build a factory site, to grow food, to locate a park)?

4. If you were going to build something here (e.g., house, factory, main road, park), where is the best place to put it? Why?

5. What do you smell at this location? What are the sources of these smells?

6. How could you improve this area environmentally? Economically? Aesthetically?

7. Can you identify a particular landform feature (e.g., a cliff, a hill, a moraine)?

8. What sorts of transportation networks can you identify?

9. What did this area look like 100 years ago? Upon what did you base your conclusions?

10. What do you think the area will look like in 10 years' time? What clues can you offer for your prediction?

11. What natural and human "hazards" can you find (e.g., erosion, flooding, fire)?

12. How does the landscape influence the way people live?

13. How have people changed the landscape? Which of these changes have been beneficial and which have not?

Study of an Issue or a Problem

A second way to organize instruction is by focusing on issues or problems that have significant geographic dimensions, such as global warming, the destruction of rain forests, and the disposal of radioactive waste. Or students could study local problems of pollution and land use such as deciding whether a shopping mall should be built in a particular location (for an example of a simulation where a decision has to be made concerning the location of a facility, see Chapter 17). The steps in studying a problem are as follows:

1. Identify the problem. Clarify any terms in the problem statement. Identify for whom it is a problem and why.

2. Identify the site(s) of the problem. In some contexts, such as a drought or an earthquake, the exact location can be determined. With a crisis such as global warming, the location is impossible to determine, so students should note the places that generate the majority of the pollutants that, in turn, create the warming conditions.

3. Describe the geography of the site(s).

4. Determine the consequences of the problem. Explore the intended and unintended consequences over the short and long term. For example, clear-cutting of forests creates jobs and is apparently less expensive than other logging methods. However, erosion of the logging site is likely. The consequences of droughts or floods may be far-reaching; crops grown in the area may no longer be available, leading to price increases and product shortages.

5. Research possible solutions. Collect information to identify possible solutions, and the benefits and disadvantages of each.

6. Decide on the most defensible solution.

7. If feasible, take action. Write letters to relevant organizations, publicize concerns through displays and letters to newspapers, and carry out activities such as recycling cans and bottles, cleaning up streams and parks, and reducing consumption of non-recyclable products.

Study of Regions

This is usually based on a descriptive study of identifiable regions such as sub-Saharan Africa, the Amazon rain forest, or the Canadian Shield. However, regions do not exist in the natural order of things. Regions are human constructions, and different people have different ideas about what constitutes a region. Students might consider questions such as these: What would Canada look like if it were divided into regions based on the popularity of various kinds of pop music? Why would regions based on landforms make sense? To whom? Where does one draw a line to divide one region from another? Answering these questions helps students realize that people can have different ideas about what constitutes a region.

Another way to organize a regional study is to divide the class into groups representing various landform regions. Each group would determine the benefits of living in the region. Groups could establish their own criteria and then score their region based on these criteria.

For studying regions in Canada, students can play *Crosscountry Canada*.[4] By playing the role of a truck driver, students learn about the geography of the area in which they are making deliveries.

Study of Global Systems

Many of the organizing ideas advanced by global educators involve teaching about **global systems** (see Chapter 19, Global Education), which include both physical and human-created systems. The point of studying these systems is to focus on interrelationships. For instance, a topic could be organized around a particular product (chocolate, orange juice) and the influences of global economic, climate, and landform patterns could be ascertained. (For ideas about how to use webs to help students make connections among these factors, see Chapter 13.) By analyzing a particular phenomenon within the broader system, students can begin to see the often complex connections with other phenomena. For example, the abundance of cheap products from certain countries is linked to child labour, whereas the provision of a well and agricultural tools from Canada can lead to a decline in diseases and improvement in the economic well-being of a village in Africa.

To help students gain some sense of relationships between physical systems, create charts such as the following:

Tropical climate				
Latitude	Countries	January temperature and precipitation	July temperature and precipitation	Vegetation
10° North to 10° South				
10° North to 20° North				
10° South to 20° South				

Activity 11-B

Look at the social studies curriculum in your province/territory and determine how learning geography is organized. Decide on the criteria that you would use to choose the best way of organizing for geography instruction. Does the curriculum match your criteria?

Because all children conceive of the world in their own ways, this is where teaching geography has to start—with what students believe about the earth and how they visualize space. This is where teaching students how to read and create maps is important.

Maps and Mapping

Maps are not only useful in finding a route from one place to another; they can also provide an enormous amount of information about a particular location. By using a variety of maps of one place, we can discover information about that area's climate, landforms, geology, demographics, economics, flora, fauna, history, and so on. Students need to understand these things in order to understand how humans relate to their environments and how particular environments can influence how people relate to one another.

Before students can use maps to obtain information, they have to experience and grasp basic topographical concepts such as open and closed curves, direction, continuity and discontinuity, boundaries and regions, points of reference, size, and area.[5] Young children comprehend these concepts at a basic level and can build on their understanding as they learn from three-dimensional models and maps.

The Globe

This is one of the first geographic models to introduce to students. Young children, through direct teaching and incidental learning, should learn that the world is a sphere and that there are continents and oceans. They should be shown that the world rotates, which is why we have night and day, and that the world revolves around the sun. In later grades, they should realize that the world is tilted on its axis, and that the Tropics of Cancer and Capricorn are where the noonday sun is directly overhead at the solstices. Without knowing this, they will not be able to explain the seasons.

Here are some activities to help students learn about the world as depicted on a globe.

1. Have students choose a place in the world where they would really like to go.

   a) Calculate the distance to this place. In the upper elementary grades, students can be shown that a great circle route is the shortest distance between two distant locations.

   b) Determine what, if any, bodies of water will have to be crossed.

   c) Determine what countries will have to be travelled through.

   d) Find the easiest route to get to the location, and decide on the form(s) of transport to be used.

   e) Have students determine whether it is daytime or nighttime at their destination when it is daytime where they live in Canada.

   f) Also, have them ascertain what season it will be at the new location.

2. Have students make their own globes by blowing up a balloon and depicting the continents with papier mâché or cutouts (shaped like continents) glued onto the balloon.

3. Give students cutouts of the continents. Have students label the cutouts and locate them on the globe.

4. Play a game in which teams are formed. Ask each team in turn to locate a place on the globe. If the team answers correctly, award a point.

5. Have students determine whether there is more land or water in the world. One way of determining this is to place cutouts of the continents in the oceans of the world as shown on the globe and then see how much space remains. This, of course, ignores the area taken up by lakes, rivers, etc., but it does provide an "eyeball" answer. The scientific way is to calculate the landmass area and the area taken up by bodies of water, and subtract one from the other. Most atlases provide the sort of information necessary to make these calculations.

6. Have students determine which is the largest continent and which the smallest one. Again, cutouts of the continents or information from an atlas could be used.

7. To find out how big certain continents are, use a world map that you can spare and cut out the continent in question and a selection of other countries with which your students are familiar and see how many countries will fit into the continent.

8. Whenever places are mentioned in stories or in current events, have students locate these places on the globe.

This last activity is a useful way of informally teaching students where places are in the world. There is no need for formal lessons, as familiarity with the globe over time will help students learn where places are located. These informal methods need to be pursued, as students don't learn location by osmosis. This was borne out in a recent assessment in British Columbia[6] where it was clear that Grade 4 students had not been formally taught, and had not learned through informal means, where the Prairie provinces are in Canada. Only 58 percent of the students tested could correctly locate them on a map of Canada.

In the intermediate grades, maps should be related to the globe because a flat map cannot give an accurate representation of shapes on a sphere. Students can discover this by drawing on an orange and seeing what happens to their drawing when the orange is peeled and the peel is flattened out.

Maps

Students will probably be more familiar with maps than with the globe and, as a result, will have distorted views of the world. For example, maps that use the Mercator projection show Europe and South America to be relatively equal in size, even though South America has twice Europe's land mass. Africa appears smaller than North America, yet Africa is 50 percent larger. Further, Eurocentric views are fostered because two-thirds of the Mercator map is taken up with the northern hemisphere, and Europe is shown in the middle. All maps distort, but some are worse than others.[7] Students need to be exposed to a variety of map projections and see the world from different perspectives. Have your students look down on the world from the North Pole and from the South Pole; have them view maps where Asia is in the centre.

Activity 11-C

In order for students to draw and read maps, certain concepts and skills will have to be taught. To discover these concepts, refer to any topographical map:

1. Choose a place on the map and determine its **grid location** (e.g., determine its latitude and longitude).
2. Choose two places and determine the distance between them.
3. See if you can locate any of the following: a river, a road, a building, a forest, a mountain, or a hill.
4. Identify the highest land shown on the map.
5. Choose two places and state what the compass direction is between them.
6. Choose any place on the map. Pretend that you are actually standing on the ground at that location. Facing in a chosen direction, draw what you would see.

The concepts of direction, grid location, symbol, scale, elevation, and perspective develop with age. The following chart indicates what map skills and concepts students should develop at different ages. It is based on a compilation of evidence from several sources.[8]

Map Skills			
Concepts	By age 7	Ages 7–9	Ages 9–11
Direction	Follows directions of left, right, etc.	Uses compass to find NEWS.	States compass bearings in degrees. Aligns maps by means of a compass.
Location	Describes location in terms of front, behind, etc. Uses globe to locate continents or countries.	Uses simple grids. Locates objects on the ground in approximate position on a map.	Uses latitude and longitude.
Symbols	Uses symbols and colour on picture maps.	Draws and recognizes some conventional map symbols. Understands the need for a KEY.	Uses KEY to locate objects on a map.
Scale	Sorts objects by size and shape. Measures distances using hands and feet.	Draws and uses large-scale maps. Measures large objects accurately.	Measures accurately. Realizes that as scale decreases, generalizations on a map increase.
Elevation		Uses colour to indicate elevation.	Reads simple contour maps.
Other	Draws routes between objects.	Draws route to school and plan of classroom. Finds countries in atlas. Understands purposes of different sorts of maps. Uses aerial photos of known areas. Compares map to globe.	Relates map to aerial photos. Aware of limitations of maps. Compares map scales. Uses Landsat maps. Infers climate from latitude, and economic activity, etc. from location in the world. Uses time zone map of North America.

Activity 11-D

Below are two maps. They show how the ability to draw maps develops. One map is drawn by a Grade 1 student, the other by a Grade 4 student.[9]

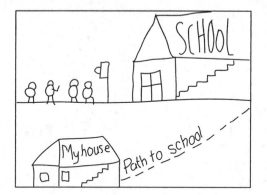

Grade 1
student's map

Grade 4
student's map

Compare these two maps. What are the differences? Why might these differences exist?

Perspective   Young children find it difficult or impossible to imagine what something would look like if they were viewing it from a pilot's-eye view. They cannot put themselves in the place of the pilot. If asked to draw a map, young children will draw it as they see it, i.e., from ground level. They also have trouble orienting objects on the ground. The maps that follow show the sorts of problems young children have.

The ability to see things from the pilot's **perspective** develops with age. By about eight years of age, most students will have this ability. To develop it further, try the following activities:

1. Have students look down on their shoes and draw them.

2. Put objects on a desk and have students draw them while looking down.

3. Ask students to draw a person while looking down on his or her head.

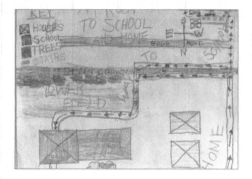

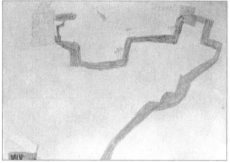

This map shows how a young child draws a straight road that goes up and down hills.

4. Have students pretend to be helicopter pilots hovering over the school; ask them to draw what they think they would see.

5. Have students pick an object on a map or aerial photo and draw it as if they were standing on the ground.

6. Obtain an aerial photo of the area in which your school is located. Have students draw a map of the area by tracing roads, buildings, etc.

Aerial photographs (such as the photo on page 142) and stereograms can be used to enhance the ability to visualize from a map what a landscape actually looks like. This entails comparing what is seen in these photographs with the map. Whenever possible, maps that show where the students are situated should be used. Students can then practise orienting the map to the direction in which they're facing, comparing the map with the landscape, and noting what is not depicted on the map, or what is on the map but is no longer on the landscape.

We all visualize space in idiosyncratic ways. When students draw their routes to school, they will include objects that are important to them, and they will perceive scale in terms of what they think are long or short distances. Even adults do this. To find out how good your spatial perception is, try the next activity.

Activity 11-E

Draw a map of Canada without reference to an atlas, globe, or wall map. When your map is complete, compare it with a cartographic representation.

1. If you live in the West, did you have problems mapping eastern Canada? Why?

2. If you live in the East, did you have problems mapping western Canada? Why?

3. Did you include provincial boundaries, capital cities, major rivers, mountain systems, major lakes, and islands such as Baffin and Victoria? Did you include Canada's newest territory, Nunavut? Why or why not?

4. Was your scale correct? Why or why not?

We each view space in our own way, based on our background and experiences. Consider young students whose parents are concerned about crime and do not allow them to travel on their own. They are not allowed to roam the neighbourhood or go off on their own to play in the local park. They are likely to have a limited view of the community in which they live. Or, if they are always transported by car, their space will be bounded by roads and highways instead of residential streets and back lanes. Consider nomadic children whose lives consist of wanderings according to age-old patterns. Their views of the spaces they occupy will be very different from those of the people who travel the same routes as traders or tourists. Consider your own experiences with places that have special salience to you: your home; the place where you were married; the hospital in which your child was born; the first cathedral, temple, famous building, or archeological site you visited; or where you saw the most beautiful sunset. And if you have travelled a lot, then your geographical horizons will likely be far broader than those of people who have never travelled outside their own communities. We should build on students' conceptions of space and broaden them through geographical studies. We can do this through field trips, through vicarious experiences such as pictures and videos, and through literature in which people describe the landscapes they live in and the meanings these surroundings convey.

Direction   Once students can use such terms as "left," "right," "in front of," "behind," and so on, and can locate objects using these terms, simple compass directions can be used. To illustrate the relationship between these terms and N, E, W, S, quickly answer this question: "If you are facing north, is west on your right or left?" As pointed out earlier, many maps have north at the top. Unless corrected, students may believe that north and south are perpendicular, not parallel, to the earth's surface. This misconception has students saying, "up north" and "down south," and believing that rivers run north–south because water flows downhill. My students always had trouble conceiving of the Mackenzie River as flowing into the Arctic Ocean, as this was toward the north and, therefore, "uphill."

One of the most useful introductions to directions is the "ME" diagram. In this activity, students draw objects that are closest to them in each direction.

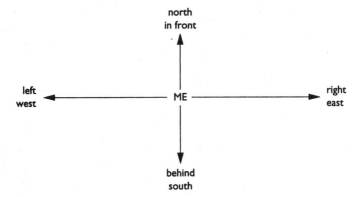

This activity can be modified to introduce other directions (NE, SW, etc.), and the concept of scale can be introduced by having students draw objects that are nearer or farther away from them.

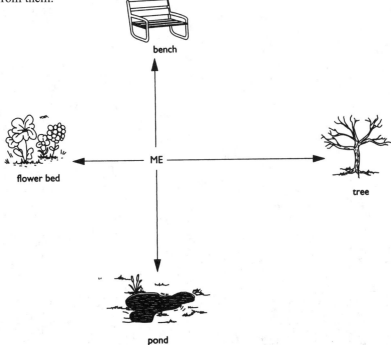

Here are some other useful activities for practising direction:

1. Locate direction using means other than the compass (the sun, stars).

2. Divide the class into pairs and have one student give directions to the other. The other student has to correctly follow the directions. ("Go three paces north. Stop. Go two paces east. Stop.")

3. Label the classroom walls with the correct compass bearings and give students directions. ("Face the north wall. Go to the west door.")

4. Hide an object in the classroom or playground and give students directions on how to find it.

5. Give each student an imaginary map, read a story, and have students draw the route taken by a character. ("John walked north to the big tree. He turned west toward the river.")

6. Have students observe a slow-moving object (person, insect) and map the moves it makes.

7. Use maps to determine directions from one place to another.

8. Ask students to plan routes between two locations on a map using various forms of transport.

9. Do simple orienteering. Give students a trundle and a map (such as the map on page XX) marked with a number of locations where students have to go. The playground could be used as the orienteering course. For example:

    a) Start at A. Walk north for 80 m. Pick up a stone.

    b) Walk west for 70 m. What is located there?

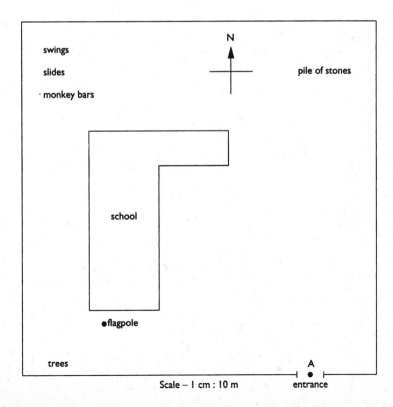

c) In what direction would you walk to arrive at the corner of the school?

d) Walk south along the side of the school for 60 m. What is located there?

Grid Location   If you wish to get from point A to point B, it is not enough to know the direction; you have to know where points A and B are located. You have to have some reference points. You couldn't do a crossword puzzle unless there were numbers across and down. You couldn't play Battleships without letters and numbers to refer to each space. With these kinds of grids, you begin locating places.

Students must realize the importance of having some kind of location system. Some ways to do this are a) ask students how they would tell their parents where they were if they got lost and were phoning to get their parents' help; b) ask students how they would tell the coast guard where they were if their boat had broken down; c) have students make a map of their classroom and ask them how they are going to correctly locate the positions of desks, chairs, etc. (For this activity, try using floor or ceiling tiles as guides, or place a grid system on the floor using chalk or tape lines.)

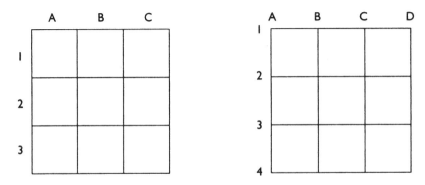

The conventional way of locating places on a map is to use latitude and longitude. These are quite complex concepts to fully understand and are not usually introduced until the intermediate grades.

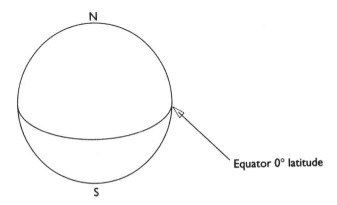

Before latitude and longitude are taught, students must know something about the world. They must understand that the world is spherical, that there are a North and a South Pole, and that the equator divides the sphere into two hemispheres. This last point is easy to perceive, as globes are manufactured in two hemispheres that join at the equator. Longitude is more difficult, as the two hemispheres of a globe are not joined at Greenwich, or the prime meridian, and it is a historical "accident" that Greenwich is 0° longitude.

Once students have grasped these basic ideas and can point out lines of latitude and longitude on a globe and a map, use some of the following ideas:

1. Hand out a map of an imaginary island like the one shown below and have students carry out these activities:

   a) Locate a town at latitude 10° S and longitude 10° W.

   b) Locate a lake at latitude 0° and longitude 10° E.

   c) Locate a boat at latitude 20° N and longitude 20° E.

   d) Put three other items on the map, give the map to a partner, and ask your partner to give the latitude and longitude of your three items.

2. Locate places using latitude and longitude. Which places are on the same latitude or longitude as St. John's, Calgary, or Tuktoyaktuk? If they are on the same latitude, will the climate be about the same? Find out what the climate is like, and if there are differences try to ascertain why (prevailing winds, closeness to bodies of water, or particular land formations). Are there climatic similarities if places are on the same line of longitude?

3. Play a game in which students, in turn, call out the location of a place using latitude and longitude. The first member of the class to identify the location receives a point. This could be modified to make it a team game.

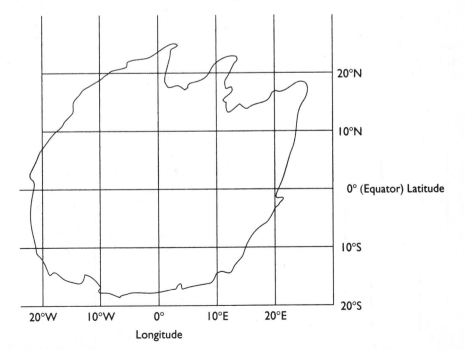

Time Zones and the International Date Line   If you landed in Fiji on the morning of your birthday, stayed overnight, and then flew to Samoa on the following day, you would arrive in time to celebrate your birthday. This fact baffles elementary school students and some adults. To teach about **time zones** and the **International Date Line (IDL)**, you have to *show* how they "work." Students in the early grades can understand that if it is daytime where they are, it will be night on the other side of the world. If they have travelled far enough east or west, they may have experienced changing the time on their watches, or may have wondered how they arrived by air in Vancouver from Toronto only an hour later than they left Toronto. And anyone who watches sporting events on television will know about the effects of time zones.

To demonstrate time zones in the classroom, use a flashlight and a globe. Assume that it is noon when the sun is directly overhead any place in the world (location A). Because lands to the east are ahead in time, and lands to the west are behind, it is afternoon to the east and morning to the west. To show this, shine the flashlight on the globe and rotate the globe 15° to the east (360° divided by 24 hours equals 15° for every hour). It will be noon at the new location (location B) and 1 p.m. at location A. If you were standing at location A, you would see the sun to the west and eventually watch it "disappear." Actual time zones do not exactly follow lines of longitude, so students will have to refer to a time zone map to find out where they are located. Places that are located midway between 15° intervals often set their times at a difference of half an hour from places east and west of them. (One example is Newfoundland.) Help students understand why time zones are not always located between each 15° of longitude and why some places choose to have half-hour differences. Once students have understood the necessity for time zones and their relative locations in the world, you can demonstrate what happens at the IDL.

For this demonstration you have to pretend that the sun and time move around the globe. Make a strip of paper that will encircle a globe one-and-a-half times at the equator. Mark off the strip for every 15° of longitude and label the beginning *Monday noon*. Roll up the strip of paper, and starting at 0° longitude (the prime meridian at Greenwich), unroll the paper moving west around the equator. Call out the time at Greenwich as Monday noon reaches each 15° interval, e.g., "It is Monday noon at 120° west; it is Monday 8 p.m. at Greenwich." As the strip of paper gets longer, have a student help you hold it. When you get to the IDL, tell students that days have to "begin" and "end" somewhere: that place is the IDL. When noon on Monday "crosses" the IDL, it "becomes" noon on Tuesday. Change *Monday noon* to *Tuesday noon* on the strip of paper. Students can see that Tuesday is to the west of the IDL (at Greenwich it is also Tuesday), and Monday to the east. Keep unwinding the strip (this is where you really need a student to help you hold the paper), remembering that the day west of the IDL is now Tuesday. When Monday midnight "crosses" the IDL, it "becomes" Tuesday midnight. As this is followed by 12:01 a.m. on Wednesday, Monday "becomes" Wednesday and a day is lost. Relabel your strip of paper to show this. (Don't worry; you "regain" it when you travel east across the IDL!) Looking at the strip of paper, you can see that you would go from Wednesday to Monday when travelling east. Remember, as soon as midnight Monday "moved" off the prime meridian, it was 12:01 a.m. on Tuesday at this same location, so the whole world doesn't miss all or any of Tuesday. You only lose one whole day if you cross the IDL at *midnight*. If you cross at other times you lose 24 hours, but not a whole day. For example, you still have 12 hours of Monday if you crossed the IDL east to west at noon, and you have 12 hours of Tuesday on the other side.

Once students can identify the time at various locations in the world, they can figure out time zones and travel time. If you left Vancouver on Monday at midnight to fly to London, England, your departure time would be Tuesday 8 a.m. in London time (there is an eight-hour time difference). If the flight took 10 hours, at what time would you arrive in London? To calculate this you have to know what time it is at your destination when you leave and add on the travel time. Thus, Tuesday 8 a.m. plus 10 hours gives an arrival time in London of Tuesday 6 p.m.

Symbols

On the imaginary island map on page 147, students will have used symbols to show a town, a lake, and a boat. Although young children may use their own symbolic representations on their maps, you should introduce conventional map symbols in the primary grades. These symbols are not always simple to understand. Some symbols represent actual objects such as buildings; others represent imaginary lines such as boundaries. Students may be surprised that imaginary objects do not actually exist on the ground; they expect to see a physical object. Some symbols look like what they represent (e.g., a blue line for a river); others do not (e.g., a red line for a road). When students are asked why some cities are in red and others are in black, they may tell you that the roofs in the two cities are made of different materials. The use of colours can also be confusing when they are used to denote elevation. Students' natural inclination is to associate colours with vegetation. So green denotes lush vegetation and lots of rain, brown denotes little vegetation and not much rain, and white represents snow. Here are some ideas to help students understand map symbols.

1. Make cards like those shown below:

   a) Fold a card in half and glue the halves together.

   b) Divide the class into four equal groups, and seat each group around a table.

   c) Place a set of cards in the middle of each table. Shuffle the cards.

   d) The first person in each group finds the symbol for a bridge and hands the card to the next person in the group. This person reads the label on the back of this card, puts the card back in the pile, and locates the card showing the correct symbol. This card is handed to the next person, and so on.

   e) With groups competing, play until one group arrives back at the symbol with which the game began.

   f) To extend what is taught through this game, add more labelled cards with symbols.

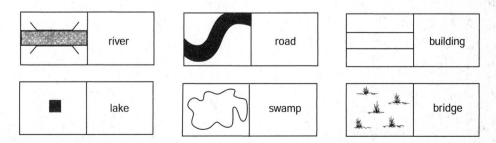

2. Make a set of cards, each card labelled with a different geographic feature such as a river, a church, a main road, and a lake. For two students to play this game, you'll need about 20 cards with different labels. If you want the whole class to play, you'll have to have 10 to 20 sets of cards.

   a) A pair of students is given a map (any topographical map, real or imaginary, will do) and a pile of cards.

   b) Each student in turn picks up a card, reads the label and, if the symbol for that label appears on the map, puts it on the map. If there is no symbol for the label, the student keeps the card. The student with the least number of cards kept wins the game.

3. Compare a photograph of an area with a map of the area. Note the map symbols and compare them with what the photograph shows.

4. Give out a blank map of the playground or part of the local community. Have students walk in the area and use symbols on the map to show what is there.

5. Give students a map and true or false statements (either in written form or stated orally), for example, "There is a river on the map" or "There is a marsh." Have students identify which statements are true and which are false.

6. Have students make up imaginary maps and invent symbols.

7. For many objects, there are no universally recognized symbols. Have students make up symbols for such places as video stores, cinemas, parking lots, etc.

Scale   Young children usually grasp the concepts of "larger than" and "smaller than." But the concept of "exact scale" is hard to grasp, as it depends upon mathematical skills that aren't taught or learned until the intermediate grades. Young children can practise using scales by doing the following types of activities:

1. Use different scales to represent actual lengths. For example, one arm's length: one paper clip; one pace: one eraser.

2. Use a length of string to measure distances from where students are located on a map or a globe to other places. When a number of distances have been calculated, students can be questioned as to which place is nearest to them and which is farthest away.

3. You could do the following activity to help students understand that when a shape is scaled up or down, it is the area that is made larger or smaller.

Activity 11-F

Work with a partner. Get a large sheet of paper and draw a simple grid on it. Have your partner lie down on the sheet of paper and draw around him or her. Get another sheet of paper that is half (or less) the size of the other one, copy the same grid onto it, and then copy your partner's outline onto it. The following diagrams show how this activity can be done using your hand.

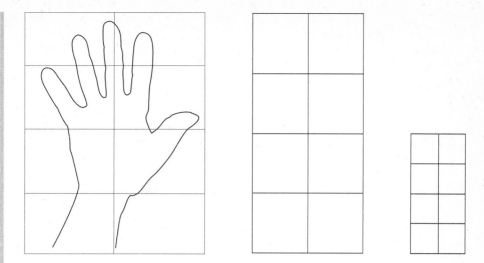

Young children find it quite fascinating to see themselves a tenth of their real size, and even more so to see themselves twice their own size when the original drawing is doubled.

4. Find distances from their present location to places mentioned in the news, in stories, etc.

5. Make maps of the same area using different scales (1 cm:1 m; 1 cm:1 km).

6. Compare maps that use different scales.

7. Work out the shortest route between two places.

Students should first learn to use large-scale maps (1:2500). These show a great deal of detail because they cover small areas. Small-scale maps like the ones found in atlases cannot show much detail because they cover large areas. To remember the difference between the two, think of *large-scale* maps as showing *large* details and *small-scale* maps as showing *little* detail.

Elevation So far, we've looked at maps as though everything were flatland. Maps also show elevation. Topographical maps use **contour lines**, but understanding these lines is an upper intermediate ability. The concept of **elevation** can be introduced by providing three-dimensional models so that students can *feel* as well as see the raised areas. Later they can use the atlas and the colour key (green for lowlands, white for the top of very high mountains) to locate various elevations. Where in the world (or in the country, or province) are there flatlands? Where are there mountains? To introduce contour lines, have students do the following:

1. Have students make a cone.

2. Instruct them to place the cone, base down, on a piece of paper and to draw around the base of the cone.

3. Have students measure halfway up the cone and draw around the halfway mark on the cone. Ask them where this line would appear on their piece of paper.

4. Have students indicate where the top of the cone would be drawn on the piece of paper.

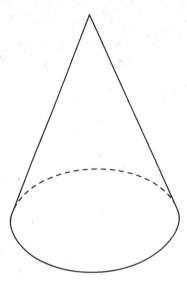

5. Students should then label the heights indicated by the lines on the piece of paper, counting the base line as sea level. They should colour in the area between the base line and the halfway mark, and then use a different colour for the area between the halfway mark and the summit.

6. Suggest that students use the elevation map to answer these questions:

   a) How high is the cone?

   b) If you were going to climb the cone, would it make any difference from which point on the base line you started? Why or why not?

Activity 11-G

Draw a contour map for the following shape, using the same procedure as outlined above.

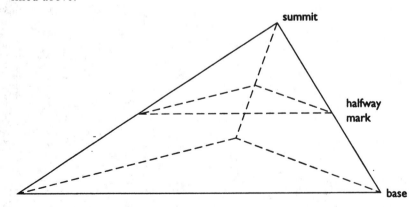

   If you wished to climb this pyramid, which route would be the easiest? Which the steepest? How can you tell?

Activity 11-H

On this map, draw contour lines linking benchmarks of the same height.

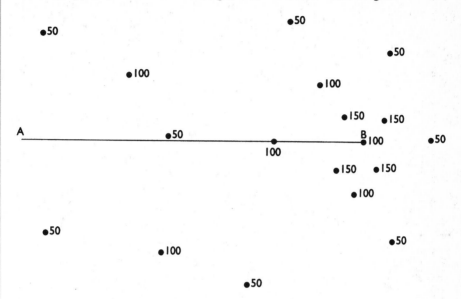

Cut out a piece of thick cardboard that would cover the area 50 m high or higher. Cut out a piece of cardboard to cover the area that is more than 100 m high. Cut out a piece of cardboard to cover the area that is more than 150 m high. Now, build your hill.

1. In order to climb this hill, what would be the least steep routes? What would be the steepest route?

2. What might you expect to find along the A–B line? How can you tell?

Elevation, however, is not a very meaningful concept unless students can relate it to something. Prairie-town students will tend to think of grain elevators as being very tall, whereas urban students will relate to skyscrapers, and students living in mountainous regions will compare the elevations of mountains. To give students a sense of the heights of various objects, give each one a copy of a large protractor as shown on the next page. Have them mount the protractor on stiff cardboard, attach a piece of wood (a ruler will do) along the top, and drop a plumb line from the centre of the protractor.

They have now constructed a **clinometer**.

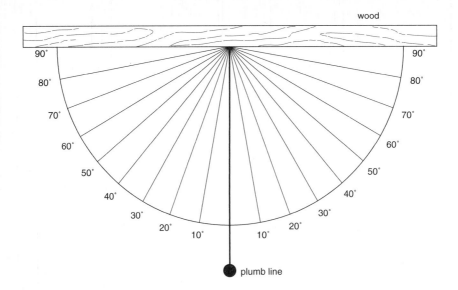

Students can find the height of an object (tree, telephone pole, etc.) by using the clinometer. Have them move away from the object and sight the clinometer to the top of the object so that the plumb line is at a 45° angle. Then measure the distance from the base of the object to where the sighting was taken.

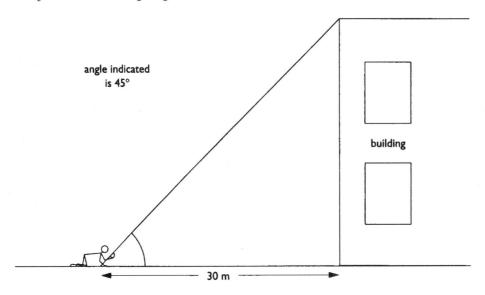

As shown in the diagram above, the height of the building is 30 m. How do you know this? Because you have an equilateral right-angled triangle.

If it is not possible to get in a position where the clinometer indicates a 45° angle, then use the following procedure.

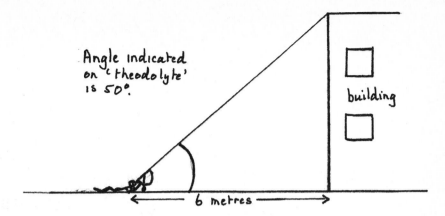

Take a clinometer sighting and note the angle. Measure the distance from where the sighting was taken to the base of the object. On a sheet of paper, draw a large right angle and, using an appropriate scale, measure the distance that you used from the base of the object to where you took your sighting. Now, using an ordinary protractor, draw the angle that was indicated by your clinometer reading.

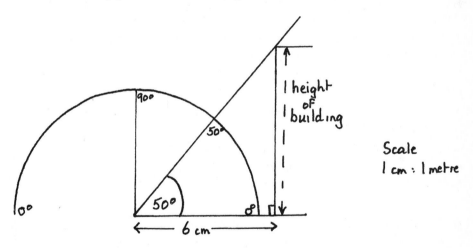

Measure from the base of the object to the top. By using the scale, students will find out the approximate height of the object. In this case, the building is approximately 70 m high.

The clinometer can also be used when students are making their own maps. Have students determine the boundaries of the area they wish to map and locate a sight line from which to measure angles. Replace the plumb line on the clinometer with a solid pointer. At a given location, students will hold the clinometer in front of them at eye level and sight the pointer at an object. They should determine the angle of the object they wish to place on the map, measure the distance from their location to the object, and plot the object on their map.

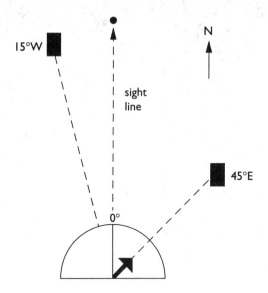

There are several other activities for students to carry out in order to learn about maps and mapping. Try the following:

1. Give students an outline map of an area in the community, take them for a walk in the area, and have them map what they see.

2. Have students decide on the best route to take to certain places using different forms of transport.

3. Have students use different types of maps and find out what kind of information is provided on each type.

4. Collect stamps and place them on a map of their country of origin.

5. Give students an incomplete map, and have them finish it and compare it to the real one.

6. Have students make land-use maps of the community.

7. Collect pictures of foods eaten by students and locate their origins on a map.

8. Where appropriate, have students make class maps showing their own birthplaces and those of their parents and grandparents.

9. Collect pictures of various places in the world and locate them on a world map.

10. Make models, draw pictures, and write descriptions or stories about various landform features, and locate them on a map.

Many of these mapping activities do not involve landscapes that students can experience by using all their senses. Most of what we teach about occurs outside the classroom. Although we bring in books, pictures, and maps that represent the world outside, whenever possible we should give students the opportunity to see for themselves whatever phenomenon is being studied. We do this by carrying out field research, which will be discussed in Chapter 12.

OTHER ACTIVITIES

1. Use a Canadian school atlas and list the geographical information about Canada that could be learned from it.

2. Identify the mistakes this Grade 4 student has made in drawing the map shown here. (See the Answers section for a list of the mistakes.) How would you help the student rectify these mistakes?

3. Have elementary school students of different ages draw maps of their routes from home to school. Compare the results. What problems do the students have? How might these be corrected?

NOTES

1. J. Bradley, "Quebec report: Whither geography?" *Canadian Social Studies* 36:1 (2002). www.quasar.ualberta.ca/css/Css_36_1/CLquebec_report_jon_bradley.htm

2. Geography Education Standards Project, *Geography for Life: National Geography Standards* (Washington, DC: National Geographic Research and Exploration, 1994).

3. Ibid.

4. D. Vincent, *Crosscountry Canada* (Burnaby, BC: Didatec Software, 1996).

5. C. Sunal and D. Sunal, "Mapping the child's world," *Social Education* 42:5 (1978), pp. 381–383.

6. C. Bognar and W. Cassidy, *Social Studies in British Columbia: Technical Report of the 1989 Social Studies Assessment* (Victoria, BC: Assessment, Examinations and Reporting Branch of the Ministry of Education, 1991).

7. G. Rice, "Teaching students to become discriminating map users," *Social Education* 54:6 (1990), pp. 393–397.

8. T. Burley and G. Atkinson, "Geographic skills: A research-based sequence for grades one to nine," *History and Social Science Teacher* 22:2 (1986/87), pp. 101–105. S. Muir and H. Cheek, "Assessing spatial development: Implications for map skill instruction," *Social Education* 55:5 (1991), pp. 316–319. J. Bale, *Geography in the Primary School* (London: Routledge and Kegan Paul, 1987). S. Catling, "Environmental perception and maps," in D. Mills, ed., *Geography Work in Primary and Middle Schools* (Sheffield, England: The Geographical Association, 1988). P. Bailey, *Teaching Geography* (Newton Abbot, England: David and Charles, 1974).

9. Drawn by Christina Disler. Used with permission.

GLOSSARY OF KEY TERMS

Clinometer — an instrument used to determine the height of objects.

Contour lines — lines on a map denoting elevation.

Elevation — the height of objects and landform features.

Global system — a network of relationships connecting a phenomenon—e.g., weather, trade—to more than one area in the world.

Grid location — a way of locating places on a globe or map, e.g., using latitude and longitude.

International Date Line — an imaginary line at 180° longitude, east of which is one day earlier than to the west.

Landscape study — the examination of a specific place.

Perspective — the ability to look at a landscape and see it from the pilot's-eye view, or to look at a map and visualize things as they are on the ground.

Scale — a representation of the size of an object or the distance between objects, e.g., 1 cm:1 km.

Time zone — an area in which the time difference from Greenwich Mean Time is established, e.g., Pacific Time zone, Central Time zone.

chapter twelve

Learning in the Real World: Field Studies and Field Trips

FIELD STUDIES

Collecting data first-hand and getting a "feel" for a place are two of the major objectives of field studies. Other important aims are to develop certain skills, such as map reading, and to stimulate interest in a topic. Field studies can also act as a catalyst for further research. They should be undertaken whenever possible because they a) reflect what geographers and social scientists do; b) are interesting for students; c) provide an ideal learning situation, especially for teaching research and map skills; and d) broaden students' horizons.

Activity 12-A

Field trips have to be as carefully planned as any lesson. Read the following paragraph and identify what the teacher has done properly but also what she has failed to do in planning a field trip. Then consult the Answers section.

A teacher has organized a trip to a local industrial site. Transportation has been booked. She has visited the site and made full arrangements (tour guide, schedule, location of washrooms, and lunch facilities). Safety concerns have been addressed. Students have been given background information, a list of questions to answer, and activities to do while en route to the site and when they are actually there. Rules have been laid down. Parent-volunteer supervisors have been contacted. Each student has brought 25¢ for transport costs and has been told what to bring on the trip (appropriate clothing, lunch, writing materials, and medical prescriptions for those requiring them). Because all of the class's subjects are taught by this teacher, there are no timetable problems. The principal has given permission for the trip.

Once a suitable field-trip location has been identified and logistical arrangements have been made, relevant activities must be prepared for the students. Below is a list of possible activities as well as questions that could be asked at various field-trip locations where the teaching and learning of geography are the focus. Which activities a particular class might carry out depends upon the objectives of the field trip.

1. Identify examples of different forms of land use: industrial, agricultural, residential, commercial, recreational. Why are particular areas used for particular purposes? Is this the best use of the land in question?

2. Note different physical landform features. Locate a cliff, lake, valley, etc. Note the climatic conditions. How do these conditions affect the area and the people living there?

3. Observe the transport networks. Do power lines, roads, and railroads follow the best routes? Why or why not?

4. Note the location of boundaries. Where are the political boundaries? What are the reasons for their location? What other sorts of boundaries are there—property, cultural, ethnic, etc.? How do these boundaries affect the movement of people or goods?

5. Compare house and house-lot sizes in places A and B. Are they different or similar? Why?

6. Find out the reasons for the locations of buildings, roads, and other features. Why is this (industry, farm, store, etc.) built where it is?

7. Find out the history of the area. Is this an old (building, farm, industry, etc.)? How can you tell? Why was it built? Where did the materials used in its construction come from? Do we build this way now? Why or why not? What did the area look like 100 years ago? Was it better or worse then? What changes have occurred in the natural environment? What changes are likely to occur in the future? Can we prevent undesirable changes? How?

8. Account for the differences in vegetation between place A and place B.

9. Identify examples of natural and human-created hazards to people, to local fauna, and to the environment in general. Can erosion pose a threat? Where has erosion occurred, and why? Was it caused by natural or other means? Could it—and should it—have been prevented? What other natural and human-created phenomena pose a hazard to the environment? Can these be prevented? How, and at what cost?

10. When studying an industry or business, find out about the site, the raw materials, the products and the markets for them, the source of power used, the transportation used, the ownership of the industry or business, and the impact it has on the environment. Find out about the workers: any health hazards they face; how much input they have into how the business or industry is operated; how they are treated (for instance, if there is discrimination on the basis of sex, ethnicity, or class); whether they are unionized; how much they earn; what hours they work; etc.

11. Draw a picture of Y (building, landform feature).

12. Sketch a map of Y.

13. What do you think the area will look like in 10 years' time? Will it be better or worse than it is now? Why? Draw a map showing how you would like the area to look in 10 years' time.

14. List all the sounds you can hear and smells you can smell. Where do they come from?

15. Write descriptive words or sentences about how you feel at the site. Does it make you feel happy, sad, angry?

16. Collect some items, if this is permissible (small rocks, vegetation); label and display them.

17. How are people using the environment? Are they harming it in any way? Are there any indications of conservation efforts in the area?

18. Carry out an environmental appraisal. Create a score sheet like the one below, pose appropriate questions, and use the sheet to evaluate an area.

Environmental Assessment							
Location:							
Date and time of assessment:							
	+3	+2	+1	0	−1	−2	−3
Overall appearance							
Architecture							
Condition of natural environment (trees, etc.)							
Condition of human environment (buildings, etc.)							
Neatness							
Traffic noise							
Traffic danger							
Traffic smell							
Ease of people movement							
Ease of parking							
Other_____							

There are three types of field studies:

1. **Field teaching:** This involves teaching students at a site other than the classroom (e.g., teaching a lesson on salmon at a salmon hatchery).

2. **Field inquiry:** Here students find out answers to questions on the field site. These questions could be posed by the teacher and/or by the students, e.g., at a museum: How many different types of materials were used in the construction of a pit house? Or at a shopping centre: How many stores cater to women exclusively?

3. **Field discovery:** In this type of study, students go to a site with no preconceived ideas of what to do when they get there. Rather, students and teachers use the site to generate interest in particular topics and to answer student-posed questions.

Field studies of any type can be carried out in three different ways:

- On a site with clearly defined boundaries (an industry, store, farm, village).
- Traversing areas that differ from one another (going from a valley to a hilltop; from a residential to an industrial area; from a rural to an urban area; from a low-cost to a high-cost housing area).
- From a vantage point (a tall building or a hill).

In all these forms of fieldwork, students can write answers to questions, draw, collect specimens, map, make graphs, take photographs, record sounds, interview people, make charts, do scientific experiments, measure things, count things, and so on.

FIELD TRIPS

Field trips need not require extended bus travel; the school environs provide a rich source of possibilities for studying the local community. Even the school itself provides a "field trip" site. In the following example, questions are raised about the geography, economics, sociology, anthropology, politics, history, aesthetics, and philosophy of a school. You are encouraged to question many of the assumptions about schools and schooling that are usually taken for granted.

Questions

1. Where is the school in relation to the community? In what surroundings? Why was it built there? What does this location suggest about the relationship between the school and the community?

2. What are the architectural features of the school? What activities might it encourage? What attitudes does it communicate?

3. How is space in the school used? Are there spaces in which students are not allowed? Are there spaces for various student activities that are determined by students (e.g., a space for skipping, for talking, for playing soccer on the playground; a space in the corridor that is only used by Grade X)? Why?

4. What kinds of special facilities does the school have? Are there rooms for specific purposes? If so, what are these purposes? What can you infer from this about the kind of activities that the school and community value most? How much space does each department have? Is the size of the classroom space a factor of grade level or subject matter? What kind of equipment is provided? Do some subjects or interests get more equipment than others? Why? What does all this tell you about what is important for the school and the community?

5. What is the interior decoration of the school? Is it aesthetically pleasing? Is it comfortable? What assumptions about school and learning does all this reveal?

6. What are the classrooms like? What furniture is provided? Do students and teachers have the same or different furniture? Why? How is seating arranged? What does this suggest about how teaching and learning are carried out, and how teachers and students communicate with one another? What behaviours does the classroom seem to encourage? What does all this assume about teaching and learning?

7. In the actual construction of the classroom, what materials were used? Where did these materials come from? Were any imported? What raw materials were used? How many different kinds of occupations were necessary to build the classroom? Where does the heating come from? Where does the electricity come from? What does all this tell us about the economics and geography of the wider community? What does it tell us about interdependence?

8. What kinds of pictures, posters, or objects decorate the walls? What do they say? What messages do they convey? Who put them there? Why? What kinds of ideas, people, and activities does the school seem to honour? Why?

9. What rituals are performed at regular intervals? Why? What are their purposes? What values do they reflect? What kinds of symbols do they involve? What roles do people play? What cultural beliefs do these rituals transmit?

10. What activities do students undertake most often? Do males and females perform the same or different activities? Why? What do students study? For how long? What does all this tell us about what the culture expects students to do when they're adults?

11. How do people dress? Do teachers and students dress differently? What influences the way people dress? What materials are used in making everyone's clothes? Where do these materials come from?

12. What cultural values can be inferred from the way the school is governed? Who has authority? Why? Who is involved in the decision-making processes?

Activity 12-B

Using your own faculty, college, or school, choose one or more of the above questions and use the following inquiry procedure:

1. Ask question(s).
2. Generate hypothesis(es).
3. Decide what data are needed.
4. Decide on method(s) of collecting data.
5. Analyze, interpret, and evaluate data.
6. Confirm or deny the hypothesis(es).
7. Conclude.

Field Trips to Special Sites

Which activities are most appropriate on trips to museums, historical sites, and other special places will depend upon the trip's objectives and the students' abilities. However, a few guidelines apply to all trips:

1. Make sure the students know what the objectives are. Carry out activities to prepare students for the trip (describe the site, tell students what to look for, have students develop hypotheses to test at the site). Then students should be encouraged to answer the following sorts of questions based on those presented in Chapter 10:

   • What is significant about this site (museum, art gallery, etc.)?
   • What is displayed and why is it displayed?

- What is not displayed even though it would be relevant to the site?
- Who chooses what to display?
- What feelings does the site engender?

2. Choose a particular object and state, where appropriate, what it is made of, what its purpose was, who made it, who used it, whether it is used today, what changes have occurred, and whether the object is better or worse than the most comparable object in our time.

3. In looking at a painting, ask whether it is an accurate representation of the subject of the painting, what could be learned about life from it, what the artist was trying to say, why it was painted, and how representations have changed over time (see Chapter 16 for ideas about examining images).

4. If there is an object that is unfamiliar to students, have them guess what it is.

At some sites, students can manipulate artifacts and participate in activities as they were practised in the past (e.g., being at a school as it was in the early 1900s or living in a pioneer home).

When a field trip is over and students return to the classroom, further work should be carried out. First, letters of thanks should be written to those who helped (guides, parent volunteers, etc.). Second, the work done on the field trip should be compiled in the form of reports, charts, and so on. The information collected should be discussed and interpreted so that generalizations can be formulated. If the field trip was a significant one, then work should be displayed and parents invited to view it. The trip should be evaluated, both by you in terms of student achievement, and by the students in terms of what they learned from it and whether they were interested or not. We should also reflect on the whole trip and consider the following questions:

- Was it well organized?
- Could it be improved next time?
- Was it the best way of getting the desired information?
- Were there too many or too few activities for students to perform?
- Did the trip cover too much or too little?
- Did anything go wrong (if so, how could this be avoided next time)?
- Were the objectives of the trip realized?

OTHER ACTIVITIES

1. Choose a location that would be worthwhile for students to study. Design three activities that students could carry out at this location.

2. Design a question sheet for students to answer when visiting a museum, an art gallery, or an industry with which you are familiar.

GLOSSARY OF KEY TERMS

Field discovery — letting students explore a site to raise their own questions and find answers.

Field inquiry — students seek answers to questions at a site, e.g., finding out about the history of a community at a museum.

Field teaching — teaching about something at the relevant site, e.g., teaching about fishing on a fishing boat.

chapter thirteen

Putting It All Together: Making Connections

If students are to learn social studies in a meaningful way, then they have to make connections between what they know and new information. They have to connect information they learn in both history and geography and then relate this information to knowledge from other disciplines. They must begin to develop powerful generalizations that synthesize large amounts of information. This may sound rather grandiose, but even Grade 1 students can begin to develop and understand generalizations such as these: all families have rules; people change their environments to satisfy their needs and wants; and families differ because of a variety of factors including their values, their economic status, their location, and how many people there are in the family.

DEVELOPING GENERALIZATIONS

The instructional procedure outlined in this book begins with the identification of concepts necessary for the study of a particular topic or question. Students then acquire information about how these concepts apply to the topic or question, through expository and/or inquiry methods. The final step in this procedure is the development of generalizations. This instructional procedure is not the only one that you can use, but it does provide an effective structure for unit planning (see Chapter 14).

Generalizations are statements about relationships between and among concepts. They summarize large bodies of information. Generalizations are useful because, once they have been verified, they make it unnecessary to carry out research in each new case that is covered by the generalization.

There are several kinds of generalizations.[1] **Universal generalizations** cover every case to which they refer. They are true for *all* times and places, and therefore they may contain words such as "all," "never," and "every." Here is an example: "Urban growth increases in relation to industrial development." **Prevalence generalizations** contain terms such as "most," "the majority of," and "usually." "The majority of cities in the world suffer from air pollution" is an example. **Probabilistic generalizations** are often identified by the word "probable," with a number attached. Gallup and other polls often state their findings as probabilistic generalizations—e.g., "This poll is accurate within 2 percent, 19 times out of 20." Finally, there are **enumerative generalizations**, which summarize data that have actually been counted. Statements about all 30 students in a particular classroom are enumerative generalizations.

Activity 13-A

Identify the generalizations in the following passage. Answers are in the Answers section.

> All countries in the world have a system of government. The form of government of each country is determined by the size of the population, its history, and its beliefs. Where there are few people, government can be simple, whereas larger countries require more complex forms of government. All governments provide certain services to people. In most countries the services are provided to all the people. In dictatorships, only people who support the government get services. In Canada, all people receive educational and medical services. What other services do Canadians receive?

Now that you have some understanding of what generalizations are, find out which generalizations are considered to be important for students to learn.

Activity 13-B

Locate, in the social studies curriculum guide in your province, the generalizations that students are supposed to learn. What sorts of generalizations are they?

We formulate generalizations through **inductive reasoning**; for example, "This A is a B, and that A is a B. Therefore, all As are Bs." Or, "Therefore, the next A will be a B." Enumerative generalizations can be verified by seeing if, in fact, all As are Bs. With other generalizations, it is usually impossible to see if every A is a B. This is why it is often said that in inductive reasoning, we "leap" from what is known to a conclusion that we cannot be *certain* is true. In our everyday lives we make a few observations about something and generalize quite reliably to all future observations. When we generalize about complex, irregular phenomena such as human behaviour, however, our generalizations have to be more tentative.

In all cases of generalization, the following criteria should be applied:

1. There are enough instances to justify the generalization.
2. The generalization fits into a larger structure of knowledge.

Here are some ways in which students can develop generalizations and begin to apply the above criteria.

In primary classrooms, we can start by collecting information about students and creating generalizations about them: we all have unique characteristics; we all share certain needs. As students become more capable of dealing with bodies of information using Taba's concept development ideas (see Chapter 6), data-retrieval charts can be used to formulate generalizations. An example follows.

Data-Retrieval Chart: Nigeria				
Climate	Landforms	Vegetation	Agriculture	Transportation
data	data	data	data	data

To encourage the formulation of generalizations, pose the following types of questions:

1. What is similar about all the items under the _____ label? Can you formulate a generalization about _____?
2. How is agriculture related to the climate?
3. How is the transportation related to the landform?
4. What has the transportation system to do with agriculture?
5. Why is the southern area of Nigeria best for growing crops?

You can modify this chart to include other phenomena for comparative purposes. Other questions can then be asked to encourage students to make more substantial generalizations by summarizing larger bodies of information.

Location	Climate	Landforms	Vegetation	Agriculture	Transportation	Other
Nigeria	data	data	data	data	data	data
Ontario	data	data	data	data	data	data

1. How are the climates of the two places similar or different? What generalizations can you make about the climates of Nigeria and Ontario?
2. What accounts for the agricultural differences between Nigeria and Ontario?

Activity 13-C

Below is a data-retrieval chart about an isolated Atlantic fishing community. The students who produced it have created maps, graphs, and pictures, and have learned how fish are caught and processed. They have written a story about life as a boy or girl in the community and have discussed the advantages and disadvantages of living in a fishing community.

Data-Retrieval Chart		
LOCATION	**CLIMATE**	**JOBS**
Atlantic coast	Hot summer	In-shore fishers
Sheltered harbour	Cold winter with heavy rains and storms	Fish-plant workers
Nearest town is 50 km away	Frequent fog	Marine outfitters
		Dairy farmers
		Retailers
BUILDING MATERIALS	**NATURAL ENVIRONMENT**	**FISHING SEASON**
Wood	Ocean	April to October for cod and halibut
Stone	Rocky cliffs	Limited mussels, crab, lobster in season
	Beach	
	Arable land	
	Trees	
BUILDINGS	**UNEMPLOYMENT**	**TRANSPORT**
Houses	40% in winter	Fishing boats
Post office	8% in summer	Pleasure boats
Fish-processing plant		Rowboats
General store		Trucks
Marine store		Cars
Church		
Elementary school		
Hotel with coffee shop		
Summer cottages		

Using the information above, answer the following questions:

1. How are jobs in the community related to the natural environment?
2. How are jobs related to the climate and unemployment rate?
3. How is the relative isolation of the community related to community services?
4. Now pose two more questions that ask, "What has _____ got to do with _____?" Answer these questions.

Answering the questions above will lead to the creation of enumerative generalizations about the community, such as those shown below.

Relationships:

• The trees and rocks provide building materials.

- Location on the ocean provides such jobs as fishing, marine outfitting, and tourist services.

Enumerative generalizations:

- Buildings in the community are built from materials found in the locality.
- Eighty percent of the jobs in the community are dependent upon the natural environment.

If the enumerative generalizations based on this village are true of other isolated fishing communities, then we could formulate a prevalence generalization. For example: "In isolated fishing communities in Canada, there will likely be high unemployment during the off-season because of the seasonal nature of job opportunities." To arrive at this prevalence generalization, students would have to identify other isolated fishing communities in Canada. From these they could draw a random selection and find out if the generalizations made about the Atlantic Coast community were also true of other communities.

Students can be helped to understand how to formulate reliable generalizations from a sample of cases by carrying out the following type of activity. Give students a statement about all students in the school: for example, "All students in the school like watching cartoons on TV" or "All students use biodegradable drink containers at lunch." Tell them that it would take far too long to ask every student about watching cartoons or to observe all students to see if they use biodegradable drink containers. What has to be done is to observe or ask a **representative sample**. This means that the sample must reflect all the different types of students in the school, using characteristics such as age, sex, ethnic group, etc. If each class in the school is fairly representative of the entire school population, then a random sample of students from each class could be observed at lunchtime or could be asked about their cartoon-watching habits. If individual students each drew a different sample, the results would be more reliable: the larger the sample, the more representative it is likely to be. For ideas about carrying out surveys, see Chapter 16.

Activity 13-D

Following is an incomplete web diagram showing relationships among various aspects of the fishing industry. Add further relationships to the diagram and then formulate generalizations. Is there enough evidence to support your generalizations? Do your generalizations fit into a wider body of knowledge about resource-based industries? To verify your generalizations, ask what would happen if a particular aspect of the generalization were modified in some way. For example, "If the government placed a ban on all fishing, what might happen?" or "If the cost of (oil, wood, etc.) went up, what might occur?" This helps students see how everything is connected and that a modification in one link in a chain creates modifications in other links. This type of web diagram is a very powerful one for helping students "see" the concepts of interdependence and interaction.

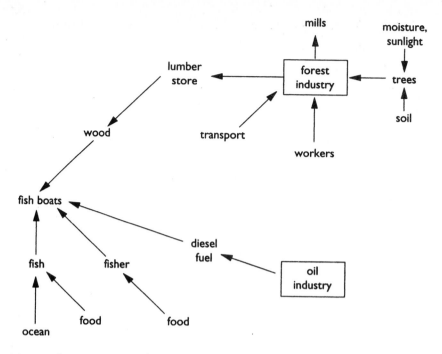

Most students appear to enjoy this activity and come to realize how complex and inter-connected the world really is. For instance, a pictorial diagram showing the purchase of a chocolate bar by a student can demonstrate how this apparently simple act is related to the wider economic system.

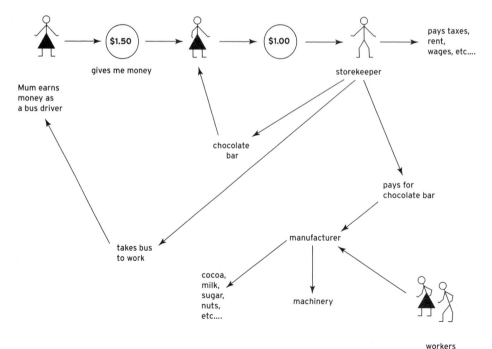

By extending this diagram, we could formulate this generalization: "All members of a society are interdependent; individual producers of goods and services exchange with others to get the goods and services they need to satisfy their basic wants." Further, we can ask questions that help students see cause-and-effect relationships. For example, if the cocoa bean crop fails, then the cost of a chocolate bar will likely increase. If there is more pocket money available, then more chocolate bars can be purchased; and if more purchases are made, the storekeeper will, all other things being equal, make more money.

Activity 13-E

Create a web starting with an item that you own. Diagram all the connections to this item. Then change one of the connections and trace the effects on all the other elements.

As an alternative to having students formulate their own generalizations, present students with generalizations and help them determine if there is evidence to support these generalizations.

Activity 13-F

Here is a universal generalization:

> Interaction between people and their environment influences the ways in which people meet their needs.

How would you discover if this were true in your own community? If this generalization is true, then...

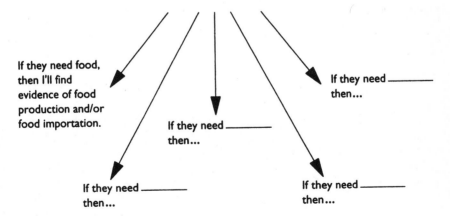

If they need food, then I'll find evidence of food production and/or food importation.

If they need _____ then...

If they need _____ then...

If they need _____ then...

If they need _____ then...

AVOIDING OVERGENERALIZATIONS

One of the most common mistakes in reasoning is overgeneralizing. We have to teach students that although we cannot possibly check the truth of all the generalizations we employ in our everyday lives, we have to be on our guard when we generalize. This is especially important in the recognition and avoidance of stereotypes.

Activity 13-G

What generalizations are being assumed in the following? Which ones are warranted? Answers appear in the Answers section.

1. I'm going to hire recent immigrants. They'll be good workers.
2. He's a boy so he won't cry.
3. The country will change culturally and economically with the arrival of so many immigrants.
4. Because she has working-class parents, I expect she'll have problems in school.
5. I'm not going to Vancouver again in the summer. Last time I went it rained all the time.
6. He's wearing a turban so he must be from India.
7. He's a boy so he won't be good at sewing.

Helping students recognize the generalizations they use is especially important when they are not warranted. For instance, in number 4 above, it is assumed that daughters of working-class parents have trouble in school. This is not necessarily true. These sorts of stereotypes can lead to prejudicial attitudes and possibly discriminatory actions. This is why it is extremely important to teach students the dangers of overgeneralization.

You can present students with examples of how overgeneralizations have created harm. For example, have students find out about the belief held at the beginning of World War II by members of the British Columbia and Canadian governments that many of the Japanese living on the British Columbia coast were real or potential enemies. This belief led to the forced removal of Japanese families from their homes. Or, in researching the role of women, students will identify the belief that women could not perform certain roles in society, which resulted in their exclusion from these roles.

OTHER ACTIVITIES

1. Develop a generalization from the following information.

The Bedouin		
February	A little rain	Move herds to spring pastures.
March		Make cheese and butter for the year.
April		Shear sheep.
May	No rain	Harvest.
June		Thresh.
July		Winnow.
August		Store grain.
September		Move herds often to new pastures.
		Water animals daily.
October	A little rain	Plant crops.
November	Some rain	Move to central camp.
December		New animals are born.
January		

2. How would you test the generalization "As the size of the community changes, the services within the community change"?

NOTE

1. R. Ennis, *Logic in Teaching* (Englewood Cliffs, NJ: Prentice-Hall, 1969), pp. 423–435.

GLOSSARY OF KEY TERMS

Generalizations:

> **Enumerative** — statements that summarize data that have been counted, e.g., "All the students in this class have English as a second language."

> **Prevalence** — statements that are mostly or usually true, e.g., "Most Third World countries do not have democratic forms of government."

> **Probabilistic** — statements about the statistical probability of an occurrence, e.g., "This poll is accurate within 2 percent, 19 times out of 20."

> **Universal** — true statements for all times and places, e.g., "All people need food to survive."

Inductive reasoning — reasoning that if this A is a B, and the next A is a B (and so on), then all As are Bs.

Representative sample — a group from an identifiable population that fairly represents the composition of that population.

chapter fourteen

Putting It All Together: Developing a Unit Plan

In this chapter we look at a framework for an entire unit plan, focusing on major concepts, specific empirical information, generalizations, inquiry skills, and intellectual standards. We need to have a unit framework so that we, and our students, know approximately what the result of our teaching is supposed to be. A unit framework gives us a map of where we want to go and how we intend to get there. By careful planning we can ensure that we have covered the important aspects of the chosen topic, that it is organized in a logical way, and that we have considered all the relevant curriculum and instructional variables.

The framework described in this chapter contains some of the key variables that have to be considered, but it does not contain them all. This is a practice run. Resource materials, evaluation procedures, integration with other subject areas, and individual lessons that teach needed skills or information are omitted or mentioned briefly.

For a more thorough review of **unit planning**, see Chapter 22. However, the present chapter's framework does provide logically and pedagogically sound formats, which can be adapted to suit specific objectives and topics of study as well as particular school, classroom, and student characteristics. One systematic format is sequenced in the following way:

1. Develop concepts appropriate for studying the topic.

2. Implement inquiry and/or expository methods to teach how these concepts apply to the topic.

3. Develop generalizations.

Suppose we want to plan a unit on a particular culture. We want to emphasize the discipline of anthropology and the concept of interdependence using "culture" as the organizer. Using the framework above, broad objectives might be stated as follows:

1. Students will be able to define concepts useful for the study of a culture (e.g., food, shelter, clothing, recreation, religion, education, language, rights, values, law, and government).

2. Students will be able to state how the above concepts apply to the culture being studied (e.g., details of how food is gathered, prepared, and eaten).

3. Students will develop the following generalizations:

   a) All people adapt their environment, and are adapted by the environment.

   b) All cultures share certain characteristics; for example, all cultures have a form of government.

   c) All people are interdependent.

4. Students will develop competency in such areas as carrying out research, using a map, etc.

CREATING A FRAMEWORK

These objectives can be phrased in more specific terms when the culture to be studied is chosen and when a grade level is specified. Activities could then be sequenced as follows:

Topic: Culture X

1. Show a picture of some aspect of Culture X. Make it as puzzling as possible to stimulate student interest. Ask students where they think this picture was taken and who are the people portrayed.

2. Using maps and the globe, locate the area of the world where the people live. Have students find out how far away it is. How could they get there—what countries, seas, etc., would they have to cross? Guess what climate, landforms, economic activities, etc., they might find there.

3. Show the students a *representative* set of pictures (showing as many aspects of the culture as possible). Show about five pictures and carry out the Taba Concept Development procedure (Chapter 6).

   a) Have students list or draw items they see in the pictures. If students notice only major features, point out the details.

   b) Have students tell you what they have noticed. List about 15 of the items on the blackboard. If the students have drawn the items, collect the pictures and display them on a bulletin board.

   c) Take the first item noted on the blackboard and ask whether anyone can see any item that would go with it, **or** have groups of students classify the items and share their categories with the class.

d) Once a group of items has been identified, ask students to label the group. When a concept label has been chosen, make sure that all the items are examples of the concept.

4. When the blackboard list has been classified, or groups of students have shared their concept labels and a common set of labels has been developed for the entire class, have students copy the classification chart into their notebooks and/or make a large classroom display chart.

Data-Retrieval Chart					
Landform	Transportation	Climate	Dress	Daily life	Other
Desert	Walking	Very hot	Long white	Children care	
Oases	Camels	during day	robes	for goats	
Rolling sand dunes	Jeeps	Sandstorms	Sandals	Worship	
	Trucks	Cold at night		each day	
		No rain			

5. If students have collected other information derived from the initial presentation, have them fit it under the appropriate concept labels. Create new categories if an item does not fit the existing concepts. Ask students what information they think visitors from another planet would want to know about this culture. Would what they want to know fit into the categories above? Do the concepts developed help describe the culture of the people being studied?

6. Each student should now have a chart identifying the major concepts that are useful for the study of the culture. From this point, a number of different approaches may be taken. You could take each concept in turn and teach about it, or students could carry out inquiry procedures (Chapter 8). The students themselves could choose a concept and questions for study.

If cooperative learning (Chapter 9) is the approach taken, the questions and activities chosen by the students could be the following:

Group One: Food

a) What do these people eat? Where does it come from?

b) How is food collected? Who collects it?

c) How is food prepared? Who prepares it?

d) Are there particular sex roles evident in how food is collected and prepared?

e) Are there traditions or customs related to eating or preparing food?

f) How are the people dependent on each other for obtaining and preparing food?

Write a hypothesis for each question and find out if your hypothesis is correct.

Presentation of conclusions:

- Make a menu.
- Prepare a meal.
- Draw pictures of the food.
- Draw a web diagram showing how food is related to jobs, roles, economic activities, religion, and so on.

Group Two: Shelter

a) What forms of shelter do they have?

b) What is used to make the shelters? Who provides the materials? Where do the materials come from?

c) How are shelters constructed? Who constructs them?

d) How is the shelter suited to the environment?

e) Who is responsible for making the shelter a home? In what ways is the shelter a home?

f) How are people dependent on each other for shelter?

Write a hypothesis for each question and find out if your hypothesis is correct.

Presentation of conclusions:

- Make a model of a house.
- Draw a chart showing how houses are built.
- Create a chart showing what adult and child males and females do in building or maintaining a home.
- Draw a web diagram showing how shelter is connected to jobs, sex roles, the environment, economic activities, and so on.

7. When students have completed their inquiries, collect their work, display it, and fill in the data-retrieval chart.

8. Ask questions that relate the various concepts to each other. ("What has climate got to do with dress?" "How is the transportation adapted to the environment?" "What part do religious beliefs play in education, daily life, etc.?" "How do male and female roles differ?" "What roles do children play?") Through this procedure, generalizations can be formulated (see Chapter 13). For instance, by noting how members of the culture have adapted to the environment and, in turn, have adapted the environment itself, your class might be able to form this generalization: "People adapt to their environment and adapt the environment to realize their needs." By noting how people are dependent on each other for basic needs, the students might develop a generalization about the interdependence of people.

9. Throughout the unit, compare the culture being studied to the students' own culture.

10. Generalizations about the culture being studied can be applied to new situations by asking hypothetical questions such as these: "What would happen if a new need or want arose in the culture?" "How would this affect how people adapted to, and adapted, their environment?" "How would this change people's way of life?" Relate changes to the students' own lives. For example, what changes occurred in their lives when they got a computer, a parent lost a job, or a new well was dug in their community?

11. Throughout the unit we need to think about how to evaluate student learning and whether students have met our objectives (Chapter 15). Groups of students might evaluate other groups by asking questions about the cultures studied and then commenting on the answers given and on the groups' displays and presentations. We also need to identify opportunities for integration. For example, do you know of any songs or folk tales from which students can learn something about musical and story forms in the culture? If so, have the students compare them with music and stories they know. Are there particular technologies used in the culture being studied that will introduce students to new ways of solving scientific or engineering problems?

12. As a grand finale, a culture fair could be held in which all student work is displayed. Here we might focus on some global education, human rights, and multicultural education objectives (see Chapters 19 and 20).

Activity 14-A

Create your own unit plan about life on a fur trading post in the 18th century. Try applying the framework outlined above.

DEVELOPING AN OUTLINE

1. Palisade/Main Gate

The current palisade has been reconstructed mostly to follow the line of the original, which was removed in the mid 1860s. The north wall actually lay a bit further north, closer to the existing railway line. The gates used to open for trade every day except Sunday, from 6 a.m. to noon and 1 p.m. to 6 p.m. The Indian Tradeshop was likely built into the north palisade line. This allowed the clerks to stay inside the fort while serving the shop's Salishan customers who came by river.

2. Bastions

Fort Langley had at least three bastions, one each at the fort's northwest and northeast corners and a third close to the southeast corner. Bastions were used as lookout stations and temporary housing. The Fraser River has always been an important transportation route for Aboriginal peoples long before it became a key link in the network of Hudson's Bay Company forts.

3. Blacksmith Shop

Taken down about 1918, an early blacksmith shop was located slightly north of the present building. The blacksmiths forged farm tools, building hardware and iron trade goods for both the fort and other trading posts that did not have blacksmiths.

4. Cooperage

Barrels were built in the cooperage to store and ship salmon, cranberries, farm produce and other goods. The original building, which was located slightly further north, was removed by the late 1860s.

5. Storehouse

The storehouse, built in the 1840s, is the only original building left on site. Used as a warehouse for most of the Hudson's Bay Company time period, it has also seen service as a cooperage, possibly a dwelling and later a barn. The building was renovated in the 1930s to stabilize the structure.

6. Theatre

Watch a video on Fort Langley's history in the theatre. A warehouse used to stand on this spot. Along with several other buildings, it provided storage for trade goods and provisions for the fort and those in the interior, as well as furs awaiting shipment to England.

7. Servants' Quarters

This building was constructed on the site of an original structure. It is believed to have been one of several used to house Hudson's Bay Company workers and their families.

8. Big House

Reconstructed for the 1958 centennial of British Columbia, the original Big House served as the fort's main office and residence of the chief trader, clerk and their families. Upstairs in the Big House, British Columbia was proclaimed a colony on November 19, 1858. The original building was replaced by a newer residence (later dismantled) in 1872.

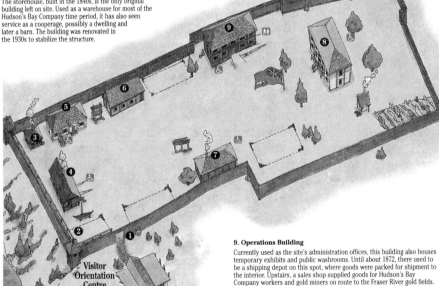

9. Operations Building

Currently used as the site's administration offices, this building also houses temporary exhibits and public washrooms. Until about 1872, there used to be a shipping depot on this spot, where goods were packed for shipment to the interior. Upstairs, a sales shop supplied goods for Hudson's Bay Company workers and gold miners on route to the Fraser River gold fields.

   ♿ **Wheelchair Entrance**

   ☎ **Telephone**

   🚻 **Washrooms**

Fort Langley

Topic: What was life like on a fur trading post in the 18th century?

Grade Level: 4 or 5

Choose your focus: A discipline, or an interdisciplinary phenomenon or issue

Choose your major objectives: Knowledge of information, information gathering and reporting, intellectual values, and social and personal values

Choose your organizer: Theme, concept, issue, inquiry, problem, project, or narrative

1. How would you motivate student interest in this question?

2. By referring to the pictures of Fort Langley, list the categories (concepts) that would be useful for organizing information. How would you get students to identify these concepts? (See Chapters 4 and 6.)

3. What questions need to be asked so that more information is collected about each category? (See Chapter 7.) How would you focus on the questions of significance, evidence, continuity and change, progress and decline, empathy and moral judgment, and agency? (See Chapter 10.)

4. How would students obtain answers to these questions? (See Chapters 8, 9, and 10.)

5. What resource materials would be needed? (See Chapter 16.)

6. How could students record their answers? (See Chapter 8.)

7. How would the data be organized so that generalizations are formulated and the topic question is answered? (See Chapter 13.)

8. How would you assess student learning? (See Chapter 15.)

What we have just done is incorporate concept development with inquiry methods and generalization development in order to write a broad outline for a unit plan. Our plan might take several weeks to implement, and it might involve a variety of teaching and learning techniques and resource materials. It may well include more than is outlined above, but we do have a valuable general framework. Here is an example using an inquiry format on Canadian agriculture:

Topic: Agriculture in Canada

Grade Level: 3 or 4

Focus: Geography

Major objectives: Knowledge of information, information gathering and reporting, and social values

Organizer: Inquiry

1. Introduce the topic by asking students where their food originates and which products they think are produced in Canada. Give students a list of what is grown and produced in Canada.

2. Have students look at a map of Canada and hypothesize where the various products are produced.

3. Divide the students into groups and have each group answer the following questions about agriculture in a given region:

   a) What type of agriculture is there in your region? Why is your region suitable for this type of agriculture?

   b) How is farming carried out? What is life like for the farmer and the farm family?

   c) How does agriculture contribute to the food you eat, to Canada, and to other countries?

4. Have students present their conclusions as an advertisement for their region's agriculture. Encourage them to try to persuade the class that their region is the most important.

5. Synthesize the advertisements, drawing students' attention to the relationships between climate, landform, and agriculture. Look at the similarities and differences between agriculture in the different regions, and compare the lives of farmers and their families from region to region. Draw out the relationships between farming and the food students eat and the contributions agriculture makes to Canadians.

6. Create a large map of Canada to locate various types of farming, and use string to link the origin of products to the students' location. Then, on a world map, link products to other countries that import them.

Story-Form Framework

There are other ways of constructing a unit. Here is one using Kieran Egan's story-telling format (see Chapter 5).[1] It is followed by an example where critical thinking is required.

   Topic: Native peoples of Canada

   Binary opposites: Survival and destruction

1. Begin with a vivid example of the concepts—tell a story of what would happen if buffalo could not be found before Plains people ran out of food, or depict the onset of an early winter for the Cree nation.

2. Link each aspect of the lives of Native peoples to the concepts: the importance of shelter as protection from the elements, the cycles of food gathering, and the impact of changes on these cycles. If there are survival relationships with other aspects of the cultures studied, they would be included here.

3. Introduce the impact of the Europeans. Show how, in many respects, the survival techniques of the Native peoples could not cope with European influences. Study the destruction of the Beothuk, and the residential schools that were designed to destroy Native cultures.

4. Show how Native peoples have met the challenge of survival and destruction.

5. Assess students on their understanding. Have them give examples of survival and destruction. Ask students to explain how the challenges of survival and destruction were and are now being met.

An Integrated Unit

Topic: Pioneers in western Canada

Grade level: 3–5

Focus: History

Major objectives: Students will use primary and secondary sources and literature to understand and empathize with the lives of pioneers in western Canada.

Organizer: Theme or survey

1. Using a story[2] or, if possible, real-life accounts of pioneer life that you often find in local museums and archives, have students trace the route of the chosen pioneers from their country of origin to western Canada. Calculate the distance and the time it took and estimate the average distance travelled per day. Compare this figure to today's travel time.

2. Discover the reasons for emigration and compare these reasons with why people immigrate to Canada today.

3. In a series of lessons, teach about life as a child of a pioneer family—the hardships, the lack of economic and political power, the joys when things went well, the building of communities, and so on. Focus on the details of daily life but relate these to the bigger concepts of adaptation and belonging. Here we can integrate some science and technology by making butter, some math by teaching about measures used at that time, art with quilting, and music by learning some folk songs of the time. And, of course, students will have to learn some geography. If we use a story we could compare it with the primary sources we use and discuss the plot line and characters from a literary standpoint.

4. As a finale, students could role-play a day in the life of a pioneer child, create a diary or a scrapbook, or develop a calendar showing the seasonal patterns of life.

Critical Thinking Activity

Topic: Who were the first people in North America and how did they get here?

Grade level: 7

Focus: History

Major objectives: Knowledge of information, information gathering and reporting, and intellectual standards

Organizer: Inquiry

Start by giving students two conflicting accounts of the arrival of the first people in North America. Ask how there could be such accounts and how the truth of the matter could be determined. Looking at a map of the world, have students suggest how people might have travelled here. Read to them the stories collected by anthropologists of First Nations people that tell of how they got here, and explain to students that anthropologists and archeologists try to answer different sorts of questions.[3] Depending on the abilities of the students, one of several approaches could be taken. If the information available is at too high a reading level for the students, then paraphrase the material and have each group look at one theory and make a chart showing the evidence for the theory and any counterevidence. If students can, have them read some of the material and create the chart. Then have each group present its theory to the rest of the class and begin the focus on the standards of weight of evidence, accuracy of evidence, corroboration of evidence, and whether the theory seems to fit into what else we know about how people travelled 10 000 or more years ago.

Have the class create a large chart of all the theories and have them make a hypothesis about which theory(ies) seem supportable.

Assess students on the basis of how well they collected the information on the various theories, how accurate their portrayal of the theory was, how well they judged the reliability of the author(s) (see Chapter 8), and how well they used the other intellectual standards (see the next chapter).

Activity 14-B

Obtain a unit plan. You can find them in journals, or your instructor or education library may have some unit plans on hand. Answer (at least) the following questions:

1. Are the objectives, content, instruction, and evaluation procedures congruent? Is each objective addressed in the teaching plan? Are students evaluated on each objective?

2. Is the sequence logical?

3. Do lessons focus specifically on the major concepts, or is it taken for granted that students will know what they mean?

4. Is there a variety of activities for students to carry out? Do these actively engage students?

5. Are there opportunities for students to work in groups? Is it assumed that students will know how to work in a group, or are there specific activities to help them do this?

6. What skills are students supposed to be able to display? Is it assumed that students will have these skills, or are there specific lessons to teach them?

7. What resource materials are required? Are these provided? If not, are they readily available?

8. Do you think the unit is worth teaching? Give your reasons.

OTHER ACTIVITIES

1. Take a textbook chapter or chapters and develop a unit plan outline where the organizer is a generalization.

2. Create a critical thinking unit on one of the following questions:

   a) How can we best find out about our local history?

   b) How can we best find out about how people in (a chosen place) live?

   c) Whose account of the Battle of the Plains of Abraham is most reliable—the French or the English?

NOTES

1. For a full account of this unit, see K. Egan, "Story forms and romantic perspectives: Alternative frameworks for planning in social studies," in R. Case and P. Clark, eds., *The Canadian Anthology of Social Studies* (Vancouver: Pacific Educational Press, 1999).

2. Two suitable stories are C. Parry, *Eleanora's Diary: The Journals of a Canadian Pioneer Girl* (Richmond Hill, Ont.: Scholastic, 1994), and C. Matas, *Footsteps in the Snow: The Red River Diary of Isobel Scott* (Markham, Ont.: Scholastic, 2002).

3. For the stories that the First Nations people tell about the first people in North America and how anthropologists and archeologists ask and try to answer different sorts of questions, see, J. Cruikshank, *Reading Voices: Oral and Written Interpretations of the Yukon's Past* (Vancouver: Douglas and McIntyre, 1991).

GLOSSARY OF KEY TERMS

Unit planning — deciding on the objectives, scope, sequence of lessons and activities, resources, teaching and learning activities, and assessment methods that are most suitable for the teaching of a given topic.

chapter fifteen

What Have Students Learned? Assessing and Evaluating Students

Although it is possible merely to measure and describe what students know and can do (assessment), we are also required to make judgments (evaluation). **Assessment** has to do with collecting data on student performance, and **evaluation** involves making judgments based on those data. In social studies, as in all subject areas, we need to know whether students are realizing curriculum objectives and how well they are achieving them. Information on students' strengths and weaknesses is needed for completing report cards, giving feedback to students, and making curriculum decisions. Assessment and evaluation, then, are ongoing processes in the classroom. Teachers frequently use **diagnostic assessments** as a means of establishing a baseline for teaching. We often observe students while they are engaged in an activity to ascertain how well they are performing. We use pre-tests to determine how much students already know, or can do, so that we can design our curriculum; we use post-tests to discover how successfully students have performed. We also want students to assess and evaluate their own progress. Thus, assessment and evaluation are key aspects in any teaching situation.

There are a number of ways evidence can be collected for evaluative purposes.[1] One of the most common is the test, whereby the student's score becomes the basis for evaluating that student. There are four basic ways of using test scores:

1. A student's score can be compared with a previous score.

2. Individual scores can be ranked from high to low.

3. A student's score can be compared using a **criterion reference** (e.g., a standard such as "Students should be able to correctly identify the latitude and longitude of places on the globe").

4. A student's score can be compared against a **norm reference**, such as an average score derived from administering the same test to other students. Standardized tests are an example of this type. Norms can be derived from various sizes of samples. Standardized tests may have provincial, national, or international norms.

The difference between a criterion and norm referenced test is demonstrated by a driving test. Here each individual is judged by his or her ability to perform certain tasks (criterion reference); whether he or she passes or fails is not based on how many other people pass or fail (norm reference).

Some situations allow us to choose the kind of assessment procedures we want to use, but sometimes others dictate the choice. If our school, district, or provincial ministry of education requires that we administer a particular test to our students, then we are contractually bound to do so.

When information has been collected, evaluations about the students' progress can be made. Suppose that student A scores 30 percent on the social studies test. Notice that this does not tell us a great deal about how well A is progressing. If the test was extremely difficult, for instance, this score might be exceptionally high. However, there is little doubt that the person who received such a score, or others who knew about the score, would conclude that this was not a good test result.

Suppose that A's score on the test is actually the lowest in the class and is below average in comparison with the provincial norm. Each of these comparisons of A's score implies an evaluation of A's progress. A's score is below the evaluative standard for each comparison group; therefore, A could be judged as not progressing well. However, perhaps A is working extremely hard and the score is a vast improvement over A's previous test result. In this case, a positive evaluation might be made, despite the low score on the test. What is important to note here is that an evaluation is, by definition, a judgment. This judgment is based on evidence, which in turn is based on value judgments about *what* information should be collected and *how* it should be collected. Thus, as teachers, we will decide on what bases students will be evaluated and what criteria we will use to evaluate them.

There are two types of criteria. One type specifies in descriptive terms what to look for. Examples of **descriptive criteria** could include these: students identify the latitude and longitude of major cities in Canada, or give three reasons for a position on an issue, or use three sources to find out about the foundation of the Hudson's Bay Company. But these criteria do not tell us what standards should be met. **Evaluative criteria** inform us that the latitude and longitude of major cities in Canada should be accurate, that the three reasons are plausible and well argued, and that the three sources are relevant and accurate. "Accurate," "plausible," "relevant," and "well argued" are evaluative terms. These are general evaluative terms that, when given more specificity, become standards. So, for example, the latitude and longitude should be accurate in degrees, minutes, and seconds; the three reasons must match those of an expert in the field. Standards are often based on **norm-referenced tests**; if a student scores 80 percent on the **standardized test**, then he or she has attained the standard of the top 10 percent of all students in Canada. If a student scores 85 percent on a classroom social studies test, then this might be B standard work.

In teaching students about criteria and in having them produce their *own* criteria for assessing their own and others' work, you might want to start off with descriptive criteria and introduce evaluative ones later on.

Before planning any assessment, we have to answer several questions:

1. On what should the student be assessed and evaluated: knowledge, skills, attitudes, dispositions, behaviour? (See Chapter 21 for a discussion of the evaluation of attitudes and dispositions.)

2. Why is it necessary to assess and evaluate the student on X?

3. Should *all* students be assessed and evaluated on X?

4. What is the best way of collecting information about X? Should the same information be collected from all students?

5. Who should collect the information: teachers, students, and/or outside agencies?

6. When will the information be collected: at the end of lessons, or units; daily, weekly, monthly, yearly?

7. How will results be recorded?

8. How will the results be used?

9. What criterion/criteria will be used to determine success?

Answers to these questions depend upon our conception of social studies. As was pointed out in Chapter 2, those who favour the Citizenship Transmission conception of social studies are likely to test for the acquisition of empirical information, using "objective" tests and ranking students on the basis of their performance. Those who hold the Reflective Inquiry conception are likely to assess student progress vis-à-vis previous performances and to test for more than the recall of specific information. Those who adhere to the Critical Reflective conception are likely to use portfolio and self-assessment methods.

Activity 15-A

What is your position on assessment and evaluation? Do you agree or disagree with the following statements? Why?

a) Students should be compared with each other on any given performance.

b) Students should be tested only on "objective" criteria.

c) Students should be assessed and evaluated on knowledge, skills, and attitudes.

d) Students should be assessed and evaluated on an individual basis—improvement vis-à-vis previous performances.

e) Students should be assessed and evaluated on the basis of results from tests that have Canadian norms.

f) Students should never be tested because tests cause anxiety.

g) Students should not be tested because tests examine only for low-level knowledge and are not objective.

h) Because parents want to know how well their child is doing in relation to other children, students should be ranked.

i) Students should be assessed and evaluated on the basis of informal observations and interviews.

j) Students should be assessed and evaluated on how they tackle a problem, not on whether they get a correct answer.

k) Test results should be used only to diagnose a student's strengths or weaknesses.

l) Test results should be used only to improve instruction and the curriculum.

Once decisions have been made about the purposes and nature of assessment, decisions concerning the methods are required. As pointed out previously, one of the most common is the test or quiz. These activities can take a variety of forms, each of which needs careful planning.

Activity 15-B

There is at least one thing wrong in the construction of each of the following test items. Note what is wrong and identify the type of test item used, i.e., multiple choice, true/false, etc. When you are done, turn to the Answers section.

1. Jacques _____ sailed up the _____ river and _____ the Native people.

2. Jean Chrétien
   a) was prime minister of Canada.
   b) wears glasses.
   c) was a good politician.
   d) Liberal.

3. Discuss pioneers.

4. The early explorers of Canada had to contend with disease, transport problems, lack of maps, hostile Native people, and difficult terrain. TRUE or FALSE?

5. Before contact with Europeans, the Native people ate
   a) spaghetti
   b) buffalo meat
   c) wild rice
   d) curry
   e) none of these
   f) all of these

6. Van Horne was born in _____.

7. Match a), b), and c) to the correct items on the left.

   _____ St. Lawrence River   a) a river in Canada

   _____ Ottawa   b) capital city of Canada

   _____ Yurt   c) a Mongolian house

The items in Activity 15-B all test for the recall of information. To assess students' acquisition of concepts requires us to pose questions that ask students to define terms, give examples of a term, and differentiate between a given term and other closely related ones. Here are some examples:

1. Give a definition of _____.
2. Use the term _____ correctly in a sentence.
3. From a list of definitions, select the one that correctly defines the term _____.
4. From the following list, select those that are examples of _____.
5. From the following pictures, identify the one that is an example of _____. For instance, which of the following is a picture of an island?

 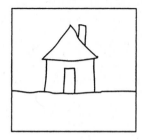 

6. From a number of examples, identify the concept.
7. Given a list of word pairs, identify the similarities and differences between the two terms in each pair, e.g., car/truck, nurse/doctor, farm/ranch, need/want.
8. Given a concept, identify examples and state what all the examples have in common, e.g., food, plant, continent, role.
9. Given a list of attributes, identify which ones are relevant to a given concept. For example: Law—
    a) Something you have to obey.
    b) Punishment occurs if you break it.
    c) Created by adults.
    d) Designed to protect people.
    e) Tells someone what should be done in a particular situation.
    f) Enforced by the police.
10. Make up a sentence in which the concept _____ is used.

Activity 15-C

Design a test for students at three different grade or age levels to determine their ability to define and use one of the following concepts: power, independence, sexism, prejudice. In your view, what would qualify as an adequate understanding of your chosen concept at each of the chosen grade or age levels?

To test for knowledge of generalizations and the ability to generalize, the following types of test items can be used.

1. Give students the following directions: Carefully study the generalization shown below. If any of the evidence below the generalization could be used to support it, indicate this by placing the letter Y (for "yes") opposite the statement. If the evidence does not support it, indicate this by placing the letter N (for "No") opposite the statement.

   Cultures change in varying degrees when they come into contact with another culture.

   a) The Native peoples of Canada were influenced by French and English fur traders.

   b) Some Australian Aborigines still maintain the same lifestyle that Aborigines practised a thousand years ago despite the influx of many Europeans.

   c) Many Inuit have replaced their dogsleds with snowmobiles.

   d) The first English settlers in Canada lived in ways to which they were accustomed.

2. Give students a number of similar cases or events and ask them to formulate a generalization:

   In place A, which relies solely on fishing, there is high unemployment during the non-fishing season.

   In place B, the mine is the major source of employment. In July, the mine was closed and heavy unemployment resulted.

   Place C is a lumber town. When lumber prices decreased, many workers were laid off.

   What generalization can be made about these three events?

Activity 15-D

Design a test item to assess student understanding of one of the following generalizations:

All families have rules.

Conflicts develop between individuals and groups when goals and expectations differ.

Contact between cultures brings changes in the social institutions within them.

Multiple choice, fill-in-the-blank, true/false, matching, short answer, and essay items can be used in a variety of testing contexts. For example, to test for the ability to draw inferences and think critically about information, we can use the following kinds of test items:[2]

Context: *Archeologists are excavating the site of an ancient Haida community on the Queen Charlotte Islands.*

1. The archeologists find a stone axe. One of them says, "The Haida knew how to make stone axes." Is the archeologist correct? Why or why not?

2. The archeologists know that the Haida made clothing out of cedar bark. They examine the trees in the area and find that only small strips of bark were taken from the trees. Why might this be done?

   a) Because cedar bark is not useful.

   b) Because taking too much would damage the tree.

   c) Because taking a lot would be too much to carry.

These kinds of items can also be used to assess students in other areas. For example, the following question is designed to find out whether or not students know where to locate information:

Question: *In which source would you look if you wanted weather information for Montreal today?*

a) an encyclopedia

b) today's newspaper

c) a magazine about Montreal

d) an atlas

To assess other intellectual standards you could use the following sorts of items:

Suppose you want to know whether an item in the newspaper is true. What would be the best way of finding out?

1. Look at two other newspapers and the TV news and see if they told the same story.

2. Phone the newspaper office and ask the reporter if his or her account is true.

3. Look at another newspaper and see if it gave the same information.

Suppose you want to know whether a crosswalk is needed to cross the street outside the school. What would be the best way of finding out?

1. Ask your classmates whether they think a crosswalk is needed.

2. Ask the teachers whether they think a crosswalk is needed.

3. Find out from the police whether there have been any accidents on the street when children were crossing.

4. Ask parents whether they think a crosswalk is needed.

Suppose you wanted to find out whether the first people got to North America across an ice-free corridor from Siberia about 10 000 years ago. What would be the best evidence that this theory may not be true? You may choose more than one answer. Pretend all the information below is true.

1. There is evidence of human beings in South America 20 000 years ago.

2. There was only a very narrow ice-free corridor 10 000 years ago.

3. Some spear points found in the eastern United States look like ones used by people in Europe 10 000 years ago.

There are several things to remember in test construction:

1. The purpose must be clear. What exactly is it we wish to test for?

2. The test items must match the purpose of the test. If we want to find out how well students can use inquiry procedures, one of the best means would be to give them an inquiry task and assess and evaluate their performance. This sort of performance measurement, or **authentic assessment**, evaluates the way(s) in which students tackle a particular problem, not just the results of the performance.

3. We must choose the most appropriate form of test (essay, multiple choice, etc.).

4. The questions should be clear and unambiguous.

5. If we wish to rank students, the test should contain questions that will differentiate between students at the high and low ends of the scale.

6. The test should be reliable; that is, if the test were given again, students should get about the same score as they obtained the first time.

7. We must have justifiable criteria for evaluating student answers.

Paper-and-pencil tests are one way of collecting information about students' performances. Another way is to observe students both in and out of the classroom. As teachers, we will be constantly observing students and making decisions on the basis of our observations. By collecting observational data in a formalized way, we will obtain more reliable data.

As with all assessments, decisions have to be made about the purposes of the observation, the method, and the timing. Observations can be carried out by time sampling, in which a sequence of behaviours is recorded (e.g., how a student acts in a given period of time), or by observing a particular event, such as the behaviour of a student in a discussion group. To record these data, we will need to keep checklists. These checklists may require a *yes* or *no* for the behaviour being recorded, or they may contain a rating scale, or a space for anecdotal comments. Checklists can be **quantitative** or **qualitative**. Here is an example:

Names of students	Uses card catalogue	Uses table of contents	Uses index	Uses internet

When a student is observed using the card catalogue, a check mark is put against the student's name (quantitative). You could also evaluate students' use of the card catalogue by rating their performances as *excellent*, *good*, *fair*, or *needs improvement* (qualitative).

The following type of checklist could be used if group work is to be evaluated:

	Alice	Ingrid	Lieh	Rashad	Rob
Expresses support for others					
Asks for information					
Gives help to others					
Encourages others to contribute					

When a rating scale is necessary, a checklist could be constructed as in the examples below:

Group Work

Name of student:

Enthusiastic	1	2	3	4	5	6	7	8	9	10	Unenthusiastic
Confident	1	2	3	4	5	6	7	8	9	10	Apprehensive
Responsive	1	2	3	4	5	6	7	8	9	10	Reticent
On task	1	2	3	4	5	6	7	8	9	10	Not on task
Cooperative	1	2	3	4	5	6	7	8	9	10	Uncooperative
Respectful	1	2	3	4	5	6	7	8	9	10	Disrespectful

Picture Studies

Rating Scale:

1 = can do this only with prompts

2 = can do this with few prompts

3 = can do this independently

Name of student	Accurately describes what is in the picture	Generates plausible inferences from the picture
Abby	3	2
Alice	2	3

Inquiry Checklist

	Good	Adequate	Causes concern: remedial action needed
Understanding the question	Knows what the question means. Can paraphrase the question.	Has adequate grasp of the concepts contained in the question.	Has insufficient understanding to make sense of the question.
Generating hypotheses	Can generate several plausible hypotheses.	Can generate one or two plausible hypotheses.	Generates no hypotheses or implausible ones.

To evaluate an oral presentation, the following chart could be used.[3]

	Excellent	Good	Adequate	Needs help
Content · is accurate · covers the main points · is detailed · is interesting				
Organization · effective introduction · logical sequence · effective ending				
Delivery · easily heard · looks at audience · expressive voice				

Activity 15-E

Design a checklist for a particular behaviour. Identify the specific behaviours you would observe and state why you think these are the crucial ones. State what your criteria would be for excellent performance.

These sorts of checklists, along with other techniques such as student–teacher interviews, can be used in "authentic" or performance assessment in which students are evaluated on the way(s) they perform a task. They can perform these tasks either on their own or in a group situation. During careful observation—listening to student discussion (in a group task), having students talk about what they are doing and why, and through teacher questioning—students can display what they are capable of doing in a "real" situation.[4] In a formal testing situation, students may not perform as well as they are able, so their results may not accurately reflect their competence. Although an authentic assessment tries to avoid these problems, it does have one drawback: it is time-consuming. Teachers in England who use it as part of the National Testing Program complain about the amount of time it takes and the amount of paperwork it entails.[5]

Each student should be encouraged to judge his or her own performance. If we want students to take responsibility for their learning, then we have to provide them with opportunities to evaluate their own performances. When given the chance to assess their strengths and weaknesses, students can begin to make their own decisions about what and how they should study. They can use a self-evaluation checklist like the following:

	All the time	Most of the time	Occasionally	Never
I listened to others				
I shared ideas				
I worked hard				

In all the above, **rubrics** were used to evaluate student performances. Case[6] provides guidelines for developing rubrics:

1. Brainstorm possible criteria.

2. Prioritize the criteria by selecting those that are most important and relevant for the purpose of the assignment.

3. Consolidate the criteria by organizing them around themes, e.g., reasoning ability, presentation, research skills, etc.

4. Establish levels by deciding how many would be appropriate. Is three enough? Would five be better?

5. Draft polar descriptors starting with what the highest and lowest levels of performance would look like.

6. Write the "in-between" intermediate descriptors.

7. Refine the rubric by checking to see if the descriptors are precise and mutually exclusive and that the levels are approximately equivalent.

8. Finalize the rubric and attach a weight to each criterion. Where appropriate, assign a grade for each level, e.g., if a student scores 9/10 on criterion one, 3/5 for criterion two, and 18/20 on criterion three, is the final mark of 30/35 worth an A+, an A–, or something else?

9. Pilot the rubric. Try it out on a sample assignment or have your peers critique it.

A great deal of information is needed to evaluate students thoroughly. Information can be collected from test results, observations, and interviews with the student. Especially useful in this regard is a **portfolio** that contains a comprehensive collection of the student's work, including written work, photographs of projects, audio or video recordings of presentations, and self-evaluations. All these items should be collected throughout the school year. For teachers, the portfolio provides a great deal of data on which to base evaluations and diagnose instructional weaknesses. In parent–teacher interviews, the portfolio provides a picture of the kind of work the student has done over time. Confidence is fostered when students know the objective for having a portfolio and have been helped to create one.[7] Students should be encouraged to select the work they wish to include in the portfolio. They should establish their goals and decide which pieces of work best reflect those goals. A self-assessment is also useful:

Portfolio topic: _____

The two pieces I selected for my portfolio are _____ and _____.

I chose them because _____.

I do well at _____.

I could improve in _____.

I intend to improve by _____.

Students might compare their portfolios with others' so that they can evaluate their own work. They can use the portfolio to report to teachers and parents/guardians. Students can also use it as a basis for developing a plan of action for future improvements.

Evaluating student progress is only one reason for collecting data. Another reason is to help us improve our instruction. If on the basis of test results we find that students are unable to answer certain questions, then we should ask ourselves why this is so. Was the content or skill beyond the students' capabilities? In this case, the curriculum needs to be changed. Was our instruction inadequate? If so, it should be improved. Was the test item ambiguous or badly worded? In this case, we need to write better test items. Whenever test results do not measure up to our expectations, we must question them, and question the accuracy of our own expectations.

Case[8] provides a set of criteria for evaluating assessments:

a) The assessment focuses on the important goal.

b) It provides valid indications of student ability.

c) It supports student learning.

d) It uses teacher time efficiently.

Assessing and evaluating students are complex tasks. What is assessed, how information is collected, what criteria are applied, what the purposes are for the assessment, and how results are used are questions that need careful consideration.

OTHER ACTIVITIES

1. Choosing a grade level for each objective below, design ways of assessing student performance based on the following objectives:

   a) The student should know the names of four continents.

   b) The student should understand the concept "interdependence."

   c) The student should use a map of Canada to locate Toronto.

   d) The student should work cooperatively in a group activity.

   e) The student should state what is unique about herself/himself and what characteristics she/he shares with others.

   f) The student should give an example of a case that would support this generalization: "Technological development contributes to the nature and extent of cultural change."

   g) Given a picture and a number of statements about the picture, the student should identify which are observation statements and which are inferences.

2. How would you find out whether students knew

   a) how to critically assess an advertisement in a newspaper?

   b) the events leading to the election of a provincial premier?

   c) how an Egyptian pyramid was built?

   d) how to use a video camera?

   e) how to conduct oneself on a field trip?

   f) how to behave in a discussion group?

NOTES

1. T. Fenwick and J. Parsons, "Nine modes that evaluate individual student learning in social studies," *Canadian Social Studies* 31:4 (1997), pp. 178–180.

2. Adapted from C. Bognar and W. Cassidy, *Social Studies in British Columbia: Technical Report of the 1989 Social Studies Assessment* (Victoria, BC: Assessment, Examinations and Reporting Branch of the Ministry of Education, 1991).

3. P. Clark, "Escaping the typical report trap: Learning to conduct research effectively," in R. Case and P. Clark, eds., *The Canadian Anthology of Social Studies* (Vancouver: Pacific Educational Press, 1999).

4. J. Myers, "Assessment and evaluation in social studies," in I. Wright and A. Sears, eds., *Trends and Issues in Canadian Social Studies* (Vancouver: Pacific Educational Press, 1997).

5. J. Clanchy, "Tests: The final straw," *The Observer: Schools Report* (May 16, 1993), pp. 3–6.

6. R. Case, "Principles of authentic assessment," in R. Case and P. Clark. eds., *The Canadian Anthology of Social Studies* (Vancouver: Pacific Educational Press, 1999), p. 407.

7. T. Fenwick and J. Parsons, "A note on using portfolios to assess learning," *Canadian Social Studies* 33:3 (1999), pp. 90–92.

8. R. Case, p. 396.

GLOSSARY OF KEY TERMS

Assessment — collecting data about student performance.

Authentic assessment — assessing students while they are actually engaged in a task, e.g., solving a problem.

Criterion reference — a standard against which a student is assessed, e.g., that the student can correctly identify the latitude and longitude of major cities in the world.

Descriptive criteria — what to look for in assessing a student's performance, e.g., that the student has written a paragraph or has used the internet to obtain information.

Diagnostic assessment — determining what students already know and can do, in order to plan or improve instruction.

Evaluation — making judgments on the basis of an assessment.

Evaluative criteria — the criteria that state what standards are to be met in a given performance, e.g., the student's paragraph is *coherent*, and the information obtained from the internet is *reliable* and *relevant* to the task at hand.

Norm-referenced test —a test where the standard (often numerical) is based on results from other assessments.

Portfolio — a collection of student work over time.

Qualitative checklists — checking how well a student exhibits a specific behaviour, e.g., using a rating scale.

Quantitative checklists — checking how many times a student exhibits a specific behaviour.

Rubric — a framework of criteria for ranking student performance.

Standardized test — a test where the norms are based on provincial, national, or international results.

WEBSITES FOR PART 2

Ancient Egypt

www.ancient-egypt.org/bib/pyramids.html
www.crystalinks.com/egypt.html
www.eyelid.co.uk/pyramid3.htm
www.guardians.net/egypt
http://homepages.tcp.co.uk/~nicholson/egypt.html
www.kingtutone.com
www.pbs.org/wgbh/nova/pyramid
http://pharoah.heavengames.com/egypt/history/pyramids/into/shtml
www.touregypt.net
http://users.eihost.com/ata/egypt.htm

Ancient Greece

www.ancientgreece.com
www.arwhead.com/Greeks
www.bbc.co.uk/schools/landmarks/ancientgreece/main_menu.shtml
www.historyforkids.org/learn/greeks
www.pbs.org/empires/thegreeks

Archeology

www.archaeologica.org

Archeology network:
archnet.uconn.edu

Cooperative Learning

A to Z Teacher Stuff Network:
www.atozteacherstuff.com/articles/cooperative.shtml

California Department of Education:
www.cde/gov/iasa/cooplmg2.html

Cooperative learning elementary activities:
204.184.214.251/coop/ecoopmain.html

Cooperative Learning Center:
www.co-operation.org

Cooperative Learning Network:
www.sheridance.on.ca/coop_learn/cooplm.htm

Instructional Strategies Online:
http://schools/sped.sk.ca/DE/PD/instr/strats/coop

University of New Brunswick cooperative learning modules:
http://cspace.unb.ca/nbco/pigs/modules

Critical Thinking Organizations

Critical thinking books and software:
www.criticalthinking.com

Critical Thinking Consortium, Richmond School Board, BC:
https://public.sd38.bc.ca/RTRWeb

Critical Thinking Cooperative, BC:
www.tc2.ca (in progress as of June 2004)

Ohio Center for Critical Thinking Instruction:
www.acorn.net/lists-ht/occti.htmlPhilosophy for Children:chss2.montclair.edu/ict

Richard Paul and Linder Elder's Critical Thinking consortium:
www.criticalthinking.org

University of Melbourne's critical thinking site:
www.philosophy.unimelb.edu.au/reason/critical

First Nations

Assembly of First Nations:
www.afn.ca

Indian Affairs Select Bibliography of Children's Books about Aboriginal Peoples for Ages 4–14:
www.ainc-inac.gc.ca/pr/lib/bib

McGill First Peoples' Library:
www.mcgill.ca/fph/library

Ministry of Indian and Northern Affairs Canada, Kids' Stop:
www.inac.gc.ca/ks

Geography

Geography resources:
www.ola.bc.ca/ou/links/g.html#geog

Discovery Channel:
www.school.discovery.com

Geoworld:
http://home.istar.ca/~whamilto

National Geographic:
www.nationalgeographic.com

History

Ancient Civilizations:
www.cuneiform.org

Canadian Children's Museum:
www.civilization.ca/mce_ccm/mce_ccne.asp

Canadian Heritage Information Network:
www.chin.gc.ca

Canadian museums:
www.virtualmuseum.ca

Canadian Museum of Civilization:
www.civilizations.ca

Eyewitness History through the Eyes of Those Who Lived it:
www.ibiscom.com

Historica:
www.histori.ca

History Channel:
www.historychannel.com

Memory Project:
www.thememoryproject.com

Parks Canada:
www.parkscanada.ca

The Vikings:
www.pbs.org/wgbh/nova/vikings
www.pastforward.co.uk/vikings
www.bbc.co.ca/history/ancient/vikings

Virtual Mueum of New France:
www.civilizations.ca/vmnf/vmnfe.asp

Women in world history:
womeninworldhistory.com

Women's History:
womenshistory.about.com
archnet.uconn.edu

Inquiry Learning

Inquiry learning:
www.thirteen.org/edonline/concept2class/month6

Inquiry Learning Forum:
http://ilf.crlt.indiana.ed

Inquiry page:
http://inquiry.uiuc.edu

Maps and Mapping

Atlas of Canada:
www.atlas.gc.ca

Canadian Geographic Map Maker:
www.canadiangeographic.ca/mapping

Houghton Mifflin Publishing:
www.eduplace.com/ss/ssmaps/index.html

Mapquest:
www.mapquest.com

Multimap, Online Maps from Everywhere:
http://uk2.multimap.com

National Geographic:
Plasma.nationalgeographic.com/mapmachine

Tom Snyder Productions, Neighborhood Map Making Machine:
www.teachtsp.com

University of Texas Collection of World Maps:
www.lib.utexas.edu/maps

US National Oceanographic and Atmospheric Administration:
www.ngdc.noaa.gov/seg/topo/global/shtml

Xerox Corporation:
mapweb.parc.Xerox.com/map

Yahoo:
maps.yahoo.com/py/maps.py

World History Charts

www.hyperhistory.com
www.historychart.com

Where's the Information? Obtaining, Analyzing, and Evaluating Information

Students need information, both print and visual, with which to test hypotheses, learn history and geography, and deal with social issues. Similarly, teachers will need information in order to teach a given topic. Although texts and other books suitable for elementary school children exist (see Chapter 5), you may find that schools don't have many resource materials, or that available resources are out of date or unsuitable on other grounds. Therefore, it is often necessary to locate recent information, much of which is "fugitive," that is, you won't find it all in libraries or even on the internet. It includes information published by museums, industries, government agencies, chambers of commerce, tourist bureaus, or private organizations. In this chapter, you will find out how to access some of these sources of information. What is included here is only a beginning. You should also be on the lookout for the many excellent materials that are available at the local level. In most cases, you will have to write a letter stating that you are a teacher requesting information for your class(es). Some organizations will send materials only to a school address, so, if you are a student teacher, you'll have to find a friendly school librarian or teacher to act as a go-between. And when you want to copy information from the internet for classroom use, make sure you do not violate copyright laws. This applies to all copying.

BIBLIOGRAPHIES

There are several useful bibliographies to which you should refer when looking for particular resource materials. Websites for some of these can be found at the end of this chapter.

- D. Ferguson, ed., *Children's Book Review* (Detroit: Thomson Gale, 2002).
- J. Gillespie, *Best Books for Children: Preschool through Grade 6* (Westport, Conn.: Bowker Greenwood, 2002).
- S. Peacock, ed., *Children's Literature Review* (Detroit: Thomson Gale, 2002).
- S. Egoff and J. Saltman, *The New Republic of Childhood: A Critical Guide to Canadian Children's Literature in English* (Don Mills, Ont.: Oxford University Press, 1990).
- R. Jones and J. Scott, *Canadian Children's Books: A Critical Guide to Authors and Illustrators* (Don Mills, Ont.: Oxford University Press, 2000).

Also check your library's reference section for other indexes, your province's curriculum guides for references, and teacher magazines for advertisements on recent publications.

SCHOOL BOARDS

School boards often have resource centres, and they also publish catalogues. Find out if your school district has such a centre, and locate the appropriate catalogue (each school should have one). To order materials, you must use an authorized form and request that the materials be sent to your school.

SCHOOL LIBRARIES

Libraries vary in quality and not all schools have them. Some contain not only books but also audio-visual resources (audiotapes, videotapes, pictures, and CDs) as well as files of newspaper clippings and other materials. Conduct a thorough search of the library and ask the librarian (where one is available) to help you. Often, on request, librarians will collect materials on a given topic and place them in a particular location so that students may use them.

TEACHERS' ORGANIZATIONS

These organizations often produce journals and newsletters and may have professional libraries. In British Columbia, the British Columbia Teachers' Federation also has a Lesson Aids Service.

MUSEUMS

Museums often provide services to schools: resource materials (pictures, booklets, and pamphlets), guided tours, and workshops for teachers and students. Contact your local museum(s) to discover what is offered and visit the Canadian museums website (see the websites section at the end of Part 2).

GOVERNMENT (FEDERAL, PROVINCIAL, AND LOCAL)

Governments produce a host of documents, some of which are suitable for elementary school use. Just be sure to contact the appropriate office. Useful government websites are listed at the end of each part of this book. A useful sourcebook is *Scott's Canadian Sourcebook* (Don Mills, Ont.: Southam Information Products Group, 2002). Provincial and foreign governments also have websites that can be located by keying in the name of the country or province in the Search box along with the words "and government."

TELEPHONE DIRECTORIES

These are a great source of information. Use them to find out the number of industries, businesses, and services in a particular area.

MAGAZINES AND JOURNALS

The list of magazines useful for social studies is huge. Only a few are highlighted here. For children, there are *Owl* and *Chickadee* (publications of the Young Naturalist Foundation), *Highlights for Children*, *National Geographic World*, and *Sesame Street*. For your own professional development, the Canadian journal for social studies is called *Canadian Social Studies*, formerly *The History and Social Science Teacher*. The journal is online, and you can access it at the address listed at the end of this chapter. Many provincial teachers' organizations have social studies professional groups that publish their own journals or newsletters. The North American social studies organization is the National Council for the Social Studies (NCSS). It publishes *Social Education, Social Studies and the Young Learner*, as well as bulletins, newsletters, and other publications that you receive as a member of the NCSS. Another journal is *The Social Studies* (available from Heldref Publications, 4000 Albermarle Street NW, Washington, DC 20016). Other teacher education journals also publish articles about social studies. These include *The Instructor*, *Educational Leadership*, *Child Education*, *Junior Education*, and *Young Children*.

EMBASSIES

Embassies often provide information to schools. Quantity and quality vary, so contact the embassy or local consulate (see the telephone directory) to discover what materials, if any, are available. To obtain materials about any country, conduct an internet search keying in the name of the country followed by an "and" with the category you wish to explore, e.g., Italy and tourism, Brazil and forestry.

TOURIST OFFICES

Each province has its own tourist agency that publishes advertising material. Some provinces produce high-quality booklets, brochures, and maps. Some towns and cities also produce tourist literature. Again, an internet search will disclose this information.

NEWSPAPERS

There is a wealth of information here. Have students collect information on current events and, where possible, on topics addressed in social studies. Try to obtain newspapers from the area under discussion. A list of websites is included at the end of this chapter.[1]

Here are a few ideas for using newspapers as a teaching and learning tool.

1. Look at advertisements. Have students prepare a list for a week's groceries for a family of three with a budget of $50 and $100. How easy or difficult is it to feed a family on these amounts?

2. Compare the same news story in two or more newspapers. How are they similar or different? Why? Trace the same news story over a period of time in several newspapers. Compare the amount of space devoted to the story, the headlines used, any evidence of a positive or negative bias, and a list of empirical and value claims. Decide which of these claims are supportable. Students could also compare two newspapers to ascertain how much space in each is devoted to different types of stories—crime, disasters, politics, etc.—and whether the newspapers report on the same major stories in similar ways. Editorials can also be compared. The same comparisons can be applied to radio and television news.

3. Read aloud a newspaper story about a particular event and have students make a picture of it. Compare pictures. Why are there differences? If a photograph was taken of the event, what might the photographer want to show? Would another photographer want to show the same thing? Why or why not? How could a photograph influence people to think in a certain way about an event?

4. Collect pictures of prominent people. Quiz students to check recognition.

5. Graph weather information.

6. Make up headlines for pictures. How could a headline influence how you feel while viewing the picture? How could the use of emotional words make a difference to your interpretation of the picture?

7. Make a class newspaper. Ask students to decide on the stories to be featured and the space that will be devoted to each. Have them give reasons for their choices.

8. Obtain newspapers from other countries and compare them. What is reported? How is a story about one's own country handled by the foreign press?

VIDEOTAPES, MOVIES, AND TELEVISION PROGRAMS

A useful source guide is *Bowker's Complete Video Directory* (New Providence, NJ: R.R. Bowker, LLC, 2002), which lists videotapes classified by country and by discipline (e.g., history, geography, sociology). The National Film Board of Canada has a website (see the end of this chapter) listing all its movies and videos.

Many excellent television programs can be found on the US Public Broadcasting System (PBS) and on The Learning Channel. The Canadian Broadcasting Corporation (CBC) often has programs that are useful in the context of the social studies. Recently, their *Canada: A People's History* series proved to be a great educational tool. If you tape any programs, make sure that you are not breaking copyright laws when you broadcast them in your classroom. As many schools are now wired for cable, you can take advantage of the services provided by Cable in the Classroom. This organization produces a quarterly publication that lists programs on a variety of networks. These programs can be taped and then used copyright-free in a classroom for at least a year. Programs are chosen by educators and then described and classified according to their subject matter; some come with lesson plans. Cable in the Classroom's website is listed at the end of this chapter.

SPEAKERS AND INTERVIEWS

Many organizations will provide speakers for schools. Contact the relevant agencies to ascertain if someone is available. Sometimes, you may wish to invite someone in the community to come and talk to your class, or you may have your students interview someone away from the classroom. Parents can often be a rich source of information. Interviewing people on a particular topic is a valuable activity for students. It can teach them how to structure questions, listen carefully, collect first-hand information, and interact responsibly with others. Students can improve their communication and social skills and won't be tempted to plagiarize from texts to get information. Their interviews can be interesting and revealing.

Interviews have to be planned carefully.[2] Students must have sufficient background information and must know the purpose of the interview and what questions to ask. Teachers have to set up the interview and ensure that the person being interviewed is suitable and will be comfortable with the sorts of questions students ask and with the way students record the responses (e.g., tape recorder, written notes). When the interview is over, students should thank the interviewee and then send a written letter of appreciation.

OTHER SOURCES OF FREE INFORMATION

Flyers, free magazines, pamphlets, mail-order catalogues, calendars from banks and businesses, newsletters, etc., can provide valuable information for social studies. So, collect and file all the materials you can. You'll be surprised at how much of it can be used.

VISUAL IMAGES

Pictures must be "read." Children have to note not only the major aspects but also the small items. Probably because of television viewing, children tend to skim pictures very quickly, failing to observe important details. Children will also tend to concentrate on what is important to them. As students are attuned to images, they can be used in many powerful ways.[3] A good idea when introducing a new topic is to place pictures around the classroom and use them to raise questions about the new topic. The following activities focus attention on how pictures can be used.

Activity 16-A

How could these pictures be used to teach social studies?

Where do you think the picture above was taken? What is happening?

Looking at the clothing and the ship, in what decade do you think this photo was taken?

The people are watching a ship carrying Canadian soldiers sailing from Vancouver. Given your estimate of the date of the photo, where might these soldiers be going? Check your response in the Answers section.

Walt Werner points out that visual images may be read in numerous ways.[4] Take another look at the picture of Bill Miner in Chapter 10. We can look at it through many different lenses:[5]

Empathetic   Here we would ask students to imagine how Miner felt as a prisoner. We could give students sentences to complete, such as, "If I were William Miner I would feel _____."

Narrative   Students would place the photo within the context of Miner's life.

Editorial   What is the photographer trying to say about Miner? Does she sympathize with this train robber? Is she trying to show him as a notorious criminal?

Instrumental   Here we would have students look at the details in the photo to learn something about Miner and his times. What is he wearing? What are his clothes made of? With other photos we can often make inferences about climate, the economy, people's lifestyles, and so on.

Iconic   Some photos have iconic status as they come to represent something significant in a culture. Although Bill Miner did not have the same status as Robin Hood, he did represent an outlaw who pulled off some daring train robberies and was regarded with a degree of awe by some people.

Oppositional and Evaluative   Students would look at other photos of Miner and compare the portrayals. They would judge the messages that they think the photographers were making.

Activity 16-B

Take a suitable photo in a social studies text or in this text, and pose questions in each of the above categories. Give your questions to a peer and have him or her answer them. Evaluate the responses and discuss your evaluation with the peer.

Werner also suggests that students consider the viewpoint of the image. Where is the viewer positioned and what effect does that have? For example, looking at Photo 5 in Chapter 6, we can imagine the different effect if the photographer had been standing off to one side. Images can also be rhetorical. Cartoons are a clear example. Sometimes, symbols can be used rhetorically. Can you find any photos in this text that you would consider symbolic? Sometimes images are shown in binary juxtaposition to display competing ideas such as old/new or developed/undeveloped. An example of this would be the placing of the photo of the classroom in Chapter 10 next to the photo of the classroom in Chapter 7. This intertextuality can be used with great effect. Witness the three photos of Vancouver in

Chapter 10. By placing them in a particular order, I am showing you changes that have occurred and asking you to consider these in terms of judging continuity and change. When you look at these images, how do they influence the way you read the printed text? Have students look at the images in the textbook before reading the text and ask them what they expect the text to say.

The captions are also important here. How does a caption affect the way we look at an image? What caption would you write for a given image? For example, the photo of the students in a classroom in China (Chapter 7) has elicited captions ranging from "Happy students" to "They only smile because they are told to." Have students write captions for a given image and share them. What are the similarities and differences, and what might be the causes of these? As with any caption, a picture can in itself have a powerful effect. It may persuade us to act in certain ways. Advertisements are a prime example here as they are meant to separate us from our money. But other images with other purposes can move us; witness photographs of Holocaust victims. We should help students reflect on the images they see. What are our reactions to the image? Why did an image move us? Was the image as we expected it to be?

The sorts of questions and ideas above are not meant to be applied to every image. Rather, we should introduce them when appropriate.

Activity 16-C

Select a particular topic you are likely to teach and locate five different resources: textbook, novel, video, newspaper article, magazine, etc. Choose one image and design an activity incorporating some of the ideas mentioned above.

COMPUTERS AND THE INTERNET

One of the most significant and problematic changes in social studies over the last 10 years has been the introduction of computers and digital technology, which are found in just about every elementary school and often in every classroom. They are ubiquitous in our lives and revolutionary in their applications. More and more, schools are being asked to ensure that students are technologically literate, and this usually translates into the use of computers in the classroom. Computers will not go away; as social studies teachers, we will have to critically examine their use and their impact not only in our classrooms but also on the world in general. What is at stake here?

There is debate about a number of concerns:[6]

1. Do computers help students think with ideas rather than with "mere" information? Does the weight of information that is now available, especially on the World Wide Web, prevent students from developing their own ideas? On the other hand, does it help students build frameworks for solving problems and organizing information?

2. Does computer use inhibit face-to-face interaction in the classroom? Will computer use reduce the development of social skills?

3. Does computer use diminish the teacher–student relationship, with students now relating to a machine rather than the teacher?

4. Will the computer help the at-risk and special needs student, or will it be used more for the average student?

5. Do computers really help students collect information from a variety of sources so that they can begin to grapple with contradictory evidence?

6. Is the ease of obtaining information from the internet turning students into mindless information gatherers?

7. Will computer use mean that "old-fashioned" writing will disappear from the curriculum?

8. Will reading information with flashy graphics and video clips from the computer screen mean that students will not read other texts?

9. Will computer use broaden the gaps between the rich and the poor? Between male and female? Between those who have home access to computers and those who do not?

10. Will the World Wide Web lead to information control by a few or increase the number of alternative perspectives?

11. Will students regard what they see on the screen as "the truth"?[7] We know that students view the textbook as a source of truth; will this belief now be transferred to information on the computer screen?

12. In a similar vein, will the computer promote the view that the individual is a detached observer acquiring objective information from the screen? Will the student fail to see the human interests that are bound up in what is available on the screen?

13. With the strong interest (especially by boys) in video games, many of which contain violence, will students themselves become more violent?

14. And with the amount of pornography on the web, what effect will this have on young minds? Should the web be censored? What do we as teachers do when, even inadvertently, students log onto a pornographic site?

15. Privacy issues also arise. How much do others know about us because we use email, log onto sites that post a cookie, use credit cards to make purchases or buy a service, and communicate in a chat room?

These questions need to be raised in classrooms. The computer is not benign. It is the product of human beings with their own agendas. We need to understand what these agendas are and critique them so that students become wise users of technology.

Research evidence suggests that students do learn via computer technology:[8] they are motivated to learn; their self-esteem may rise because they are in charge of their own learning; and they learn social skills such as taking turns and cooperating with others.[9] Teachers also find that they, too, have become more productive through computer use. They can store mark sheets, handouts, and quizzes; post assignment information and reference material;[10] and find information for their lessons.[11]

Computers were first used for running simple skill-building programs and for writing reports. Social studies teachers can use computers to enhance instruction in several basic ways.

Student Presentations

Students can create and edit their own writing and, if the software is available, use graphics and desktop publishing programs to produce their own reports. With the sophistication of these programs, text in multiple styles and sizes, graphs, and pictures can be incorporated into stylish presentations. I have found, however, that students using these computer resources are likely to spend far more time on the *style* rather than the *substance* of a presentation. However, some research suggests that students learn to write better on the computer than they do through more conventional ways.[12]

There are hundreds of programs available for use as instructional resources. A useful guide, even though it is a bit dated now, is *Education Software Institute 1998 Resource Guide* (Omaha, Nebr.: The Institute, 1998). As there are so many programs on the market now, the best ways of finding out what is available is through the school library or district resource centre, and through reviews in teacher journals.

Tutorials

Tutorials are designed to present factual information and to teach rules, principles, and problem-solving strategies. The usual format of these programs is 1) an introduction to outline the objectives; 2) the presentation of information; and 3) the posing of a question, which if answered correctly, allows the student to proceed to the next lesson. The student can enter or exit these programs at any point. There are also drill programs that provide repeated practice in learning a specific rule, skill, or set of facts. Research evidence[13] suggests that computer-based instruction holds a very small advantage over other methods in the teaching of particular knowledge and skills. This evidence, however, is based on numerous studies whose points of reference may not be comparable. Because students learn in different ways and computer programs tend to vary in quality, it should not be assumed that computer-based instruction is always more effective than other means of instruction.

CD-ROMs

CD-ROMs can store encyclopedias and allow students to listen to famous speeches, music, and animal sounds to augment text and pictures. Students can also use links to connect bits of information. Here are some sample CD-ROMS that teachers have found useful:

- *Cabot: The Discovery of the New World* (1997). National Research Council of Canada. St John's: Media Touch Technologies Inc.
- *Canada's Visual History* (1994). National Film Board of Canada.
- *Canadian Encyclopedia* (1998). Toronto: McClelland & Stewart.
- *Canadian Geographic Explorer Kit* (1996). Royal Canadian Geographical Society. IQ Media Holdings Corporation.
- *Canadian Visual Images* (1996). Edmonton: Arnold Publishing.
- *Egypt and the Fertile Crescent* (1995).Washington, DC: National Geographic Society.
- *Geobee Challenge* (1997). Washington, DC: National Geographic Society.
- *Greece and Rome* (1996). Washington, DC: National Geographic Society.
- *India and China* (1996).Washington, DC: National Geographic Society.
- *John Cabot* (1997). St John's: Media Touch.
- *Klondike Gold: An Interactive History* (1996). Whitehorse: Hyperborean Productions; Vancouver: Multimedia Corporation.
- *Maya Quest* (1995). Minneapolis: MECC.

- *The Metis* (2000). Gabriel Dumont Institute. Edmonton: Arnold Multimedia: Department of Canadian Heritage.
- *Parliament Hill: An Interactive Tour* (1997). Sydney, NS: Voyageur Interactive Technologies.
- *The Peopling of Atlantic Canada* (2001). Sydney, NS: Folkus Atlantic Productions (www.folkus.com).[14]
- *World Fit for Children* (2002). Ottawa: Health Canada.

Simulations and Games   Some of the most popular programs are simulations and games. These include simulations of how particular things "work," e.g., how a glacier is formed and how it moves, and games such as *Battleships* and simulation games. Some recommended computer games include the following:

- *Crosscountry Canada*—for Grades 4 and above. In the role of a truck driver, students learn about the geography of the areas in which they make their deliveries. Available from Didatech, Burnaby, BC.
- *SimCity. The original city simulation* (1995). Irvine, Calif.: Interplay Productions.
- *My City: What Would You Change If You Were Mayor?* (1997). Toronto: McGraw-Hill Ryerson.

Photo CDs   Using photo CDs,[15] students can store, view, and print pictures for their presentations.

Database Programs

Students can use **database programs** to obtain information. With some programs, such as *PC Globe* or *World Atlas for Macintosh*, they can manipulate data to create their own graphs and charts.[16] Given that much statistical information in textbooks is out of date, database programs are an important source of current information.

Email

Computers can also be used for intercommunication, and even as the means for a modern version of pen pals. Through electronic mail, your students can communicate with students in other locations and trade information for the price of an internet connection. Classes have exchanged information with students in other countries and have produced virtual comparative textbooks.[17]

The World Wide Web

Probably the most significant use of computers is obtaining information from the web. With a modem, students have at their fingertips more information than they will ever need. We can put this to good use through WebQuests. Milson and Downey[18] define these as "inquiry oriented activity in which most or all of the information used by learners is drawn from the Internet." To facilitate a WebQuest, we would identify the websites to be used in a particular inquiry and create a website page that would consist of the following: an introduction containing the key background information and the question(s); an outline of what students are expected to do; the process(es) they are expected to use and a list of the resources; an explanation of how students are to be evaluated; and finally, a statement of the goals of the inquiry and any additional investigations students might carry out.[19]

Search engines, such as Yahoo, Altavista, and Google, allow us and students to enter a search word to discover information that relates to that term. For example, entering <Pyramids and Egypt> using the Yahoo search engine produced this list (only the first 10 results are listed here):

- Pyramids: The Inside Story
- Egypt: Construction of the Egyptian Pyramids
- Egyptian Mysteries
- Egypt Pyramids Pharaohs Hieroglyphs—Mark Millmore's Ancient...
- Egypt Pyramid Index
- Photographs of Egypt—Photographic Images of Ancient Egypt
- Cyber Journey to Egypt—Guardian's Egypt
- King Tut One
- The Ancient Egypt Bibliography—Pyramids
- Pharaoh Heaven—Egypt/History/Pyramids

Activity 16-D

Look at the list above and, on the basis of reading what is presented here, hypothesize which sites are likely to be useful for upper-intermediate students who are studying how the pyramids were constructed. Then look at the Answers section to find out what these sites contain.

The majority of references on the internet are not categorized or evaluated, and students have to search through the list to find what they want to know, without the benefit of a teacher's asking them whether the information they are using is reliable. At least with textbooks, there is careful attention to standards of accuracy; not so on all websites. So students have to be disposed to ask critical questions about the information and know what criteria to use to judge the truthfulness of the information they are reading. Below, you will find questions that you and your students should ask about a website.

For both students and teachers, there is a plethora of useful websites. Some are transient; others will stay around. Websites that my students have found useful are listed at the end of this chapter.

Students have to be taught how to use the internet. Although browsing can be fun, we (or librarians) have to teach students how to use search engines and the logic required to locate information efficiently (e.g., using "and," "or," "not"). We can also search out websites for student use and bookmark them for easy reference.

Although it is clearly advantageous to have a vast range of resources, it is always important to evaluate them before they are used. Below is a list of factors that should be taken into consideration when choosing a website for student use. Students should also be encouraged to ask many of the same questions:[20]

- When was the website produced and how often is it updated?
- Who are the authors and what are their qualifications?
- Who is sponsoring the website and what impact does this have on its content?
- What is the purpose of the site and who is the intended audience?
- How easy is it to gain access to the website and to navigate it?
- Are there links to other sites and can these be accessed easily?
- Is additional software required to use the site and is this provided?
- What level of ability (reading comprehension, technical knowledge) is required to obtain information from the website?
- Has the site been evaluated by any external agency and, if so, how is it rated?
- What are the strengths and weaknesses of the website?
- Is the reading level suitable?
- Are the pictorial items clear and bright?
- Is the print size appropriate?
- Are the index and glossaries useful?
- Is the information accurate and up to date?
- Is the information biased in an inappropriate way?
- Is the information logically sequenced?
- Is the information representative of the topic?
- Is the language even subtly sexist or racist?
- Are any stereotypes presented? For example, are females shown pursuing activities that were once male-dominated as well as those that have been traditionally female-dominated?
- How are seniors, children, and disabled people portrayed?
- If there are student activities, are they appropriate?
- Is the material interesting?
- Do students have the necessary prerequisite knowledge and skills to use the material?
- Can students with differing abilities use the materials?
- Is the material easily accessible?
- How easy is it to navigate the material?

Activity 16-E

Locate a website that you think would be useful in your teaching and evaluate it using the questions listed above.

USING GRAPHS AND SURVEYS

Teachers using either expository or inquiry methods to teach history or geography can make good use of graphs and survey information. Students can also use graphs to present what they have learned and can carry out surveys to ascertain answers to questions.

If you look at nearly any newspaper or textbook, you will find graphs. Because graphs can display a great deal of information in a more understandable form than a list of numbers, they are important tools in social studies (e.g., young children can "see" how big numbers are and can "see" relationships among sets of data).

Block Graphs

The simplest form of graph is a **block graph**. Young children can actually construct these graphs by using objects like wooden blocks or coloured stickers. For example, if you were to graph the information about pets discussed in Chapter 17, your graph could show Grade 1's most popular pets.

Number of Students

5		
4		
3		
2		
1		
Cats	Dogs	Rabbits

Most Popular Pets in Grade 1

Another way of building the graph is to use student names. Here is an example using the same popular pet information:

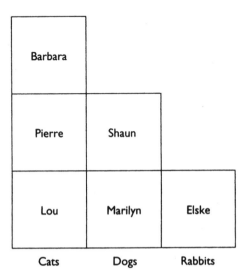

Barbara		
Pierre	Shaun	
Lou	Marilyn	Elske
Cats	Dogs	Rabbits

Student Choices of Most Popular Pets in Grade 1

Once students can make graphs and use equal intervals, they can draw the intervals or measures on graph paper with large squares.

Activity 16-F

In a group, have each member draw a graph based on the following information, each using a different scale on the population figure axis. What different impressions do you get with the different scales? If there is a large interval, do the differences between the cities seem larger than when the interval is smaller? How could advertisers or others use graphs to influence your beliefs and attitudes?

Population of metropolitan areas, 2002 (to nearest thousand):

St. John's	177 200
Halifax	363 200
Montreal	3 548 800
Toronto	5 029 900
Winnipeg	685 500
Regina	197 000
Edmonton	967 200
Vancouver	2 122 700

Line Graphs

When children can "read" points on a line, **line graphs** can be introduced. The same information on a block graph can be used to show how a line graph is constructed. Here is an example using the popular pet data:

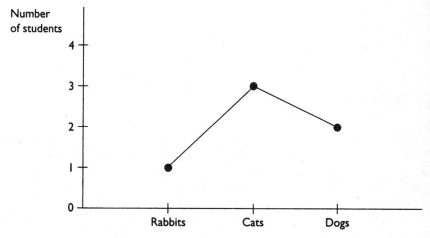

Most Popular Pets in Grade 1

Once students can construct graphs (this can be done by integration with math lessons), they can learn to interpret them. Interpretation involves translating (reading) the data, as well as using data to draw inferences and create hypotheses, which can then be checked by recourse to other information.

Activity 16-G

Interpret this graph:

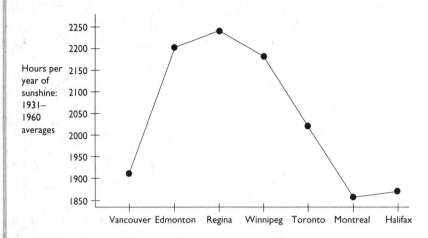

a) Which city has the most hours of sunshine per year?

b) Which city has the fewest hours of sunshine per year?

c) What is the difference in hours of sunshine between Montreal and Regina?

d) What factors account for Regina having the most hours of sunshine?

e) What accounts for Montreal having the least hours of sunshine?

f) If 1960–1993 averages were graphed, do you think the graph would be different from the one above?

Graphs can be created using any numerical data—temperatures in various cities in Canada, favourite television shows of the class, population figures, results of traffic surveys, different kinds of products in a supermarket, and so on.

Circle Graphs

Circle graphs are the most complicated for children to comprehend, as they must first understand angles in a circle. Once they can comprehend the clock face, they may be able to construct simple circle graphs, but more complicated ones have to be left until the intermediate grades. A simple circle graph might consist of information about how children spend their time in a 12-hour period between 8:00 a.m and 8:00 p.m.

Complex circle graphs may involve showing percentages. If this is done, children have to divide a 360° circle into 100 parts. Because this is fairly complex, it has to be left until ratio skills are mastered.

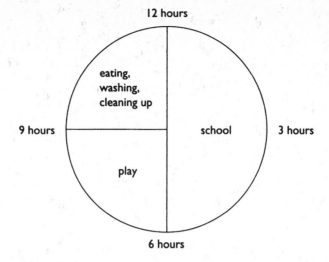

Opinion Surveys

Opinion surveys are not only an important source of existing information but also a means of finding out new information. Surveys are used to discover people's opinions, beliefs, or knowledge about a particular topic. Suppose you wanted to find out what your peers' attitudes are toward the teaching of social studies in the elementary school. First, you would have to determine what question(s) to ask. Respondents could be asked an open-ended question, such as "How do you feel about teaching social studies?" Or they could be asked to choose from a list: "I feel _____ about teaching social studies."

happy	*nervous*	*frightened*	*confident*

Another format that could be used is a scale.

	Strongly agree	Agree	Undecided	Disagree	Strongly disagree
I feel confident about teaching social studies.					

Once the question(s) have been posed and are judged to be clear and unambiguous, then you have to decide how to conduct the survey. This could be done by conducting individual interviews or by using a questionnaire. In both cases, you have to decide who is to be surveyed. If there are only a small number of potential respondents available, everyone could be questioned. However, if the population is large, you'll have to use a sample. To choose a *random* sample, you can put all the names of potential respondents in a hat and draw out as many names as you think feasible to survey. You might also wish to find out information about the persons surveyed. For example, age might be important, or gender, or whether respondents are in the first, second, third, or fourth year of university. Once you have determined what demographic data you require, then you can conduct the survey, collect and classify the responses, and interpret the results.

Activity 16-H

Conduct a survey to determine the favourite TV show, movie, book, or hobby of your peers. Design a questionnaire and collect, graph, and interpret the results. Design your survey to answer the following questions:

a) Do males and females differ in their preferences? Can you explain the difference or similarity?

b) Is age a significant variable in explaining preferences? Why or why not?

Do you think the results are representative of people who share the same characteristics as you (that is, as a pre-service or practising teacher)? Why or why not? How would you find out?

When students are conducting surveys, they should learn how to make sure that questions are understandable and do not contain ambiguous words like "some" and "many." They should divide complex questions into smaller, more specific ones and decide the best way of obtaining responses. After conducting the survey, they should interpret the results. Make sure that students recognize the limits of their data. For example, ensure that they understand that people who volunteered to fill out their survey forms do not represent the entire population of their community, or even of their school.

Activity 16-I

Design a lesson plan to teach students how to conduct a survey. State what the survey question would be. Describe how you would get students to design a questionnaire, carry out the survey, tabulate the data, and interpret the results.

OTHER ACTIVITIES

1. Select a book, movie, videotape, or instructional software program. Evaluate it using the questions discussed in this chapter. Is the material suitable for your purposes?

2. Select a series of visual images about one person, place, or event. Using the categories suggested by Werner, pose a number of questions that relate the images to each other. For example, if there are two pictures of the same person, then ask questions such as these: How do the images differ? How are they the same? What might account for the differences? What is the image maker trying to say in each image?

3. Locate an appropriate governmental or non-governmental organization in your area, and collect whatever information it has that would be useful in your teaching. Evaluate this information using the questions previously listed.

NOTES

1. For a list of specific sites, see D. Hicks and E. Ewing, "Bringing the world into the classroom with online global newspapers," *Social Education* 67:3 (2003), 134–139.

2. A. Sears, "Enriching social studies through interviews," *History and Social Science Teacher* 25:2 (1990), pp. 95–98.

3. P. Clark, "Training the eye of the beholder: Using visual resources thoughtfully," in R. Case and P. Clark, eds., *The Canadian Anthology of Social Studies* (Vancouver: Pacific Educational Press, 1997).

4. W. Werner, "Towards visual literacy," in A. Sears and I. Wright, eds., *Challenges and Prospects for Canadian Social Studies* (Vancouver: Pacific Educational Press, 2004). Also see W. Werner, "Reading visual texts," *Theory and Research in Social Education* 30:3 (2002), pp. 401–428.

5. W. Werner, "Towards visual literacy."

6. R. Pahl, "Digital technology and the social studies," in B. Massialas and R. Allen, eds., *Critical Issues in Teaching Social Studies* (Belmont, Calif.: Wadsworth, 1996).

7. C. Luke, S. De Castell, and A. Luke, "Beyond criticism: The authority of the school text," *Curriculum Inquiry* 13:2 (1983), pp. 111–127.

8. S. Gibson and R. McKay, "How research on the use of computer technology can inform the work of social studies educators," *Canadian Social Studies* 35:2 (2001). www.quasar.ualberta.ca/css/Css_35_2/research_computers_technology.htm

9. R. Pahl. See also H. Smits, "Is there a legitimate 'Luddite' response to technology in the social studies?" *Canadian Social Studies* 35:2 (2001). www.quasar.ualberta.ca/css/Css_35_2/legitimate_luddite.htm, and J. Dale, "A case against the internet," *Canadian Social Studies* 35:2 (2001). www.quasar.ualberta.ca/css/Css_35_3/FTinternet_resources.htm

10. J. Eaton, "The social studies classroom on the eve of the cyber century," *Social Education* 63:3 (1999), pp. 139–141.

11. S. Gibson, "Integrating computer technology in the social studies: Possibilities and pitfalls," in R. Case and P. Clark, eds., *The Canadian Anthology of Social Studies* (Vancouver: Pacific Educational Press, 1999).

12. R. Pahl.

13. S. Alessi and S. Trollip, *Computer-Based Instruction: Methods and Development,* 2nd ed. (Englewood Cliffs, NJ: Prentice-Hall, 1991).

14. For a description of this CD, see G. Reynolds, "Making Canadian history more inclusive through the multi-media: The peopling of Atlantic Canada," *Canadian Social Studies* 36:1 (2001). www.quasar.ualberta.ca/css/CSS_36_1/ARpeopling_atlantic_Canada.htm

15. C. Jackson, "A note on photo CDs: A valuable resource for the classroom," *Canadian Social Studies* 30:1 (1995), pp. 28–29, 32.

16. H. Riggs, "Computer database activities in upper elementary school social studies," *History and Social Science Teacher* 25:3 (1990), pp. 145–150.

17. C. Risinger, "Instructional strategies for the World Wide Web," *Social Education* 62:2 (1998), pp. 110–111.

18. A. Milson and P. Downey, "WebQuests: Using internet resources for cooperative inquiry," *Social Education* 65:3 (2001), p. 144. Also see P. Molebash and B. Dodge, "Kickstarting inquiry with WebQuests and web inquiry projects," *Social Education* 67:3 (2003), pp. 158–162.

19. For an example of a WebQuest on ancient Greece, see C. Reid, R. Labonne, and S. Gibson, "Engaging students in problem solving using a Webquest," *Canadian Social Studies* 35:2 (2001). www.quasar.ualberta.ca/css/Css_35_2/engaging_students_webquest.htm

20. Note that the evaluative questions posed about textbooks in Chapter 5 are also of concern here. For a comprehensive list of evaluative criteria, see http://schooldiscovery.com/schrockguide/evalelem.html.

GLOSSARY OF KEY TERMS

Block graph — data displayed in plane or three-dimensional shapes, usually squares, rectangles, or cubes.

Circle graph — data displayed as segments of a circle.

Database programs — computer programs containing factual information, especially maps and statistics, that can be manipulated to create charts, graphs, etc.

Line graph — data displayed in line form.

WebQuest — an inquiry activity where all or most of the information is from internet sources.

WEBSITES FOR PART 3

Bibliographies

Canadian Children's Book Centre:
www.bookcentre.ca

Canadian Materials:
www.umanitoba.ca/cm/index.html

National Library of Canada:
www.nlc-bnc.ca

Reviews of Children's Books:
www.Friend.ly.Net/scoop

Saskatoon Public Library–How Novel! Canadian Young Adult Literature:
www.publib.saskatoon.sk.ca/kids.html

Email Links

Intercultural Email Classroom:
www.iecc.org

Journals

Canadian Social Studies:
www.quasar.ualberta.ca/css/

Lesson Plans

Alberta Social Studies Council:
www.socialstudies.ab.ca

BC Teachers' Association Lesson Plans:
www.bctf.bc.ca/LessonAids

Canadian Social Studies Lesson Plans:
www.canadaonline.about.com/cs/socialstudies/index.htm

Canadian Social Studies Supersite:
www.ualberta.ca/~jkirman

CanTeach:
www.canteach.ca/elementary/canada.html

Community Learning Network:
www.cln.org

Historica:
www.histori.ca/teachers

Nova Scotia Social Studies Teachers' Association:
http://ssta.ednet.ns.ca

Ontario Association for Geographic and Environmental Education:
http://oagee.org

Ontario History and Social Sciences Teachers' Association:
www.ohassta.org

SchoolNet:
www.schoolnet.ca

Social Studies Lesson Plans:
www.usask.ca/education/ideas/tplan/sslp/sslp.htm

Telus Resources:
http://2learn.ca

Media

Cable in the Classroom:
www.cableducation.ca

Canadian Broadcasting Corporation:
www.cbc.ca

CBC Newsworld:
www.newsworld.cbc.ca

National Film Board of Canada:
www.nfb.ca

World newspapers:
www.ipl.org/div/news
www.onlinenewspapers.com

Social Studies Resources (General)

Discovery Channel:
www.discoveryschool.com

National Council for the Social Studies:
www.socialstudies.org

Social Studies Resources:
www.usask.ca/education/ideas/socstud.htm

Schoolnet:
www.schoolnet.ca

Yahoo's site for children:
www.yahooligans.com

What Are Values and What Have They Got to Do with Making Decisions in Social Studies?

VALUES IN DECISION MAKING

In Part 2, we were concerned with teaching concepts, empirical information, and intellectual standards. Throughout this discussion, decisions were made about what to teach, how to teach, what to evaluate students on and how we should carry this out, and what resource materials to use. Teaching requires that decisions be made about these matters, as well as about what rules of behaviour students should observe. We cannot avoid values in teaching; there is no such thing as value-free teaching or a value-free school. In Part 4, we focus on decision making and the social and personal values on which we base our decisions. As you will see in the activity below, value judgments cannot be avoided in decision making.

Activity 17-A

Read the following vignettes and decide whether the decision maker has made a good decision or a bad one. On the basis of your evaluations, identify the criteria that should be used to judge (and make) decisions.

A. I decided to buy this car. I can afford it. I need a car to get to work; the bus service where I live is terrible. According to the motoring column in the local newspaper, this car has the lowest gas consumption of all cars of its type on the market. It has all the accessories I want. It's a safe car to drive. It's my favourite colour. It has the latest pollution-control devices. Servicing will not be a problem, as there's a service centre three blocks away that specializes in repairing this type of car. And, being a sports car, it'll suit my lifestyle.

B. I've been offered a one-year teaching position in Nigeria. I've decided to accept it, as an immediate reply was required. I would love to go to Africa; here's my golden opportunity. I haven't discussed this with my wife, who is pregnant and hates hot weather, but I'm sure there'll be good medical facilities in Nigeria and she'll get used to the heat. Anyway, I'm sure she won't want to stay in Canada on her own for a year, and when I explain to her why I've accepted the position, I'm certain she'll understand.

C. I've decided not to introduce decision making to my Grade 2 students for a number of reasons. First, my students need to learn the basics, and decision making isn't part of the basics. Second, decision making is far too difficult for my students to grasp—they'll be incapable of understanding words like "alternative" or "consequence." Third, decision making always involves controversy. I don't want parents breathing down my neck or my students getting upset because there are no right answers. And fourth, I haven't got time to introduce something new into an already overcrowded curriculum.

The following criteria should be used for evaluating decisions:

1. The evidence used by the decision maker should be true or well confirmed.

   In Vignette C, for example, there is ample evidence to suggest that children in Grade 2 can understand the term "consequence." Thus, the contrary argument is not a reason that would support the decision. If the evidence used is suspect or false, then the decision may not be a good one. This is why we emphasized intellectual standards in Part 2.

2. The decision maker should consider all the relevant evidence.

   The decision maker in Vignette B has not considered other relevant evidence, such as housing in Nigeria, the cost of living, the salary he would receive, and especially the feelings of his wife.

3. The decision maker should consider all reasonable alternatives.

   In Vignette A, the decision maker might be faulted for not considering the use of a bicycle to get to work. By not considering all reasonable alternatives, the decision maker might ignore the best choice.

4. The decision maker should use concepts accurately.

   In Vignette C, it could be argued that the "basics," by definition, do include decision making. If the concepts involved in the decision are not used in an accurate way, then the decision may not be justifiable.

5. The decision maker should base his or her decisions on values that are justifiable.

   In Vignette A, the decision maker appears to have satisfied his/her personal values, having considered his/her own self-interest. In Vignette B, the teacher's lack of concern for his wife is not justifiable; he has not considered the well-being of another person.

In the above vignettes, the decision makers have made their decisions on the basis of certain values and preferences. While certain decisions can be based on preferences alone, in decision-making contexts where there are serious consequences for the decision maker and/or others, the consideration and justification of all relevant values and information are required. This is where critical thinking becomes so important.

WHAT ARE VALUES?

All values share some common characteristics. **Values** are "things" that are deemed to be of significant worth in a person's life. They guide and influence behaviour. For example, if wealth is valued, then actions are taken to obtain it. If people value political freedom, they may try to overthrow oppressive regimes. Often, when people are strongly committed to a value, they will make efforts to persuade others to accept it. Preferences, on the other hand, are expressions of taste. Unlike values, they need not be based on firm convictions, nor need they be necessarily justified. Usually, if I said that I preferred vanilla to chocolate ice cream, no justification would be necessary. (Can you think of a situation in which you would want someone to justify this preference?) On the other hand, if I said that I preferred you to act in a certain way, then it would be legitimate to ask for justification. Smoking is a clear case of personal taste becoming a social value issue. In Part 4, the focus is on values because they are significant in human affairs.

The values people hold can be expressed in three ways:

1. **Simple value statements:** X is good/ugly/efficient, etc.

2. **Comparative value statements:** X is better/worse/more beautiful, etc., than Y.

3. **Prescriptive value statements:** X ought to be done. People should do Y.

In justifying values, people formulate arguments in which some empirical claim about the value is linked to a value conclusion. For example, if we believe that students should learn about significant events in the history of Canada, then we may decide they should learn about Louis Riel and the 1885 resistance. Our decision, written in argument form, will look like this:

Value Premise (Standard): Students should learn about events in Canadian history that historians consider significant.

Empirical Premise: The 1885 resistance is an event in Canadian history that historians consider significant.

Value Conclusion: Therefore, students should learn about the 1885 resistance.

If we were asked why students should learn about events in Canadian history that historians consider significant, we might formulate another argument and appeal to another value. For example:

Value Premise (Standard): Students should learn whatever is required to foster good citizenship.

Empirical Premise: Learning about events in Canadian history that historians consider significant is required to foster good citizenship.

Value Conclusion: Therefore, students should learn about events in Canadian history that historians consider significant.

This type of argument—two premises that lead logically to a conclusion—is called a **syllogism**. It has the same form as the well-known argument below. Notice, however, that in the arguments above, the conclusion and the major premise are value judgments, whereas in the argument below, the conclusion is an empirical claim.

Major Premise: All persons are mortal.

Minor Premise: Socrates is a person.

Conclusion: Therefore, Socrates is mortal.

Activity 17-B

Fill in the conclusions for the following syllogisms. When you are through, refer to the Answers section.

1. **Value Premise (Standard):** Students should engage in activities that help them respect one another.

   Empirical Premise: Having students work in cooperative groups will help students respect one another.

   Value Conclusion: _____.

2. **Value Premise (standard):** Students at age nine should learn whatever mapping skills they are capable of learning.

   Empirical Premise: Students at age nine are capable of learning conventional map symbols.

   Value Conclusion: _____.

3. **Value Premise (Standard):** Students should come to understand whatever is necessary to become good citizens.

   Empirical Premise: Students have to understand the Canadian Charter of Rights and Freedoms to be good citizens.

   Value Conclusion: _____.

Good arguments are those in which conclusions follow logically from the premises, and the premises are believable or defensible. This is why the first part of the book is devoted to empirical and conceptual matters; value judgments are based on these matters. If the empirical claims are not supported, or if concepts are used inappropriately, then the value conclusions may not be justifiable.

Often, our value premises are not explicitly stated when we argue for something. We might argue that students should be engaged in group learning activities because this will encourage mutual respect, and simply take for granted that mutual respect is desirable. Or we might claim that students shouldn't damage school property because it's against the school rules, and merely assume that school rules should be obeyed. To justify the conclusion of a value argument, we must also be able to justify the value standard in the major premise. Note how important this discussion of arguments is when we are trying to justify what and how we teach, how we evaluate student learning, and how we expect students to behave.

People can be committed to a plethora of different values. They can value justice, wealth, pleasure, beauty, equality, physical health, salvation, antiques, and so on. Some of these will be **ultimate values** and some will be **instrumental values**. If one's "ultimate" value is personal pleasure, then collecting antiques may be "instrumental" in realizing this value. These values can be personal in that we accept them for ourselves. Examples would be persistence and intellectual curiosity. Social values are about others and include such values as respect and justice. Of course, what one accepts as a personal value can also be a social value. What is important to note is that different **types of values** demand different justifications.

In the decision-making vignettes at the beginning of this chapter, the teacher in Vignette B clearly valued his own interests over and above the needs and feelings of his wife. In this case, **moral values** (having to do with how people ought to be treated) were overridden by **prudential personal values** (having to do with self-interest). Simply put, moral values are *other-regarding*, whereas prudential values are *self-regarding*. Young children (and some older children as well as some adults) tend to confuse these two categories, using prudential arguments to justify a moral decision—it's OK to break the law so long as you don't get caught. In such cases decision makers use a prudential point of view when a moral one is clearly required.

I use the term **point of view** here to refer to the *kind* of value judgment being made, or the *kind* of reasons and value standards needed to justify them. Although the number of different points of view is a matter of debate, most experts in this area recognize the following points of view: **prudential**, **moral**, **religious**, **aesthetic**, **environmental**, and **intellectual** (those having to do with logic, reliability, and validity were discussed in Part 2 of this book). Many people now place environmental values in the moral category as they view what happens to flora and especially fauna as a moral matter. The decision maker in Vignette A has used the aesthetic, environmental, and prudential points of view. Notice that something can be judged negatively from one point of view and positively from another. As pointed out above, an action can be both prudentially acceptable and morally unacceptable.

There are hundreds of opportunities for students to make decisions and learn and practise critical thinking. When students are given a choice of which book they will read, or whom they will research, students have to make a decision. In any project where research is required, students could judge the quality of the resources they use not only on the basis of intellectual values such as accuracy and clarity, but also on aesthetic grounds, and then decide which resources are the best. In a study of Canada, students could decide which province they would like to live in, or which area of the country they would like to visit. In studies of ancient civilizations, students could decide which civilization made the greatest contribution to our way of life, or which artifact of a civilization was the most significant, or which civilization had the best human rights record or treated women or children in an acceptable manner. In studying explorers, students could decide which explorer was the greatest.[1]

WHY TEACH VALUES?

Both in and out of school, students make value judgments and act on them. They make judgments about environmental concerns; they judge actions according to their conceptions of fairness; they make choices as consumers; and they have conceptions of honesty, discrimination, justice, fairness, and so on. As they mature, they begin to make decisions and take actions within the political arena. Because the content of social studies is centred on people, moral values cannot be avoided in the classroom. How people are treated, and how they relate to their physical and social environments, are fundamentally moral concerns.

The fact that students make value judgments, however, does not mean that such judgments will be well considered. Just as we help students deal with empirical and conceptual matters, so we must help them grapple with the myriad value questions that impinge on their lives and foster the values that are part of the school mandate.

Activity 17-C

In your social studies curriculum guide, identify the values that are to be fostered. What sorts of values are there (moral, prudential, aesthetic, environmental, religious)?

Not everyone agrees that it is important to help students develop the abilities necessary to make defensible value judgments. Reasons advanced for *not* focusing on teaching values in schools include the following:

a) Students may not be comfortable with discussing certain sensitive values such as those concerned with sexuality.

b) Values taught in school may conflict with those taught at home.

c) Teachers may feel that they cannot raise certain value issues if the community has strongly entrenched views.

d) Teachers may try to indoctrinate students into accepting inappropriate values. Witness Jim Keegstra in Alberta, who for years taught that the Holocaust was a Jewish conspiracy.

e) Parents may feel that the role of the school is to teach "facts," not "values."

Therefore, we have to be diligent and think carefully before we introduce value issues into the classroom. However, as mentioned earlier, we cannot avoid values in our teaching, and we have a responsibility to help students develop those values required for responsible citizenship.

IDENTIFYING VALUES

How can we help students identify the values that they or others hold? One way is to use the following type of activity:

- What do you think is happening in the photo on the next page?
- How do you think this person feels?
- Would you feel this way if you were in this situation?
- Do you think the person likes feeling this way?
- What do you think is important to this person?

Create a chart to show responses. For example, someone feels happy about having a lot of money if having a lot of money is a value. Someone feels angry because of a lack of fairness, but only if fairness is held as a value. See the chart below:

FEELINGS	VALUES
happiness	wealth
anger	fairness

If you hold a particular value, do you feel positive about it? If you have a particular feeling, do you value it?

Feelings and values are linked. If we hold a value, then we have a positive feeling, but the reverse isn't necessarily true. We might have a feeling of anger, act on it, and then regret it because after reflecting on it we don't think that anger was the appropriate reaction in this situation. Our immediate feelings overrode our usual judgments about the justification for being angry and what constitutes defensible behaviour in such situations.

Other ways can be used to help students identify values. For example, we could ask students to analyze their classroom situation and identify what is important (e.g., respect, safety, learning, kindness, competition, etc.). We could use Values Clarification activities as outlined in the next chapter. Or we could ask explicitly what students value and compile a list of their values. If we decide to carry out this activity, we should be careful not to invade the students' right to privacy.

We could also use stories and have students identify the values that characters in the stories hold.

When studying cultural groups, students can note what values people have by inferring those values from what people do. Here, the focus should be on similarities, not differences. Rather than emphasizing the different ways people practise religious beliefs, we can focus on the way all cultures value some form of spirituality.

In using social studies textbooks, we can help students identify the values people hold or held: What motivated Canadian fur traders? Why did the English invade Quebec? Why did the French oppose the British?

TEACHING DECISION MAKING

When students have identified some of the values they hold and are aware of the values that should be considered in a particular decision-making situation, we should have them weigh the advantages and disadvantages of acting on any particular alternative. There are many opportunities in the social studies curriculum and in the daily interactions in the school for decision making. For example, many social studies curricula call for students to make decisions about community, provincial, Canadian, and international questions. In the classroom students may be called upon to help make rules, or in conflict resolution cases to decide how to resolve a problem (see the next chapter). The **decision-making procedure** has four steps:

1. Definition of the problem.

2. Identification of alternatives.

3. Identification and evaluation of the consequences of acting on each alternative.

4. Making a decision.

It should be noted that this is not a lock-step model. A decision maker may consider one alternative, decide that the consequences are unacceptable, and then consider another alternative until a desirable one is found.

In the first step, the decision-making situation is presented. This could be in print or pictorial form. It could arise from a current event or it could be an actual classroom or school situation. For example, what should the class do to celebrate Christmas or Hanukkah? How can fighting be stopped on the school playground? How should the class help starving children in Ethiopia? The situation has to be clarified so that students understand what the problem is. Terms may have to be defined and research may have to be carried out in order to comprehend the background to the problem.

To ensure that it is a *decision-making* situation, rather than one where a mere choice would suffice, the problem has to be significant in terms of curriculum content or to students in the class. Although the terms "choose" and "decide" are often used interchangeably, the term "decision making" will refer in this book only to significant contexts where substantial thought is required. The distinction between "choose" and "decide" can be noted in the following examples: The judge *chose* to sentence the accused to life imprisonment. The judge *decided* to sentence the accused to life imprisonment. In the second example, it is implied that the judge thought seriously before acting, whereas the first example could imply mere whim.

The second step involves the generation of alternative solutions. Sometimes there are only two alternatives, as in deciding whether to *tear down* or *renovate* a historical building, or deciding to do *something* rather than *nothing*. In other situations, there may be several alternatives, as shown in the Incinerator Simulation Game on pages 231–233.

Sometimes the alternatives will have to be generated by the decision makers. For example, if we ask students to make a decision about how to make the community a better place in which to live, it will be up to them to generate the alternatives.

In the third step, the consequences of each alternative are identified and evaluated. This will entail asking "What might happen if A is done?" and tracing possible consequences for both the short and long term. A good idea here is to use a web diagram showing the short-term and long-term consequences. For instance, if one possible solution for making the community a better place in which to live is the building of a swimming pool, the short-term consequence may be that people will be happier and jobs will be created, but in the long term taxes may be increased. In this case, a choice has to be made between community satisfaction and increased taxation. In the Incinerator Simulation Game on pages 231–233, a student may have put prudential values (e.g., NIMBY—Not In My Backyard) ahead of consideration for the well-being of the entire community.

The decision-making procedure is an extremely useful one in the study of current events. Students can identify the issues and conflicts that are germane to the event, find out what alternative courses of action are proposed, generate their own alternatives, determine what they think the consequences of acting on the various alternatives will be, and arrive at their own decisions. For example, students in schools in Vancouver are involved in making decisions about environmental issues and are taking practical actions to alleviate pollution and garbage problems. This type of action is discussed at greater length in the next chapter.

DECISION-MAKING LESSON PLAN

What would make the best pet for me?

Goals: Personal and social values

Strand: Interdisciplinary concern

Organizer: Problem

Objectives:

1. The students should arrive at a decision using the following procedure: a) define the problem, b) generate alternatives, c) identify the consequences of each alternative, d) evaluate the consequences.

2. Students should consider their own situations and the effects of their choices on others who live with them.

3. Students should give defensible reasons for their decisions.

Tell students that they are going to make a decision. Outline the problem by having students state what pets they have and what it is like to have them. Discuss the benefits of having pets and any problems there are—dogs attacking people, pets having to be looked after when the family goes away.

1. Identify the decision to be made by stating that there are many pets students could have, but which one would be best?

2. Students list the pets that they think are suitable. Where there is argument about whether a pet is suitable or not, the pet is left on the list so that students can eventually decide. Then, either individually or in groups, they research what each pet on the list will need in terms of food, exercise, space, medical care, and accessories, and the cost of these in

terms of time and money. The amount of detail and research required here will depend on the maturity of the students. They can consider their own family situations and make a chart showing the benefits and disadvantages of owning the pet they have initially chosen. The findings on each pet are then shared and a large chart is constructed showing the information collected. Questions are posed about the consequences of owning a pet. For example, if a disadvantage of owning a dog is that it might bite someone, then ask how that might be avoided. If the disadvantage of owning a cat is that there would be problems when the family went away, then ask whether a friend or neighbour might look after the cat. Each student decides on the best pet for himself or herself, and writes a sentence stating the reasons. Class results are then graphed (see Chapter 16).

If you are teaching primary school students, you may want to engage them in the following decision-making situation. Read this story to them or, if possible, have students read it for themselves.

> Geraldine is Alice's best friend. One day Alice forgets to bring her lunch to school, and although Geraldine shares her lunch with Alice, Alice is still hungry. She asks Michelle, who has four chocolate bars, if she can have one of them. Michelle says, "No, I want them." When Michelle isn't looking, Alice takes two chocolate bars. She goes back to Geraldine and says, "I took Michelle's chocolate. She's greedy. She doesn't need four chocolate bars. Don't tell anyone." Michelle notices that her chocolate bars are missing and tells the teacher. In class, the teacher says, "Someone has taken Michelle's chocolate bars. Does anyone know who took them?" Geraldine knows that Alice took them. Should she tell the teacher?

Now, ask the following questions:

1. "What is the problem?" (Students clarify the problem.)
2. "In what ways could the problem be solved?" (Students list the alternatives.)
3. "With each of the solutions, who is worst off?" "What sort of harm could occur to this person?" (Students discuss the answers.)
4. "If you were the worst-off person, would it be right for you to take the proposed action?" "What would be the consequences if everyone in a similar situation acted in this way?" (Students imagine the consequences and state what they are. Students then write down their own solutions and justify them.)

USING SIMULATION GAMES TO TEACH DECISION MAKING

One effective technique to help students begin to make responsible decisions is to have them play **simulation games**. Unlike games such as Twenty Questions or Word Bingo, simulations try to be as true to real-life events as possible. Although they cannot take the place of real situations, simulations offer students a safe environment where they can test solutions to problems, make decisions, and not suffer the actual consequences. Here is one simulation game in which students take on the role of a property owner and make a community decision.

Activity 17-D

Try the Incinerator Simulation Game in your class. On the map on the following page, designate a town lot for each member of the class. If there are fewer than 36 students, spread ownership over the entire map.

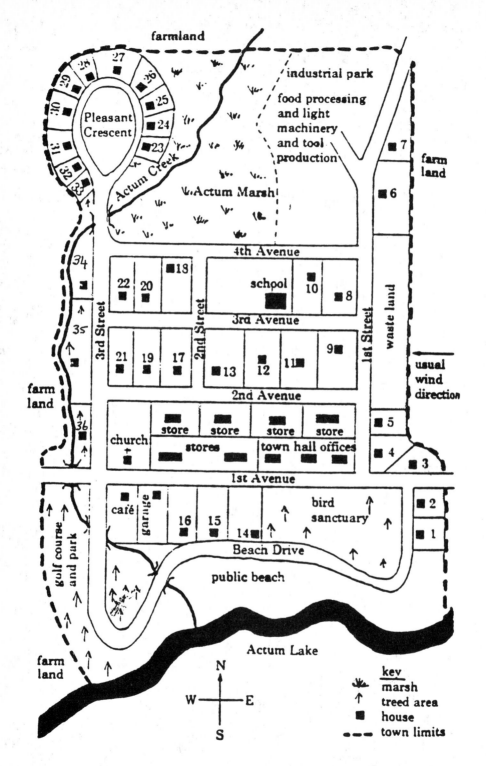

BACKGROUND: The town of Actum, a small tourist resort, has a garbage problem. All the landfill sites outside the town limits are full, and garbage must now be disposed of within the town limits. The town has been granted federal money to build a garbage incinerator. The incinerator will have a 20-m chimney and will take up space equivalent to one house lot. The problem is where, within the town limits, to locate the incinerator. As there is no alternative to garbage disposal, the incinerator *must* be built.

Each individual should choose a site for the incinerator. Then hold a town meeting and decide where to locate the incinerator.

The following questions should be asked on completion of this simulation:

1. What influenced your choice for the site of the incinerator (wind direction, aesthetics, transportation routes, proximity to houses, stores, parks, and farmland)? What values did you appeal to? What point(s) of view did you adopt? Did prudential concerns outweigh concerns for the well-being of the community? What values are likely to be in conflict in this situation? Should what is best for the entire community override an individual's prudential interests?

2. How did the town decide (voting, compromise, total agreement of all concerned, being "ordered" by someone)? Would you want all similar decisions to be made in the same way?

3. What is the best way to make such decisions? Is there any way such decisions can be made without disadvantaging someone? If we accept a democratic form of government, do we then have to accept the fact that we will not always have our wishes acted on?

4. If your choice was not accepted and the incinerator location is disadvantageous to you, how do you feel? As a member of a minority, could you do anything? Should you do something?

5. Should people get involved in planning their communities, or should they leave it to elected (or unelected) officials?

6. Do situations like this really occur? Where? How are they resolved?

Primary grade children can also play this game, but instead of a map use a model of the community. The children can actually *see* the incinerator and, by moving it to different sites, *see* the consequences of their decisions. The game can be adapted for different situations: where to locate a new swimming pool, industry, park, store, fire hall, community centre, ice rink, and so on.

There are some possible pitfalls in the use of simulation games. If competition will win the game, then discussion should ensue on the justification for this. If the game is oversimplified, then students might get the impression that solutions are easy. If students can win by doing something immoral (such as taking resources away from another player), this should also be discussed. In simulations that involve role-playing, students may not take their roles seriously. And, as alluded to above, there may be discipline problems or occasions when there is a great deal of emotion involved; these situations will need defusing. However, with careful planning and adequate debriefing, these pitfalls can be avoided. Simulations are a powerful way to teach particular values and foster certain positive attitudes. They are extremely motivating for most students.

USING ROLE-PLAYING TO TEACH DECISION MAKING

Another effective technique for teaching students decision making is to engage them in **role-playing**, which allows students to explore alternative solutions. Here are the steps to follow:[2]

1. Present a decision-making situation and ask students how they would feel in this situation and what solutions are possible.
2. Select role-players who will play the participants in the situation. The rest of the class will act as observers. They are given questions to focus their attention on the role play (see below).
3. Have the role-players enact one possible solution. Ask the observers to evaluate the solution and generate other solutions.
4. Have the same role-players, or new ones, enact these other solutions.
5. Evaluate the activity. Did the role-players play their parts in realistic ways? Which is the best solution? Why?

Role-playing has several benefits. It helps students try out alternative behaviours in a safe context while avoiding "real-life" consequences. It gives them opportunities to express feelings that they might not otherwise express.

Great care has to be taken in role-playing, however. Decision situations should be carefully chosen. Unwilling students should not be forced to participate, and those who love "acting" should not be allowed to dominate. In role-play situations where negative behaviour is exhibited, it is important to discuss with the class how they felt about it and the justification (if any) for it. But if role-playing is implemented in a pedagogically sound way, it can provide students with many insights into human behaviour and decision making. Furthermore, students usually enjoy the activity.

Role-playing can be incorporated into many situations. For example, in the Incinerator Simulation Game (above), students could act out the roles of residents who live in various areas of Actum and argue their cases for where the incinerator should be built. In a study of a community in which a "big box" retailer wishes to locate, students could take on the roles of the potential new store's owner, a local store owner who thinks his business will be destroyed if the new store is built, a consumer who wants more choice and cheaper merchandise, and a local resident who is concerned about the increase in traffic that the store will bring to the neighbourhood. When examining the forest industry in Canada or elsewhere, students could play the roles of a forest company owner who wants to clear-cut a forest, a forest worker who needs work, an environmentalist who is against clear-cutting, and a local resident who is worried about the effects of logging on her property as clear-cutting will create erosion problems. In a study of Canada, students could role-play family members who each wish to spend a summer holiday in a different province. In the section on law-related education in Chapter 19, there is an opportunity for students to take on the roles of a plaintiff, a defendant, and a judge. In a mock trial, students could also act as witnesses, jury members, and lawyers. Where an issue is being examined, students could be asked to play the role of a person who is opposed to their position, thus developing more open-minded attitudes.

Activity 17-E

Create an activity where a decision is required in which students engage in role-taking. For example, in a unit on another culture, students could take on the role of a member of the culture who is trying to persuade a tourist to decide to visit that culture.

The question that arises in all the above examples is, "Is there a *right* decision, and if so, what is it?" The next chapter is devoted to approaches you could take in answering this question.

OTHER ACTIVITIES

1. Identify the value standard in each of the following arguments. Check your responses in the Answers section.

    a) Because children are people, they should be treated with respect.

    b) Hitting a child is morally wrong because it's a form of child abuse.

    c) Students who wear glasses in my classroom should not be given special consideration. They're not disabled.

    d) Watching TV for five hours a day is harmful to children, so they should not be allowed to do it.

2. Design a lesson plan using the decision-making procedure for a primary class. Choose an appropriate decision situation and outline how you would teach the lesson.

3. Critique the following lesson on decision making and compare your critique with the one in the Answers section.

    TEACHER: Today, class, we're going to help someone make a decision. Please read the story and then we'll help Alice decide what to do. *[She hands out the story to the class.]*

    Sharon is Alice's best friend. They walk to school together every day. They play together at recess; they roller skate and go swimming together. Sometimes older kids tease Sharon, who wears a hearing aid because she can't hear very well. They make fun of her and whisper nasty things that she can't hear. This always upsets Sharon and that makes Alice angry. But Alice is not sure what to do when kids start teasing Sharon.

    Alice's mother tells her to ignore the teasers and they'll soon stop.

    Alice's father advises her to ask the teasers how they would feel if someone were teasing them.

    Alice's sister tells her to go the school principal.

    Alice's brother tells her he will beat up the kids who are teasing Sharon.

    TEACHER: What's Alice's problem?

    STUDENT: She has to decide whether to ignore the teasing or tell the principal about it.

TEACHER: Good. Now, let's consider what Alice could do. What are her alternatives? As I write them on the blackboard, I want you to copy them down in your notebooks.

STUDENT: She could get her brother to punch out the teasers.

STUDENT: She could ignore them.

TEACHER: OK, let's not have any more. Let's see what the consequences would be if she acted on either of these.

STUDENT: Her brother might get beaten up.

TEACHER: I don't think that will happen. Her brother is much bigger then the teasers. Anyway, it's not a good idea to beat up people.

STUDENT: Her teasers might stop if they knew her brother would beat them up.

TEACHER: Do you all agree?

CLASS: Yes.

TEACHER: Would that be a good consequence?

CLASS: Yes.

TEACHER: What if she ignored the problem?

STUDENT: The teasers would get fed up and stop.

STUDENT: No, they would just keep doing it.

TEACHER: Let's take a vote. Who thinks the teasers will stop teasing Sharon? *[10 hands go up.]* Who thinks they'll keep on teasing Sharon? *[15 hands are raised.]* So, we've decided that won't work. What should Alice do?

STUDENT: She should tell her teacher and get the teacher to stop it.

TEACHER: Yes, I think that would be a good idea. So, have we decided that Alice should talk to her teacher?

CLASS: Yes.

4. Modify the Incinerator Simulation Game for a Grade 1 class to involve a decision about where to put a new park.

5. Create some decision-making vignettes for a Grade 3 class that will introduce them to the standards of good decision making.

6. Create a role-playing activity that will help students understand that different people can have different values and that these values have to be taken into account in a decision-making situation.

NOTES

1.   For decision-making ideas framed as critical challenges, see J. Harrison, N. Smith, and I. Wright, *Critical Challenges in Social Studies for Upper Elementary Students* (Richmond, BC: The Critical Thinking Cooperative, 1999).

2.   F. Shaftel and G. Shaftel, *Role Playing in the Curriculum,* 2nd ed. (Englewood Cliffs, NJ: Prentice-Hall, 1982).

GLOSSARY OF KEY TERMS

Comparative value statement — statements that evaluate the comparative worth of two or more things.

Decision-making procedure — a procedure wherein students clarify the decision to be made, generate alternatives, identify the consequences of acting on each alternative, evaluate the consequences, and make a decision.

Point of view — used in this text to denote the type of value claim, e.g., the moral point of view, the environmental point of view, etc.

Prescriptive value statement — a statement that dictates what *ought to be* or what *ought to be done.*

Role-playing — an activity in which people enact a scenario by playing the characters in a given situation.

Simple value statement — a statement that evaluates the worth of something.

Simulation game — a game where the situation is as lifelike as possible.

Syllogism — an argument in which two premises lead logically to the conclusion.

Types of Values:

> **Aesthetic** — having to do with beauty, form, and texture.
>
> **Environmental** — having to do with how the natural environment is treated; now often viewed as part of the moral domain.
>
> **Instrumental value** — a value that is held in order to realize some higher or ultimate value.
>
> **Intellectual** — having to do with truth, logic, clarity, etc.
>
> **Moral** — generally speaking, having to do with how others are treated and how disputes are resolved.
>
> **Prudential** — having to do with self-interest.
>
> **Religious** — having to do with a set of beliefs concerning the nature, cause, and purposes of the universe, especially as these relate to a superhuman agency or agencies; spirituality.
>
> **Ultimate value** — the most fundamental value; all other values are instrumental to this one.

Value — something that is deemed important in a person's life and that motivates the person to behave in certain ways.

chapter eighteen

Approaches to Teaching Social and Personal Values

In the last chapter, we saw that value judgments cannot be avoided in teaching social studies. Teachers do attempt to instill values in students, especially in young children. Two justifications can be advanced for this. The first is that there are some values to which children must be committed to ensure their continued well-being and that of others in society. The second justification is that young children cannot understand the often complex reasons certain values ought to be acted upon. Reasoning may not persuade children to act in a particular manner; they may have to be convinced in other ways.

Children obtain their values in two basic ways. One way is through reinforcement. A child is praised for virtuous behaviour and punished for behaviour that is contrary to what is desired. Reinforcement can take the form of exhortations, lectures, rewards, the removal of privileges, or the use of facial expressions to show approval or disapproval.

The second way children learn values is by modelling behaviour. Through interaction, children "pick up" the values of their families, their peer groups, and the society in which they live. In the classroom, teachers either consciously or unconsciously exemplify acceptable values. Literature, textbooks, and the media can also exemplify values that students pick up.

You may remember that when you were at school, certain people were regarded as heroes and heroines, whereas others were viewed as villains. You may also recall the fables, parables, and stories read to you that were designed to teach you particular moral lessons. Today, children's exemplars are often media stars, and their moral lessons derive from television.

Activity 18-A

Think back to your elementary schooling. List the names of those who were regarded as the heroes and villains in the school curriculum and what their claims to fame were. Now list those whom *you* regarded as heroes and villains, and indicate their claims to fame. How are the two lists similar and different?

Now do the same for the heroes and villains in contemporary elementary texts and stories and, separately, those in the mass media. Again, analyze the similarities and differences.

As children mature, they develop reasoning abilities and start using arguments to defend their value positions. How they argue depends, in the main, upon their developmental level, how they are taught, and what models of good reasoning they have.

Activity 18-B

In a group, divide up a social studies curriculum guide so that each group member analyzes approximately the same number of pages. Then identify the values that are emphasized. Classify these, where possible, into moral, prudential, aesthetic, and intellectual categories. Share your list with your peers. What values are given most emphasis?

As teachers, you might find that among members of your community there is basic agreement about certain values. Parents will want their children to value respect for siblings; likewise, we will want respect for each other in our classrooms. However, other values may be controversial. Witness the recent controversy in Surrey, BC, where the school board banned elementary school books that portrayed same-sex families.

Whatever values we wish to foster, we can teach them either explicitly or through our modelling and the classroom climate we develop. In the latter case we can have students help make and enforce classroom rules, have them engage in conflict resolution activities (see Chapter 20), and have them participate in activities that involve students helping other students (for ideas here, see Chapter 9). As teachers we must model the kind of values we want our students to adopt so that they do not receive contradictory messages. Explicit teaching can involve decision making and other values-education activities such as role-playing, engagement with movies and literature, and service learning (see below) or social action projects (see Chapter 19).

This chapter examines the various approaches to the explicit teaching of values. The brief summaries provided here cannot do justice to all the complexities involved in values education—there are no "quick fixes." Readers should consult the references listed at the end of this book for further guidance.

THE CHARACTER EDUCATION APPROACH

Activity 18-C

What values do you think your students ought to act upon in the classroom? Make a list of these and share your list with your peers. Do you agree or disagree? Why? What implications do your agreements or disagreements have for your conduct as a teacher? What points of view (moral, prudential, aesthetic, etc.) did you use to justify your decisions?

The purpose of the **Character Education** approach is to instill in students certain values that are considered desirable. These often include virtues such as tact, honesty, perseverance, obedience, and courtesy. In a review of the virtues proposed by three experts in the area of Character Education, Leming[1] found that they disagreed more than they agreed. However, most character educators in the United States defended teaching certain virtues on the basis of the rise in juvenile crime, drug use, vandalism, and gang wars. It is assumed that if children are taught the "right" values, then these phenomena will decrease. Such values may be those deemed to be universally acceptable, or they may be those shared by a society or particular group within a society. The values could be moral, prudential, religious, or aesthetic. In many cases they will be enshrined in law or in a religious code.

Proponents of this approach regard the individual as a reactor rather than an initiator. The individual is to be taught the values thought desirable in much the same way as the three Rs were traditionally taught. Proponents may also believe that desired values should be instilled in children through indoctrination—initiation into fixed, doctrine-like beliefs held without a basis in evidence or consideration of alternative positions.

This approach uses several teaching/learning strategies. All are based on behaviourism and social learning theory. One strategy is to use literature in which characters exemplify desired values. A story is presented that illustrates the adherence or non-adherence to a particular virtue (modelling); then students are led through questioning and discussion to arrive at the "correct" answers (reinforcement). The same intent is present when stories of heroes, heroines, and villains drawn from history are presented. In these cases, students are rarely told *why* they should admire the heroes and heroines or that many of them had less-than-desirable traits. When controversial issues are taught, this approach entails avoidance of presenting all sides of an issue. Students receive only evidence and arguments that support the "right" answer; the teacher's questions about the issue are designed to lead students to this answer. Often, where the intent is to have students avoid certain actions, such as smoking or taking drugs, scare tactics are used. The student is denied any opportunity to question the evidence or the arguments presented. Or children are taught to "just say no," without consideration of *why* they should say no. Sometimes, the desired virtues are acted on. Students carry out **service learning**[2] in which they help out at food banks, coach ESL students, or volunteer in senior citizens' centres. They also get involved in social action projects in which they try to resolve a social issue through actions such as cleaning up a polluted river or restocking a salmon stream.[3] They may not be told why they should engage in these activities or have any choice in the matter.

Before using this approach, we should consider several questions: a) Who is to decide what values to instill? b) What should be done when two acceptable values are in conflict? For example, should a person refrain from stealing food when that is the only way of saving somebody's life? c) In a multicultural classroom, how does a teacher deal with values that may conflict with those of the dominant society, or school values that conflict with parental ones? A further consideration is the efficacy of this approach. If the right values are instilled in children, will children act on them? For example, there is evidence that children do not always interpret stories in the way that was intended by an author and do not always act on the values that are espoused in stories or activities designed to influence them.[4] In fact, traditional approaches to sex and drug education have been found, in some cases, to increase sexual[5] and drug-taking activities,[6] and zero tolerance policies do not seem to be working in Canadian schools.[7] Yet we do want children to accept such virtues as responsibility, honesty, and tolerance, and we want to warn them of the dangers of drugs. We can do so, when Character Education is tempered with reason, where the classroom and school climate are democratic (see Chapter 19), when rules are fair and fairly enforced, where students are involved in helping resolve conflicts[8] (see Conflict Resolution in Chapter 20), and where students are treated with respect.

THE VALUES CLARIFICATION APPROACH

Rather than instilling values in students, the **Values Clarification** approach aims to help students identify their own values and act on them.

Activity 18-D

Below are a variety of Values Clarification activities. All are adaptations of activities proposed by Simon et al.[9] Try several of these activities and then answer the questions at the end.

1. Rank the following behaviours from the most reprehensible to the least.

   a) Hitting a child who is misbehaving _____

   b) Being sarcastic to a child _____

   c) Ignoring a child who needs help _____

2. On your retirement from teaching, your students present you with a scroll. If you were to write the words on this scroll, what would you like them to say? For what would you like to be remembered?

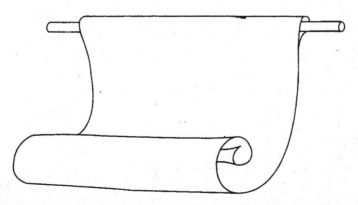

3. What is your attitude toward the use of snowmobiles in national or provincial parks? On a continuum from "banning completely" to "allowing unlimited use," where would your position lie?

4. Complete this sentence: I wish the federal government would _____.

5. Reflect on what you have done so far this week. What made you happy? What made you upset? What are you proud of having done? Could your week have been better? How?

6. Let's suppose you expect your students to work very hard for you and to attain very high standards. Your students always do well on tests. Your principal decides to give you a class of intellectually immature students, but you like working only with better-than-average students. Your principal, however, is adamant.

   a) In what different ways might this be resolved?

   b) What might happen as a result of each solution?

   c) Which solution do you think would be best?

7. A friend of yours in a university course has copied an assignment from a student who did a similar course at another university. He/she obtained a very high mark, whereas you obtained a very low mark, despite the fact that you spent a great deal of time and effort on the assignment. Would you tell your instructor? What would be the advantages and disadvantages of telling?

8. Choose any value issue and discuss it with a group of your peers. When statements are made that positively or negatively evaluate the issue, use these questions, where appropriate, to further clarify the statement(s):

   a) Are you glad about that?

   b) What do you mean by _____?

   c) What would be the consequences of that?

   d) Have you thought of any other possibilities?

   e) Are you going to act on that idea?

Having considered these activities, answer the following questions:

1. What do you think the aim(s) is/are for each of the activities above?

2. Do the activities help you clarify your own values?

3. What procedures did you follow to arrive at answers in the activities above?

4. What types of values are to be found in these activities?

5. Rank the activities in terms of the importance of the value issue. Which activity focuses on the most important value(s)? Which focuses on the least important?

6. If you disagreed with a peer regarding the solution to one of the above activities, would it matter? Why or why not?

7. What would be the advantages of having a clear set of values? Would there be any disadvantages?

Values Clarification is premised on four key points:

• There is a focus on students' own lives.

- There must be a non-judgmental acceptance of other students' values.
- Students must carefully consider their values.
- There is the assumption that students who know what they value will be empowered.

According to Values Clarification theory,[10] to have a value, one must do the following:

1. *Choose* freely from alternatives after thoughtful consideration of each alternative.
2. *Prize* and cherish the choice; be happy with it and be willing to affirm the choice publicly.
3. *Act* by doing something with the choice, repeatedly, in some pattern of life.

The approach relies on the individual, who must decide which values are positive and, to demonstrate his or her acceptance of them, must act on them.

This approach can be used to clarify all types of values (moral, prudential, aesthetic, etc.), as well as tastes and preferences. As preferences are a matter of personal opinion, Values Clarification can become relativistic in the manner of "Your preference is as good as my preference." Extreme proponents of Values Clarification take the view that all values are relative, but most agree with this statement made by Louis Raths:[11]

> If, for any reason, we do not want a child to choose a particular alternative, like setting fire to a house, we should let him/her know that this is not within the realm of choice.

The research evidence for the efficacy of Values Clarification is not strong.[12] Further, the use of this approach raises questions about whether values and preferences ought to be justified in the same way; whether values are, or ought to be, relative to the individual; and whether the three steps of Values Clarification always produce values that are morally defensible.

THE COGNITIVE-DEVELOPMENTAL APPROACH

Neither of the above two approaches says anything about how students reason about value issues. Lawrence Kohlberg[13] addresses this question in his six-stage model of moral reasoning. In Stage 1, children reason on the basis of concerns of reward and punishment and pleasing authority figures. In Stage 2, they serve their own needs while realizing that other children have their own interests, reasoning in effect that "I'll scratch your back if you'll scratch mine." In Stage 3, children try to live up to conventional standards of their group or the wider society. And in Stage 4, children show a concern with maintaining society; this is referred to as the "law and order stage." Stages 5 and 6 are found only in adults. The stages are sequential—you cannot skip a stage—and hierarchical, with each stage representing an improvement over the previous one and building toward the next higher stage. The reasoning at each stage is a product of both environmental and genetic stimulants. Development depends on a person's maturity and the social milieu, with "intelligence" and role-taking ability being especially relevant.

This stage-developmental theory has been applied in moral education programs. Here is an example:[14] Students are given a story in which a young girl promises her father not to climb trees. Her friend's kitten is caught in a tree and she is the only one who can rescue it. Should she climb the tree to save the kitten? If she climbs, she breaks a promise; if she doesn't, the owner of the kitten will be heartbroken because his mother has told him that if the kitten gets into trouble once more, the kitten will be given away.

Once the dilemma has been posed, the class is divided into groups of students. To ensure that there is initial conflict in the groups, each group should have students who either reason at different stages of moral reasoning or disagree on whether the girl should climb the tree. It is assumed that if students at a given stage are exposed to arguments at the next-highest stage, they will be stimulated to begin to think at this higher level. The groups discuss their responses to the dilemma, and then state their conclusions and the reasons for them. The following questions are posed:

- Would it make any difference if the girl's father didn't know whether she climbed the tree?
- Would the girl's father understand if she did climb the tree?
- Should all promises be kept?
- How will the kitten's owner feel if the kitten is (is not) rescued?
- Suppose the girl doesn't like the kitten's owner. Should that make any difference to her decision?
- How would you feel if you were the girl? Or the owner of the kitten?

This approach has been criticized from the perspective that most moral problems are not dilemmas. It is not always the case that someone will be disadvantaged whatever action is taken, and there are often more than two alternative courses of action in actual moral problems. There is also the problem of having all the facts of the case presented in the dilemma. In real life we may need to discover the facts and evaluate them, and it is often the case that the facts are in dispute.

Feminist scholars have criticized Kohlberg's theory for being male-oriented. (Kohlberg did base his theory initially on research involving only male subjects.) These scholars claim that females tend to use an ethic of caring and are concerned with mutually satisfying relationships rather than with justice.[15] Recent research has indicated that reasoning about moral problems is complex and context-bound.[16] Thus, we have to take this complexity into account and help students reason well about the moral problems they all face in their day-to-day lives by utilizing a variety of methodologies rather than relying on just one.

THE VALUES ANALYSIS APPROACH

Values Analysis is based on the assumption that there are rational ways to resolve value issues. The focus is on the logic of arguments, the truth of empirical claims, the clarification of concepts, and the justifications for the value principles, rules, or standards that are used to arrive at a decision.

Here is an example: Students have been asked to collect money for UNICEF when they are trick-or-treating at Halloween. They debate whether to do this; the question is raised about the need to give aid to other countries. The teacher poses the question "Should we (members of the class) give aid to other countries?" She decides to use a case study of a village in Somalia. The students read about the problems the villagers face and list the types of aid they receive. Clarifying the concept of "aid" by discussing examples, they eventually arrive at a list of what they would qualify as aid (see Chapter 6 for ideas about clarifying concepts). In inquiry groups (see Chapter 9), students then carry out research about other countries that receive aid from Canada. They draw up a list of reasons for its provision and create a chart.

Should we give aid to other countries?	
We should give aid.	**We should not give aid.**
Giving aid will prevent starvation.	Giving aid will mean poor people in Canada won't be helped.
It'll help people who are ill and can't get medicine.	It'll result in people not helping themselves—they'll rely on aid all the time.
It'll provide schools for children.	Some children in class can't afford to give money, and they'll feel badly if everyone else does.

The students evaluate the reasons for and against giving aid. Would students who cannot afford to give money feel badly when other students give? Does aid prevent starvation? Here, you can use the standards for assessing the reliability of empirical claims outlined in Chapter 8. "Truth" may well be difficult or impossible to establish in some cases, and teachers must use their judgment about the level of reliability required. For example, there is no way that students can *check* how many people are actually starving. Students will have to rely on figures from UNICEF and other relief agencies. These figures are likely to be reliable; if relief agencies were found to be untruthful, it is unlikely that people would continue to give money to them.

The next step consists of identifying the value standards to which students have appealed. These are the standards behind the reasons above for giving aid: we should prevent starvation; we should help people who are ill; and we should provide schools for children. Next, identify the value standards behind the reasons for *not* giving aid.

The final step is to "test" the value standard. This is where the Values Analysis approach differs fundamentally from the other approaches. In the Character Education approach, the standard is taken for granted if it is socially acceptable. According to the Values Clarification approach, so long as the steps of the valuing process have been carried out, the standard is acceptable. According to the Cognitive-Developmental approach, the value standard is based on the stage of reasoning attained.

In the Values Analysis approach, the justification for the value standard or principle is judged by applying four **principle tests**:[17]

The Role Exchange Test: When, as a child, you had hurt someone else in some way, you may remember being asked, "How would you like it if somebody did that to you?" The point of this question is that if you would not want the action to be performed on you, then you should not do it to someone else. This is the basis for the Role Exchange Test. The question, however, should be posed as "Would it be *right* for you in the role of the other person to do X?" It is not just a question of liking. A child may not *like* to go to the dentist, but it would be *right* for a parent to insist that the child go. These are the steps to follow:

1. Imagine what it would be like in the other person's situation and to experience the consequences the action would have on that person.

2. Consider whether it would be right for the other person to take the action if you were the one experiencing the consequences.

3. Decide whether to accept or reject performing the action because of the consequences to the other person. This test is most powerful when the consequences to the other person are undesirable.

The Universal Consequences Test: You may also remember from your childhood being asked, when you had done something wrong, "What if everybody did that?" This question's point is that if the consequences of everybody's performing a particular act would be disastrous, then *you* should not do it. In this test, the decision maker has to imagine the consequences if everyone who could perform the same action for the same reasons were to do so. For example, can a motorist justify driving well above the speed limit with the argument that he was late for an extremely important meeting? We can imagine a number of motorists wanting to use this as a reason, and we can imagine the consequences if they were all to speed. Although this reason does not justify speeding, the justification offered by an ambulance driver carrying a critically ill patient might be acceptable for every ambulance driver in a similar situation. The steps in this test are as follows:

1. Imagine the consequences if everyone who might perform the same action for the same reason were to do so.

2. Consider whether the imagined consequences would be acceptable.

3. Conclude that the action is right if the consequences are acceptable, and then subject the decision to the other principle tests, or conclude that it is wrong if the consequences are unacceptable.

The New Cases Test: A third question that you may have been asked when you were engaged in some bad behaviour is this one: "Would you do the same thing in another similar situation?" This question focuses on the presumption that people ought to be consistent in their judgments. In this test, a standard that has been accepted is applied to new, logically relevant cases. The power of the test depends on applying *difficult* cases. If students have said that stealing from someone in the class is wrong, it is probably ineffective to ask whether they would steal from friends, relatives, other children in the school, etc. Rather, pose a problem where stealing would lead to desirable consequences, such as saving a life. Then students must determine whether they think the principle "In no circumstances whatsoever should people steal" is justifiable or whether another principle is more acceptable, such as "People should not steal except in circumstances where a life is at stake." The latter principle would need to be tested with new cases in order to determine whether the person doing the reasoning is willing to hold to it consistently. The steps are as follows:

1. Choose a case that logically falls under the value standard being appealed to.

2. Consider whether to judge this case in the same way as the original decision was judged.

3. If the case is judged in the same way, and it is the hardest case that can be imagined, then accept the decision.

The Subsumption Test: This last test is different from the other three. It is designed to determine if the value standard in question falls under and is consistent with a more general, higher principle that the decision maker accepts. It is useful in discerning the general value principles on both sides of a conflict. For example, in the foreign aid case, the more general principle might be that we should help *all* people who are worse off than we are. The decision maker then has to decide whether or not this general principle is acceptable by applying the other three tests.

It may appear that all this is far too complex for elementary school students. But we do ask young children, "How would you like that done to you?" "What if everybody did that?" and "If you would do that in this situation, would you do it in X situation?" These questions are the bases for the Role Exchange, Universal Consequences, and New Cases tests. Of course, elementary students cannot apply these tests in a sophisticated way, but they can be asked to consider the consequences of their actions for other people. Even though primary-grade children will have difficulty applying the Role Exchange test—because they will believe that other people share their perspective—this does not mean that they should not consider the effects of their actions on others. By about age seven, children do realize that others can have different perspectives, and that these have to be taken into account when interpersonal decisions are made.

Here is an activity that asks you to apply the principle tests.

Activity 18-E

Read the following vignette and answer the question that follows.

> The Fraser family—a mother, a father, a three-year-old, and a five-year-old—is looking for an affordable place to rent. The parents are getting quite desperate, so when they see an advertisement for an affordable duplex they hurry over to look at it. The parents decide that it is just what they are looking for, and they tell the owner, who gets out a rental contract and starts to fill it in. He asks them if they have children. They reply that they have two. The owner tells them that they cannot rent the duplex, for he does not rent to families with children. He claims that children make too much noise and are likely to damage his property.
>
> Should the owner have the right to refuse to rent the duplex to the Fraser family?

Suppose you argue that the owner should have the right to refuse to rent the duplex because it's his property and he has the right to do what he likes with it. The value standard is "Property owners ought to be able to do whatever they like with their own property." How would you answer the following questions?

1. Imagine you are a member of the Fraser family. Would the owner's decision be right if you were the one experiencing the consequences?

2. What would be the consequences if every property owner in the city refused to rent to couples with children because children create noise and might damage property? Are these consequences acceptable?

3. Suppose a man comes to the owner and is told that the duplex is available for rent. The owner asks for his name and is told that it is Levin. The owner asks if he is Jewish. The man's answer is yes. The owner says he does not rent his duplex to Jews. Should the owner have the right to refuse to rent the duplex to Jews? Suppose a person in a wheelchair wanted to rent the duplex but is told by the owner that he does not rent to people who are physically challenged. Should the owner have the right to do this?

4. If you were asked to justify the principle that property owners can do whatever they please with their property, what higher principle would you use?

Suppose you argue that the owner should not have the right to refuse to rent to the Fraser family because that would be discriminatory. The value standard would then be "People should not have the right to discriminate." How would you answer the following questions?

1. Suppose you were the owner. Would it be right for you to experience the consequences of having renters who you believe will be noisy and will damage your property?

2. Would the consequences be desirable or undesirable if no property owners were allowed to choose their tenants?

3. Suppose two young males who have a reputation in the community for drug dealing and gang warfare wish to rent the duplex. Should the owner have the right to refuse to rent it to them?

4. If you were asked to justify the non-discrimination principle, to what higher principle might you appeal?

The Values Analysis approach demands that critical thought be applied to value questions. Difficult as it may be, it is not beyond the capabilities of students to begin to grasp some of the complexities of value reasoning. As Beck[18] says:

> While value questions are indeed complex and subtle, they are not beyond the capacity of ordinary adults and children. In fact, we all solve hundreds, perhaps thousands of value problems quite successfully every day.

Several questions can be raised about this approach: What role should emotions play in reasoning about value issues? What does one do in situations where, after applying the principle tests, there is still disagreement about the right thing to do? Is this approach appropriate in a multicultural society where there are different conceptions of what is morally correct?

Activity 18-F

Identify a value issue in a social studies curriculum guide or text.

a) Do you think students will find this issue significant? Is it relevant to their lives? Should it be relevant?

b) Do you think students are mature enough to make decisions about the issue?

c) If there are activities for students to carry out or questions for them to answer that are meant to help them examine or resolve the issue, evaluate them. What approach do these activities or questions seem to take? What assumptions are being made about the nature of values, how students learn them, and how value questions ought to be resolved?

d) If there are no activities or questions, design some so that students can be helped to examine the issue and arrive at their own conclusions.

VALUES, TEACHERS, AND THE CURRICULUM

Despite the fact that all teachers are value educators, values education is a contentious issue in Canada. Few provinces have a well-thought-out policy or program. This is because, as with all curriculum decisions, politics is involved. Whatever stance a governing body takes seems to raise the ire of at least some people. Some parents do not want their children to be exposed to any form of values education, believing that it is the task of parents or the church to do this. Others want the schools to take a particular approach to values education. Teachers are caught in the middle. Yet values cannot be ignored, especially in social studies, where one of the major foci is on how people interact with one another. It is not enough to merely identify the values people hold and the things that influence people's interactions—we must also help students make rational decisions about actions that affect their lives and the lives of others. Issues of violence, environmental degradation, genetic engineering, sexism, and racism confront us all. We need to learn how to deal with them, which requires that we develop particular areas of knowledge, abilities, and dispositions. Coombs[19] has described the attainments of the morally educated person.

1. *Knowledge of what one's society regards as morally right and wrong.*

    Thinking about moral questions takes place in a society that has a moral code. Making moral judgments is more a matter of rethinking that moral code than it is of devising a completely new one. Therefore, students need to know what the moral rules of the society are and why a system of public morality is necessary. Such knowledge is gained by teaching children that there are some values, such as not killing, deceiving, or lying, which, in the main, are morally justifiable.[20] Through activities that focus on the consequences of not having moral rules, children can realize that they are better off in a society that upholds such rules than one that does not. A further justification for this attainment is that we cannot stop every minute to consider the moral acceptability of our actions. Some value judgments have to be habitual. Here character education can play a key role.

2. *Knowledge of moral concepts such as equality, justice, stealing, cheating, lying, prejudice, discrimination, and so on.*

    Concepts determine how we see a situation. If shoplifting isn't viewed as "stealing," then it is unlikely to be viewed as wrong. If a situation in which a person is denied something on the basis of race, gender, or religion is not perceived as "discrimination," then it is unlikely to be regarded as immoral. Further, by grasping moral concepts, students become more morally sensitive. Having a profound understanding of "discrimination" will lead students to be on the lookout when it occurs. They will also be more likely than less sensitive students to view a discriminatory situation as one of discrimination. Concept attainment activities (see Chapter 6) can be used to help students grasp key moral concepts.

Activity 18-G

In this activity, you will present students with a problem in which the application of a particular concept is fundamental to its resolution.

Which of the following would qualify as an act of cheating? In which situation(s) would the action be wrong?

a) **A** looked at **B's** quiz and copied down **B's** answers.

b) **A** happened to see the quiz on the teacher's desk and looked at the answers. When **A** did the quiz, **A** remembered the answers he'd seen and used them.

c) **B** told **A** that he'd seen the answers on the teacher's desk and told **A** the answers. **A** used what he'd been told to answer the quiz questions.

    d) To answer the quiz questions, **A** needed to remember where various countries were located. The teacher had forgotten to take the world map off the classroom wall. **A** used the map to answer the questions.

    e) By mistake, the teacher gave **A** a quiz sheet on which the answers were pencilled. **A** copied the pencilled answers, then erased them.

    f) **A** had missed a lot of school because of illness, but her parents insisted that she do the quiz and do well on it. So **A** wrote the information she needed on a piece of paper that she hid up her sleeve. **A** then used this information to take the quiz.

1. Is there intent to deceive in the vignettes above? Are they all cases of cheating? If not, what attribute of "cheating" is missing?

2. If a student states that a clear case of a moral concept is X, then pose other relevant examples to see whether the student accepts these as being cases of X.

3. If a student accepts that a particular attribute of a value concept should apply, then use the Role Exchange and Universal Consequences tests to see if the student would abide by the decision. For example, if the students say that it would be fair to cheat because everyone else does (i.e., the principle is "Whatever everyone else does is acceptable"), then ask whether the consequences of holding this standard would be acceptable in all cases.

Activity 18-H

Design an activity that would help students clarify a particular moral concept such as fairness. Create cases in which the concept might or might not apply so that students are encouraged to discuss what constitutes fairness in any particular case.

3. *Ability and inclination to apply principle tests to the rules and standards used in making moral judgments.*

This includes the ability to role-take (and this requires the disposition to empathize with others), the ability to imagine the consequences if everyone who might perform a particular action actually did so, and the ability to understand what harms people, both physically and emotionally. Literature is a valuable tool here, as is the fostering of a classroom climate where students care about each other and where reason-giving is rewarded.

4. *Ability and inclination to seek all information relevant to a value question.*

Too often we make judgments based on either incomplete or false information. For example, in a discussion I held with a Grade 6 class, it was widely believed that shoplifting didn't harm anyone (the store owner had insurance, or wouldn't miss the item). These students did not realize that shoplifting created additional costs for the store owner that, ultimately, would be passed along to consumers. So, in tackling any value question, we need to collect information about the facts of the case, and about alternative solutions and the consequences of acting on them.

5. *Resolution to do what one has decided is a right action, and to refrain from doing what one has decided is wrong.*

It is all very well to make decisions about what is right and wrong, but we also have to act. Thus, we have to encourage students to participate in social action projects (see Chapter 19) and, as teachers, we have to create a classroom and school environment in which right actions are encouraged.

6. *Ability to clarify personal values using appropriate activities.*

Many of the Values Clarification techniques encourage reflection on the values that are important to a person.[21] For example, the "Twenty Things You Love to Do" activity asks students to list things they love to do and then divide them into those costing money, those done alone, those done five years ago, those done daily, weekly, monthly, or yearly, and so on. Reflecting on their lists can give students an insight into what they think is of value.

Have students list their needs. What could they do without in order to survive? Extend the basic needs of food, shelter, water, and air to include basic human goals—freedom, security, wealth, self-respect, and pleasure. What would life be like without these goals? Inquire into whether people in Canada and in other parts of the world can fulfill their needs and goals. What happens when they can't? To what degree do all people require freedom, security, and so on? To what extent do individual students realize these human goals? Instruct students to list a) what they are free to do and whether or not they want to pursue these freedoms, and b) what they are *not* free to do and the reasons why. Ask students to identify constraints in their lives and discuss whether these constraints are justifiable. Can or should we do anything when people's needs and goals are not being met?

To help students develop a positive self-concept, we can encourage, praise, listen to, and respect student contributions. We can also carry out activities such as "Pride Time," an activity in which students write about something they are proud of.[22]

This list of attainments raises many questions about both theory and practice. You are advised to consult the bibliography for further guidance. All these attainments, however, are crucial when we focus on how to help students make decisions.

If values education is to have any effect, then we, as teachers, must exhibit the following characteristics:[23]

a) We must be perceived as possessing a high degree of competence, status, and control over resources.

b) We must be perceived as caring people.

c) The benefits of our modelled behaviour must be apparent.

d) The modelled behaviours must be shared by other significant people.

e) The desired behaviours must be reinforced and repeated.

OTHER ACTIVITIES

1. State how you would apply one of the approaches to values education (Character Education, Values Clarification, or Values Analysis) in the following situation:

Jack is the star player on the school baseball team. It is mainly due to his pitching and batting that the team is in the league finals. The day before the championship game, Jack is showing off to his friends by swinging his bat around. He has been warned on two previous occasions not to do this, and he's been told he'll be punished if he's caught. Other members of Jack's class have also warned him about his bat swinging. But Jack is on top of the world because he's in the championship game. In swinging his bat around, he hits Bill on the head. Bill isn't too badly hurt, but he'll have a large bruise on his temple. The teacher sees the incident and immediately suspends Jack from the championship game. The team members circulate a petition asking the school principal to cancel Jack's suspension, allow him to play in the game, and give him some other punishment. Should Bill sign the petition?

2. Create a chart identifying the major characteristic of each of the approaches to values education.

	Purposes	Assumptions	Teaching activities	Critique
Character Education				
Values Clarification				
Cognitive-Developmental				
Values Analysis				

3. What approach(es) will you use in your classroom? Why?

NOTES

1. J. Leming, "Teaching values in social studies education: Past practices and current trends," in B. Massialas and R. Allen, *Crucial Issues in Teaching Social Studies* (Belmont, Calif.: Wadsworth, 1996).

2. E. Bloom, "Service learning and social studies: A natural fit," *Social Education: Middle School Learning—A supplement* 67:4 (2003), M4–M7.

3. For a discussion of social action projects, see P. Clark, "All talk and no action? The place of social action in social studies," in R. Case. and P. Clark, eds., *The Canadian Social Studies Anthology* (Vancouver: Pacific Educational Press, 1999).

4. J. Leming.

5. J. Stout and F. Rivera, "Schools and sex education: Does it work?" *Pediatrics* 83 (1989), pp. 375–379.

6. E. Schapps, E. Dibartalo, J. Mortimore, C. Palley, and S. Churgin, "A review of 127 drug abuse prevention program evaluations," *Journal of Drug Issues* 11 (1981), pp. 17–43.

7. S. Cole, "Saying no to zero tolerance," *The Globe and Mail*, August 30, 2003, F6.

8. For example, the Alberta Teachers' Association has a Safe and Caring School Project that is used in about one third of the province's schools and takes a comprehensive approach to values education.

9. S. Simon, L. Howe, and H. Kirschenbaum, *Values Clarification: A Handbook of Practical Strategies for Teachers and Students* (New York: Hart, 1972).

10. L. Raths, M. Harmin, and S. Simon, *Values and Teaching,* 2nd ed. (Columbus, Ohio: Charles E. Merrill, 1978).

11. Ibid., p. 32.

12. J. Leming, p. 153.

13. L. Kohlberg, *The Psychology of Moral Development: The Nature and Validity of Moral Stages* (San Francisco: Harper and Row, 1984).

14. One of a series of dilemmas posed in *First Things: Values* (New York: Guidance Associates, 1979).

15. C. Gilligan, *In a Different Voice: Psychological Theory and Women's Development* (Cambridge, Mass.: Harvard University Press, 1977).

16. L. Walker, C. Russel, K. Hennig, and M. Mastuba, "Reasoning about morality in real life moral problems," in M. Killen and D. Hart, eds., *Morality in Everyday Life: Developmental Perspectives* (New York: Cambridge University Press, 1996).

17. These tests were developed by the Association for Values Education and Research at the University of British Columbia.

18. C. Beck, *Better Schools: A Values Perspective* (New York: Falmer, 1990), p. 2.

19. Adapted from J. Coombs, "Attainments of the morally educated person," in D. Cochrane and M. Manley-Casimir, eds., *Development of Moral Reasoning: Practical Approaches* (New York: Praeger, 1980).

20. See B. Gert, *The Moral Rules* (New York: Harper and Row, 1966).

21. S. Simon, L. Howe, and H. Kirschenbaum, *Values Clarification: A Handbook of Practical Strategies for Teachers and Students* (New York: Hart, 1972), pp. 30–34.

22. J. Canfield and H. Wells, *100 Ways to Enhance Self-Concept in the Classroom* (Englewood Cliffs, NJ: Prentice-Hall, 1976).

23. J. Leming, p. 169.

GLOSSARY OF KEY TERMS

Character Education — an approach to teaching values (virtues) that relies upon the reinforcement and modelling of those values.

Cognitive-Developmental approach to moral education — an approach to values education in which students, through discussion, are stimulated to reason to their next highest stage of moral development.

Principle tests — four tests applied to a decision to evaluate its moral acceptability:

New Cases Test — seeing whether, in relevantly similar situations, you would act in the same way as you would in the original situation. If you would not, then the decision needs to be reconsidered.

Role Exchange — placing yourself in the position of the most disadvantaged person in the situation and asking whether it would be right for you, in that position, to act on your decision. If it would not be right, then the decision needs to be reconsidered.

Subsumption Test — determining whether your decision fits in with the rest of your value system. If it does not fit, then the decision needs to be reconsidered.

Universal Consequences — seeing whether you are willing to universalize your decision in all relevantly similar situations. If you are not, then the decision needs to be reconsidered.

Service learning — activities designed to encourage students to help the disadvantaged in their community, thereby realizing the objectives of character education.

Values Analysis — an approach to values education that encourages the application of critical thinking and principle tests to issues.

Values Clarification — an approach to values education that encourages students to choose freely from alternatives after considering the consequences, prizing their choices, and acting on them.

chapter nineteen

Values in Citizenship, Global, and Law-Related Education

In the next two chapters, our concern is with various curriculum areas that are generally included in social studies: in this chapter, citizenship, law-related, and global education; and in Chapter 20, multicultural, human rights, peace, gender, and conflict resolution education. All of these areas are fraught with significant value questions. Indeed, how each is conceptualized is a value question in itself. In the discussion on the nature and purposes of social studies (Chapters 1 and 2), the point was made that the way social studies is conceptualized depends, in large part, on the judgments made about what students should learn. If we believe that students should memorize a multitude of facts about Canadian history, then what is done in social studies will be influenced by this belief. Similarly, if we think that a good citizen is someone who is patriotic and always obeys the law, then what is done in the name of citizenship education will be based on this belief.

Each of these curriculum areas rests on assumptions about how people ought to be treated. In **citizenship education**, we focus on how people should be governed and how people ought to act either as citizens of Canada or as citizens of the world. In **law-related education**, we examine the laws that govern people's behaviour, who should create laws and enforce them, and what procedures should be used to resolve disputes. In **global education**, our concern is with all of us on this planet. All of these areas involve profound value questions. Although questions of how people ought to be treated require empirical information, information alone will not suffice.

This chapter introduces three of these curriculum areas and outlines broad objectives for each. Chapter 20 does the same for other areas. As you work through both chapters, you will notice that the boundaries between the curriculum areas under discussion are often quite flexible and that sometimes it is only the degree of emphasis that differentiates one from another.

CITIZENSHIP EDUCATION

The primary focus in Canadian social studies is education for citizenship.[1] However, what this means is subject to continuing debate.[2] What is clear is that it is a complex notion with interrelated components of national identity; a system of rights; political and civic participation; and social, cultural, and supranational belonging.[3] Each requires understanding if citizenship education is to move beyond slogans and beyond memorizing the three levels of government in Canada. Government, in a broad sense, is a matter of how people relate to one another in families, places of worship, labour unions, businesses, industries, and recreational and community-organizational settings, as well as classrooms. In all these social contexts, notions of identity, rights, responsibilities, rules, authority, justice, and power arise. Citizenship confers a particular status on a person. It entitles that person to certain rights and privileges and, in turn, entails particular responsibilities that often manifest themselves in participation in political and civic affairs. And all of this is tied up with notions of who we are—the question of Canadian identity.

It is not enough to transmit knowledge about these concepts or to inform students about politics, government, law, and the norms of society. If we assume that people in a democracy have a right to make up their own minds, then students should be taught how to deal intelligently with a broad range of issues such as these:

- whether money collected from a school fundraiser should be given to the Food Bank or spent on a class field trip
- how to deal with bullying in the school playground
- whom to vote for as class president
- how to welcome a refugee to the class

Activity 19-A

Using the four components of citizenship education—national identity; a system of rights; political participation; and social, cultural, and supranational belonging—create a list of what you would consider relevant to citizenship education in a grade level of your choice. How do these four components relate to the curriculum and to the classroom in general? Share your list with a partner. Do you agree or disagree? Why?

What is taught in the name of citizenship education will depend on our philosophy of social studies (see Chapter 2). If we accept the Citizenship Transmission approach, then we will take a conservative view and foster the values of loyalty and participation in elections. A Reflective Inquiry proponent will take a more liberal view and help students participate democratically in society, whereas a Critical Reflective approach will entail teaching students about social justice and oppression at the national and/or international levels. In applying any of these conceptions, the following guidelines for citizenship education are suggested. Students should begin to

- learn how to locate and use information about governance situations
- acquire competency in decision making
- acquire competency in communicating effectively with decision makers
- know the main structures and functions of government
- understand the function of laws and know about the main features of the Canadian Charter of Rights and Freedoms
- acquire competence in cooperating and working with formal and informal organizations involved in promoting one's personal interests and the interests of others
- explore the concept of Canadian identity

Each of these goals has to be translated into appropriate objectives. For example, in a primary class, students can identify services provided by the government in their community. They can examine laws, such as traffic regulations, that directly impinge on their lives. They can become involved in decision-making situations in which their decisions are acted upon, such as choosing where to go on a field trip; deciding how to raise money for a particular school project; or deciding how to celebrate a special day (Canada Day, etc.). They can begin to learn about Canadian symbols and their origins.

Students might also be involved in "action" projects such as helping people in need, visiting people in hospitals, or collecting for charity.[4] They might even lobby for something—a crosswalk at a dangerous intersection near the school or the better treatment of zoo animals. (Both of these examples stem from actual cases in which elementary school students were involved.) Note that there is sometimes controversy about whether or not students should be involved in social action projects like these. Student maturity, the level of student commitment to the action as a follow-up to their own decision, parental expectations, and institutional rules and regulations should all be carefully considered before embarking on such projects. Clark[5] provides the following criteria for judging the worth of a social action project:

1. Will the project promote a sense of empowerment on the part of students?
2. Will the project develop a range of civic competencies?
3. Will the project promote academic learning?
4. Is there a high degree of student interest and personal commitment?
5. Is the cost in teacher time worth the potential benefits?
6. Is there a high probability of achieving what students will deem a success?

In the intermediate grades, students can begin to examine levels of government, how governments are formed, how representatives are elected, how governments and the judicial system function, and how laws are made and enforced. They can also continue to explore the notion of Canadian identity. They can come to understand, at a relatively sophisticated level, concepts like justice, authority, rights, responsibilities, and freedom.

For all of these objectives, the best teaching method is actual participation. Form a classroom government; simulate different forms of government and see how students like living under them; formalize and enforce student-created rules. Students do not learn how to be responsible in a system based on punishment and obedience; they learn how not to get caught.[6] When students are involved in the formation of rules and are taught the reasons behind the rules, they are more likely to behave responsibly and democratically.

Intermediate students should begin to study local, national, and world issues. Where feasible, they should become involved in events that are important to them. If social action is not appropriate, students can at least be given the opportunity to make judgments about policy questions. Here, some of the activities already mentioned can be used, such as the Incinerator game in Chapter 17.

Activity 19-B

This activity could be used with elementary school students by changing the question to "What are the characteristics of a good Canadian elementary school citizen?" The activity, however, is for you, and these are the questions:

- What is a "good citizen"?
- What is a "Canadian"?
- Is there a rule or law that covers the characteristics you identified in the first question? For example, you may state that a good citizen should vote in elections, but there is no Canadian law that enforces voting.
- Whether or not there is a law/rule that defines a "good citizen," should there be? Why or why not?
- If there is a law/rule, or you decide that there should be one, who should enforce it?
- What should be the penalty for not upholding the law/rule? Why?
- Is being a Canadian merely a question of legality or has it got a deeper meaning?
- How do you intend to act on your beliefs about the characteristics of a good citizen? Are these questions relevant to the other curriculum areas discussed (e.g., multicultural, peace, or global education)?

Citizenship education is the responsibility of the whole school, but it has to be emphasized in social studies. We cannot expect students to "pick up" the requirements for good citizenship; they have to be formally taught and practised.

GLOBAL EDUCATION

Activity 19-C

In what ways are other nations involved in, or connected with, each of the following:

a) the room you are in now

b) the clothes you wear

c) the language you speak

d) the weather you are experiencing

  e) the income tax you pay

  f) the TV you watch

  g) the requests you receive for charitable donations

  h) the food you eat

In 1964 there was one TV for every 20 people in the world; now there is one for every four. It took 13 years for TV to acquire 50 million users; the internet did it in five. It is estimated that there were once 10 000 languages; fewer than half are likely to survive this century. English is now spoken by about one fifth of the world's population. In China, 260 000 women read *Cosmopolitan* magazine, and there are 92 000 Amway sales representatives.[7]

As the world becomes increasingly interdependent, social studies educators have begun to aim for a global perspective in curricula. There is dispute about the goals and meaning of global education. Some view it as a means to enhance people's ability to compete in a global economy; others perceive it as a stepping stone to world government; and some include human rights, multicultural, and environmental education under the global education umbrella.[8] However, most proponents emphasize the study of world history, world systems and institutions, world cultures, and world issues. Students are asked to consider themselves as world citizens. To bring this about, educators such as Kniep[9] have proposed the following objectives:

1. Students should, through historical studies, understand the development of humankind, the rise and fall of civilizations and empires, and the causes of contemporary global problems. At the elementary school level, students should be exposed to more than just the history of Canada or Western Europe. They should also study the history of other cultures, looking at events in one part of the world in light of what was happening elsewhere. For example, in studying the first European explorers of Canada, we should emphasize the events that led to these expeditions so that students begin to understand causation and interconnectedness. If students in Canada are constructing time lines of their own or other people's lives, they should also construct a time line showing what was occurring in other parts of the world. Further, any historical topic we are teaching should be put in a global context. If we are studying ancient Greece, let's also ask what was happening in North America at that time (see Chapter 10).

2. Students should understand how Canada relates to the rest of the world, and how they themselves are part of various global economic, political, technological, and ecological systems. A start can be made by having students identify products they use that are of foreign origin, a language they speak other than French or English, or a media or sports star they admire who is not Canadian. They can make a list of 10 words they use frequently and then find out the derivation of those words. In the intermediate grades, students can begin to understand world geographical patterns (see Chapter 11), to learn about international organizations such as the United Nations, and to look at the provisions of the Universal Declaration of Human Rights and the Declaration of the Rights of the Child.

3. Students should be aware of various world views—political, economic, spiritual, aesthetic, and moral. Students in the primary grades can begin to understand that although there are fundamental similarities among people, there are also some deep differences. Students in the intermediate grades can start to look for world patterns by extending

the topic they are studying to the rest of the world. For example, if students are studying a country that has a predominantly Muslim population, they should identify the key tenets of this faith and find out which other countries have large Muslim populations.

4. Students should realize that their actions can contribute both to world problems and to their solutions. There are several ways to show students how they can do this. One way is to focus on development projects sponsored by Canada and supported by Canadian charitable donations. Students could be given scenarios such as the following:

> You are _____ years old. You live in _____. The landscape looks like this: _____. The climate is _____. You have these tools: _____. You have no _____ (e.g., water supply close to where you live). How would you cope? What skills would you need to overcome the problem?

Students could then suggest solutions, which need to be evaluated carefully. Giving money to people or sending in foreign experts may not be the best course of action.

5. Students should avoid stereotyping other people and countries. As we have seen, stereotyping can lead to prejudice and discrimination. To challenge student stereotypes, teachers have to first identify them. Teachers can do this by asking students to write down what they think they know about a particular country or group of people. Where appropriate, students should then compare lists. Ask them where they acquired their information and whether they think it is true. Then have students find evidence for their statements. If many students share the same beliefs, they could work together. When they have located evidence to support or reject their initial beliefs, they should present it to the rest of the class. Care should be exercised here. Teachers should first check to see whether the students have written racist or other derogatory statements. If they have, the teacher should question the student about the derivation of these statements and attempt to persuade the students that they are not justifiable.

6. Students should understand "interdependence" as it relates to themselves and the physical and social world. This requires teachers to draw relationships between the immediate world of the student and the rest of the planet. In the elementary grades, students can begin to compare their own families and communities with those in other countries and see that people share many common needs, goals, and problems. Students can also draw connections between themselves (the food they eat and so on) and the rest of the world. In the intermediate grades, you can discuss global issues and the role that Canada plays (and that students play) in international affairs. By studying other cultures, past and present, students can further develop such fundamental concepts as interdependence, change, conflict, scarcity, and culture.

One significant concept is **sustainable development**. Although this is usually explained as "development which meets the needs of the present without compromising the ability of future generations to meet their own needs,"[10] what qualifies as sustainable development in any particular instance is often a matter of dispute. A basic introduction to the concept, however, is relatively straightforward. Students can be made aware that many of the world's ecosystems are in danger; that the world's population will probably double in 50 years' time; that 20 percent of the world's population consumes 80 percent of the world's goods; and that the gap between rich and poor nations is growing. This information can provide a background to the study of global issues and international development initiatives.

The following activities will help realize the goals of global education:

1. Create webbing diagrams showing how students interact with one another and with other persons in the school. Do the same for the community in which students live, the country, and eventually the world. For an example, continue the chocolate bar diagram in Chapter 13, linking the various phenomena to the rest of the world.

2. Have students trace the origins of the food they eat, the clothes they wear, the toys they play with, etc. Show how all these are dependent on the labour of workers (and sometimes indentured or slave workers), raw materials, transportation, and so on (in effect, a global economic system).

3. Have students trace the origins of the words they use. How many different languages are represented in the languages students speak in the school?

4. Examine social problems in Canada and have students inquire into the roles that various people, including them, will have to play if pollution or poverty is to be reduced.

5. Inquire into particular aspects of foreign aid and foreign development. How is Canada trying to help the less fortunate? Are these efforts worthwhile? Are they well designed? Are they working?

6. Inquire into particular situations in which Canadians are in need of help. Can students do anything to alleviate the suffering of their fellow citizens?

7. Examine a global problem—for example, forest depletion—and have students inquire into the suggested causes and solutions. Can students be part of the solution? How? When choosing problems to study, remember that the objective is not to create the impression that students are powerless or that the problem is too complex to be resolved. Choose problems that provide a chance (if students decide to take it) for some kind of action, even if it is only informing others about the problem.

In all of the above activities it is necessary to engender certain dispositions in students so that they move from a narrow, parochial viewpoint to a more global one.[11] These dispositions include open-mindedness, empathy, the inclination to look beyond simplistic accounts and solutions to complex problems, and the willingness to put aside (where appropriate) personal and national self-interest. Case[12] indicates three forms of bias that are significant in global education: **ethnocentrism**, where one's own culture is viewed as superior to all others; **national fanaticism**, which refers to the view that one's country's interests come before those of other countries; and **presentism**, where the concern is with the interests and well-being of people of today rather than those of future generations. A global-oriented disposition, so as not to be biased, cannot be taught directly. It has to be modelled by teachers in the classroom and supported by the wider community.

LAW-RELATED EDUCATION

Given that social studies is concerned with the study of relationships among people and that many of these relationships are regulated by rules and laws, law-related education has an obvious part in the curriculum. The focus should extend beyond the *what* and *how* of specific laws, to include an understanding of *why* we have a particular system of law. In addition to specific content—such as statutes and regulations and how they are enacted, the court system, and the roles of judges and the police—we need to study the very idea of law and the principles that lie behind it. This will entail understanding some basic legal and moral concepts such as authority, freedom, rights, and justice. How these concepts are defined and applied will help students see how a legal system is justified.

Understanding legal and moral concepts will help students develop the ability to determine whether a particular action is an instance of a concept under consideration. Suppose we are concerned with the concept of justice. Suppose, further, that a student is accused of breaking a school rule. What would constitute justice in such a situation? Is the student given a fair hearing? Can the student call witnesses? Is the student deemed innocent, and is it up to the "authorities" to prove guilt beyond a reasonable doubt? Or is the student deemed guilty before a hearing, with the responsibility placed upon him or her to prove innocence? This type of reasoning is common to situations in which a decision has to be made about whether a particular action falls under a particular rule or concept. So, in baseball, was X a foul ball? In school, was Y a case of cheating? (See Activity 18-G). The point of this type of activity is not to produce student lawyers. Rather, it is to help students understand our law-governed society and to reason about the complex conflicts and issues that face us all.

Law-related educational objectives can be realized not only through the direct teaching of law but also by applying a legal perspective to other social studies content. This can be carried out in numerous ways. Students can begin to understand

- how rules and laws impinge on their lives in the classroom, in the family, in the community, in industry, and in government
- how the court system operates, as well as the roles of the police, the judiciary, and legislators
- what rights and freedoms Canadians have under the Canadian Charter of Rights and Freedoms
- such concepts as human rights, authority, power, democracy, responsibility, freedom, justice, equality, and rules
- how laws are made and what influence the public can have in making and changing laws
- that law is closely bound up with conceptions of morality, and that laws can be changed in response to changing public views of what is immoral

Activity 19-D

Have students try to identify the laws related to the following activities (try this one yourself):

a) buying food at the supermarket

b) mailing a letter

c) having a meal at a restaurant

d) walking a dog

e) buying clothing at a local store

f) telephoning a friend

g) driving a car or riding a bicycle

h) watching TV

We can help students realize law-related educational objectives through activities such as these:

1. Play a game in which the rules are unclear, unfair, or changed arbitrarily. Have the students sit in groups of five or six. Give one student in each group a ball. Tell the students that the first team to pass the ball around the group will win. Before any group completes this task, stop the game and tell the students that the ball must be passed with the left hand only. When group members complete this task, tell them that they are disqualified because they passed the ball clockwise (or counter-clockwise). You can now add other rules that are unclear (pass the ball vigorously) or unfair (only students who are blue-eyed can play). By this time, the students will be thoroughly frustrated and a fruitful discussion about rules can be held.

2. Assign or read students a story where it is unclear whether a particular legal or moral concept applies. For example, was it "fair" on the school's sports day that younger students started a race 10 metres in front of older students?

3. Have students discuss cases where it is unclear whether a rule applies. For example, suppose the rule chosen is "No vehicles in the park." Could a child on a tricycle be arrested? Could an ambulance driver who enters the park to help an injured person be charged? Would the driver of the garbage truck picking up litter have to park his truck outside the park and carry out the garbage?

4. Identify rules that directly impinge on students' lives. Identify the purpose of each rule. Ask what would happen if nobody obeyed the rule. Should there be any exceptions to the rule? Who should enforce the rule? Should there be some kind of penalty if the rule is broken? Who should decide the penalty?

Activity 19-E

Which of the following would be good classroom rules? Why? What purposes do they serve?

> *Nobody shall talk in class.*
>
> *You should enjoy what you do in class.*
>
> *Don't interrupt when someone is talking.*
>
> *Keep your desk tidy.*

a) Could the purposes be better achieved by means other than formal rules?

b) What will be the effects of the rules?

c) Identify the strengths and weaknesses of each rule:

> Is it well designed?
>
> Is it understandable?
>
> Is it clear what is expected?
>
> Is it fair?
>
> Is it designed to minimize infringement of important values?

5. Play a "desert island" game in which the class is marooned. You can decide what food and shelter are available and what the landscape and climate are like. Have the class decide what they'll need to survive, how they'll organize themselves, and what rules or laws they'll need. Or give students a list of rules and have them decide which ones would be good rules. For example:

    a) Females/males shall do all the cooking.

    b) The strongest male/female will be the leader.

    c) Everyone should be allowed to speak and vote on decisions that affect the whole society.

    d) There shall be no stealing of other people's property.

    e) The people who do the most work shall receive the most food.

6. Students could make up their own rules prior to any group discussion. Copies of the rules would be distributed to the class and these would form the basis for the decision-making activity. The rules could be compared to the rights listed in the Universal Declaration of Human Rights and the Canadian Charter of Rights and Freedoms.

7. Hold a **mock trial**. Students can try Goldilocks for eating the bears' porridge. They will be assigned the different roles (the judge, jury, witnesses, defence lawyer, and so on) and will act out the trial procedure.

8. Give students situations in which a legal decision is required. In the following vignette, one student plays Nick, another plays Lorne, and a third is the judge who has to make a decision. Nick and Lorne argue their cases to the judge. They use the following information:

    Nick lends 10 comic books to Lorne.

    Lorne promises to return them in one week.

    Nick warns Lorne to take care of them.

    The comic books cost Nick $1 each.

    Lorne returns the comic books at the end of the week.

    Five comic books are torn and unreadable.

    Lorne says that his younger brother (age three) took the comic books from his room and tore them up.

    Nick demands Lorne pay him $5 to replace the damaged comics.

    Lorne refuses to pay.

    Based on this evidence, the judge decides how this matter should be resolved.

9. When studying other nations or cultures, whether contemporary or past, have students find out about the legal system. For example, when studying ancient Babylon, look at Hammurabi's Code. It is a fascinating vehicle for discussion, containing such laws as this one: "If a man accuses a man, and charges him with murder but cannot convict him, the accuser shall be put to death."

10. Study laws that directly impinge on students' lives. Are these laws

    a) a means of social control over antisocial behaviour?

    b) an effective means of resolving disputes?

c) a means of providing social benefits?

d) a means of providing guidance in daily social affairs?

It appears that young students differentiate between two kinds of rules: conventional mores (e.g., eating food with a knife and fork) and moral rules.[13] The former they view as conditional; the latter they view as absolute even if there is no law. To further develop this distinction, show pictures in which a social custom is displayed (e.g., shaking hands with someone) and ask, "Would it be all right to bow, to rub noses, or to embrace when greeting someone?" Then show pictures of scenes in which a moral rule is violated (e.g., a child hitting another) and ask, "Would it be all right to do this even if there is no rule against it?"

OTHER ACTIVITIES

1. Look at a social studies curriculum and note how citizenship education is conceptualized. Then look at the rest of the curriculum and determine where citizenship education is addressed. Do the content, activities, etc., match the conceptualization?

2. How could law-related education be related to the goals of citizenship education?

3. Design an activity that would help students realize the following objective: Students should understand how the law impinges on them.

NOTES

1. V. Masemann, "The current status of teaching about citizenship in Canadian elementary schools," in K. McLeod, ed., *Canada and Citizenship Education* (Toronto: Canadian Education Association, 1989).

2. I. Wright, "The centrality of critical thinking in citizenship education," *Canadian Social Studies* (2003). www.quasar.ualberta.ca/css/CSS_38_1/ARcentrality_of_critical_thinking.htm

3. F. Gagnon and M. Page, *Conceptual Framework for an Analysis of Citizenship in the Liberal Democracies,* a report to the Multiculturalism Directorate, Citizen Participation Directorate, and Strategic Research and Analysis Directorate, Department of Canadian Heritage, Government of Canada, May 1999.

4. C. Chamberlin, "Citizenship as the goal of social studies: Passive knower or active doer?" *Canadian Social Studies* 26:1 (1991), pp. 23–26. Reprinted in R. Case and P. Clark, eds., *The Canadian Anthology of Social Studies* (Vancouver: Pacific Educational Press, 1999).

5. P. Clark, "All talk and no action: The place of social action in social studies," in R. Case and P. Clark, eds., *The Canadian Anthology of Social Studies* (Vancouver: Pacific Educational Press, 1999).

6. J. Sweeney and F. Monteverde, "Creating a civic culture: Questioning classroom assumptions," in B. Massialas and R. Allen, eds., *Crucial Issues in Teaching Social Studies* (Belmont, Calif.: Wadsworth, 1996).

7. All information taken from *National Geographic* 196:2 (1999).

8. W. Werner, "Whither global education?" *Canadian Social Studies* 27:3 (1993), pp. 121–122.

9. W. Kniep, "Social studies within a global education," *Social Education* 53:6 (1989), pp. 399–403.

10. D. Roche, "The impact of sustainable development on development education," *Institute Newsletter,* Institute for the Humanities, Simon Fraser University, 5:1 (1992), pp. 15–17.

11. W. Werner and R. Case, "Themes of global education," in I. Wright and A. Sears, eds., *Trends and Issues in Canadian Social Studies* (Vancouver: Pacific Educational Press, 1997).

12. R. Case, "Global education: It's largely a matter of perspective," in R. Case and P. Clark, eds., *The Canadian Anthology of Social Studies* (Vancouver: Pacific Educational Press, 1999).

13. L. Nucci, "Conceptual development in the moral and conventional domains: Implications for values education," *Review of Educational Research* 52 (1982), pp. 93–122.

GLOSSARY OF KEY TERMS

Citizenship education — a term used to denote a focus on how people should be governed and how people ought to act as citizens of a country or of the world.

Ethnocentrism — the view that one's own culture is superior to all others.

Global education — a term used to denote a variety of different programs and approaches that focus on developing global understandings, concepts, and perspectives.

Law-related education — a term used to denote a variety of programs and approaches that focus on legal concepts, understandings, and issues.

Mock trial — a simulation of a real legal trial.

National fanaticism — the view that one's own country's interests come before all others.

Presentism — concern with the interests and well-being of people today rather than those of future generations.

Sustainable development — development that meets the needs of the present without compromising the ability of future generations to meet their needs.

chapter twenty

Values in Multicultural, Human Rights, Gender, Peace, and Conflict Resolution Education

In this chapter, we continue the theme of the values inherent in other curricula areas that fall under the social studies umbrella. As you will note, there is considerable overlap between multicultural and human rights education and between these and global education as outlined in the previous chapter. And all of them have to do with citizenship education in its broadest sense.

MULTICULTURAL EDUCATION

Canada's population is ethnically and culturally diverse. According to the 2001 census,[1] 5 978 875 of us identify ourselves as having English origins; 4 668 410 have French roots; 4 157 210 Scottish; 3 822 660 Irish; 2 742 765 German; 1 270 370 Italian; 1 071 060 Ukrainian; 1 094 700 Chinese; 1 000 890 North American Indian; and 713 330 identify ourselves as East Indian.

This diverse population has created both problems and opportunities for educational policy-makers in Canada. For much of the last century, the educational policy was to assimilate new immigrants into Canadian society. Immigrants were encouraged to cast off their cultural roots and live like "Canadians." The same Citizenship Transmission approach was used when Native children were forced into residential schools.

Fortunately, this extreme assimilation/citizenship approach is no longer viewed as justifiable. However, a certain degree of assimilation must take place if society is to operate; new immigrants have to accept the basic tenets of Canadian democracy and the ethical principles of the society, and society has to react to the justifiable demands of minorities.

We all must remember that multiculturalism is official government policy and that discrimination on the basis of race or ethnicity is illegal. The aim in Canada is to

> recognize and promote the understanding that multiculturalism reflects the cultural and racial diversity of Canadian society and acknowledges the freedom of all members of Canadian society to preserve, enhance, and share their cultural heritage.[2]

And Section 15 of the Canadian Charter of Rights and Freedoms states:

> Every individual is equal before and under the law and has the right to equal protection and equal benefit of the law without discrimination and, in particular, without discrimination based on race, national or ethnic origin, colour, religion, sex, age, or mental or physical disability.[3]

With these policies in mind, educators have developed multicultural curricula (some of which include issues of sexism or are placed in a global education framework) and specific anti-racist and anti-prejudice programs for schools. Some educators differentiate between anti-racist programs and multicultural education. Multicultural education focuses more on learning about cultures and celebrating cultural traditions. **Anti-racist education** aims to help students understand the history and contemporary nature of discrimination, and the unequal social and power relationships in institutions and in society in general. It also aims to help students take personal or collective actions to redress inequitable practices. There is intense debate about which of the two approaches should be emphasized.[4] In my view, there is no compelling evidence at present to favour one over the other. For purposes of this chapter, they are treated together since both have significant contributions to make.

Banks[5] outlines four ways that multicultural education could be conceived.

1. **The Contributions Approach:** Here, ethnic heroes are added to the curriculum without changing the basic scope, sequence, or goals. This approach is easy to implement, but students do not gain a comprehensive view of the role that ethnicity plays in Canada. Rather, they see ethnicity as an addendum to Canadian history and present-day society.

2. **The Additive Approach:** Multicultural content, concepts, and perspectives are added to the curriculum without changing the basic structure. Thus, a story about the experiences of a newly arrived immigrant is incorporated into a unit on citizenship; or the history of the first Ukrainians who settled on the prairies is added to the unit on western expansion. This approach is also easy to implement but does not give students a rich sense of multiculturalism.

3. **The Transformation Approach:** This approach infuses the curriculum with multicultural concepts, themes, and issues. It exposes students to a variety of perspectives and would give them a rich sense of the multicultural nature of Canada.

4. **The Social Action Approach:** This approach builds on the Transformation Approach by incorporating components that help students deal with current issues and take actions to bring about a more just society.

Activity 20-A

Given that various approaches can be taken toward multicultural education, which approach(es) would you take?

Examine your answer by carrying out the following activity. Let's say that in the community in which you teach there is an ethnic minority group. Members of the group have been living in the community for 50 years and have been attempting to maintain their ethnic identity. A majority of members of the larger community are prejudiced against them, and there have been overt acts of discrimination and harassment.

Your objective with your class is to attempt to reduce this prejudice. Which of the following approaches would you emphasize? Why?

a) teaching about the culture so that students realize that the group is very different from the majority

b) teaching about the culture to show that the group shares the same basic needs as all other people but has different practices

c) teaching that many of the statements made about the group by members of the majority group are erroneous

d) teaching about the culture by going on a field trip to the group's neighbourhood so that students can have some actual experience of how the group lives

e) presenting cases in which the group was discriminated against

f) having students role-play as members of the group by dressing up, eating their food, dancing, etc.

g) having students read accounts of the life of the group written by the group's own members

h) teaching about the contribution the group has made to Canada

i) taking students to the museum to see artifacts used by the ethnic group in the past

j) teaching students about the nature of prejudice and why it is unjustified

Notice that having information about this group is not enough to reduce the prejudice in the community. This is not to say that knowledge isn't necessary; however, multicultural education must consist of more than teaching and learning information.

Although knowledge of cultures other than one's own can reduce prejudice,[6] it can also engender negative attitudes in students. If we take an outsider's perspective and compare the culture being studied with our own, we may emphasize differences rather than similarities, thereby creating an "us versus them" mentality. Even if an insider's perspective is taken—learning about the culture through the eyes of the participants—students may still judge the culture to be inferior. This perspective, however, does allow for a more realistic view because members of the culture can recount their own version of their ideals and problems. However, we must remember that the accounts we read or the speakers we listen to are not necessarily representative of all the members of the group. This is significant when we come to teach about First Nations people as there are "fifty plus Aboriginal linguistic communities and cultures."[7]

Since young children tend to judge negatively what is unfamiliar or what they find ambiguous, information can certainly help the unfamiliar become familiar and the ambiguous become clear. Children make mistakes when defining racial categories;[8] reliable information will help them create categories that are accurate and non-stereotypical. This explains why it is worthwhile to teach about other ways of life and to participate in the songs and dances of other cultures.

What then should be done? According to Aboud,[9] propositions about how children become prejudiced should guide the development of multicultural education programs. These propositions relate to age groups.

Propositions related to four- to seven-year-olds:

- Prejudice is based on a polarized and simple dichotomy of positive and negative emotions. Greater differentiation among emotions will reduce prejudice.
- Prejudice is based on the egocentric judgment that only one way of experiencing the world is the right one. Learning that there are many ways of being right reduces prejudice.

Propositions related to seven- to twelve-year-olds:

- Judging people on the basis of internal rather then external criteria increases with age and is inversely related to prejudice.
- Attending to between-group similarities and within-group differences increases with age and is inversely related to prejudice.
- Recognizing that one's own perspective may differ from another's and that both perspectives can be valid increases with age and facilitates the acceptance of ethnic differences.

Activity 20-B

Individually, prepare a list of such items as likes and dislikes, what you're good at, and what hobbies or interests you have. Identify your country of origin or the ethnic group(s) to which you belong. Share your list with someone from another country of origin or ethnic group, and with someone who is from your country of origin or ethnic group. Do you share anything with either person? Do you think that if you're a member of some identifiable group, you will necessarily share the same characteristics? What characteristics are you likely to share? What characteristics might differ? Do you think that you and a member of a group to which you don't belong will necessarily share *no* common characteristics?

Children of about three years of age begin to be aware of racial and ethnic characteristics. The type of activity above can demonstrate that there are both within-group and between-group similarities and differences.

We should encourage our young students to recognize a range of feelings and emotions. We should show them that although feelings such as anger and happiness are universal, the same things can affect different people in different ways. (For example, what makes one person happy can create feelings of dislike in another.) Children should be helped to realize that we can experience mixed emotions. One way to do this is to use examples from the students' lives, such as "How would you feel if your best friend won the race that you wanted to win?" or "Can you be glad that you got a present from your aunt even though it wasn't exactly what you wanted?" Make your students aware of other universal characteristics of people. All of us are vulnerable—we can all be injured or killed. All of us are fallible—we can all make mistakes. Each of us has limited knowledge and skills; we each have conflicting desires and wants; and we all make choices. All students should be encouraged to look at people as individuals and to judge on the basis of internal rather than external criteria. Let our students understand that there are as many differences within a group as there are between groups. Encourage them to see that different ways of living can be perfectly acceptable.

All of Aboud's propositions have been applied in curriculum materials developed by Alternatives to Racism.[10]

Among the other guidelines proposed by the many educators working in the area of multicultural education are the following:

1. Accentuate similarities rather than differences between people. The message to be conveyed here is not that we should all be treated the same in every respect and that any differences are aberrations. Rather, it is that we share fundamental characteristics, including certain rights, and that we all should be treated as "persons." A focus on the similarities between people can reduce children's tendencies to negatively evaluate what is different.

2. Students often tend to stereotype others. The realization that there are both within-group and between-group similarities and differences can help students avoid stereotyping, as can the following activities:

   a) Categorize people under a variety of labels to show that a member of a particular group can be classified in a number of ways.

   b) Where a stereotype does exist, show exceptions to that stereotype.

3. Use cooperative learning groups in which there is an ethnic mix to foster positive attitudes toward members of those different ethnic groups. Research studies have indicated that cooperative learning can lead to the reduction of prejudice and the fostering of positive attitudes toward other cultures (see Chapter 9).

4. Have students understand the nature of prejudice and discrimination. Students should understand that prejudice is a positive or negative attitude based on inadequate or erroneous evidence. Discrimination involves acting on prejudices so that individuals, or groups of people, are denied fair and equal treatment. These acts consist of physical attack, verbal hostility, avoidance, and unjust treatment. Ask students to identify examples of each of these types of behaviour and those against whom they are directed. Have students write a story about an act of discrimination, identifying the feelings experienced by the people involved. Use puppets to enact the story. (Using puppets encourages spontaneity. Students are more willing to express themselves freely with puppets because "the puppets" are doing the talking, not the students.) Literature can also be a valuable tool. For example, reading the story of a First Nations elder in northern Manitoba and her friendship with a young boy teaches students not only about Aboriginal culture but also about friendship and trust between old and young.[11] To use literature effectively requires that books be carefully chosen. Bainbridge and her co-authors[12] provide a list of criteria that include these: characters are authentic; members of the minority portrayed feel pride in their background; and the story increases acceptance and understanding.

5. Encourage students to learn how to reason well about empirical, conceptual, and value matters. Value judgments about other cultures are based on beliefs about those cultures as well as the value standards held by students. Principle-testing the value standards used by students (see Chapter 18) has been shown to reduce prejudicial attitudes.[13]

Activity 20-C

Avoiding mistakes in reasoning can help students avoid erroneous beliefs. In this activity, state what fallacies are being committed. Check your responses in the Answers section.

a) New immigrants are really hard-working. My next-door neighbour, who is a new immigrant, works from dawn to dusk seven days a week.

b) The unemployment rate is higher now than it was in 1960. As there are more immigrants now than there were in 1960, the high unemployment rate must be due to immigration.

c) In the past, the majority of immigrants came from Europe. Therefore, the majority of new immigrants should come from Europe.

d) In a recent poll, it was found that a majority of business executives thought that the federal government should cease giving money to ethnic groups for cultural activities. We must take these important people's views seriously and stop giving money to these groups.

e) Unless we stop all immigration, Canada's economy will crumble.

f) If we allow Native peoples to govern themselves, then the Hutterites will want self-government, and soon every group will want self-government and Canada will cease to exist.

In classrooms where student self-esteem is fostered, where there is equality of opportunity, and where students are encouraged to judge others on the basis of internal rather than external characteristics, there is less likelihood of racism and prejudice. When an entire school is committed to the aims of multicultural education, and attempts are made to communicate effectively with minority parents and students, then those aims are more likely to be realized.[14]

This approach requires that the hidden curriculum be in tune with the aims of multicultural education. Teachers and administrators must also become knowledgeable about the beliefs, values, and socio-linguistic conventions of students in the school and learn how best to communicate with students of minority groups. The school is a microcosm of the larger society. If students and teachers can bring about a "society" in which diversity is accepted within a unified and cohesive "nation," then many of the aims of Canadian multiculturalism will have been realized.

HUMAN RIGHTS EDUCATION

The concept of **human rights education** is involved implicitly or explicitly in all the curriculum areas discussed in this and the previous chapter. Citizenship is bound up with the rights accorded members of a nation state; multiculturalism with the rights of ethnic groups; law-related education with rights within a legal system; and global education with universal human rights.

While issues of human rights have been of concern for centuries, it was not until 1948 that the nations of the world, under the auspices of the United Nations, adopted a Universal Declaration of Human Rights. In this declaration, nations committed themselves to the advancement of such rights as equality, life, liberty, freedom of speech, education, and justice. Similarly, the UN Declaration of the Rights of the Child affirms that all children are entitled to such rights as "love and understanding and an atmosphere of affection and security, in the care and under the responsibility of their parents whenever possible," and "protection against all forms of neglect, cruelty and exploitation."

While these declarations have no legal force, the Universal Declaration of Human Rights has been influential. Its principles are evident in the Canadian Charter of Rights and Freedoms, which was entrenched in the Canadian constitution in 1982. However, knowing that the Universal Declaration of Human Rights exists and knowing that the Charter of Rights and Freedoms guarantees certain rights is not enough. Students need some understanding of why we have rights and what having certain rights entails. Thus, students should understand

- the importance of human rights and the consequences of not having them
- the basic tenets of the Universal Declaration of Human Rights, the UN Declaration of the Rights of the Child, and the Canadian Charter of Rights and Freedoms
- the distinctions between types of rights such as equality rights, language rights, and religious rights
- the fact that having rights carries with it the responsibility to uphold the rights of others

The examination of children's rights is an ideal way to study contemporary issues. Because rights cross all realms of human experience and directly concern children as individuals and as members of a group, students can easily understand their importance.

In the primary classroom, activities that focus on basic human needs and goals—and the consequences of not being able to fulfill them—can help students begin to realize the import of human rights. (It is noteworthy that young children *do* think that there are rights to which all people are entitled.[15]) Cooperative learning activities can help students come to this realization and accept responsibility for upholding the rights of others (see Chapter 9). In the intermediate grades, students can begin a more formal examination of human rights documents and start to consider the rights of minorities, people who are physically challenged, and so on. They can begin to understand some of the complexities involved in resolving cases of discrimination. Students can also consider foreign aid programs and how they are influenced by concerns for human rights. Furthermore, they can study problems where human rights are at issue within their own community and within Canada as a whole. In all cases, they should consider the ways in which people have acted to protect or gain human rights, and how people have organized programs to alleviate human suffering on a local, national, or international basis.

All this has to occur in a classroom where rights are respected. How teachers handle disagreements between students, discuss political issues, and react to students from backgrounds different from their own is crucial.

Gender Issues

Sexism is a human rights issue. Issues of gender, therefore, have an important place in social studies. Although gender education encompasses both males and females, for too long females have been relegated to a minor role in social studies curricula and textbooks. Whereas there has been some improvement in the number of females and males depicted in non-traditional roles, especially in elementary textbooks, there is still the problem of reverse stereotyping.[16] This is demonstrated in the way that females are often portrayed in textbooks as *only* being involved in traditionally male roles. There are few portrayals of women engaged in housekeeping, or girls playing with dolls, because these are viewed as reinforcing a stereotype. Further, women are often included only because they were married to men who were famous, or they excelled in roles normally reserved for men. There has been progress but, as Noddings[17] points out, merely showing pictures of women or mentioning them doesn't move us very far toward an inclusive curriculum. She points out that "mentioning women for achievements that would go unrecognized if the subjects were male is demeaning to women and trivializes the history under examination."[18] She argues that the curriculum needs to be radically altered.

> First, there might be much more emphasis on what we once called "private life" as contrasted with "public life." As we know, the sharp separation between the two breaks down under analysis, but the tradition that sustains the separation is still dominant.[19]

Noddings calls for an emphasis on family membership and homemaking, by which she means the study of what constitutes a home, who would count as members of a home, and why a nation is often referred to as a homeland. Like Tupper,[20] who argues that in Canada there is a male bias in conceptions of citizenship education, Noddings asserts that instead of the traditional focus on citizenship education, we need competent parents, homemakers, friends, etc., and that an inclusive curriculum would deal with these "private" matters. As I pointed out in the discussion of the cognitive-developmental approach to moral education in Chapter 18, an approach that seems to favour justice reasoning (viewed as a more male trait) over the ethic of care (viewed as more of a female trait) does not do justice to the complexities of moral reasoning. Yet we see little if anything in social studies curriculum guides about care. In fact, as students move from the study of the family and community, where one would expect there to be a focus on caring, to the study of large geographical regions and the history of Canada, there is more and more emphasis on the "public" sphere than on the "private." How then do we address the "gender gap" in our curriculum? There are several approaches that can be taken.[21]

The Comparison Approach   In the **comparison approach**, the lives and accounts of women are compared with those of men. For example, the lives of pioneer women are contrasted with the accounts of pioneer life written in textbooks by male historians. Comparisons focus on both similarities and differences among a variety of voices. The strength of this approach in the elementary grades is that students are very familiar with identifying similarities and differences. However, its potential weakness is that students may see things in black and white and may not realize the complexity of human lives. Yet we can present the lives of women in their families, in their communities, in the past, and around the world and contrast these to the lives of males. And we can ask students to consider these comparisons and begin to think about questions of sexism.

The Segregated Approach   In the **segregated approach**, women are treated as a separate topic. So, in a community study, the roles of women are examined; in a unit on Canada,
famous and not-so-famous women can be the focus. For example, we could examine the
lives of women during the Cariboo or Klondike gold rush, or the experiences of women during the expulsion of the Acadians, or the life of a farmer's wife on the prairies. The strength
of this approach is that women are seen as deserving special attention; the weakness is that
women are not mentioned except when they are the subject of a special topic.

The Integrated Approach   As the title suggests, in the **integrated approach** women
are incorporated into all aspects of the curriculum. This approach gives women a central
place, socializing students to the equal importance of males and females. It is also likely
to increase self-esteem in girls. However, this approach is difficult to implement because
of a lack of materials. Existing textbooks, despite improvements, often continue to portray
males as the "movers and shakers" and relegate women to sidebars.

These approaches can be put into practice through activities such as these:

1. Have students state what they like and dislike about being a boy or a girl. Compare
   their statements and have students identify which things, if any, could be changed. Are
   their likes and dislikes things that girls or boys are "supposed to" like? In the intermediate grades, have students pretend that they are parents and state what behaviours they
   would expect from their sons and daughters.

2. Give students the following letter, modelled on the type one reads in a popular advice
   column, and have them answer it.

   > Dear Abby,
   >
   > In my class, the girls get to set up the science experiments and supervise the use of the com-
   > puters. We boys get to wipe tables and clean the sink. It should be the other way round. What
   > should we do?

3. Provide students with pictures of various occupations and sports. Students should state
   whether males and females could be involved in these activities. If students say that only
   one sex can be involved, they usually make the claim that there is some difference between
   males and females that precludes the other sex from participating. Have students carry out
   some research and collect evidence about men and women engaged in non-traditional roles.

   Another idea is to ask students what they want to be when they are adults. Can both
   men and women occupy their chosen roles? Are there equal opportunities for both
   sexes to train for their chosen jobs? With primary school children, discuss who does
   what jobs in the home and whether both sexes can do the same jobs.

4. When discussing historical topics, ensure that the role of women is given consideration
   equal to that of men. Have students focus on the role of women in Native cultures; in
   the first European settlements and in all subsequent settlements; and in politics, the
   arts, and science. When students discuss the topic of famous women (see Kirman[22]),
   they could role-play an interview with one of the women, or write a diary as if they
   were that person. In preparing a family history (see Chapter 10), students could focus
   on the history of a female relative. As pointed out in Chapter 5, students could analyze
   their textbook and determine the number of times women are mentioned, who those
   women are, and what they are doing or had done. In the later grades, students could be

encouraged to rewrite a part of the textbook by including women. An interesting historical topic is "costume." Have students find out what men and women wore at different times, the trends in fashion, how these trends were advertised, and what effects fashion had on how men and women portrayed themselves. For example, Victorian middle- and upper-class women wore clothes that restricted their freedom of movement, demonstrating that they did not perform "menial" tasks.

Study the clothing worn by students. With the advent of jeans, have gender differences in clothing been reduced? When studying other cultures, look at clothing and relate it to how males and females view themselves, or are viewed by others. Why do men wear skirts in some cultures? Why do women wear trousers? For further ideas, especially on how women have been treated in the curriculum, see Tetreault.[23]

5. Read stories or biographies of women. Show how both "ordinary" and famous women have made a difference.[24]

6. To help students understand the role played by the media in **sex-role stereotyping**, have students watch television programs and complete the following chart.

Activity 20-D

Try this activity for yourself. Watch a couple of programs and complete the chart.

	Women	Men	Boys	Girls
Activities carried out				
a) for fun				
b) as work in the home				
Occupations				
a) Who was in charge?				
b) Who needed help?				
What people worried about:				
What decisions people made:				

After watching the programs, what general statement can be made about how males and females are portrayed in television programs?

Ask your students to answer the following questions when they watch commercials:

- To whom was the product being sold?
- Whom will the product help?
- Who was shown using it?
- Who was talking about the product?
- What activities were males and females shown doing?
- What message was conveyed about what males and females should be like?
- What values were seen to be important to males and females?

Students could also inquire into how cartoons portray males and females. Are women or girls still viewed as being weaker and less intelligent than men or boys? Do women have jobs? Do they make important decisions?

Primary students could discuss the portrayal of men and women in fairy tales, stories, and nursery rhymes. What do girls and boys do? Who is strong? Who is weak? Would the story be equally sensible if the roles were reversed, for example—a boy being scared by a spider? In the European version of Little Red Riding Hood, the main character is rescued from the wolf by the woodcutter. In the Chinese version, the female character, Lon Po Po, triumphs over the wolf by herself. Teachers could read stories to students in which there are strong female characters or where girls perform roles once reserved for boys. Or students could make up a story in which traditional sex roles are reversed. Telling children stories that lack sex-role stereotyping results in less sex stereotyping by children.[25]

Sex roles are learned early in childhood and are reinforced by society. Students need models. Therefore, the school must be conscious of its role and be careful not to perpetuate sex-role stereotyping. We must be especially aware of the vital role we play in modelling non-sexist behaviour and fostering it in students. We should ask ourselves whether

- we seat and group students by sex
- we have different expectations for boys and girls
- girls and boys are allowed to participate equally in all classroom and school activities
- the roles of women in the curriculum are given equal consideration to those of men
- there is a focus on non-traditional sex roles

PEACE AND CONFLICT RESOLUTION EDUCATION

Peace education, like the other curriculum areas discussed in this chapter, is conceptualized in various ways. For some people, it concerns disarmament and the avoidance of war; for others it relates to conflict resolution in general. Peace may be seen as an ultimate goal or as a means to achieve human rights. The organization InterPares puts it this way:

> Peace is rooted in justice. It is rooted in the principle of self-determination of all people and peoples, free of coercion, acting in their own name. Peace implies, therefore, profound respect for people, their places, their ideas, their aspirations, and their actions to realize the world they imagine. Peace means the acceptance and nurturance of diversity. It means openness to embrace others as ourselves. Peace means dialogue, within and among diverse societies and cultures.[26]

Whatever conception of peace is adopted, peace education should at least introduce students to the following sorts of questions:

a) What is the student's conception of peace?

b) How do other people conceive of peace?

c) What would be the benefits of peace?

d) Is preserving peace more important than fighting for liberty or security?

e) Is the use of force ever justified?

f) Can the use of force (in a particular situation) be avoided? How? Does playing with war toys or watching violent TV programs lead to aggression?

g) What causes wars? What are the effects of war?

h) Is a peaceful life possible without having basic human rights?

Students should not be required to give firm answers to all these questions but rather encouraged to think about peace. The purpose of peace education is to encourage students to reflect on this significant human concern. It is noteworthy that boys in Grades 5 and 6 demonstrate the most interest in war. It is also this age group that shows the most tolerance of other people. This seeming paradox has yet to be explained, but it does suggest that boys at this age may be disposed to reflect on issues of war and peace and how people ought to be treated.[27]

One key way to encourage the resolution of conflicts is to focus on conflict resolution. Bickmore[28] defines this as the "process of seeking to understand conflicts and their sources and to nonviolently resolve them." She describes two dimensions: the substantive one, which involves learning what conflict is about and how it comes about, and the procedural one, focusing on the managing and resolving of conflicts and the resources required. As with any form of values education, we can explicitly teach these dimensions or we can do so indirectly. Explicit teaching can involve helping students understand how conflicts occur in the family, the community, the country, and in the wider world. Existing curriculum content often involves the study of conflicts. They are found in the areas of multiculturalism, gender, citizenship, law, human rights, global studies, and history. Here we can have students analyze the conflict in terms of how it occurred, whose interests are involved, what the various interests are and how these might have emerged, what the relationships are between the people involved, and how the conflict was resolved—if it ever was. Students, where possible, could evaluate the resolution and determine if it was the best one possible. This kind of analysis is also useful in looking at current events and in resolving real problems.[29] Students can be taught to act as peer mediators and can be involved in the establishment and enforcement of classroom rules. Students also learn about conflict resolution indirectly by observing how their parents, teachers, peers, and world leaders deal with conflict. However, not all of these may be justifiable, and students should be encouraged to evaluate them where appropriate.

A simple idea is to have students identify conflict situations that they have experienced and note how they felt, what they thought, and what they did or thought of doing. If what they felt and did was not likely to resolve the conflict, then have students arrive at other actions they might perform to resolve the conflict. For example, if you are pushed, you might feel angry and push back. This might escalate into a conflict. How could this be prevented? This seemingly simple situation has parallels in international affairs; when the World Trade Center was attacked, the reaction of the US was to "push back." Role-playing is another powerful strategy for teaching conflict resolution, since to deal with conflict students need to learn about other people's points of view. For example, the activity where students play the plaintiff, the defendant, and the judge (see the section on Law-Related Education in the previous chapter) can help students realize that a story can have many interpretations and that resolutions to conflicts can vary depending on who is making the resolution. Probably the best strategy that can help students resolve conflicts peacefully is to teach them how to be peer mediators. Bickmore[30] has carried out research in this area in Toronto and has demonstrated its effectiveness. To ensure that peer mediation realizes social studies knowledge objectives, students should learn about the causes of conflict and some of the history of conflict resolution.[31]

Note how interrelated peace and conflict education is with other areas such as citizenship, law-related, global, gender, and multicultural education, and how interrelated all these are with each other. In the introduction to Chapter 19, it was pointed out that the boundaries between the curriculum areas discussed here are flexible. What is common to each is the question of how human beings ought to be treated. Whatever the specific objectives of citizenship, multicultural, global, law-related, human rights, and peace education, they are (or should be) concerned overall with helping students understand themselves and others in many different types of relationships.

OTHER ACTIVITIES

1. State whether you agree or disagree with the following proposition and present your reasons. Share your reasons with a peer, and if you disagree with each other, argue your case. If you agree, do you share the same reasons? Which reasons do you think are most compelling?

   > Having global, human rights, multicultural, law-related, peace, citizenship, conflict resolution, and gender education is confusing. We should incorporate all of them in social studies without giving them separate labels.

2. Analyze a social studies curriculum guide or textbook and ascertain whether any of the subjects discussed in this chapter are mentioned. If they are mentioned, what is the focus—information giving, conceptual understanding, issue resolution?

3. Analyze an elementary social studies textbook for its depiction of women. How many are mentioned? What are their roles? Are they portrayed in non-traditional roles? Are they integrated into the text or do they appear as sidebars? How does their depiction differ from that of males?

4. Create an activity based on a conflict incident in which students have to analyze the conflict, determine what ways are available to resolve it, and decide which way would be the most justifiable.

NOTES

1. Statistics Canada 2001 Census. www.statcan.ca/english/Pgdb/demo28a.htm

2. From Bill C-93, *An Act for the Preservation and Enhancement of Multiculturalism in Canada*, House of Commons, July 12, 1988.

3. *Canadian Charter of Rights and Freedoms*, Constitution Act, 1982.

4. J. Kehoe, "Multiculturalism in social studies," in I. Wright and A. Sears, eds., *Trends and Issues in Canadian Social Studies* (Vancouver: Pacific Educational Press, 1997).

5. J. Banks, *An Introduction to Multicultural Education*, 2nd ed. (Boston: Allyn and Bacon, 1999).

6. J. Banks, "Multicultural education: Its effects on students' racial and gender role attitudes," in J. Shaver, ed., *Handbook of Research on Social Studies Teaching and Learning* (New York: Macmillan, 1991).

7. J. Orr, "Teaching social studies for understanding First Nations issues," in A. Sears and I. Wright, eds., *Challenges and Prospects for Canadian Social Studies*, 2nd ed. (Vancouver: Pacific Educational Press, 2004).

8. N. Wyner and E. Farquhar, "Cognitive, emotional and social development: Early childhood social studies," in J. Shaver, ed., *Handbook of Research on Social Studies Teaching and Learning* (New York: Macmillan, 1991).

9. F. Aboud, *Children and Prejudice* (Oxford: Blackwell, 1988).

10. These include *Alternatives to Racism: New Friends* (1984); V. Bowers and D. Swanson, *More Than Meets the Eye* (1989); V. Rogers, *All the Colours of the Rainbow: A Multicultural Storybook* (1990); and V. Rogers, *Apple's Not the Only Pie: A Multicultural Storybook* (1990). All have accompanying teachers' guides and all are available from Pacific Educational Press, University of British Columbia, Vancouver, BC V6T 1Z4.

11. P. Eyvindson, *Red Parka Mary* (Winnipeg: Pemmican Publications, 1996).

12. J. Bainbridge, S. Pantelo, and M. Ellis, "Multicultural picture books: Perspectives from Canada," *The Social Studies* 90:4 (1999), p. 185.

13. J. Kehoe and F. Echols, "Educational approaches for combatting prejudice and racism," in S. Shapson and V. D'Oyley, eds., *Bilingual and Multicultural Education: Canadian Perspectives* (Avon, UK: Multilingual Matters, 1984).

14. J. Kehoe, *A Handbook for Enhancing the Multicultural Climate of the School* (Vancouver: Pacific Educational Press, 1983).

15. L. Stone, "Intercultural and multicultural education," in V. Atwood, ed., *Elementary Social Studies: Research as Guide to Practice* (Washington, DC: National Council for the Social Studies, 1986).

16. P. Clark, "Between the covers: Exposing images in social studies textbooks," in R. Case and P. Clark, eds., *The Canadian Anthology of Social Studies* (Vancouver: Pacific Educational Press, 1998).

17. N. Noddings, "Social studies and feminism," in E. Ross, ed., *The Social Studies Curriculum: Purposes, Problems and Possibilities* (New York: State University of New York, Albany, 1997).

18. Ibid., p. 59.

19. Ibid., p. 63.

20. J. Tupper, "The gendering of citizenship in social studies curriculum," *Canadian Social Studies 36:3*, www.quasar.ualberta.ca/css/Css_36_3/ARgendering_of_citizenship.html

21. L. Bloom and A. Ochoa, "Responding to gender equity in the social studies curriculum," in B. Massialas and R. Allen, eds., *Crucial Issues in Teaching Social Studies* (Belmont, Calif.: Wadsworth, 1996).

22. J. Kirman, "Women's rights in Canada: A sample unit using biographies and autobiographies in teaching history chronologically," *Social Education* 54:1 (1990), pp. 39–42.

23. M. Tetreault, "Rethinking women, gender, and the social studies," *Social Education* 51:3 (1987), pp. 170–179.

24. S. Hart, "Listening to a different voice: Using women's stories in social studies," *Canadian Social Studies* 31:2 (1997), pp. 90–92, 96.

25. J. Banks, "Multicultural education: Its effects on students' racial and gender role attitudes," in J. Shaver, ed., *Handbook of Research on Social Studies Teaching and Learning* (New York: Macmillan, 1991), p. 465.

26. InterPares, *Annual Report 2002* (Ottawa: InterPares, 2002), p. 1.

27. L. Stone, p. 36.

28. K. Bickmore, "Education for peacebuilding citizenship: Teaching the dimensions of conflict resolution in social studies," in A. Sears and I. Wright, eds., *Challenges and Prospects for Canadian Social Studies*, 2nd ed. (Vancouver: Pacific Educational Press, 2004).

29. For an example of a unit dealing with violence, see R. McBee, "Can controversial issues be taught in the early grades? The answer is Yes!" *Social Education* 60:1 (1996), pp. 38–41, and for one on conflict in general, see K. Bickmore, "Conflicts global and local: An elementary approach," *Social Education* 66:4 (2002), pp. 235–238.

30. K. Bickmore, "Peer mediation training and program implementation in elementary schools: Research results," *Conflict Resolution Quarterly* 20:2 (2003).

31. K. Bickmore, "Conflicts global and local: An elementary approach," *Social Education* 66:4 (2002), pp. 235–238, and K. Bickmore, "Student conflict resolution, power 'sharing' in schools, and citizenship education," *Curriculum Inquiry* 31:2 (2001), pp. 137–162.

GLOSSARY OF KEY TERMS

Anti-racist education — designed to help students understand the history and contemporary nature of discrimination and the unequal power relationships in society so that they will take action to bring about social justice.

Comparison approach to gender studies — comparisons between male and female experiences, how males portray females, and vice versa.

Conflict resolution — a process of seeking to understand conflicts and their sources and to resolve them non-violently.

Human rights education — a term used to denote a variety of programs and approaches that focus on human rights concepts, understandings, and issues.

Integrated approach to gender studies — the experiences and actions of women are incorporated into all facets of the curriculum.

Multicultural education — education to develop understanding and respect for other cultures and their contributions. There are four approaches:

> **Additive** — multicultural concepts and understandings are added to the curriculum without changing the basic structure of the curriculum.

> **Contributions** — accounts of heroes who belong to ethnic minorities are added to the curriculum without changing the scope, the sequence, or the goals.

> **Social action** — focusing on helping students bring about a more just society.

> **Transformation** — infusion into the curriculum of multicultural concepts, understandings, and issues.

Peace education — a term used to denote a variety of programs and approaches that focus on peace and conflict resolution.

Segregated approach to gender studies — the experiences and actions of women are treated as a separate topic in the curriculum.

Sex-role stereotyping — the view that only one gender can perform certain tasks or occupy particular roles.

chapter twenty-one

How Good Are Students at Decision Making? Assessing and Evaluating Students

In Chapter 15, several different assessment procedures were discussed. All of them can be used to evaluate students in the areas of decision making and valuing. For example, we can test steps in the decision-making procedure using a variety of methods already outlined.

The first step is *clarification of the problem*, which could be assessed by using the following type of scenario:

> On Saturday, Judy has been invited to a) attend a birthday party, b) go swimming, and c) go to a movie. She doesn't have time to do all three, and she doesn't like swimming. What is Judy's problem?

Another item could consist of a vignette such as the following ones, in which students have to identify the decision that has to be made:

> Your class has decided to have a bake sale next Thursday. Everyone has offered to do something to help with the sale. Which of the following is the most important decision that has to be made next?
>
> a)   when to have the bake sale?
>
> b)   who will buy the food at the sale?
>
> c)   whether you want to have a bake sale?
>
> d)   who will bring what food to sell?

Fur traders who are buying furs are deciding whether to canoe from one fur-trading post to another much farther up the river or to return to the main fort. Which of the following is the most important decision to be made?

a) whether there will be enough food for the trip

b) whether there will be enough furs to buy at the post

c) whether the river will be rough

d) whether the mosquitoes will make the trip really uncomfortable

Activity 21-A

Create at least one test item that would test students' ability to clarify the potential problems of "latchkey children" (children who are at home alone when they leave for school and/or when they return from school).

To test for student competency in *generating alternatives*, students can be presented with a particular event and asked to list as many alternatives as possible. Alternatives can be evaluated on the basis of quantity and plausibility. Here are two examples:

> Your baseball team needs new uniforms, but the team has no money. List as many ways as you can think of to get the money to buy new uniforms.

> You are Simon Fraser and you are travelling down the Fraser River with three canoes when you come to a very steep canyon with very dangerous rapids. What could you do?

Activity 21-B

Create at least one test item to determine how well students can generate alternatives for solving one of the following problems: a) too much traffic in the downtown area; b) fighting in the school playground; c) girls' not being involved in after-school baseball because the boys make fun of them; or d) homelessness in the community.

The following examples of items might be used to assess student ability in *identifying consequences*:

a) You have to decide what to do during the summer. In the left-hand column of the following chart is a list of choices. On the right is a list of the benefits you might gain from each choice. Match each choice with its *most likely gain*.

Choices	Gains
Taking swimming lessons	Rest
Getting a babysitting job	A healthier body
Taking art classes	Money
Relaxing at home	New skills

b) List as many consequences as you can of the following event:

> If the Great Lakes dried up, then _____.

Activity 21-C

Create at least one test item to determine if students can identify the consequences of taking the proposed courses of action in the following situation:

> In order to make it safer for students to cross a busy intersection, the following proposals have been made: a) hire a crossing guard; b) build an overpass or underpass; c) put in traffic lights; d) put up warning signs for motorists; e) give all students instructions on how to cross the road safely.

These sorts of items are fairly straightforward, and good answers are not difficult to determine. However, the criteria for determining good answers to value questions are sometimes more difficult. This does not mean that students' reasoning, or the products of their reasoning, cannot or should not be evaluated. The following type of "test" can be administered, and the teacher can use the criteria outlined below to evaluate student responses.

A vignette is presented in which someone has to make a decision that concerns other people. The following questions are then posed:

a) What decision should you make?

b) What, if any, would be the benefits to you?

c) What, if any, would be the disadvantages to you?

d) What, if any, would be the benefits to the others involved?

e) What, if any, would be the disadvantages to the others?

f) If you were the disadvantaged person, would it be right to act on the decision? Why or why not?

g) Here is a similar case. Would you make the same decision in this case? Why or why not?

h) Would you want everyone to make the same decision in this case? Why or why not?

Evaluation of responses should be based on the chart on page 284:
Here is an example that incorporates many of the questions posed above.[1]

> In the town of Actum there is a downtown area that contains many heritage houses. A developer approaches the town council seeking permission to build a much-needed shopping centre that will revitalize the downtown area. If the shopping centre is built, the business community will be delighted. But the people who live in the heritage houses do not wish to move.

1. If the shopping centre is built, what problem would this cause?

    a) There would be too many shops.

    b) People would lose their homes.

    c) There would be too many people in the downtown area.

2. If the shopping centre is built, who will be most disadvantaged?

    a) The people who live in the heritage houses.

Excellent	Good	Fair	Needs help
Can identify the consequences to self and others	Identifies major consequences	Identifies a few consequences	Cannot identify consequences
Has fairly clear ideas of what is in one's own best interest	Identifies what is in one's own best interest	Has difficulty identifying what is in one's own best interest	Cannot identify what is in one's own best interest
Is able to put self in the shoes of the other person and consider that person's needs, interests, and feelings	Can identify other person's needs, interests, and feelings	Can identify some of other person's needs, interests, and feelings	Cannot identify other person's needs, interests, and feelings
Can consider universal consequences of acting on the decision	Can generalize the decision to other cases	Can generalize the decision to one other case	Cannot generalize the decision
Is able to consider other similar cases and state why the decision applies or does not apply in the new cases	Can give plausible reasons the case applies or does not apply to several new cases	Can give plausible reasons the case applies or does not apply in another case	Is unable to see relevance of a new case to the one being considered
Is willing, where appropriate, to put aside prudential concerns and make decisions that do not harm others	Puts aside prudential concerns	Cannot decide whether prudential concerns outweigh moral concerns	Acts solely on prudential concerns
In group decision-making sessions, is willing to seek advice and consider the views of others in the group	Seeks advice and considers others' viewpoints in a consistent way	Occasionally considers others' viewpoints and seeks advice	Rarely, if ever, considers others' viewpoints or seeks advice

   b) The developer.

   c) The shoppers.

3. If the shopping centre were built, how would you feel if you were one of the people who lived in the heritage houses?

   a) Happy because you would get a new house.

   b) Unhappy because you do not want to move.

   c) Happy because you would have more stores to shop in.

   d) Unhappy because you like the furniture in your house.

4. What is the best way to make the decision?

   a) Let everyone in the town decide.

   b) Let the developer decide.

   c) Let the business people decide.

   You could then pose other questions about alternative solutions to this problem and about the best solution, and ask students whether their decision would be different if the facts of the case were different. For example: Suppose the heritage houses were the only examples of this type of house left in Canada. Would this make a difference to your decision?

You can use this type of item as the basis for a **performance** or **authentic assessment**. Listen to a group of students and keep a record of their deliberations as they try to resolve the problem. Place particular emphasis on how well they define the problem, generate alternatives and consequences for proposed actions, and argue for a particular solution. In the intermediate grades, students could write a letter to the editor of their local newspaper stating how they would resolve the issue. Evaluate the letter using the criteria outlined above.

Activity 21-D

This test is for you.[2] It is designed to assess how well you would lead a class discussion on a value issue. For each example, decide which is the best question to ask.

Example 1

TEACHER: Students shouldn't take school paper home for their personal use.

STUDENT: Well, our parents pay for it, so why shouldn't we?

What should you (as teacher) say?

   a) Let's take a vote. Who agrees with that and who doesn't?

   b) How many of you take paper home for your personal use?

   c) What would happen if the principal caught you?

   d) Your parents also help pay for the video machines. Should you take them home for your personal use?

Example 2

TEACHER: Should you help other people even if it inconveniences you? Suppose a person in a wheelchair needs help getting the chair into a building and you are in a rush to get to a movie. Should you help?

STUDENT: No, the person in the wheelchair shouldn't go places where it is difficult for wheelchairs.

What should you (as teacher) say?

   a) Would you think it was right if nobody helped you if you were in a wheelchair?

   b) Should there be laws to make all buildings wheelchair accessible?

   c) *[To another student]* Would you help?

Example 3

TEACHER: Don't walk on the running track. It's against the school rules.

STUDENT: But what harm does it do if I walk on the track?

What should you (as teacher) say?

   a) I'm telling you it's against the rules.

   b) But what would happen if everyone did that?

   c) Are you saying it's not against school rules?

   d) How would you feel if you were me?

Example 4

TEACHER: Should we allow more refugees into Canada?

STUDENT: They would take jobs away from Canadians.

What should you (as teacher) say?

   a) Have you any evidence for saying that?

   b) Does it matter if they take jobs away from Canadians?

   c) Do you all agree that they take jobs away from Canadians?

   d) Do you have any other reasons?

Example 5

TEACHER: Is it fair that Derek chose Alex for the team, and not Ian, even though Ian is the better player?

STUDENT: Yes, because Alex is Derek's brother and Alex would be upset if he wasn't chosen.

What would you (as teacher) say?

   a) Do you think Ian is the better player?

   b) Ian, do you think it's fair?

   c) Alex, do you think it's fair?

   d) Suppose Derek was in charge of surgery at a hospital and chose his brother to perform an operation even though another doctor was a much better surgeon. Would this be right?

Wherever judgments are made, attitudes will be brought into play. As teachers, we may wish to find out what attitudes students have toward a particular issue, and we may want to change students' attitudes. The following types of attitude measures should not be used to *evaluate* students. They should be used a) to find out what individuals think so that what is taught takes into account students' attitudes and b) to discover whether attitudes change over time. Attitude measures are administered in a pre- and post-test format. They should be anonymous so that students will be more likely to divulge their true feelings and not simply write what they think the teacher wants them to write.

Here are some examples of ways in which student attitudes can be determined.

1. On meeting a uniformed member of the police force, I feel…

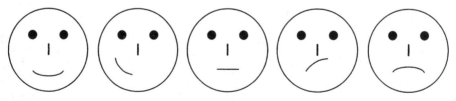

2. Members of the police force are friendly.

Strongly agree	Agree	Don't know	Disagree	Strongly disagree

3. Members of the police force are...

___ bad   ___ good

___ hard-working   ___ lazy

___ stupid   ___ clever

___ brave   ___ cowardly

4. Circle the words that tell what you feel about the police force:

interesting	worthwhile	necessary
important	exciting	dull

5. If you were to study the police force, what topics would interest you? Put a 1 against your first choice, a 2 against your second, and so on.

___ Police Dog Handling and Training

___ Police Cars

___ How the Police Are Trained

___ A Typical Day in the Life of a Police Officer

___ Crime Fighting

6. When I see a member of the police force, I think...

Activity 21-E

Create an instrument to determine students' attitudes toward one of the following: the study of Canadian history or geography, gun laws in Canada, recycling, or violence on television.

One other assessment technique is to observe students' behaviours. Here we infer students' motivations, feelings, and attitudes from their speech and behaviour and note them down, either as anecdotal records or on a checklist. However, we must remember that what is in students' minds cannot be accurately identified by simple observation of their actions. We have the problem of how to determine that a given observable action is an example of a particular sensitivity, disposition, attitude, or trait. Suppose we are interested in ascertaining how respectful students are. We can observe a student hitting another child, but the act of hitting is not a trait; a trait is the *interpretation* of an action, which, in this situation, fits under our concept of non-respect.

We cannot observe responsibility, caring, etc. We can only *infer* them from certain actions. Are our inferences valid? There are three concerns here:

1. Do we have a clear concept of the trait, disposition, or attitude? Suppose a student always puts his hand up in class when he wishes to speak. Suppose he does this out of fear of punishment, or because he wants to please the teacher, or because he realizes that this rule respects the rights of others. Perhaps he does it out of habit and has forgotten the reason he does it. Are all of these reasons examples of respect? Would we want to say that the student is a respectful person? Suppose a student considers a school rule to be a violation of her rights. Would it be *responsible* behaviour for her to protest against the rule?

2. How many examples of the exhibition of the trait do we need in order to say that someone is respectful or responsible? Will one example suffice?

3. To what extent do personality traits play a role in how students behave? Certainly we want students to be respectful and responsible, but an introvert may well display these traits in idiosyncratic ways. In a group project, should we assess the shy child in the same way as the outgoing child?

There are thousands of studies, from before Piaget's time to the present, demonstrating that children develop in their social reasoning. Thus a seven-year-old will keep a promise because she wants to please her parents, or because she fears punishment if she does not. A nine-year-old will keep a promise because he wants others to keep their promises to him. A thirteen-year-old will keep her promise because this is the convention of her peer group. Would we say that a thirteen-year-old who is using a seven-year-old's reasons for keeping promises is as responsible as a thirteen-year-old who appeals to developmentally appropriate reasons? That is, do we say that someone is acting in a socially acceptable way for the wrong reasons?

Clearly, we must be very careful in assessing student attitudes and sensitivities. This does not mean that assessment is impossible or that it should not be carried out. As the example below attests, we can create rubrics that can be used to assess students in a responsible way.

Responsibility (Grades 3 to 4)		
Poor	**Moderate**	**Good**
Rarely helps others	Sometimes helps others	Usually helps others
Needs to be reminded of classroom rules	Sometimes needs to be reminded of classroom rules	Usually follows classroom rules
Has to be told to do chores	Sometimes volunteers to do chores	Usually volunteers to do chores
Rarely completes tasks on time	Sometimes completes tasks on time	Usually completes tasks on time
Does not accept consequences for own actions	Sometimes accepts consequences for own actions	Usually accepts consequences for own actions

OTHER ACTIVITIES

1. How would you ascertain the attitudes of Grade 6 students toward the Canadian government's immigration policy?

2. How would you evaluate the ability of Grade 1 students to make decisions?

3. How would you determine if Grade 3 students can put themselves into another person's role?

NOTES

1. Adapted from C. Bognar and W. Cassidy, *Social Studies in British Columbia: Technical Report of the 1989 Social Studies Assessment* (Victoria, BC: Assessment, Examinations and Reporting Branch of the Ministry of Education, 1991).

2. Adapted from the work of the Association for Values Education and Research, University of British Columbia.

GLOSSARY OF KEY TERMS

Performance (authentic) assessment — assessing students while they are actually engaged in a task.

WEBSITES FOR PART 4

Global Education

American Forum for Global Education:
www.globaled.org

AusAID Global Education:
www.globaleducation.edna.edu.au

Canadian Hunger Foundation Lesson Plans:
www.partners.ca

Canadian International Development Agency:
www.acdi-cida.gc.ca

Statistical Information about UN Countries:
www.un.org/cyberschoolbus

United Nations:
www.unesco.org/education/index.shtml

World Resources:
www.k-12world.com

Human Rights

Alberta Teachers Association Diversity and Human Rights:
www.teachers.ab.ca/diversity/index/html

Amnesty International:
www.amnesty.ca

Canadian Civil Liberties Association:
www.ccla.org

The Child's Rights Information Network:
www.crin.org

Girls' Rights:
www.girlsrights.org

Human Rights Education Organization:
www.hrea.org

Human Rights Resource Center:
www.hrusa.org

Law-Related Education

Centre for Education, Law and Society at Simon Fraser University and the Law Courts Education Society of British Columbia:
www.lawconnection.ca

Multicultural Education

Canadian Council for Multi/Intercultural Education:
www.ccmie.com

Canadian Multicultural Education Foundation:
www.cmef.ca

Canadian Race Relations Foundation:
www.crr.ca

Community Learning Network:
www.cln.org/subject_index.html

Diversity Learning Gateway Project:
www.diversitylearning.ca

Handbook of Research in Multicultural Education:
www.wileycanada.com

Multicultural Education Resources:
www.schoolnet.ca/home/e/resources

Skipping Stones, an International Multicultural Magazine:
www.SkippingStones.org

UN High Commissioner for Refugees:
www.un.org/Pubs/SchoolBus/index.asp

chapter twenty-two

Writing a Unit Plan

In this chapter, we synthesize all the material covered in previous/earlier chapters into a unit plan. In practice, unit planning is not a linear procedure. Although the rationale, objectives, subject matter, instructional activities, and assessment must all be logically related, this does not mean that we have to develop a unit in this order. We could start with the results of a social studies assessment, determine what students do not seem to know, and use the assessment instrument as the basis of our instruction. Or, we may determine that we really want students to learn how to use a decision-making strategy and choose the subject matter that best matches this strategy. This chapter is written on the assumption that although we often have definite plans for a particular topic, there are times when we start out with very few clear ideas.

THE CONTEXT

Choose a grade level or class. Answer the following questions:

1. What does the curriculum guide suggest that students at this grade level or in this class should learn?

2. Do you think this would be relevant, interesting, significant, and worthwhile?

3. Would it be within the students' capabilities?

4. If the curriculum guide allows you to choose your own topic, is there a skill, sensitivity, concept. problem, or generalization that seems especially relevant to you and/or your students—for example, a current event? If there is, can you give positive answers to the questions above?

5. What is my basic philosophy? What are my basic aims?

THE RATIONALE

Having chosen the topic, write down some good reasons for teaching it. You may think of other reasons as your planning becomes more specific.

Here is an example for a Grade 2 unit on the community:

Topic: The Community (Grade 2)

Rationale: The curriculum guide suggests this topic be studied in Grade 2. Given that students interact constantly with their community, it is a significant topic. The topic provides opportunities for students to learn about the interactions of people and people's interactions with the environment. This knowledge can then be built upon in later grades when students learn about other communities in the world. Students can begin to realize that a community is a microcosm of the wider world, and many of the concepts that are significant in studying communities are useful in other contexts. A community study can provide the concrete experiences that young students require. Also, a variety of skills can be developed—simple mapping, graphing, interviewing, and so on. All these skills are significant in the further pursuit of social studies goals and in everyday life. Resource materials are easily found in the community.

THE MAJOR GOALS

In broad terms, what are your goals? Will they include subject matter knowledge, information gathering and reporting, intellectual standards, personal and social values, and citizenship action? Example:

Goals for the study of a community

Subject matter knowledge: knowledge of the community (history, geography, and people); how people meet basic needs and how they are interdependent.

Information gathering and reporting: getting information on field trips, from guest speakers, and by interviewing people in the community; reporting by using simple maps and charts.

Intellectual standards: accuracy of information.

Social and personal values: appreciation for interdependence and responsibility to maintain interdependent relationships.

THE SCOPE OF THE SUBJECT MATTER

If these broad goals do not indicate exactly what subject matter should be studied, then we have to analyze it into subtopics. Given that the topic of **interdependence** in the community is broad, what subject matter could be studied? Here, a web is useful. An example of a web called "The Community" is shown at the top of the following page.

It may be impossible to study all these subtopics, so a decision has to be made about which one(s) will be included. Rather than trying to cover everything and thereby creating a kind of hodgepodge unit, choose a focus. This may already be evident in your statement of goals. If it is not, then decide to emphasize disciplinary or interdisciplinary knowledge and organize your unit around a theme, a concept, a generalization, an issue, an inquiry, a problem, a project, or a narrative.

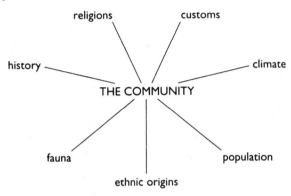

When you have identified a focus, then a rationale has to be provided for it. Of course, if you've chosen a particular focus at the outset, then you will have already settled on your rationale. However, if you've only provided a very broad rationale for your topic, then you need to give good reasons for choosing the focus that the unit will have. For example, if you decide to tackle "multiculturalism" or "pollution" as your overall topic, you have to decide what content is suitable for your particular grade or age level. If you were to select the concept of "change" as your focus, your rationale might look like the following:

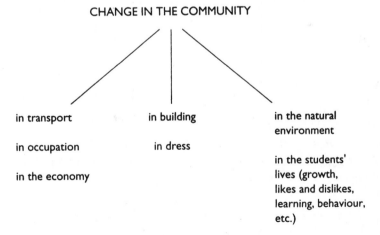

Topic: Change (Grade 3)

Rationale: Change is constant, and students should begin to consider how and why change occurs and what influence they can have on the process of change in particular contexts. Students experience change in themselves (in growth, in learning, in how they behave) and in their community (new buildings, more pollution, etc.). For this age group, both contexts are suitable vehicles through which to begin to comprehend the concept of change.

Now choose the content that will exemplify your focus. Example:

Topic: Change in the Community (Grade 3)

THE OBJECTIVES

Throughout this exercise, more specific objectives will be coming to the fore. At what stage you actually specify and articulate these objectives is a matter of judgment. Some educators like to write them early on; others like to state them after they have outlined a broad framework. I actually work by writing down my goals and then listing specific objectives as they come to mind; then I finalize the list when all the pieces are in place.

When choices have been made concerning the major goals and framework for the unit, then objectives can be stated in more specific terms. For example, if the objective is "to learn about what tasks the mayor of the community performs," it can be expressed as follows: "The student will correctly name tasks performed by the mayor." Suppose our topic is the history of the local community. We might write the objective as "Students will know about the history of the community." But this is too vague to be useful. If the objective is unclear, then so too will be your evaluation of student learning. Thus, we need to specify objectives as clearly as possible.

Activity 22-A

From the objectives below, identify the ones that are clearly stated.

a) The student will really understand the history of the Riel Rebellion.

b) The student will write a three-page essay on the life of Pierre Trudeau.

c) The student will correctly write a definition of the term "gillnetter."

d) The student will interpret a map.

e) The student, when given a map, will be able to measure accurately the distance between two points.

f) When given the name of a country, the student will identify the capital city of that country.

g) The student will know capital cities.

Clear objectives use verbs such as *list, identify, draw, explain, define, model, measure,* and *solve*. They derive from the broad aims of the unit and are statements of value judgments about what students should learn.

Activity 22-B

Specifying your objectives:

a) "Students will know about New Brunswick." Make up three specific objectives that would relate to "knowing about New Brunswick."

b) "Students will understand the economic impact of the St. Lawrence Seaway on the provinces of Quebec and Ontario." State three specific objectives that would express this major goal in measurable terms.

Having identified knowledge objectives, you are in a position to determine the information-gathering and information-processing tools necessary to attain the knowledge objectives. For example, if students use an atlas to find the distance between Montreal and Paris, they must locate the appropriate map, using the index and reference system to find Montreal and Paris. Then they must use the map scale and a suitable measuring instrument to ascertain the distance between the two cities.

Activity 22-C

For each of the following objectives, identify the information-collecting and information-processing tools that the student would be practising or learning.

Objective: Using floor plans and pictures of a Roman villa, the student will write a description of the villa.

Objective: Using library resources, the students will draw five means of transportation used to get from the British Columbia coast to the Cariboo goldfields in the 1860s.

Objective: In groups, students will tour the local supermarket and compose a list of jobs performed there.

Social studies is not only concerned with objectives about "knowing that" and "knowing how"; it is also concerned with dispositions, sensitivities, and appreciations. These objectives are often labelled "affective" objectives. Basically, affective objectives state how we want students to be disposed toward something, or what we want students to value. In the objectives above, we may wish students to *appreciate* the hardships suffered by gold miners in the Cariboo. In studies of cultures or ethnic groups, we will want students to *respect* cultural differences. In decision making, we will wish students to be *willing* to consider points of view that differ from their own. In studies of disadvantaged people, we would like students to *feel empathy*. It is often difficult to write these objectives in specific terms. For example, we could specify that the demonstration of a positive attitude toward disadvantaged people would consist of giving money to a charitable organization, but this is only one aspect of what we might consider "a positive attitude." In the case of appreciating the hardships of gold miners, we might interpret a student's statement "I'm glad I'm not him" an indication that the student has some appreciation. When stating affective objectives, you should have some idea of what would constitute successful performance, even though your criteria are "subjective."

THE SEQUENCE

Having obtained a broad perspective on the scope of the unit, you can now put it into a logical sequence.

1. What kind of prior knowledge will students need to have? Do specific concepts and skills have to be taught before the unit is actually presented?

2. Would it be best to start with something students are familiar with or something they are not familiar with?

3. Could another topic in a different subject area act as a springboard for this unit?

4. What would be a logical sequence once a starting point has been ascertained?

5. How can the unit be organized so that the major findings are synthesized?

6. Can the unit be sequenced so that the information or skills covered relate to other subject areas?

OPENERS

Whatever the sequence, there needs to be an opener so that students are motivated and excited about the unit. Stating "Today, class, we're going to study X; open your textbooks at page Y" is unlikely to stimulate students. Below are some ideas that are designed to spark student interest.

Activity 22-D

Study the photographs that follow and answer the questions below.

a) In what country were these photographs taken?

b) What led you to this conclusion? What clues did you use?

c) On the basis of your experience with the photographs above, predict how well you will do in identifying photographs of the above country X from a number of photographs that may or may not be of country X.

d) Which of the next set of photos are of country X? Consult the Answers section.

Photo 1

Photo 2

Photo 3

Photo 4

Photo 5

Photo 6

Photo 7

Why were you successful or unsuccessful in identifying these photos?

The above procedure is an adaptation of the **discrepant data technique**. First, we identify a stereotype that we think people hold. In this case, the stereotype was that certain scenes are definitely Canadian. Second, we reinforce this stereotype by showing pictures that fit the stereotype. Third, we introduce discrepant data that do not fit the stereotype, so that, fourth, we have to re-examine the stereotype and formulate a new generalization.

Suppose children have stereotypic views about the continent of Africa; for example, only black people live there, or all the people are hunters or farmers, and so on. Show pictures of people who live in Africa that fit the students' stereotypes and ask them, "Who are these people?" and "Where do they live?" Then, having ascertained that all the pictures are of people who live in Africa, say, "I'm going to show you some more pictures and I want you to tell me where *these* people live." Display pictures of people who live in Africa that do not fit the stereotype. If students incorrectly identify the pictures (and in my experience they will), then state that all the pictures were of people who live in Africa. The new information will have to be reinforced during your unit, as some students may be dubious.

Another opener is to show students an object or picture of something unknown to them. Students have to guess what the object is by asking questions that demand a *yes* or *no* answer only; i.e., the question "What is it?" is not allowed, but the question "Is it an X?" is allowed.

Activity 22-E

Using the above technique, try to ascertain from your instructor or a peer who has looked at the answer, what the picture below depicts. (The answer appears in the Answers section.)

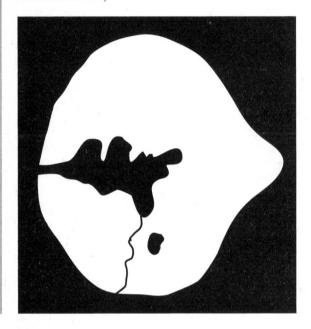

All these ideas are meant to puzzle students. The next idea can be a real puzzler if you use it when introducing a unit on culture in the intermediate grades.

Activity 22-F

Read the following passage and answer the question "Who are the Nacirema?" (The answer appears in the Answers section.)

THE NACIREMA[1]

The Nacirema inhabit a large area of the North American continent. Because of their belief that the human body is ugly and that its natural tendency is toward illness, everyone tries to avoid disease and ugliness by various ceremonies performed in a shrine. Every house has one or more of these shrines and people are judged to be wealthy if they have a lot of shrines in their homes.

The ceremonies performed in the shrine are private and secret. The most important thing in the shrine is a box, or chest, built into the wall. In this chest are kept many charms and magical liquids; no native believes it is possible to live without them. Most of these charms and magical liquids are obtained from medicine people who are rewarded with large gifts. However, the medicine people decide what ingredients should go into the liquid or charm by writing them down in a secret language that only medicine people and herbalists understand; it is the herbalist who, for another large gift, provides the actual charm.

Even after the charm has had its effect, it is not thrown away, but is placed in the charm box in the shrine. The charm box is, therefore, filled to overflowing, often with useless junk. The natives therefore must believe that old charms still protect them.

Beneath the charm box is a small basin. Every day each member of the family enters the shrine, bows his or her head before the charm box, mixes different sorts of holy water in the basin, and performs a washing ceremony.

There is also a mouth ceremony, when a bundle of small sticks is put in the mouth along with certain magical powders, and the bundle moved in a very specific way. Despite this magic to protect the teeth, once or twice a year the natives visit a holy mouth person. He or she, with a number of probes, prods, and sharp, pointed tools, puts the native through a painful ceremony. The native's teeth are prodded and decay is removed. Magic materials are put into holes and sometimes whole teeth are pulled out in a torturous way. All this is done because the natives believe that they will lose their friends unless they have these ceremonies performed.

SPECIFIC LESSONS AND INSTRUCTIONAL STRATEGIES

Once our sequence has been planned, then we have to plan the specific lessons. Here, we draw upon the objectives and decide what instructional strategy will best meet each objective. If we want students to develop a framework for the unit, then concept development will be most appropriate (see Chapter 6). If there are central concepts that need to be grasped, then concept attainment is the best strategy (Chapter 6). Having students inquire into particular questions is a good way for them to learn specific information, to apply their information-gathering skills, and to develop intellectual standards (Chapter 8). Other ways could include teacher talks, using videos, or reading stories (Chapter 5). Creating generalizations might involve the use of web diagrams (Chapter 13). Focusing on values may involve decision making and using simulation games (Chapters 17, 18, 19, and 20). In any of the above, students could present their conclusions in a variety of forms (Chapter 8).

Here is a roughed-out example based on the study of the Acadians. The broad goals are for students to gain historical and cultural subject-matter knowledge, to learn that history is interpretative, to realize that to understand the present we must look at the past, and to respect the Acadian culture. The organizer will be an inquiry question: "Who are the Acadians?" Our sequence will be chronological, tracing the history of the Acadians, culminating in a study of contemporary Acadian culture. Students have already studied the first European explorations of Canada and know of the rivalry between France and England.

Opener: Have students imagine that army officers come to their homes and tell them they have to leave the country. What might the reasons be? How would they feel?

Main body of the lesson: Use this opener to lead into the story of the Acadians: "They first settled in Acadia but were expelled in 1755." Ask students to hypothesize how the Acadians first settled in Canada, why they were expelled, and where they were sent. Tell students that Acadians now live in Nova Scotia and New Brunswick, and ask them how they think this occurred. Have groups of students use a jigsaw strategy to test their hypotheses so that each group arrives at a history of the Acadians.[2] For example, give one student an (undated) account of the founding of Acadia. Give another student a history of the period up to 1713; a third student the story up to 1755; another student an account of the expulsion; and so on up to the present. Have students share their information and create a time line. Develop a web diagram to show the connections between the various causes of the expulsion. Tell students to read both an Acadian *and* a British account of the expulsion. Ask students why these two versions would differ and have them relate other events where accounts might differ depending on observers' points of view.

This series of lessons would be followed by a series on contemporary Acadians. Groups of students would each research a particular aspect of Acadian life and create a chart showing their findings. Students would then draw connections between the history of the Acadians and their present ways of life. Students would also collect newspaper reports where Acadian concerns were mentioned. The unit would culminate in the creation of a mural answering the major inquiry question "Who are the Acadians?"

ASSESSMENT

Finally, we have to ascertain if students have realized the objectives (see Chapters 15 and 21). We have to go back to our objectives, state how we could assess students on each one, determine which ones should be formally tested, and design appropriate instruments. In the Acadian example, we might have students carry out self-assessments on their group projects and create a portfolio containing examples of their best work. We might give them a quiz on the important events in Acadian history by asking them to correctly locate the events on a time line. We could give them an account of the expulsion from the Acadian point of view and have students rewrite it from the British viewpoint. We might ask students to write a paragraph outlining what contributions the Acadians have made to Canada.

EXAMPLE OF A UNIT PLAN

What follows is an example of a unit plan in which the focus is on the concept of **interdependence** and how rules and conventions often define the roles we play and the ways we relate to others. These rules and conventions are the customary behaviours that are culturally observed but not enforced (such as shaking hands when meeting someone) and rules that are enforced by authorities (e.g., school rules, community regulations, and laws). Related to the concept of rules is "responsibility." People in interdependent relationships are responsible for upholding the rules and conventions that pertain to their roles. For instance, we as teachers are not legally bound to comfort students who are upset, but it is a convention that we do so.

Topic

Community Interdependence, Rules, and Conventions (Grade 2)

Rationale   Interdependence is a key concept in social studies and can be explored by studying the interactions between the student and the community. By studying interdependence, students can see how their actions affect others and how the actions of others affect them. This knowledge will help them realize the interdependent and interconnected nature of the world and how they can help (or hinder) progress toward a better world. Insofar as communities are rule-governed, the influence of rules on community interdependence will be explored. This understanding will lead to greater student insight into how people interact and will eventually help students evaluate the customs, regulations, and laws that impinge on their lives.

Major Goals

1. Subject matter knowledge: knowledge of a) the community and how the concept of interdependence applies; b) the services and resources in the community and how the community interacts; and c) the rules and conventions that apply.
2. Information gathering and reporting: collecting information from print sources, field trips, and interviews; reporting in print and pictorial media.
3. Intellectual standards: accuracy and plausibility of inferences.
4. Social and personal values: appreciating the importance of interdependence and the responsibilities involved in maintaining it.

Scope and Sequence   Our scope is bounded by the major goals and by the abilities of the students. We have to study at least some of the people who live and work in the community, determine the rules and conventions they operate on, and find out how they relate to each other. We will utilize interdisciplinary knowledge and will organize our unit around the concepts of interdependence and rules. Our sequence will be based on using the most familiar information first.

Because the school is a major focus and the teacher is an important person in the students' lives, one example of interdependence will be a study of the interactions between the students, the teachers, and the rest of the school. Schools are rule-governed institutions, so the effects of rules on student–school interactions can be explored. The knowledge gained can be extended by studying the police force, i.e., how police officers relate to the wider community and their role in enforcing the law. We would then need to see how we are dependent on the environment and what conventions govern the ways we interact with it. Depending on the time available, we might also look at other groups or individuals in the community and ascertain how interdependent they are. If there are ethnic groups in the community, we might want to study how they maintain interdependent relationships.

Specific Objectives   This scope and focus lead to some specific objectives:

1. Students will describe the jobs and roles of teachers, police officers, and one other community group chosen by the students.
2. Students will state why these jobs and roles are important to the community and how they relate to the concept of interdependence.
3. Students will state how different kinds of rules affect community life and how rules relate to interdependence.

Planning the Episodes of the Unit

We are now in a position to plan the individual episodes of the unit. We need to know

- the subtopic and/or questions
- the information that students will use
- the activities students will perform
- the way(s) students will present their information
- how we will assess students
- the opportunities for integration with other subject areas

The following examples consist of "bites" of content that have some structural unity. It might be possible to teach a particular episode in one lesson of 30 to 45 minutes, or a particular episode might entail several lessons.

Episode 1

Topic: School

Question: What would happen if you didn't have to attend school? Would these consequences be desirable or undesirable?

Information: Student hypotheses. Students' or teacher's list of consequences.

Activities: Discussion. Trace the possible consequences and discuss the plausibility of each. Talk about the desirability of each consequence and create a list of criteria (freedom to do whatever you like, need to be educated to get a job, etc). Students draw a picture of one consequence (for themselves, family, teachers, retailers, recreational facilities, etc.) and state why it would be desirable and/or undesirable.

Presentation: Class mural showing consequences and decisions about their desirability.

Assessment: Assess each student's drawing to ascertain if the consequence is plausible and whether his or her reasoning about the desirability/undesirability is reasonable given the criteria generated in the class.

Episode 2

Topic: Interdependence in the School

Question: How are people in the school dependent upon one another?

Information: Roles of various school personnel. Jobs performed by males and females.

Activities: Interviewing. Listening to people in the school explaining what they do. Composing a list of tasks performed by school personnel and noting whether these tasks can be performed by both males and females.

Presentation: Diagram showing how students, teachers, and others interact within the school community.

Assessment: Use a checklist to judge students' interviewing skills. Look at the list of tasks and assess for accuracy.

Integration: Stories about schools.

Episode 3

Topic: Role of Rules in the School

Question: How do rules affect school interactions?

Information: Pictures of school activities. Teacher and student contributions.

Activities: Using list of activities carried out in school (from Episode 2), discuss rules behind each activity; categorize rules as customs, school rules, legal rules, and subject-matter rules (e.g., spelling, grammatical rules).

Presentation: Role-play following or not following a particular custom, school rule, or legal rule. Inclusion of rules that exist in the interactions diagrammed in Episode 2.

Assessment: Assessment of the accuracy of the role play. Were the consequences of following or not following a particular rule realistic?

Integration: In all other subject areas, especially with regard to subject-matter rules (e.g., how to carry out addition in math, how to perform a scientific operation).

Episode 4

Topic: Rules

Question: What makes a good rule?

Information: List of rules. Criteria for good rules (see Activity 19-E).

Activities: Discussion of each rule. Students draw a picture of the consequences of not following a good rule. Relate rules to the categories generated in Episode 3. What would be the effect on interdependent relationships if rules were not followed?

Presentation: Each student takes a particular interaction (student–teacher, student–principal, etc.) and writes a sentence about a rule that affects the interaction and why it is a good (or bad) rule.

Assessment: Assess the sentence for accuracy and whether any of the criteria for a good rule have been stated.

Integration: Discussion of what constitutes good rules for safety purposes in physical education and science, and for learning in general in other subject areas. Stories of behaviour related to following (or not following) rules.

Episode 5

Topic: School Rules and Laws

Question: Who enforces school rules and who enforces laws?

Information: Series of vignettes (Example: Alice runs in the school corridor, which is against the school rules. Can the police arrest her?). Student- and teacher-generated list of rules and laws that directly affect students.

Activities: Discussion. Role play of vignettes (e.g., police officer attempting to arrest Alice, and Alice's reactions).

Presentation: Class list of rules showing who enforces each one. (Activities proposed on pages 261–264 could be carried out in this episode.)

Assessment: Accuracy of list of rules and enforcement. Plausibility of the role play.

Episode 6

Topic: Tasks of Police Officers

Question: What do police officers do?

Information: Field trip to police station.

Activities: Listen to presentations made by members of the police force. Interview police officers. Observe or take photos of the activities they perform. Find out how many female and minority-culture officers there are.

Presentation: A "radio" program in which students play the role of a police officer and are interviewed by other students.

Assessment: Self-assessment of behaviour on the field trip. Accuracy of the radio program.

Episode 7

Topic: The Relationship of the Police to the Community

Question: How do the police relate to the community?

Information: Visit by police to class.

Activities: Listen to presentation; ask questions. Discuss what would happen if there were no police in the community.

Presentation: Webbing diagram showing police–community interactions.

Assessment: Students draw a web with themselves in the middle, showing how the police relate to them and to the community. Assess for number of accurate connections made.

Episode 8

Topic: Interdependence and Rules

Question: How do students, the school, and the police relate to the community, and what effects do rules have on these interactions?

Information: All information gathered so far during the unit.

Activities: Drawing something relevant (a store, a community centre, a road, a park) in the community and a picture of a student, a teacher, and a police officer. Where there is an interaction, coloured string is used to show the links. For each link (if feasible), the rule or rules that affect the interaction are identified. Examples: students by law have to attend school; students follow certain rules in their interactions with teachers; students and teachers customarily behave in certain ways in their interactions. Students discuss what would happen if rules were not followed, if new rules were created, or if one of the components in an interdependent relationship were weakened or disappeared.

Presentation: Students write a short paragraph to demonstrate their understanding.

Assessment: Assess the paragraph for accuracy and coherence. Does it have a good introductory sentence and a good summary ending?

Extending and Modifying the Plan

The unit could be extended by studying a different group (if appropriate, an ethnic or First Nations group), noting interdependent relationships as well as the rules and conventions governing those relationships. An idea here might be to look at how greetings take place, what rituals are performed around food, or what celebrations occur in the community and what rules or conventions apply to them. Students could then compare these practices with their own and see what similarities and differences exist. The unit could also involve students looking at the natural environment of the community, how people in the community are dependent on it, and what rules govern people's interactions with the environment.

For various reasons, including unforeseen developments, most plans have to be modified in the actual implementation. For instance, a video may be unavailable on the day it is needed; students have to be taught something before the unit can continue; or (as happens frequently) students find something in the lesson very interesting and so you decide to spend more time on this topic than on the intended one.

This chapter has presented one way of unit planning—but not the only way. Students can also be involved in planning. For example, after a visit to the police station, students could pose their own questions, carry out their own research, and make a presentation. They might choose to write a poem about the police, or to find out how many police shows there are on TV. Students could read laws that affect their lives and rewrite them in language that a Grade 2 student could understand. Any of these activities could be encouraged, even though you hadn't planned for them.

Assessment

Finally, the unit needs to be evaluated. Below is a list of suggested questions:

- Was the topic worth teaching?
- Did students realize the objectives?
- Did students find it interesting?
- Could students cope with the unit? Was it within their capabilities?
- Were the resource materials appropriate?
- Was I interested in teaching the unit?
- Were the objectives congruent with the teaching/learning and evaluation procedures?
- Was the sequence logical?
- If I taught the unit again, what, if anything, would I change?

NOTES

1. Adapted from H. Miner, "Body ritual among the Nacirema," *American Anthropologist* 58:3 (1956), pp. 503–507.

2. See www.umoncton.ca/etudeacadiennes/centre/cea.html for information (in French) on Acadian history and culture. See www.schoolnet.ca/vp-pv/quiz/acadia.html for a quiz on Acadian history.

GLOSSARY OF KEY TERMS

Discrepant data technique — a technique in which a stereotype is identified and reinforced; then data that do not fit the stereotype are introduced so that a new generalization is formulated.

Interdependence — a concept of interaction and interconnectedness whereby one person's (or group's) actions affect another person (or group) and vice versa.

Answers to Activities

ACTIVITY 1-B

All the vignettes could be considered social studies activities only if the *objectives* for engaging students in the activities pertain to social studies. However, many of the vignettes may realize other goals as well. For example, creating a mural may achieve objectives in social studies and art education.

ACTIVITY 2-C

a) Teacher B	e) Teacher A	i) Teacher B
b) Teacher A	f) Teacher C	j) Teacher A
c) Teacher C	g) Teacher B or C	k) Teacher C
d) Teacher B	h) Teacher A	l) Teacher A

ACTIVITY 2-D

1. Citizenship Transmission
2. Reflective Inquiry (although it could be Critical Reflection)
3. Citizenship Transmission
4. Critical Reflection
5. Social Science
6. Citizenship Transmission
7. Citizenship Transmission
8. Reflective Inquiry (although it could be Critical Reflection)
9. Critical Reflection

ACTIVITY 3-F

a) Vertical integration

b) Subject matter integration

c) Not integration (no central idea is pursued)

d) Personal integration

e) Whole school curriculum integration

f) Unless moves are made to link the history, geography, and First Nations studies together, this would not be an example of integration.

g) Subject matter integration. Students are synthesizing information to create generalizations.

ACTIVITY 6-B

1. Hutterite *family* (Alberta)
2. Arctic hares, Leporidae *family*
3. Pauline Johnson, Canadian poet
4. Quatsino Indians at a potlatch
5. Lee Mong Kow *family* (Victoria, British Columbia)
6. Group of East Indians at North Pacific Lumber Co. (Barnet, British Columbia)

ACTIVITY 6-F

The concept is "immigrant."

ACTIVITY 6-G

The concept is "tradition." If you look at the last sentence, it sounds odd to say that watching television news every night is not a "custom" (which would be a sensible choice for all the other blanks). This practice seems to have many of the attributes of "custom" in that it is regularly performed over some extended period of time; it is an act of persons who, in most cases, can either do it or refrain from doing it; it is usually done with full awareness of what one is doing; and one may believe that one ought to do it. However, unlike some other customs where there are sanctions applied if they are not followed, refraining from watching television news is not a punishable offence.

"Tradition" has characteristics that are similar to "custom." However, a tradition may be more robust than certain customs. It may be handed down orally and deliberately from generation to generation (whereas a custom may endure for only one generation and may not be formally taught). Tradition may be based on very strong beliefs, which, if contradicted, may seriously undermine group cohesiveness and may lead to extreme sanctions (whereas not all customs have these characteristics). Also, it sounds a bit odd to say, "X is my individual tradition that no one else practises," whereas it is normal to say, "X is my custom even though no one else practises it." Yet, words change in meaning over time, and one often hears people say that they are starting a tradition just for themselves. This usage would be incorrect if a necessary attribute of the word was that a tradition had to be passed down from generation to generation. However, in ordinary language, we may find that the words "tradition" and "custom" become almost interchangeable.

ACTIVITY 6-H

Examples of "authority" are a), b), e), f), and possibly g), depending on whether the principal really has authority to do this. Notice that in the other cases there is the exercise of power without the requisite authority.

CHAPTER 6: OTHER ACTIVITIES

The teacher has implemented Taba's Concept Development procedure well. She/he has ensured that students have 1) correctly classified items, 2) decided whether items could be classified in more than one category, and 3) created categories useful for study of the topic.

ACTIVITY 7-D

As I find many problems in using Sanders's and Bloom's taxonomies, the answers provided are, in some cases, debatable. The highest level of question is indicated.

a) Empirical Memory

b) Empirical Memory

c) Empirical Synthesis

d) Empirical Translation

e) Conceptual Memory

f) Conceptual Analysis

g) Value Evaluation

h) Value Evaluation

i) Value Evaluation

j) Empirical/Logical Analysis

If you accept the two premises in j), then logically you must accept the conclusion.

ACTIVITY 8-A

The following assumptions would be made: b), c), e), f), g), h), i), and j).

ACTIVITY 8-B

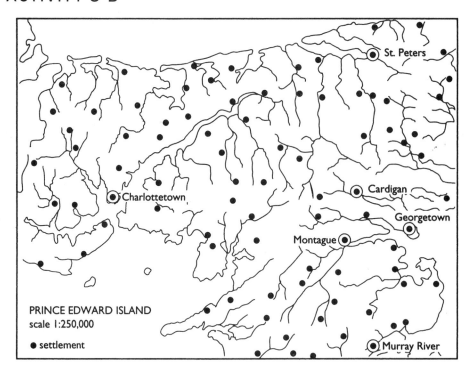

The map depicts part of Prince Edward Island.

ACTIVITY 8-C

In 1818, the British government helped army personnel settle in Canada. Settlers received free transportation and some food for the first year, and privates were given 40 hectares (100 acres) of free land. According to Andrew Haydon, *Pioneer Sketches in the District of Bathurst* (Toronto: Ryerson Press, 1925, p. 64), the head of each family was entitled to receive 1 axe, 1 broadaxe, 1 mattock, 1 pickaxe, 1 spade, 1 shovel, 1 hoe, 1 scythe, 1 drawknife, 1 hammer, 1 handsaw, 2 scythe stones, 12 panes of glass, 0.5 kg (1 lb.) of putty, 5.4 kg (12 lb.) of wrought-iron nails in three sizes, 1 camp kettle, 1 bed tick, and 1 blanket.

ACTIVITY 8-E

1. Option a) is a credible source. It is up to date, relevant to the topic, and representative. It (probably) does not provide a political message (bias).

2. Option a) is representative and is a credible source. It is up to date and will have been carefully reviewed by the publisher (textbooks are not adopted by ministries of education or school boards if they do not meet certain standards). However, given that it is a textbook, the topic may not be covered in depth. *If* it is representative of the topic, the CBC documentary would be an equally appropriate source. Given a forced choice, I would opt for the textbook.

ACTIVITY 8-F

1. a) The umpire is credible. The umpire is in a position to see the event and is unbiased.

2. c) The cyclist is most reliable. The cyclist was not involved in the accident and had no conflict of interest. He/she was in a good position to see the accident and was presumably paying attention to the traffic lights.

3. a) The police used the most accurate method of measuring the skid marks.

CHAPTER 8, PAGE 98

The person described on page 98 is Kim Hunter who at the time of writing was a young woman of 11 years of age.

ACTIVITY 8-H

Primary sources are a) and d).

ACTIVITY 8-I

The inference statements are c), d), f), and h). All are plausible.

ACTIVITY 10-D

William Miner was born in 1847 in Bowling Green, Kentucky. He executed a series of robberies in the American West and was released from San Quentin prison in 1904. He came to Canada in that year and robbed a CPR train near Mission, British Columbia. On May 8, 1906, Miner and two accomplices were captured by the North West Mounted Police when they botched the robbery of a CPR train near Kamloops. He was sentenced to 25 years in the penitentiary in New Westminster, British Columbia, but escaped in August 1907. He fled to the United States and continued to carry out robberies. He died in prison in Georgia in 1913. A movie, *The Grey Fox*, was made about his life in Canada.

CHAPTER 11: OTHER ACTIVITIES

The scale is incorrect. The room would be 5 km long. Further, the chair is bigger than the bed. The scale should read 1 cm: ___, not 1 cm = ___. If South is at the top of the room, then East and West are incorrect; if East and West are correct, then North and South are reversed. The perspective is confused; the bed, chair, and pictures are not drawn from the pilot's-eye view.

ACTIVITY 12-A

The teacher has forgotten to obtain permission from parents or legal guardians for their children to go on the field trip. This is a legal requirement and thus is obligatory before any field trip is undertaken.

ACTIVITY 13-A

Every sentence, bar the last one, is a generalization. Each one is presumed to be universally true.

ACTIVITY 13-G

The following generalizations are assumed:

1. All recent immigrants are good workers.
2. Boys don't cry.
3. Immigrants create cultural and economic change.
4. Working-class girls have problems in school.
5. It rains all the time in the summer in Vancouver.
6. People from India wear turbans.
7. Boys aren't good at sewing.

ACTIVITY 15-B

1. Far too many correct answers are possible.
2. Stems a), b), and c) are possible answers; d) does not grammatically follow from the question. Also, c) is a value statement and can be "right" or "wrong" only on the basis of a value principle or standard.
3. Far too broad—what would count as a good answer?
4. Some explorers might have had to contend with all these factors, whereas others did not. The entire statement is neither true nor false.
5. Confusing—doesn't state which Native peoples are being discussed. If f) were the correct answer, this would include e) and would be illogical.
6. A crib? A house? May? 1860? What would count as a correct answer?
7. Bad matching—far too obvious.

ACTIVITY 16-A

The first photo is of the Dragon Dance in Chinatown in Vancouver. The dance is performed at special events, especially at Chinese New Year. The second photo was taken in 1918. It shows the Canadian Expeditionary Force sailing to Vladivostok, Siberia, to join with forces from the United States, Britain, France, and Japan, ostensibly to protect supplies that had been sent to Russia when Russia was allied with England and France. The real reason might have been to support the White army that was dedicated to overthrowing the Bolsheviks.

ACTIVITY 16-D

Pyramids: The Inside Story. PBS's Nova program provides reliable and interesting information on several topics, including the construction of the pyramids.

Egypt: Construction of the Egyptian Pyramids. As the title indicates, this site includes information on the construction of the pyramids, with the ramp theory taking pride of place.

Egyptian Mysteries. Discussion of several theories of pyramid construction, including the theory that they were built by aliens.

Egypt Pyramids Pharaohs Hieroglyphs—Mark Millmore's Ancient.... A personal site covering many aspects of Egypt—you can write your name in hieroglyphics—but with little information on construction of the pyramids.

Egypt Pyramid Index. Various theories on how the pyramids were built are considered. Links to new discoveries are included.

Photographs of Egypt—Photographic Images of Ancient Egypt. As the title indicates, this site contains photos taken while the photographer was on a tour of Egypt in 1996.

Cyber Journey to Egypt—Guardian's Egypt. A personal homepage of a chiropractor with a great interest in Egypt. Nothing on construction of the pyramids.

King Tut One. A site for children is included, and there is information on pyramid construction.

The Ancient Egypt Bibliography—Pyramids. In association with Amazon.com. Not a very useful site.

Pharaoh Heaven—Egypt/History/Pyramids. A commercial site that includes a game involving the building of a city. Users have to log in.

ACTIVITY 17-B

1. Value conclusion: Students should work in cooperative groups.
2. Value conclusion: Students at age nine should learn conventional map symbols.
3. Value conclusion: Students should understand the Canadian Charter of Rights and Freedoms.

CHAPTER 17: OTHER ACTIVITIES

1. a) People should be treated with respect.
   b) Child abuse is morally wrong.

c) Students who wear glasses should not be given special consideration in school class-rooms. OR: Only disabled people should receive special consideration in classrooms.

d) Children should not be allowed to do things that are harmful to them.

3. The teacher did not implement the decision-making procedure in an appropriate way. The teacher allowed the problem to be wrongly defined; limited the number of alternatives to be considered; invented new information; held a vote when it was inappropriate (to decide whether an empirical claim concerning the teasers is true); and imposed his/her own decision on the class, cutting off any further discussion.

ACTIVITY 20-C

a) Overgeneralization. Just because one recent immigrant is hard-working does not mean that all recent immigrants will be.

b) False cause (*post hoc ergo propter hoc*). There are other reasons for the high unemployment.

c) Appeal to tradition. Just because immigrants came from Europe in the past, it does not follow that they should today.

d) Appeal to authority. Are business people experts on whether the government should give money to ethnic groups?

e) "Black or white" (either this or that). This form of argument presents an oversimplification: Canada's economy could crumble (if it were going to crumble) for a variety of reasons.

f) Slippery slope (in which it is argued that you must not accept as desirable the first event in a supposed chain of events that will lead eventually to something undesirable). In this case, you could agree to allowing Native peoples to govern themselves without agreeing to the rest.

ACTIVITY 22-D

Photographs 1 to 4 were all taken in Canada: Photo 1, Quebec City; Photo 2, Vancouver; Photo 3, Toronto; Photo 4, Ottawa.

Photo 5 was taken in Beijing, China.

Photo 6 was taken in Quebec City.

Photo 7 was taken in Dr. Sun Yat-sen Gardens, Vancouver.

ACTIVITY 22-E

Map of the world as known to Europeans, 1398.

ACTIVITY 22-F

Nacirema = American (spelled backwards).

A Selected Bibliography

GENERAL ELEMENTARY SOCIAL STUDIES METHODS TEXTS

Banks, J. *Teaching Strategies for the Social Studies: Decision-making and Citizenship Action.* New York: Longman, 1999.

Case, R., and P. Clark. *The Canadian Anthology of Social Studies.* Vancouver, BC: Pacific Educational Press, 1999.

Chapin, J., and R. Messick. *Elementary Social Studies: A Practical Guide,* 4th edition. New York: Longman, 1999.

Ellis, A. *Teaching and Learning Elementary Social Studies,* 7th edition. Boston: Allyn and Bacon, 2002.

Farris, P. *Elementary and Middle School Social Studies: A Whole Language Approach.* Boston: McGraw Hill, 1997.

Hage, J. *Effective Elementary Social Studies.* Belmont, Calif.: Wadsworth, 1996.

Kirman, J. *Elementary Social Studies: Creative Classroom Ideas*, 3rd edition. Toronto: Prentice-Hall, 2002.

Martorella, P. *Social Studies for Elementary School Children: Developing Young Citizens.* New York: Merrill, 1998.

Maxim, G. *Social Studies and the Elementary School Child,* 6th edition. New York: Merrill, 1999.

Nelson, M. *Children and Social Studies: Creative Teaching in the Elementary Classroom.* Fort Worth, Tex.: Harcourt Brace Jovanovich, 1998.

Parker, W. *Social Studies in Elementary Education,* 11th edition. Upper Saddle River, NJ: Merrill, 2001.

Savage, T., and D. Armstrong. *Effective Teaching in Elementary Social Studies,* 4th edition. New York: Merrill, 2000.

Seefeldt, C., and A. Galper. *Active Experiences for Active Children: Social Studies.* New York: Merrill, 2000.

Sunal, C., and M. Haas. *Social Studies and the Elementary/Middle School Student.* Fort Worth, Tex.: Harcourt Brace Jovanovich, 1993.

Welton, D., and J. Mallan. *Children and Their World,* 6th edition. Boston: Houghton Mifflin, 1999.

PART 1: THE NATURE AND PURPOSES OF SOCIAL STUDIES AND THE CONTEXTS IN WHICH IT IS TAUGHT

Barth, J. "Social Studies: There is a history, there is a body, but is it worth saving?" *Social Education* 57:2 (1993) 56–57.

Brophy, J., and J. Alleman. "Elementary Social Studies should be driven by major social education goals." *Social Education* 57:1 (1993) 27–32.

Clark, P. "Whither social studies?" *Canadian Social Studies* 33:2 (1999) 42–43.

Coffey, A., and S. Delamont. *Feminism in the Classroom: Research, Praxis, and Pedagogy.* London: Falmer Press, 2000.

Cruz, B., J. Nutta, C. Feyten, and J. Govini. *Passport to Learning: Teaching Social Studies to ESL Students.* Silver Spring, Md.: National Council for the Social Studies, 2003.

Levesque, S. "History and social studies in Quebec: An historical perspective." In A. Sears and I. Wright, eds. *Challenges and Prospects for Canadian Social Studies.* Vancouver: Pacific Educational Press, 2004.

Martino, W., and B. Meyenn. *What about the Boys? Issues of Masculinity in Schools.* Buckingham, England: Open University Press, 2001.

Schrug, M., and B. Cross. "The dark side of curriculum integration in social studies." *The Social Studies* 89:2 (1998) 54–57.

Sears, A. "What research tells us about citizenship education in English Canada." *Canadian Social Studies.* 30:3 (1996) 121–127.

Shields, P., and D. Ramsay. "Social studies across English Canada." In A. Sears and I. Wright, eds. *Challenges and Prospects for Canadian Social Studies.* Vancouver: Pacific Educational Press, 2004.

Social Studies Curricula in Canada. Special issue of *Canadian Social Studies* 31:1 (1996).

PART 2: EMPIRICAL AND CONCEPTUAL CLAIMS AND INTELLECTUAL STANDARDS

Exposition and Narrative

Egan, K. *Primary Understanding.* New York: Routledge, 1988.

McGowan, T., L. Erickson, and J. Neufeld. "With reason and rhetoric: Building the case for the literature–social studies connection." In M. Haas and M. Laughlin, eds. *Meeting the Standards: Social Studies Readings for K–6 Educators.* Washington, DC: National Council for the Social Studies, 1997.

Textbook Analysis and Use

Baldwin, P., and D. Baldwin. "The portrayal of women in classroom textbooks." *Canadian Social Studies* 26:3 (1992) 110–114.

McCabe, P. "Working with the textbook: How to enhance student motivation," *Social Education* 67:5 (2003) 274–277.

Concept Teaching and Learning

Hughes, A. "Getting the idea: An introduction to concept learning and teaching in social studies." In I. Wright and A. Sears, eds. *Challenges and Prospects for Canadian Social Studies.* Vancouver: Pacific Educational Press, 2004.

Wilson, J. *Thinking with Concepts*. Cambridge: The University Press, 1969.

Critical Thinking and Inquiry

Dhand, H. "The source method to teach social studies." *Canadian Social Studies* 26:4 (1992) 165–169.

Fowler, R. "Inquiry in social studies." In I. Wright and A. Sears, eds. *Trends and Issues in Canadian Social Studies*. Vancouver: Pacific Educational Press, 1997.

Hunkins, F. *Teaching Thinking through Effective Questioning*, 2nd edition. Norwood, Mass.: Christopher-Gordon, 1995.

Shively, J., and P. Van Fossen. "Critical thinking and the internet: Opportunities for the social studies classroom." *The Social Studies* 90:1 (1999) 42–46.

Wright, I. "Critical thinking in social studies: Beliefs, commitments and implementation." *Canadian Social Studies* 29:2 (1995) 66–68.

Wright, I. "Critical thinking and social studies." In I. Wright and A. Sears, eds. *Trends and Issues in Canadian Social Studies*. Vancouver: Pacific Educational Press, 1997.

Cooperative Learning

Morton, T. *Cooperative Learning in Social Studies*. San Clemente, CA: Kagan Cooperative Learning, 1998.

Myers, J. "Cooperative learning: Putting the 'social' into social studies." In I. Wright and A. Sears, eds. *Trends and Issues in Canadian Social Studies*. Vancouver: Pacific Educational Press, 1997.

Stahl, R. *Cooperative Learning in Social Studies*. Menlo Park, CA; Addison Wesley, 1994.

History

Barton, K. "A picture's worth: Analyzing historical photographs in the elementary grades." *Social Education* 65:5 (2001) 278–285.

Bednarz, S. "Using geographic perspectives to enrich history." *Social Education* 61:3 (1997) 139–145.

Clark, P. "Clio in the classroom: The jury is out." *Canadian Social Studies* 32:2 (1998) 45–48.

Clarke, G., and J. Smyth. "Stories in elementary history and the social studies." *Canadian Social Studies* 27:2 (1993) 76–78.

Hatcher, B. "Children's homes and neighborhoods: Untapped treasures from the past." In M. Haas and M. Laughlin, eds. *Meeting the Standards: Social Studies Readings for K–6 Educators*. Washington, DC: National Council for the Social Studies, 1997.

Kirman, J. "Teaching about local history using customized photographs." *Social Education* 59:1 (1995) 11–13.

Lee, P. "Making sense of historical accounts." *Canadian Social Studies* 32:2 (1998) 52–54.

Maxim, G. "Time capsules: Tools for the classroom historian." *The Social Studies* 88:5 (1997) 227–232.

Osborne, K. "History as storytelling." *Canadian Social Studies* 35:1 (2000). www.quasar.ualberta.ca/css/css_35_1/CLvoices_from_the_past.htm

Schick, C., and W. Hurren. "Reading autobiographies, memoirs, and fictional accounts in the classroom: Is it social studies?" *Canadian Social Studies* 37:2 (2003) www.quasar.ualberta.ca/css/Css_37_2/ARreading_autobiographies.htm

Seixas, P., with C. Peck. "The place of history within social studies." In I. Wright and A. Sears, eds. *Challenges and Prospects for Canadian Social Studies*. Vancouver: Pacific Educational Press, 2004.

Smith, J., and D. Dobson. "Teaching with historical novels: A four step approach." *Social Studies and the Young Learner* 5:3 (1993) 19–22.

Thornton, S., and L. Levstik, eds. "Teaching history in a changing world." Special issue of *Social Education* 61:1 (1997).

Geography

Canadian Council for Geographic Education. *Canadian National Standards for Geography: A Standards-Based Guide to K–12 Geography*. Ottawa: Royal Canadian Geographic Society, 2001.

Deir, E. "The place of geography within social studies." In I. Wright and A. Sears, eds. *Trends and Issues in Canadian Social Studies*. Vancouver: Pacific Educational Press, 1997.

Geography Education Standards Project. *Geography for Life: National Geography Standards*. Washington, DC: National Geographic Research and Exploration, 1994.

Holloway, S., and G. Valentine. *Children's Geographies: Playing, Living, Learning*. London: Routledge, 2000.

Hurren, W. "School geography and academic geography: Spaces of possibility for teaching and learning." In A. Sears and I. Wright, eds. *Challenges and Prospects for Canadian Social Studies*. Vancouver: Pacific Educational Press, 2004.

Maier, J. "Relating here to there: Globes and world maps as advanced organizers." *Social Studies and the Young Learner* 5:3 (1993) 9–11.

Muir, S., and H. Cheek. "Assessing spatial development: Implications for map skill instruction." In M. Haas and M. Laughlin, eds. *Meeting the Standards: Social Studies Readings for K–6 Educators*. Washington, DC: National Council for the Social Studies, 1997.

Natoli, S., ed. *Strengthening Geography in the Social Studies*. Bulletin No. 81. Washington, DC: National Council for the Social Studies, 1994.

Ouzts, D., and L. Walsh. "Connecting literature with K–8 National Geography Standards." *The Social Studies* 90:2 (1999) 85–92.

Pickford, F., D. Granley, R. Christian, and P. Roduta. "Our school's paths and places: An introduction to maps." *Canadian Social Studies* 29:1 (1994) 38–39.

Svingen, B. "New technologies in the geography classroom." In M. Haas and M. Laughlin, eds. *Meeting the Standards: Social Studies Readings for K–6 Educators*. Washington, DC: National Council for the Social Studies, 1997.

Thompson, G. "'I thought the world was flat, like the map showed.' Building geographic understanding with elementary students." *Social Education* 63:5 (1999) 269–273.

PART 3: OBTAINING, ANALYZING, AND EVALUATING INFORMATION

Berson, J., and D.Stuckart. "Promise and practice of computer technologies in the social studies: A critical analysis." In W. Stanley, ed. *Critical Issues in Social Studies: Research for the 21st Century*. Greenwich, Conn.: Information Age Publishing, 2001.

Braun, J., and F. Risinger, eds. *Surfing Social Studies: The Internet Book.* Washington, DC: National Council for the Social Studies, 1999.

Crowley, T. "Understanding Canada's aboriginal people: A regional guide." *Canadian Social Studies* 27:2 (1993) 71–74.

Gibson, S. "Computer technologies as supportive tools to enhance learning in social studies." In A. Sears and I. Wright, eds. *Challenges and Prospects for Canadian Social Studies*. Vancouver: Pacific Educational Press, 2004.

Martorella, P., ed. *Interactive Technologies in the Social Studies*. Albany State University of New York Press, 1997.

Special issue of *Social Education* 61:3 (1997). "A new view of the world: Using technology in social studies education."

Waters, S. "Children's literature: A valuable resource for the social studies classroom." *Canadian Social Studies* 33:3 (1999) 80–83.

Wilson, E., and G. Marsch. "Social studies and the internet revolution." In M. Haas and M. Laughlin, eds. *Meeting the Standards: Social Studies Readings for K–6 Educators*. Washington, DC: National Council for the Social Studies, 1997.

PART 4: DECISION MAKING, SOCIAL AND PERSONAL VALUE CLAIMS, AND QUESTIONS

Decision Making and Values Education

Evans, R., and D. Saxe. *Handbook on Teaching Social Issues.* Washington, DC: National Council for the Social Studies, 1996.

Hartoonian, H., and M. Laughlin. "Decision-making skills." In M. Haas and M. Laughlin, eds. *Meeting the Standards: Social Studies Readings for K–6 Educators*. Washington, DC: National Council for the Social Studies, 1997.

King, R., and J. King. "Is group decision making in the classroom constructive or destructive?" *Social Education* 62:2 (1998) 101–104.

McBee, R. "Can controversial topics be taught in the early grades? The answer is yes." In M. Haas and M. Laughlin, eds. *Meeting the Standards: Social Studies Readings for K–6 Educators.* Washington, DC: National Council for the Social Studies, 1997.

Rossi, J., ed. "Teaching controversial issues." Special edition of *Social Education* 60:1 (1996).

Sheppard, S. "Facing an issue through critical thinking and decision making in social studies." In W. Cassidy and R. Yates, eds. *Let's Talk about Law in the Elementary School*. Calgary: Detselig, 1998.

Wade, R. *Building Bridges: Connecting the Classroom and the Community through Service-Learning in Social Studies*. Silver Spring, Md.: National Council for the Social Studies, 2003.

Citizenship Education

Chamberlin, C. "Citizenship as the practice of deep ecology." *Canadian Social Studies* 31:3 (1997) 142–144.

Dynneson, T., and R. Gross. "An eclectic approach to citizenship: Developmental stages." In M. Haas and M. Laughlin, eds. *Meeting the Standards: Social Studies Readings for K–6 Educators.* Washington, DC: National Council for the Social Studies, 1997.

National Council for the Social Studies. *Civitas: A Framework for Civic Education.* New York, 1992.

Orr, J., and R. McKay. "Living citizenship through classroom community." *Canadian Social Studies* 31:3 (1997) 131–134.

Osborne, K. "Citizenship education and social studies." In I. Wright and A. Sears, eds. *Trends and Issues in Canadian Social Studies.* Vancouver: Pacific Educational Press, 1997.

Parker, W. "Why ethics in citizenship education?" In M. Haas and M. Laughlin, eds. *Meeting the Standards: Social Studies Readings for K–6 Educators.* Washington, DC: National Council for the Social Studies, 1997.

Ross, D., and E. Bondy. "Classroom management for responsible citizenship: Practical strategies for teachers." In M. Haas and M. Laughlin, eds. *Meeting the Standards: Social Studies Readings for K–6 Educators.* Washington, DC: National Council for the Social Studies, 1997.

Sears, A. "In search of good citizens: Citizenship education and social studies in Canada." In A. Sears and I. Wright, eds. *Challenges and Prospects for Canadian Social Studies.* Vancouver: Pacific Educational Press, 2004.

Sherman, A. "Democratic experiences for early years students." In A. Sears and I. Wright, eds. *Challenges and Prospects for Canadian Social Studies.* Vancouver: Pacific Educational Press, 2004.

Smits, H. "Citizenship education in postmodern times: Posing some questions for reflection." *Canadian Social Studies* 31:3 (1997) 126–130.

Yeager, E., and D. Silva. "Activities for strengthening the meaning of democracy for elementary school students." *The Social Studies* 93:1 (2002) 18–22.

Multicultural Education

Bainbridge, J., S. Pantelo, and N. Ellis. "Multicultural picture books: Perspectives from Canada." *The Social Studies* 90:4 (1999) 183–188.

Banks, J., and C. Banks, eds. *Multicultural Education: Issues and Perspectives.* New York: Wiley, 2001.

Kehoe, J. "Multiculturalism in social studies." In I. Wright and A. Sears, eds. *Trends and Issues in Canadian Social Studies.* Vancouver: Pacific Educational Press, 1997.

Ladson-Billings, G. "I don't see color, I just see children." In M. Haas and M. Laughlin, eds. *Meeting the Standards: Social Studies Readings for K–6 Educators.* Washington, DC: National Council for the Social Studies, 1997.

Varma-Joshi, M. "Understanding multiculturalism in the social studies classroom." In A. Sears and I. Wright, eds. *Challenges and Prospects for Canadian Social Studies.* Vancouver: Pacific Educational Press, 2004.

Walsh, D. "Critical thinking to reduce prejudice." In M. Haas and M. Laughlin, eds. *Meeting the Standards: Social Studies Readings for K–6 Educators*. Washington, DC: National Council for the Social Studies, 1997.

Global Education

Ashford, M.-W. "Youth actions for the planet." In R. Fowler and I. Wright, eds. *Thinking Globally in Social Studies Education*. Vancouver: Research in Development in Global Studies, University of British Columbia, 1995.

Case, R. "Nurturing a global perspective in elementary students." In R. Fowler and I. Wright. eds. *Thinking Globally in Social Studies Education*. Vancouver: Research in Development in Global Studies, University of British Columbia, 1995.

Case, R. "Promoting global attitudes." *Canadian Social Studies* 30:4 (1996) 174–177.

Darling, L. "Deepening our global perspective: The moral matters in tricksters' tales." *Canadian Social Studies* 30:4 (1996) 180–182.

Richardson, G. "Global education and the challenge of globalization." In A. Sears and I. Wright, eds. *Challenges and Prospects for Canadian Social Studies*. Vancouver: Pacific Educational Press, 2004.

Werner, W. "Starting points for global education." *Canadian Social Studies* 30:4 (1996) 171–173.

Werner, W., and R. Case. "Themes of global education." In A. Sears and I. Wright, eds. *Trends and Issues in Canadian Social Studies*. Vancouver: Pacific Educational Press, 1997.

Law-Related Education

Cassidy, W. "Law and social studies: Preparing students for citizenship." In A. Sears and I. Wright, eds. *Challenges and Prospects for Canadian Social Studies*. Vancouver: Pacific Educational Press, 2004.

Cassidy, W., and R. Yates, eds. *Let's Talk about Law in the Elementary School*. Calgary: Detselig, 1998.

Norton, J. "The State vs. the big bad wolf: A study of the justice system in the elementary school." In M. Haas and M. Laughlin, eds. *Meeting the Standards: Social Studies Readings for K–6 Educators*. Washington, DC: National Council for the Social Studies, 1997.

O'Brien, E. "We must integrate human rights into the social studies." *Social Education* 63:3 (1999) 171–176.

Tibbits, F. "On human dignity: The need for human rights education." *Social Education* 60:7 (1996) 428–431.

York Board of Education. "These shoes could be yours: A model Grade 6 integrated unit" (on the Holocaust). *Canadian Social Studies* 29:4 (1995) 159–162.

Gender

K. Greenspan, *The Timetables of Women's History: A Chronology of the Most Important People and Events in Women's History*. New York: Touchstone Books, 1994.

Loutzenheiser, L. "Gender and sexuality in the social studies curriculum: Bound and undetermined." In A. Sears and I. Wright, eds. *Challenges and Prospects for Canadian Social Studies.* Vancouver: Pacific Educational Press, 2004.

Turner, J., and P. Clark, "Move over, buster: Women and social studies." In R. Case and P. Clark, *The Canadian Anthology of Social Studies*. Vancouver: Pacific Educational Press, 1999.

Peace and Conflict Resolution Education

Avery, P. "Teaching tolerance: What research tells us." *Social Education* 66:5 (2002) 270–275.

Carson, T., and E. Lange. "Peace education in social studies." In I. Wright and A. Sears, eds. *Trends and Issues in Canadian Social Studies.* Vancouver: Pacific Educational Press, 1997.

Hargraves, S. "Peace education: Politics in the classroom?" In R. Case and P. Clark, eds. *The Canadian Anthology of Social Studies*. Vancouver: Pacific Educational Press, 1999.

Johnson, D., and R. Johnson. *Reducing School Violence through Conflict Resolution*. Alexandria, Va.: Association for Supervision and Curriculum Development, 1995.

Levin, D. "Building a peaceable classroom: Helping young children feel safe in violent times." In M. Haas and M. Laughlin, eds. *Meeting the Standards: Social Studies Readings for K–6 Educators.* Washington, DC: National Council for the Social Studies, 1997.

Shiman, D., and R. Fernekes. "The Holocaust, human rights, and democratic citizenship." *The Social Studies* 90:2 (1999) 53–62.

Totten, S. "Teaching the Holocaust: The imperative to move beyond clichés." *Canadian Social Studies* 33:3 (1999) 84–87.

Walter, V. *War and Peace: Literature for Children and Young Adults*. Phoenix, Ariz.: Oryx Press, 1993.

Assessment

Canadian Social Studies 34:1 (1999). Special issue on standards and assessment.

Fenwick, T., and J. Parsons. "Using dynamic assessment in the social studies classroom." *Canadian Social Studies* 34:1 (1999) 153–155.

Myers, J. "Assessment and evaluation in social studies classrooms: A question of balance." In I. Wright and A. Sears, eds. *Challenges and Prospects for Canadian Social Studies.* Vancouver: Pacific Educational Press, 2004.

Nickell, P. "Performance assessment in principle and practice." In M. Haas and M. Laughlin, eds. *Meeting the Standards: Social Studies Readings for K–6 Educators.* Washington, DC: National Council for the Social Studies, 1997.

Special issue of *Social Education* 63:6 (1999). "Authentic assessment in the social studies."

Special section in *Social Education* 56:2 (1992). "Student Assessment in social studies." 89–111.

Photo Acknowledgments

Agriculture and Agri-Food Canada, page 180, PEI #79, #64. Courtesy of Agriculture and Agri-Food Canada.

British Columbia Archives, page 61, HP006603. Courtesy of BC Archives.

City of Vancouver Archives, page 123, SGN 1586; pages 124–125, William Bros. AIR P108.1 (c. 1966), William Bros. CVA 23-12 (1973), William Bros. CVA 586 (WB40356-25) (1982); page 142, William Bros. CVA 586 (WB38829-26); page 206, MIL.P.13 N225 #1; page 228, CVA 32692. Used with permission.

City of Whitehorse Tourism Department, page 61. Courtesy of Terry Parker. Courtesy of Wayne Towriss. Courtesy of Sheila Dodd. Courtesy of Leo Boon, Big Bear Adventures. Courtesy of the City of Whitehorse.

CN Tower, page 297. Courtesy of CN Tower, Toronto, Ontario.

Government of Nunavut, page 77. Photo of Iqaluit harbour by Mary Ellen Miley.

Ives Tessier/TESSIMA, page 296, Quebec City 2023K532. Courtesy of Ives Tessier/TESSIMA.

National Archives of Canada, page 61, Kryn Taconis/75-1339KC, George Hunter/75-2267K. Used with permission.

National Gallery of Canada, page 100, 62-6673. Ted Grant. *Aboriginal Girl in Traditional Costume, Calgary, Alberta.* Gelatin silver print/épreuve argentique. Used with permission.

Ottawa Tourism and Convention Centre (photo from National Capital Commission), page 297. Used with permission.

Parks Canada, page 298, Louis Jacob (1988) 100/00PR-7/SPO.0001. Used with permission.

Parks Canada, Fort Langley National Historic Site, pages 178–179. Courtesy of Parks Canada—Fort Langley National Historic Site.

R. Rustad, page 298. Used with permission.

Vancouver Public Library, Special Collections, page 61,—VPL 9430, VPL 14082, VPL 7641; page 128—VPL 749; page 129—VPL 8371; page 228—CVA 32692. Used with permission.

A. Wootton, page 299, Dr. Sun Yat-sen Gardens, Vancouver, BC. Used with permission.

All other photographs by the author.

Index